QUEEN
A PEOPLE'S HISTORY

Richard Houghton

First published in 2021 by Spenwood Books Ltd,
2 College Street, Higham Ferrers, NN10 8DZ.

A CIP record for this book is available from the
British Library.

ISBN 978-1-9168896-1-3

Printed and bound in Scotland

Design by Bruce Graham, The Night Owl.
Photo copyrights: As captioned.

BY THE SAME AUTHOR

You Had To Be There: The Rolling Stones 1962 - 69

The Beatles - I Was There

The Who - I Was There

Pink Floyd - I Was There

The Rolling Stones - I Was There

Jimi Hendrix - The Day I Was There

Led Zeppelin - The Day I Was There

The Smiths - The Day I Was There

The Jam - The Day I Was There (with Neil Cossar)

Black Sabbath - The Day I Was There

Rush - The Day I Was There

The Wedding Present - Sometimes These Words Just Don't Have To Be
Said (with David Gedge)

Orchestral Manoeuvres in the Dark - Pretending To See The Future

Simple Minds - Heart of the Crowd

Shaun Ryder's Book of Mumbo Jumbo

Cream - A People's History

CONTENTS

INTRODUCTION

I SHOULD HAVE been a punk. But less than five weeks before buying the newly released 'New Rose' by The Damned for 55p from Clarks Records in 1976, I had attended the free concert given by Queen in London's Hyde Park. I was conflicted, as the largely hostile music press said these well educated college boys clearly weren't a serious rock band when the guitarist played a homemade guitar with a sixpence and the singer camped it up outrageously with his long hair and painted fingernails. I was so conflicted that in 1978 my best friend taped *Jazz* on one side of a C90 cassette for me and put the first Clash album on the other.

I saw Queen four times in total, downsizing each time from Hyde Park to Earls Court to Wembley Arena to the Rainbow. If they'd continued downsizing, they'd have been playing in my local pub. But Queen's career wasn't spiralling downwards. After the Seventies, they played on bigger and bigger stages to bigger and bigger audiences – at Wembley Stadium, on the beach at Rock in Rio, at Knebworth Park. And at *Live Aid* they played to the biggest audience of all – the whole world.

Queen were a band greater than the sum of its parts, and in Freddie Mercury possessed one of the most charismatic front men in rock. Critically rehabilitated with the passing of time, Queen are much missed as a live act and Freddie much mourned. Stick on your copy of *Live Killers*, turn up the volume and turn the page to enjoy a trip back in time with the memories of over 400 fans as they remember the dry ice, the white lights, the outrageous costumes and the scintillating performances of one of the greatest rock and roll bands of all time.

As with other books I've written, I'm indebted to others for the work they've done in cataloguing Queen's concert history, especially the website queenconcerts.com. If anyone has information about Queen shows, including memories they'd like to contribute, I'd love to hear from them at *iwasatthatgig@gmail.com*.

I'd like to thank my many contributors for sharing their memories with me. And I'd like to thank Bruce Graham for his design expertise, and the lovely Kate Sullivan for keeping the ship on course as always.

Richard Houghton,
Manchester, UK.
September 2021

EARLY SHOWS

THE REACTION
1965 – 1968, CORNWALL & DEVON, UK

WHILE STILL AT school, Roger Taylor's first semi-pro band The Reaction play several hundred gigs. Winning Cornwall's prestigious Rock and Rhythm Championship in 1966 makes The Reaction one of the busiest bands on the Cornish music circuit.

IMPERIAL COLLEGE
13 MAY 1967, LONDON, UK

JIMI HENDRIX IS booked by student Brian May to perform at Imperial College for a fee of £1,000. Brian is on the college Entertainments Committee and his band 1984 play support.

OCTOBER 1967

ROGER TAYLOR MOVES to London from Cornwall to study dentistry at the London Hospital Medical School in Whitechapel.

IMPERIAL COLLEGE STUDENTS' UNION
SUMMER 1968, LONDON, UK

ROGER IS LIVING with Truro schoolfriend, Les Brown, who spots a 'drummer wanted' notice left by astrophysicist Brian May on the union noticeboard. Smile are formed, with Roger on drums, Brian on guitar and Tim Staffell on vocals and bass.

Brian always had that very distinctive guitar sound, even back then

Roger Taylor

IMPERIAL COLLEGE
26TH OCTOBER 1968, LONDON, UK

SMILE – A FOUR piece comprising Brian, Roger, Tim Staffell and keyboard player Chris Smith - make their debut supporting Pink Floyd.

VARIOUS VENUES
1968 – 1969, CORNWALL, UK

SMILE TRAVEL TO Cornwall roughly once a month, performing in Penzance, Redruth and St Minver among other locations, often accompanied by Freddie Bulsara.

ROYAL ALBERT HALL
27 FEBRUARY 1969, LONDON, UK

SMILE ARE ON the bill for a benefit concert for the National Council for the Unmarried Mother and her Child, above the newly-formed Free. They part company with keyboardist Chris Smith.

IMPERIAL COLLEGE
15 MARCH 1969, LONDON, UK
SMILE SUPPORT FAMILY.

PJ'S
29 MARCH 1969, TRURO, CORNWALL, UK
SMILE DEBUT AT PJ's, billing themselves as a 'tremendous London group'.

SPEAKEASY
10 APRIL 1969, LONDON, UK

SMILE ARE OFFERED a one off singles deal by Lou Reizner, A&R man for Mercury Records.

KENSINGTON MARKET
1969, LONDON, UK

Phillip Robbins met Freddie at Kensington Market

I WAS THERE: PHILLIP ROBBINS, AGE 15
I WAS A 15-year-old boy serving a four year apprenticeship at the Savoy Hotel. Often in the afternoon I would go in the flea market and get chatting to stall holders. He was on the first floor, at the top of the stairs on the right, selling African masks and fascinating carved stuff. I bored him with tales of my family down in Sussex who I missed. I would go anywhere but back to the hostel in Bramham Gardens, where I was bullied from the ages of 15 to 19. Freddie was a kind face in a wonderfully exotic place, and an ear for a very lonely soul. I valued that he spoke to me and that he was kind. He paid for the teas I would go and fetch from downstairs, bringing back his change. He invited me to a bar one evening called The Pink Elephant. I went with the sister of a friend and had to leave before he arrived because of the curfew at the boys' hostel I was staying in. He was always kind and generous to me.

TRIDENT STUDIOS
JUNE 1969, LONDON, UK

SMILE RECORD 'EARTH', 'Step on Me' and 'Doin' Allright', produced by John Anthony as a promotional single for Mercury Records in the United States.

DE LANE LEA STUDIOS
SEPTEMBER 1969, LONDON, UK

MERCURY RECORDS BOOK Smile into the studio again.

MARQUEE
DECEMBER 1969, LONDON, UK

SMILE ARE BOOKED as support for Nick Lowe's band, Kippington Lodge.

FEBRUARY 1970

TIM STAFFELL LEAVES Smile and Freddie Mercury joins. The various acts he's been involved with – Ibex, Wreckage and Sour Milk Sea – have all disintegrated. Mike Grose is recruited to play bass.

British Red Cross Society
1870-1970
Truro Detachment have invited

SMILE
to play on
Saturday, JUNE 27th, 1970
We invite YOU to come and DANCE.
Further announcement next month.

They were billed as Smile but appeared as Queen for the first time

CITY HALL
27 JUNE 1970, TRURO, UK

QUEEN PLAY THEIR first ever gig, billed as Smile. The line up comprises Brian May on guitar, Roger Taylor on drums, Freddie Mercury on vocals and Mike Grose on bass. 'Stone Cold Crazy' features in the set.

We were paid £50, which was quite a lot of money back then. I'm not sure many people turned up though **Roger Taylor**

IMPERIAL COLLEGE
18 JULY 1970, LONDON, UK

QUEEN MAKE THEIR London debut.

PJ'S CLUB
25 JULY 1970, TRURO, UK

I WAS THERE: WENDY MITCHELL, AGE 18

MY FRIENDS AND I saw Queen live at a club called PJs. Roger Taylor lived in Truro and went to school in the city. They had just changed their name from Smile to Queen. We paid two shillings and sixpence (12½p) to go and see them. I know it seems odd now but we did not take much notice of them as they played at various venues in and around Truro. We used to go along to different places because they used to advertise in the local paper where they would be appearing.

1971, LONDON, UK

JOHN DEACON JOINS on bass.

THE GARDENS
17 JULY 1971, PENZANCE, UK

I WAS THERE: GRAHAM DAY

DURING 1970, I holidayed with my friends Dave and Kevin in Torquay. It had not been a wholly successful week as, returning to the campsite in a farmer's field in Torbay after a Monday night out, the car hit some concrete blocks in the dark, with the result that when we got up next day and tried to take the car out, the wheels had an elliptical rather than a circular motion. Tuesday to Thursday was spent walking to a scrap yard, identifying some track rods, taking them off the scrap car and replacing the bent ones on our Ford 100e Popular. That left one day before returning home.

In 1971, me and my friends Dave and Kevin decided to go on holiday to North Devon and Ilfracombe with our student friend Clint, a guitarist who was really into underground/progressive music. The original idea was to stay for the fortnight, but with a paucity of nightlife, we decided to break camp and head down to Penzance in Cornwall, arriving on the Thursday of the first week, camping at Perranuthnoe, and existing in the main on a diet of Cornish pasties and pints served in the village pub.

Penzance was well served with entertainment facilities, notably The Garden, rebranded from the Winter Gardens by the owner John Adams in the late Sixties. It was essentially a very well appointed ballroom and in the Seventies the concentration was mainly on rock and progressive rock. We spotted a poster for The Garden and saw that our heroes at the time, the Canterbury Band Caravan, were performing at The Garden on Saturday 17th July. 'What a treat,' we thought, and made sure we were there early enough on the night to get in.

In the dim light on the stage were a four piece band with a strangely dressed lead singer

After a quick pint at the Alexander Inn next door, we ambled into the ballroom to see if the support band were any good. In the dim light on the stage were a four piece band with a strangely dressed lead singer. They started their set with some rock 'n' roll classics – 'Jailhouse Rock', 'Be-Bop-a-Lula' and 'Shake, Rattle and Roll' come to mind. Three of us were not at all impressed at all. This was not our kind of music, and belonged to another era. However, Clint was transfixed and decided to sit crosslegged on the floor (there was plenty of room to do so!) to watch them perform, whilst we three went back to the Alexander next door. When we decided that Caravan would soon be on, we returned to The Garden, which by now was beginning to fill up as everyone was anticipating them. Clint said the other band had been called Queen and they had been brilliant. It later transpired that Caravan always had a support band and John Adams on this occasion had been offered Queen for a fee of £25.

A couple of years later, we wished we had stayed to watch and listen to Queen, as their fame had begun to grow. They returned to The Garden as a thank you to John Adams for giving them a break. Being in our early twenties, we thought we knew everything. How wrong we were!

THE GARDEN
29 JULY 1971, PENZANCE, UK

I WAS THERE: TRISH BEARD

THEY PLAYED AT the Winter Gardens (also known as The Garden) in Penzance in Cornwall. I worked there collecting glasses and was able to speak to them. I remember the place being packed.

> Trish Beard was at The Garden when Queen played there

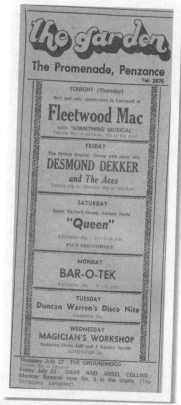

DRIFTWOOD SPARS
9 AUGUST 1971, ST AGNES, UK

I WAS THERE: JOE WEBSTER HAINES, AGE 18

I WAS ON holiday with my best friend Ricky. The pub just down the road from where we were staying was called the Driftwood Spars, right by the beach. We were told there was a live band playing that night so we went along to see. It was amazing and they were brilliant. It wasn't a massive room and not a high stage. It was quite intimate and we were very close to them. Freddie was oozing charisma even then.

Joe Webster Haines and her friend Ricky saw Queen playing in a Cornish pub

BEDFORD COLLEGE
28 JANUARY 1972, REGENTS PARK, LONDON, UK

I WAS THERE: RICHARD LUETCHFORD

I WAS IN the support band Prairie. It's mentioned in several Queen biographies as being the one where only six people turned up. In actual fact, no one turned up. The six people mentioned as being in the audience were the five members of my band plus our roadie! In 1971, my day job was working for the Social Services Department of Westminster City Council at City Hall in Victoria Street. Coming up for Christmas, we had a few students working there during their holidays, including a very attractive and stylish young woman student in the accounts department. I struck up a conversation with her and discovered that she was the Social Secretary for the student union at Bedford College. Hoping to impress her, I explained that I was in a band and that we were looking for our first gig. She said she'd like to hear us and I invited her to a band practice, held in the basement of my former employers, a music shop in West Street, WC2. She came along and, on the strength of our audition, she said she would book us, and that we would be support to another new band, called 'Queen'. The name Queen was the source of some amusing and rather homophobic remarks from my band mates.

The gig was scheduled to be at the beginning of the new college term. I am not sure why it was so badly attended, as college gigs then were usually packed, not only with students but also with music fans as the gigs were always advertised in the music press. It should have been a prestigious and well attended gig, but was a big let down for both bands, as we each played to a very big but very empty hall. We were trying out our newly acquired Sound City 100 watt stacks and mostly original material, and we were amazed to see Queen were still using battered old Vox AC 30s and playing rock 'n' roll covers.

We each played to a very big but very empty hall

After our set had ended, we had a few drinks in the bar and listened to Queen, as they had listened to us while we were on, and then we packed up and went home. I recall Brian May being particularly friendly and interested, and he came to see us when we played The Greyhound in Fulham later that year. I believe we both got £20 for the gig. Later that year, we were to hear a lot more of Queen. Prairie broke up and the members formed or joined new bands, none of which were ever to be heard of again.

MARQUEE CLUB
20 DECEMBER 1972, LONDON, UK

I WAS THERE: IAN NICHOLSON

I GOT TO see Queen live five times between 1972 and 1980, and two of those shows were for free! The first time was at the Marquee Club. Sparks were playing a number of shows at the venue, and tickets were given out free to these shows in *Sounds* magazine. A mate and I decided to check out one of these shows, so on a cold and wet Wednesday evening, we set out from South London to Wardour Street in the West End. As it turns out, we never got to see Sparks, but we did witness what was to us an unknown, but very impressive new band. Queen, even then, looked like rock stars, especially the visually and vocally impressive singer. The band played a good rocking set of songs from what was to become their debut album. My mate and I must have been impressed, as we did not bother with the arty Sparks (I kind of regret that now). This show was actually my second ever gig. Earlier that summer I had seen Alice Cooper, supported by Roxy Music at the Empire Pool, Wembley for my first ever live show. Two days after Queen, it was my third gig, Led Zeppelin at the Ally Pally. Not bad for my first three gigs.

BBC MAIDA VALE STUDIOS
5 FEBRUARY 1973, LONDON, UK

NOT YET SIGNED to EMI, Queen record 'Keep Yourself Alive', 'My Fairy King', 'Doing All Right' and 'Liar', to be broadcast on 15 February 1973.

QUEEN MARY'S COLLEGE
13 JULY 1973, BASINGSTOKE, UK

I WAS THERE: JANETTE BOYD-MARSHALL

THE FIRST TIME I saw them was at Basingstoke Tech. I was in my last year at Basingstoke High School for Girls and it was the last week of term. I can remember the sound being deafening, so that you could hardly hear for a few days afterwards. It was also hard to see much for the smoke. I seem to remember it being over 16s only - but it was the week before my birthday! I also saw them at Southampton Gaumont in 1974. A group of us went on motorbikes to see Deep Purple and Black Sabbath in the same week around Easter, and booked to see Queen later in the year. It must have been the *Sheer Heart Attack* tour. I remember it being winter and freezing, riding on the back of a bike on the way home. I was quite the hippy, so I would have been wearing flares and a sheepskin coat. Queen were louder than Purple or Sabbath and it was the first time I remember a decent light show. That was it for me until a year ago, when I saw them in Rotterdam. But things have changed and it seemed very tame and quiet in comparison.

Queen were louder than Deep Purple or Black Sabbath

QUEEN RELEASED
13 JULY 1973

I WAS THERE: MARTIN DAVIES

I REMEMBER LISTENING to Radio Luxembourg under the bedsheets with my tiny tinny pressed to my ear. The DJ announced the first release from a 'new' band by the name of Queen. From the very start I could hear that this was something out of the ordinary, not easy at a time when there were so many remarkable new

Martin Davies remembers hearing Queen on Radio Luxembourg

songs coming out nearly every week it seemed. By the time the drum solo came up, I was hooked. I can't remember when I bought the single - I still have it - but I made sure that their debut album was top of my Christmas list that year. I've still got that too!

MAYFAIR
3 AUGUST 1973, NEWCASTLE, UK

I WAS THERE: JIM HORROCKS

I SAW THEM about six months before they got into the charts. I'd gone to the City Hall with three mates to see a top band but couldn't get in so we ended up at the Mayfair. We were blown away with the Queen performance. I had never heard of them before but knew they would be big from that day. Not bad for £5 each to get in.

GOLDERS GREEN HIPPODROME
13 SEPTEMBER 1973, LONDON, UK

QUEEN RECORD AN 'In Concert' show for the BBC. Six songs that they are working on are eventually broadcast.

In November 1973 Queen embark on their first major tour, supporting Mott the Hoople

---

GAUMONT THEATRE
15 NOVEMBER 1973, WORCESTER, UK

I WAS THERE: MICHAEL WILLIAMS

ADMISSION WAS JUST £1.30. It was their first UK tour, to coincide with the pending release in February 1974 of what was to be their first hit single, 'Seven Seas of Rhye'. Top of the bill was Mott the Hoople with Ian Hunter. Freddie Mercury had long black hair and Brian May had far more curls than he does now, and was far less grey. They wore skin tight trousers and platform boots and we knew

very little about them as they had
no back catalogue. But what they
did do was to perform 'Seven
Seas of Rhye', announcing it
to us as their first single release.
It was obvious from their stage
persona and their music that
they were different to any other
group of that time. They did a
good set and went straight to a
bar café along Worcester's main
street, Foregate Street, and we
saw them there when we came
out of the theatre. They never

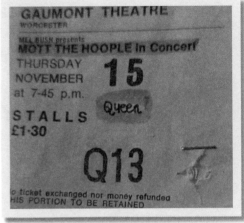

Michael Williams was at the Worcester Gaumont

played support again. They didn't need to. They were superstars in
their own right!

I WAS THERE: MIKE LANE, AGE 14

THE LOCAL CITY of
Worcester had big stars playing
at the Worcester Gaumont in
those days including The Beatles,
Jimi Hendrix and Rod Stewart.
I was astonished when I saw
Bowie on *Lift Off with Ayshea* on
TV and became besotted with
him. I asked my mum to get me
a ticket to see the Ziggy Stardust
show at the Worcester Gaumont.
It was sold out but she bought

Mike Lane was hoping to see Ziggy but
got Mott – and Queen

me a ticket to see a local band at the same venue - Mott the Hoople.
The gig was on 15 November 1973, my 14th birthday. I went with a
school friend, the first live music I had ever seen. The support act came
on with a fantastic loud entrance, and in a black and white skin tight
catsuit Freddie Mercury introduced me to the delights of Queen. I don't
remember the full playlist but the band were awesome. They finished
up with the single 'Liar' which I then bought at the venue. The gig was
awesome, as was Mott's performance. Queen of course later wrote the
lyric 'down in the city just Hoople and me'. I went on to see Queen two

more times, in the early 1980s at Milton Keynes and at *Live Aid* and in the early 1980s in Milton Keynes. It wasn't Ziggy Stardust, but my introduction to live music was still pretty amazing!

LIVERPOOL STADIUM
17 NOVEMBER 1973, LIVERPOOL, UK

I WAS THERE: ELAINE ANDERSON, AGE 13

I WENT WITH my then best friend Amanda Bennett. We used to get the ferry over every Saturday night as they had great bands on and cheap too. All our friends went even though we were so young. Queen were way better than Mott the Hoople, who we had gone to see, and I fell in love with them, especially Freddie. I just knew they would make it big, as the atmosphere was electric when they were on.

CIVIC HALL
19 NOVEMBER 1973, WOLVERHAMPTON, UK

I WAS THERE: AIDAN MULLINDER, AGE 18

MOTT THE HOOPLE had recently had a hit with 'Roll Away the Stone'. I'll always remember being so impressed by Queen's performance. The next I heard of them was in the spring of 1974 when I heard 'Seven Seas of Rhye' played on BBC Radio 1. I was then telling people I had seen them in November of the previous year. When I tell people nowadays that I saw Queen before they were famous, I sometimes wonder if they believe me - but it's true!

I WAS THERE: MARTIN ASTLEY

IN THOSE DAYS there was no internet, etc. so the news of any upcoming gigs was got from the music press ie, *Sounds*, *Melody Maker* or *NME*. Tickets would have to be purchased in person at the relevant box office or, if you felt lucky, by sending off a cheque and a self-addressed envelope.

Martin Astley went to see Mott the Hoople, not Queen

I bought the tickets on the strength of it being Mott. Finding Queen were supporting was a bonus. I guess the ticket price was somewhere in the region of £1.25. As the Civic Hall in Wolverhampton was local to where I lived, I bought the tickets direct from the box office. They also used to put up any future gigs on the notice board at the back of the box office with the stick on letters, so you would find yourself spending your £5 paper round money on two or possibly three other upcoming gigs as well! You could tell that Queen were certainly going to make it, and you couldn't say that for most of the support acts I've seen. They finished their set with a full version of 'Seven Seas of Rhye'.

NEW THEATRE
20 NOVEMBER 1973, OXFORD, UK

I WAS THERE: SIMON ELEMENT, AGE 17

A FEW DAYS before I had seen them on the *Old Grey Whistle Test*. Up until then I hadn't heard of them. After that short performance, I was really looking forward to seeing them and I wasn't disappointed. Freddie wore that black and white chequered outfit and ruled over the New Theatre in Oxford. The capacity is only around 2,000 but there must have been a lot of people who had watched the *Whistle Test* performance as it didn't take long for Freddie to command the audience. Brian May's guitar work was amazing. I have never thought he received the credit he deserved. The highlight for me was when they did 'Liar'. That still remains to this day as my favourite track. From their performance that night, you would think they'd been around for years. They blew Mott off the stage.

CITY HALL
22 NOVEMBER 1973, NEWCASTLE, UK

I WAS THERE: JOHN HALL

THE EARLY SEVENTIES in the UK is truly the golden age of rock and roll for teenagers like me. And tonight, my 18th birthday, it's off to the City Hall for another rock and roll celebration. Headliners are Mott the Hoople, a band I have seen multiple times, from their more underground rock and roll beginnings through to their metamorphosis into chart topping dudes, which is somewhat in conflict with my hippie sensibilities.

I catch the bus into Sunderland and then the train into Newcastle for the gig at the City Hall, my favorite venue in the North East. Arriving after a quick pint in the City Tavern, we take our seats. I always arrive in time to catch the support band. Not everyone does, but tonight is a bit different. The opening act is Queen. There is buzz in the media about this emerging act and you can feel it in the audience.

The band takes the stage. They already look like rock and roll stars and from their walk on music, 'Procession', and opening cut, 'Father to Son', they mean business. And it gets better. They move into 'Son and Daughter', 'Liar' and 'Keep Yourself Alive' via a rock and roll medley. Wow - this is rock and roll. They get a solid reaction from the audience but then all too soon it's over. After all, they are the opening act and they make way for Ian Hunter and the boys. It's my first exposure to the band who, even as relative unknowns, look and sound like a major act.

The following week I go to our local record store in Sunderland - Bergs (they also sell bikes) to buy their album. They don't have it in stock and have never heard of Queen, but will order it for me. I tell everyone I know about this great new band I have just seen – 'a glam Led Zeppelin' is how I describe them - and how big they are going to be. When the record finally arrives, I play it constantly, especially 'Son and Daughter', 'Liar' and 'Keep Yourself Alive' - and hope to catch the band live again soon. Live gigs are what it's all about.

I WAS THERE: JOHN PEACE

I HAVE TO confess that I wasn't much impressed with them. I stayed for the first couple of songs, neither of which I remember now, and then retired to the bar. If it's any consolation, I didn't care much for Mott the Hoople either but the ticket price was probably only a quid. I think it was Freddie Mercury's silver jump suit that started me thinking 'wtf is this crap?' Bear in mind the previous gigs I'd seen included Deep Purple, Sabbath, Groundhogs and Hawkwind.

I WAS THERE: ALAN HARDINGHAM

I WENT TO the City Hall in Newcastle to see Mott the Hoople before they became a pop group. I watched in amazement when the support group went through their set. In the end we didn't even stay for Mott. Afterwards the bar was full of people saying how we were looking forward to Queen coming back.

I WAS THERE: KAREN FAGAN

IT WAS BEFORE Freddie buffed up. He had long hair, a black cloak and black nail polish. They were brilliant - I loved their early stuff.

I WAS THERE: ROBIN RUMBLE, AGE 15

I WAS LIVING in Hartlepool, County Durham and attending Henry Smith's Grammar school with my friend David Wise (who went on to become an excellent photographer). I had an idea to go to the City Hall Newcastle to watch Mott the Hoople. Out of my pocket money, I paid the princely sum of £1.25 for a ticket.

On the day, after walking home Dave and I got the bus to West Hartlepool in order to catch the train to Newcastle, 30 miles away. We arrived in Newcastle around 6pm and did what any teenager of that time would do – we headed to a bar near the concert venue. The City Tavern is only a very short stroll from the Newcastle City Hall, and after a couple of drinks it was time to go and attend our first ever live concert. We had not heard of Queen before buying the tickets. There was no ability to research groups or who was appearing pre the internet. So the music started and – wow - what a sound and what a lead singer, who even at this stage of his career had such stage presence you just knew would be a star.

So much of that night has eroded with time but a memory that has stayed with me is Freddie dressed in his black and white harlequin outfit singing 'Liar'. I am very privileged to have memories of Queen as a support band. The Mott the Hoople aspect of the concert just does not remain in my mind, as all we spoke about on the walk back to the station to catch the last train to Hartlepool and the three mile walk from the station to the Headland was Queen and Freddie Mercury.

I WAS THERE: PETER SMITH

THEY HAD JUST released their first album and there was already a great buzz about this new band. 'Keep Yourself Alive' was played a lot in the local Sunderland Mecca ballroom that we all frequented every weekend and people were keen to see them live. 'Would Queen blow Mott off the stage?' was the question we were all asking, this intrigue ensuring that the hall was crammed, a rarity for a support act.

They were excellent, much better than many of the bands I'd seen supporting major tours. It was obvious even then that this was a band who could well make it big, although few would have predicted just how successful they would ultimately become. It was clear that Freddie Mercury was already a star in his own head which manifested itself through his incredible stage presence. Brian May's guitar playing was excellent, his unique custom (self-made) instrument adding an extra dimension of interest.

So did they outshine Mott the Hoople? Well, both bands were great. However, there was an air of excitement surrounding Queen as everybody in attendance undoubtedly felt like they were experiencing something special. For once, the 'next big thing' prophecy did of course turn out to be true and I was to see Queen a further eight times in gradually bigger and bigger venues. Things in the Mott camp were however not so good, and the pressures of success, years on the road and big egos were soon to come to a head and I saw the band only once more before the end came for them.

APOLLO THEATRE
23 NOVEMBER 1973, GLASGOW, UK

I WAS THERE: BILLY COYLE, AGE 13

BECAUSE WE WERE younger and couldn't go to the pub to drink, we thought 'we might as well just go in and watch the support'. We always read the *NME*, *Melody Maker* or *Sounds* to check who the support was and see if it was worth going early. I'd never really heard of them because their first album was just coming out. They played 'Liar' and 'Seven Seas of Rhye' that I can remember of the eight or so songs they played. Even then Freddie's presence was something. He was wearing sleeves with wings but we thought it was a cape. By the time they finished, everyone knew they were going to be a massive band. When Mott the Hoople came on, it was a bit of an anti-climax. It was the first time I ever saw the support band blow the main band away.

After Freddie died, the Brian May Band played the Barrowlands in Glasgow. We were in the pit doing the security. We were told to sit down because they weren't expecting the punters to jump on the stage. I looked up and Brian May was stepping out. He stood on my mate's head. I had to grab his leg, turn him and put him back on the stage. I said to the tour manager afterwards, 'What the fuck happened there?' It turns out there was a bit of perspex that Brian stands on which went across the pit, but it had broken the night before and they forgot to tell him, so he walked out to play a guitar solo and stood on my mate's head instead. By way of an apology, he gave my mate the sixpence he'd used that night as his plectrum.

I WAS THERE: KENNY HARVEY, AGE 18

I FIRST SAW them the week after my 18th birthday. I then saw them in their own right as the headline act over the next three years and for the final time in 2008, when they were fronted by Paul Rodgers at the SECC in Glasgow. Each concert was excellent.

Kenny Harvey first saw Queen supporting Mott the Hoople

CALEDONIAN PICTURE HOUSE
25 NOVEMBER 1973, EDINBURGH, UK

I WAS THERE: CHRISTINE ROBERTSON

I SAW QUEEN on *Old Grey Whistle Test* performing 'Seven Seas of Rhye' and was immediately hooked. I went out and bought their album. I was also into Mott the Hoople and 'All the Young Dudes' is still one of my favourite tracks of all time (I'm also a big Bowie fan). When the chance to see both bands in a local venue - know locally as The Caley on Lothian Road - came up, my friends and I managed to get tickets really near the front. They were all going to see Mott so when Queen came on (all in black and white in those days) with Freddie strutting his stuff, I think I was the only one in the whole place that was standing up and singing along to the songs as no one else knew them. My friends were mortified and kept saying to me to sit down as I was embarrassing them. These days I don't care about being embarrassing. I'm too old to bother.

TOWN HALL
27 NOVEMBER 1973, BIRMINGHAM, UK

I WAS THERE: ANITA SZOLOMICKI

I CAN'T CLAIM to be a fan of theirs particularly; I just used to go and see a lot of bands when I was younger. But later in the Seventies I met Queen at the Albany Hotel in Birmingham when I went there for a job interview. I can't remember what the job was, although it wasn't anything to do with the hotel itself. I never actually got interviewed. I was too busy ingratiating myself with Freddie. Youth, eh?

I WAS THERE: GERALD CLEAVER

I HAD SEEN Mott many times; they were one of my favourite acts. Because of the timing of the trains from my home, I always arrived in good time to see the support act at Birmingham Town Hall. That wasn't always a good move, as some supports were dire. Anyway, Queen were different. The sound and lights were good for a start, which wasn't always the case for the support act. Secondly, they had some interesting songs, given most of the audience had never heard them before, and they could play their instruments, also not always a given in those days. Lastly, the band knew how to put on a show, and did so. Audiences in Birmingham were quite prepared to walk out if they didn't warm to a support act in 1973, but they were equally ready to respond enthusiastically and loudly if the band were trying. Queen went down very, very well, and needless to say, this was their only tour as a support act.

BRANGWYN HALL
28 NOVEMBER 1973, SWANSEA, UK

I WAS THERE: WAYNE OLIVER

I FIRST SAW Queen in the Brangwyn Hall, Swansea as support act for Mott the Hoople. They were very flamboyant, all dressed in black and white. They were great songs and Brian May did an amazing segment with an echoplex. I had never heard of them prior to the gig but after seeing them I went to the local record shop and bought the first album, which I loved. The ticket was 75p, a bargain. I saw them again at the same venue a year later. They were headlining then and were even better. Plenty of gigs had honed their stage craft.

The next time I saw them was at Cardiff Castle in 1976, and by then they were a well polished live act. The last time I saw them with Freddie was at Wembley following *Live Aid* which was another superb concert and probably in my all-time top three. I saw them with Paul Rodgers on vocals in Cardiff, and again they were really good but it was not the same without Fred, although he did make an appearance via video. I have yet to see them with Adam Lambert, but I am planning to.

COLSTON HALL
29 NOVEMBER 1973, BRISTOL, UK

I WAS THERE: ANNABEL MARSHALL

I SAW QUEEN as support act to Mott the Hoople at Bristol's Colston Hall. Of course, it's not allowed to be called that now – it's now the Bristol Beacon. I thought Queen were terrific, very impressive for a support act, and I bought their first album, which I loved, and still do, although after that I didn't really care that much for them.

Annabel Marshall saw Queen on their breakthrough tour supporting Mott

WINTER GARDENS
30 NOVEMBER 1973, BOURNEMOUTH, UK

I WAS THERE: JULIA COLLINS, AGE 19

I WENT EITHER with my friend Christine, or another friend Theresa. I saw lots of bands at that venue, from around 1970 to the early Nineties. Now it's just a car park next to the Bournemouth International Centre. Queen had just released 'Seven Seas of Rhye' and they were absolutely amazing! They were definitely a hard act to follow and Mott were just an anti-climax. Queen were far superior.

WINTER GARDENS BOURNEMOUTH
Exeter Road   Telephone 26446

Mel Bush presents

MOTT
THE HOOPLE

plus supporting act

Queen

Friday 30th November at 7.30pm
Tickets : £1.10, 80p
Box Office open 10am to 5pm   (10am - 8.30pm concert dates) Sundays Concert Dates only 2pm - 8.30pm

Julia Collins saw Queen supporting Mott the Hoople

I WAS THERE: MICK SEARLE, AGE 14

I HAD JUST turned 14 and spend most of my time hanging around with my next door neighbour, Paul Smart, who was a couple of years older than me. My first recollection of Queen was hearing 'Keep Yourself Alive' on the radio, although we thought the DJ said Cream which was odd as not only had they split up but it sounded nothing them. Further plays on the radio obviously confirmed it was by a band called Queen not Cream! Soon after, Paul bought the album and we spent many hours listening to it and gradually learning more about Queen. If my memory serves me correctly, John Deacon was listed as Deacon John on the back of the album sleeve. Towards the end of the summer, we learnt with great excitement that Queen were coming to Bournemouth Winter Gardens as support to Mott the Hoople, who we were also fans of.

November 30th arrived and with massive excitement we caught the bus to Bournemouth and made our way to the venue. When Queen hit the stage, we left our seats and ran to the front of the stage, along with a few others who had also obviously come to see Queen. At the start of the concert they played a few songs that had not previously heard as they were from *Queen ll* which had not yet been released. Of these, 'Ogre Battle' stood out.

When Queen hit the stage we ran to the front of the stage

As the concert progressed they played more from the first album and I particularly remember 'Liar' and 'Keep Yourself Alive' going down well. I also recall two encores which included a fantastic version of 'Big Spender'. The feeling at the end was one of amazement at how good they had been. Sadly, in comparison Mott the Hoople were a disappointment. I bought *Queen ll* when it was released and I thought it was brilliant. Although I quite liked much of the albums that followed, I never thought it matched their early stuff.

Mick Searle thought he'd heard
that Cream had reformed

KURSAAL
1 DECEMBER 1973, SOUTHEND-ON-SEA, UK

I WAS THERE: BRIAN JONES

I WAS 16 going on 17. 'Seven Seas' had not long come out but I was there to see Mott as I was - and still am - a big Bowie fan, and of course he gave them 'All The Young Dudes'. My only memories of Queen really were of Freddie having a hole in his tights – I think he was wearing his harlequin outfit - and of me being close enough to the front to see Freddie and Roger in the wings doing backing vocals to 'Dudes'.

Brian Jones was at the Kursaal

CENTRAL HALL
2 DECEMBER 1973, CHATHAM, UK

I WAS THERE: TONY YEO

I WAS INFLUENCED by my elder brother musically, so tended to like groups that maybe friends of my age didn't. In 1973 Bowie was to play at Chatham Central Hall but my brother pulled out of going to see him due to some work exams so I didn't go, one of my biggest regrets ever. Later on, it was announced that Mott the Hoople were to play at CCH and that a group called Queen were the support act. At that point, no one had of them much, but I was determined not to miss out on seeing Mott. My brother had bought the first Queen album. It was great and

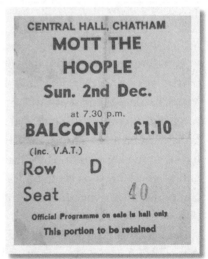

CENTRAL HALL, CHATHAM
MOTT THE HOOPLE
Sun. 2nd Dec.
at 7.30 p.m.
BALCONY £1.10
(Inc. V.A.T.)
Row D
Seat 40
Official Programme on sale in hall only
This portion to be retained

Tony Yeo saw Queen supporting Mott the Hoople at Chatham's Central Hall

had an instrumental of 'Seven Seas' on it. Myself and a friend travelled to Chatham by train to queue for tickets outside CCH on a Saturday morning.

We even got on the wrong train going home and ended up in Bromley South - but we were only 14.

On the night of the concert, Queen came on to the stage with Freddie wearing a pair of what looked like satin flared trousers with one black leg and the other white and already using his long mic. I don't really remember the songs that well, as they weren't familiar at that time, but we all knew we were watching a class act. They were absolutely brilliant and really knew how to rock the stage.

Mott came on stage after to do their gig but Queen weren't finished. When Mott sang 'Roll Away the Stone', Queen came on to do the 'Sha la la la push push' part of the song. Next day at school, I told everyone how good Queen were. As a footnote, my brother was walking up Chatham High Street and saw Overend Watts through the window of a Wimpey, with his white platform boots on. A brilliant night, never to be forgotten.

HAMMERSMITH ODEON
14 DECEMBER 1973, LONDON, UK

I WAS THERE: JOHN BISHOP, AGE 18

THE GIG WAS the late one, starting at 8:30 pm. They were the supporting act to Mott the Hoople. I liked David Bowie then so went to see Mott due to their Bowie connection. I had not really heard of Queen. At that time, my friends and I were forming a band and were busy practising to start gigging in pubs and clubs at first, just like how Queen started. The concert started and on came 'The Hoople' as some people called them. After half an hour or so, some of the crowd started chanting 'we want Queen'. This went on during most of their set. They finished their set and then there was an interval. Then on came Queen, the audience erupted, and all stood up, including me. I'm not quite sure why.

When they started played, I could see why. They were excellent, and as I like rock music, I thoroughly enjoyed their set. At the end of the concert I was buzzing as I had not heard such a variation in music before. Having been to a few concerts before, this was by far the most enjoyable and superior one so far!

In a way, I felt sorry for Mott the Hoople, but they so far had had a good run. Now it was Queen's turn!

I WAS THERE: CHRIS NAYLOR, AGE 19

I WAS SO excited to be heading for the Hammersmith Odeon in London to see my favourite band at the time, Mott the Hoople. They were going to be singing their new single, 'Roll Away the Stone', and I couldn't wait. The warm up act was a band I had never heard of, called Queen, but of course with all bands you have to give them a chance. Well, I didn't know what to say. They completely, totally and utterly blew my mind. I loved them. The set was a mixture of their own music and a number of covers, and when Mott the Hoople

Chris Naylor was really excited to be seeing Mott - and then he saw Queen!

came on, it was like a side show. I still loved their set, but all I could talk about afterwards was Queen. Since that day, they have always been my favourite band and I have all their albums. Sadly, I never got to see them again while they were at the peak of their power, though I did see them with Adam Lambert a few years ago at the O2. My love of the music and the way it was presented, combining videos of Freddie with the live music, left my love of the music undiminished. Adam Lambert is an incredibly good replacement. Queen are my favourite band, and always will be.

I WAS THERE: GARY T EVANS, AGE 15

I'D NEVER BEEN to a live gig before. I went with a friend from school. We had got tickets to see Mott the Hoople, who were a top group at the time, recording hit after hit – 'All the Young Dudes', 'All the Way from Memphis', 'Roll Away the Stone.' Ian Hunter was their lead singer, with his long, permed hair and dark glasses, and Mick Ralphs, their lead guitarist in his long-legged boots. The Hammersmith Odeon was a converted cinema. Queen were the support act, unknown at the time, and a very heavy rock group. Freddie wore black back then, but was still full of his alter ego, and they all had long hair. Little did we know where they were going to be heading in the history of the music world. From that night I was hooked on their, as I liked there raw, earlier music and collected their first four LPs.

I went to see them again when they released *A Night at the Opera*. They had completely changed to the more subtle music that generations know them for. Freddie had changed from black to white in his stage costumes, strutting more and posturing to the crowd. By then they had a list of hits. I felt the music after that LP became more commercial. The rawness had gone and it was all very polished.

I stopped buying their LPs but when Freddie took to the stage, he had the audience eating out of his hand with every movement. Freddie was before his time, a showman of the highest degree and a tragic loss to the music world. But his music lives on, as will Freddie in music lovers' hearts.

I WAS THERE: DAVID NEWTON

I WAS VERY impressed by them. Freddie was a great front man and even in the early days you could see they were going to be something special.

I WAS THERE: SALLY ATKINS

I FIRST HEARD Queen's 'Seven Seas of Rhye' and loved it so I bought the first LP. I remember thinking it was amazing - Freddie's voice, the sound, everything. I used to follow Mott the Hoople and when I heard Queen were supporting, I was really pleased. A friend and I saw them at Hammersmith. I remember Freddie standing in the spotlight holding a mic stand over his head. The music was fantastic - we were hooked! I remember them wearing black and white and people painting their nails to match Freddie's. The whole band was just streets ahead.

I managed to see them a few times and particularly remember a concert they did in London on Christmas Eve. It was magical, and they did an encore. I bought all their albums, they were always progressing and had something new. Freddie had such charisma. He really did hold the audience in the palm of his hand. As they got more and more famous, we weren't able to afford the tickets. I got married and had children but still loved Queen as did my husband. I watched them on *Live Aid* and they were so polished. My daughters loved 'Bohemian Rhapsody'. It was a sad day when Freddie died and all that talent was gone. I can't think of another band that had four such talented members, musicians and songwriters.

UNIVERSITY OF LEICESTER
15 DECEMBER 1973, LEICESTER, UK

I WAS THERE: PETER RODGERS

IT WAS MY first Christmas at Leicester Uni and it was the Stamford Hall Christmas party. There could only have been a couple of hundred people there at most. People didn't really know who they were. They gave a really good set and I remember thinking that they had a very good guitarist but that the lead singer was not very happy to be there, because we students were just standing looking at them and he kept telling us off for not dancing. It was

Peter Rodgers was in an audience of only 200 for Queen

only a little later that I got to know them and, unfortunately, my (now) wife fell for Brian May and so we bought all of their albums over the years and, later on, those of Brian himself. We saw Brian and his band live in Nottingham some years later and my wife was shocked by the bad language. We still have the vinyl albums and my wife's 62nd birthday present from our younger son was *The Platinum Collection*.

In January 1974, Queen flew out to Australia to play the Sunbury Festival

---

SUNBURY FESTIVAL
27 JANUARY 1974, SUNBURY, AUSTRALIA

I WAS THERE: PAUL DOWLING, AGE 16

I ACTUALLY SAW Queen live in Australia on two occasions in their early days. The first was in 1974 at Sunbury Festival. The second was at Festival Hall in 1976 as part of their *Night at the Opera* world tour. Sunbury was less memorable that the Festival Hall concert as it was an outside venue, pouring with rain and the schedule was behind. This caused some fans to become irate and I personally think Australia wasn't quite ready for a band like Queen. I also feel that Queen, at that time, were not the type of band that could keep a crowd like that entertained. The lads received a hostile reception and were actually booed when they left the stage, but I could see then that they were going to be big.

Jump forward a little over two years and Queen triumphantly returned to Australia. I attended their concert at Festival Hall in Melbourne in April 1976 and was completely blown away. Queen had transformed themselves into one of the most

Paul Dowling saw Queen twice

amazing bands I have ever seen – even to this day. From the very outset Freddie had the full house in the palm of his hands. It was certainly a night that will live long in my memory. They were the only two occasions I managed to see this magnificent band live. The two performances were vastly different but they still managed to influence my taste in music and became my favourite band of all time.

TOP OF THE POPS
21 FEBRUARY 1974, LONDON, UK

I WAS THERE: DAVE HOLLAND

IT WAS A dark and wintry Thursday night as a 13-year-old weed, having skilfully faked doing his homework and polished off his Findus Crispy Pancakes and chips, settled down in front of the television to absorb the movers and shakers on that week's essential programme for music lovers; *Top of the Pops*. I was that weed. Emperor Rosko was mien genial host, an exotic American DJ currently plying his trade with Radio 1. He kicked off proceedings by introducing David Bowie, swiftly followed by Alvin Stardust. So far so good. I was a 13-year-old weed who had been brushed by the glittery wand of glam rock and was now firmly under its spell.

And then we were all ushered to the BBC weather studio. This was where a band making its debut had pre-recorded a performance due to a BBC technicians' strike. Come on, it was the 1970s; of course there was a strike. A crazed piano intro that sounded like a sped-up fairground nightmare ushered in a bunch of hairy musicians, draped in black with serious looks on their faces, who began to deliver an aggressive hard rock number with a weird time signature. The bass player had a bow tie on. 'What a rebel' I thought gleefully. Then the singer preened into view and filled the family television screen with the future of music for this teenage weed. I was hooked by the time the rest of the group paused for this tousle-haired gothic stick insect to deliver the chorus: 'I'll take you to the Seven Seas of Rhye'.

'Bunch of idiots,' proclaimed my dad. He said that a lot whilst watching *Top of the Pops*. I didn't care, these were now my bunch of idiots and I needed to go to the Seven Seas of Rhye immediately.

EARLS COURT
EARLY 1970s, LONDON, UK

I WAS THERE: TILLY VACHER

MY FLATMATE IN the early 1970s taught in the same primary school as Veronica, John Deacon's wife, although she may still have been his girlfriend at that point. She and John plus Roger Taylor came to one of our bottle parties in Earls Court. We had a record player for dancing and too many people squeezed into the flat! It was nothing glamorous. I know they had just been for a fitting for their costumes for a *Top of the Pops* appearance. When Veronica left that school in Fulham, I took over her class. I remember John was quiet, and Roger was equally quiet.

'SEVEN SEAS OF RHYE'
RELEASED 23 FEBRUARY 1974

WINTER GARDENS
1 MARCH 1974, BLACKPOOL, UK

I WAS THERE: TIM PEKAREK

IT WAS THE Freshers Ball. 'Seven Seas of Rhye' had just come out. Queen cost £300 and were brilliant. We all said 'these lot are gonna make it!'

FRIARS
2 MARCH 1974, AYLESBURY, UK

ROSEMARY BAXTER, AGE 16
THEY'D BEEN ON the *Old Grey Whistle Test* and I liked their set so I managed to get right to the front up against the stage. I was having a great time until Freddie swung his head and I got covered in his sweat so I backed off quickly! I really can't remember much more apart from being squashed up against the stage close enough to be able touch them if you wanted. But it just didn't happen, as Friars was not for teeny boppers!

GUILDHALL
3 MARCH 1974, PLYMOUTH, UK

MY BROTHER WAS THERE: LYSETTE ANTHONY
MY BROTHER SAW them at Plymouth Guildhall in 1974. He was 14 and says Queen were great - and very loud! Nutz were support.

LOCARNO BALLROOM
8 MARCH 1974, SUNDERLAND, UK

I WAS THERE: JOHN HALL
QUEEN RETURN TO the North East in March of '74 and play our local ballroom in Sunderland - the Mecca, as we call it - for another great show. I don't recall too much about the set except that they play my three favourites ('Son and Daughter', 'Liar' and 'Keep Yourself Alive') and the rock and roll medley, plus some tracks from *Queen II* with 'Modern Times Rock 'n' Roll' as an encore. Oh, and of course 'Big Spender', which is a bit different. The word spreads, this band is the real deal. I continue to be an evangelist for the cause. This band is going to be big. 'Seven Seas of Rhye' gets some airplay and even makes an appearance on *Top of the Pops*, which is okay.

Then, unexpectedly, disaster strikes. The band feature on *Top of the Pops* in October '74 with their new single 'Killer Queen', with its Noel Cowardish lyrical leanings. What is this? I am appalled. What happened to my glam Led Zeppelin? They sold out, man. I give my album away in disgust. Despite my excitement around the subsequent single, 'Now I'm Here', I remain unconvinced. I would not see the band again until 2006 in Washington DC, as Queen+Paul Rodgers. (Aah, the impetuousness of youth).

Over the years a few funny things happened. Following my massive and genuine promotion of the band after that '73 show, so many people have followed up with me saying 'you were right John, they are a great band' and 'you called it right John, they made it big'. And - of course - they became superstars. Even more interestingly, just a few months ago, I watched an interview with Brian May in which he said that when 'Killer Queen' came out, many of their original fans weren't too comfortable with this change in direction. Thanks for the validation, Brian. Maybe I was wrong but at least I was not alone.

I WAS THERE: PETER SMITH

A FEW MONTHS after seeing Queen for the first time, as support for Mott the Hoople, they were back in the region, playing to a packed Sunderland Locarno. This, their first headline tour, was at the time of the *Queen II* album, which was released in the UK on the very same day as the Sunderland gig. The single 'Seven Seas of Rhye' had been released a few days earlier, and became the band's first hit, reaching number 10 in the UK charts. The big show-stopping number was 'Liar', which extended to around 10 minutes live and was a massive favourite at the time.

Everyone I knew attended and talked about this gig for months - if not years - afterwards. Queen were starting to make a big name for themselves. Their set was amazing, full of energy and an enigmatic quality that left us feeling sure that we'd witnessed something special. Like other bands at the time, Queen possessed all the sensibilities of a rock line up. However, Freddie's showmanship and vocal power elevated them to a whole new level. Their energy gave you the impression that they were destined for big things and the band's image, along with May's home-made guitar, added a peculiarity to the performance. We were all transfixed.

GREYHOUND
10 MARCH 1974, CROYDON, UK

I WAS THERE: DAVID NEWTON

MY REGULAR SUNDAY night haunt was The Greyhound in Croydon, where from 50p to £1.50 we were treated to an array of all the top bands of the Seventies, one of which was Queen. It was a small sweaty venue with a small stage and it had a great buzz about it. We saw they were coming up and, having seen them supporting Mott, got our tickets in advance. We were totally blown away by their energy - Brian May's guitar work and Freddie wielding the half mic stand. This would have been around 'Seven Seas of Rhye' time.

The next time I saw them was back at Hammersmith for the Christmas shows and, sad to say, I was slightly disappointed. I don't know why, and it was nothing that I could put my finger on. Maybe it was because I'd seen them in smaller venues and it was something exciting and new, but I wasn't a great lover of *Night at the Opera* at the time.

I WAS THERE: KATANA SUZUK PETE

ME AND A couple of mates used to roadie at the Greyhound. We'd turn up in the morning, help the roadies set up and then we used to get in for nothing. I remember that after setting up for Queen we were all sitting in the bar area trying to figure out how to get to the beer bottles behind the closed grille. Freddie walked past with a big fluffy jacket on. I don't know why I remember it but it just stuck in my mind. They played a blinding gig that night. They hit the big time shortly afterwards.

QUEEN MARGARET UNION UNIVERSITY OF GLASGOW
15 MARCH 1974, GLASGOW, UK

I WAS THERE: ROBERT FIELDS

MY BEST FRIEND John was single. He bought a stereo with a cassette deck. We'd chip in £1.50 each a week. He'd pick an album one week and I'd get a tape of it and next week I'd pick an album and he'd do a tape of that. That was how I bought Queen's very first album. I bought *Queen I* and I never even had a record player, so I'd go and visit friends and have them play the album for me. They were vibrant - the vocals, the three part harmonies. I honestly thought Queen were absolutely special.

I bought tickets for Mott the Hoople and told John, 'The band supporting them is called Queen. Their new single's called 'Liar'.' I'd heard it on John Peel. Alan 'Fluff' Freeman played it on his Saturday afternoon show on Radio 1. Kid Jensen played it too. But the Apollo never had a bar and John had this terrible habit of not going to see support bands so he missed out on Queen and I never let him forget it.

Three or four months after that, they announced they were playing the Queen Margaret Union. Because I'd worked on the Queen Margaret Union as an apprentice when it was being built, I had the principal's phone number. Any time there were any leaks or anything, I was always the person who got sent into the main hall or one of the lecture rooms to sort it. And the principal said, 'Any time you're wanting a gig in here, I'll get you in.' There were no tickets for that gig and no guest list because it was for students only and you needed a student card to get in. You signed in and paid your money. The principal put me on to two girls who signed us in, so we bought them a couple of pints as a thank you and just wandered up to the front. There was nobody there.

They were 30 to 45 minutes late coming on and looked very dishevelled. The *NME* and *Sounds* reported at the time that they'd had a massive fight in the dressing room regarding hairspray, mascara and make up. They were lucky if there were 60 people there. Me and John were down the front with about another 20 people. People were singing 'God Save the Queen' to welcome them on stage. When they came on, I shook Brian's hand and then Freddie's. They only did four or five songs before they overloaded the power circuit and blew the PA, but they were phenomenal. Very few bands get the hairs to stand up on the back of your neck. Queen did that to you. John and I lived eight miles outside of Glasgow and had to walk home afterwards.

Very few bands get the hairs to stand up on the back of your neck. Queen did

---

The next album was *Sheer Heart Attack* and I never saw Queen again after that. When they rocked, they rocked. But having four different songwriters with different styles, their music no longer appealed to me. They had a couple of good rockers on every album but there was a lot of *Sgt. Pepper-*type, vaudeville jazz stuff. There wasn't a lot to keep my attention.

Although we only saw four or five songs that night, it was a piece of history that will live with me forever.

UNIVERSITY OF STIRLING
16 MARCH 1974, STIRLING, UK

I WAS THERE: TJ MACJEE

THEY PLAYED IN the dining hall. The stage was a makeshift construction made of lab tables tied together covered with a tarpaulin. Queen played four encores, but it wasn't enough for the culture-starved locals and a riot ensued. Roadies were hospitalised as bikers and boot boys fought it out, with Queen retiring to the kitchen until escape was possible. I hid under the stage until the riot petered out. It was 55 pence a ticket, and an entertaining night to say the least.

WINTER GARDENS
29 MARCH 1974, PENZANCE, UK

QUEEN'S FINAL CORNISH appearance sees their set include 'Keep Yourself Alive', 'Liar' and two performances of 'Jailhouse Rock'.

RAINBOW THEATRE
31 MARCH 1974, LONDON, UK

I WAS THERE: IAN NICHOLSON

MY SECOND QUEEN show was at the Rainbow Theatre. This tour was for the *Queen II* album, and here we were starting to witness the rise of a band that was maturing into a major live act. It was quite remarkable how they had grown since that first Marquee show I'd seen. Freddie was certainly starting to really stamp his identity as one of rock music's finest, and most unique, front men. My memory of the songs played that night is sketchy, although I do recall the excellent rock and roll medley that brought the show to a climax, along with 'Big Spender'! Most of all, I was left with the impression that here was a band that was going to become huge.

I WAS THERE: JOHN SPENCER

THE FIRST TIME I saw Queen, they were the warm up act for Mott the Hoople at Hammersmith Odeon. At the start of their act, they were so unknown I was sat on the edge of the stage, until some roadie type guy told me to get off!

In March 1974 they were back in London at the Rainbow, which actually wasn't that far from where I grew up, and by this time they were the headline act. As was the way in those days, you phoned the box office to find out when tickets would go on sale and then you went to the venue, queued up and hopefully bought your tickets.

Early Queen were something different, with Freddie running all over the place being very flamboyant. Brian's guitar work was like nothing I'd ever heard before, John was doing the usual bassist thing, standing quite still but you could see he was a rocker, and Roger at the back was making lots of noise.

In April 1974, Queen embarked on their first North American tour, supporting Mott the Hoople, as they had in the autumn of 1973.

KIEL AUDITORIUM
18 APRIL 1974, ST LOUIS, MISSOURI

I WAS THERE: LOU BABINGA

I WAS ON the fourth row. It was a really short set, maybe 35 minutes at the most, but the first LP had come out around Christmas time over here and then seeing they were opening for Mott in April, who I had been a longtime fan of, was a bonus.

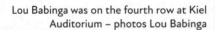

Lou Babinga was on the fourth row at Kiel Auditorium – photos Lou Babinga

URIS THEATRE
10 MAY 1974, NEW YORK, NEW YORK

I WAS THERE: JIM MORRIONE

MY VERY FIRST concert experience was seeing Mott the Hoople at the Uris Theater in NYC. This was the first time a rock show was playing Broadway. Queen were the opening act. I'd never heard of anything by Queen at that time and didn't know what to expect. My music tastes at that time were more towards glam/art rock - Alice Cooper, Roxy Music, Yes, etc. - and so I was pleasantly surprised. They handled the crowd, which naturally was waiting for Mott, well. I remember Freddie prancing around in a one piece jumpsuit in black and white checkerboard pattern, and I was pleasantly surprised to see that costume again in the movie *Bohemian Rhapsody*. Although I did enjoy their show, I never became a record buying fan of theirs. In hindsight, I should have really liked them, but they never caught on for me.

Years later, and as an out gay man then living in LA, I actually met Freddie twice in the early Eighties. The first time was in the nightclub called Probe in LA. He was just off with his group and people were stopping by, saying hello. The second time I saw him was at The Saint disco in NYC, the old Fillmore Theatre). That time, he was again with a small group. My friend and I approached him to talk. This time, he was very social and spoke several minutes with us and his friends. He was real nice.

TOP OF THE POPS
11 OCTOBER 1974, LONDON, UK

QUEEN RETURN TO the *Top of the Pops* studio to perform 'Killer Queen'. It's a performance that enraptures thousands of British teenagers and properly introduces Queen to the world.

Sheer Heart Attack *was released on 8 November 1974 by EMI Records in the UK and by Elektra in the USA. The album was supported by a 19 date UK tour that started in Manchester at the Apollo Theatre on 23 October 1974 and concluded with two shows at London's Rainbow Theatre.*

EMPIRE THEATRE
1 NOVEMBER 1974, LIVERPOOL, UK

I WAS THERE: LEO PHILLIPS, AGE 20

I SAW THEM at Liverpool Empire in 1974 on the *Sheer Heart Attack* tour, and then again in 1975 on the *Night of the Opera* tour. They were brilliant both times of course, but the 1974 tour was absolutely stunning and Mercury and May were stupendous. In my humble opinion Queen are the best band since The Beatles, and I saw them too (in 1964). Queen were on form before they got global attention. The '75 tour was brilliant, but I'm a fan of *Queen II* and *Sheer Heart Attack*. On the first album, they were finding their feet and were a little Led Zep, which is fine by me.

Leo Phillips thought Queen were the best band he'd seen since The Beatles

COVENTRY THEATRE
3 NOVEMBER 1974, COVENTRY, UK

I WAS THERE: BOB DIXON

MY FIRST MEMORY of seeing Queen was on the *Old Grey Whistle Test* on BBC2. They sang a song called 'Liar' while on tour supporting Mott the Hoople. I was still at school and waited patiently for the release of their first LP. I didn't get to see Queen until November 1974 and I then saw them seven times in total. The Coventry Theatre show was followed by Coventry (again) and Birmingham in '75, New Bingley Hall in '77, and the NEC in Birmingham in '79 and again in '84, for the outstanding *Works* tour. We weren't to know Knebworth was going to be Freddie's last, but I was there for what was billed as *A Night of Summer Magic*. I remember being blown away by Brian May's guitar solos as well as Freddie's stage presence. The early gigs at small theatres were far more intimate than the later shows in vast arenas such as the NEC and Knebworth. Freddie was the ultimate frontman and a joy to watch throughout his and the band's career together. Many friends were made along the journey and even more since, when talking to people and finding that new friends were at the same gigs 40 years ago. Although I won't be there to hear it, I plan to have Freddie sing at my funeral.

CITY HALL
5 NOVEMBER 1974, SHEFFIELD, UK

I WAS THERE: RUSSELL MORGAN

LONG AGO IN a village just down the road a bit, a pal of mine moved away with his parents to a neighbouring village. It was only a bus ride away and we were able to visit each other from time to time. Steve made new friends and would bring one or two of them over when he visited. One day Steve turned up and with him was a lanky kid with black, shoulder length, corkscrew hair. Under his arm was an LP. Steve knew I was a rock music nut and introduced us (his name escapes me unfortunately as I never saw him again). The young man presented me with the LP and the cover showed a grainy image of a figure in a spot light accompanied by the heading 'Queen'. I asked him what he had brought and he replied, 'This is the new album from one of the biggest bands this country's ever gonna see.' Always up for a new musical experience, I invited them in and put the album on our new Bush stereogram. The opening track was 'Keep Yourself Alive' and the result was that I was gobsmacked. The funny thing is, the fact that this kid was a dead ringer for Brian May meant nothing to me because I'd not seen any images of Brian at this point.

A few years later, my mates and I saw Queen for the first time on the *Sheer Heart Attack* tour at Sheffield City Hall and the support act was a band called Hustler. We had seen Hustler several times at a local venue called the Golden Diamond and they always delivered a cracking set. This made the Queen gig even more tantalising. And sure enough, Hustler played out of their collective skin to a roaring reception. I felt proud of them in some odd way. Then, after the changeover, Queen took the stage and, just like the lanky kid with the corkscrew hair said, I knew I was in the presence of greatness. The rest as they say....

ST GEORGE'S HALL
6 NOVEMBER 1974, BRADFORD, UK

I WAS THERE: DEREK COLE, AGE 16

TICKETS WERE £1. It was my first big live concert. I had heard 'Seven Seas of Rhye' on the radio and, as a lover of heavy rock and prog, I loved this new sound so I bought a ticket and took a punt on this new band on the scene. Hustler came on and they were great. Then the curtains went up and Queen played an ear blistering intro for Freddie. There was

Derek Cole saw Queen at Bradford's St George's Hall

smoke, explosions and white spots before Freddie emerged through the clouds of white smoke in a white leotard and full red cloak with ermine edges and a coronation crown. The crowd was gobsmacked. They just blew us all away. We came away saying, 'What a band, what a night!' The rest is history.

Freddie emerged through the smoke in a white leotard

CITY HALL
7 NOVEMBER 1974, NEWCASTLE, UK

I WAS THERE: JOHN PAUL PHILLIPSON, AGE 22

THE NEWCASTLE CROWD would not let Freddie go. He kept singing Elvis hits as encores. He was loved by women as well as men. I remember a sexy young woman crawling over my head trying to reach the stage.

APOLLO THEATRE
8 NOVEMBER 1974, GLASGOW, UK

I WAS THERE: DAVID FINLAY, AGE 16

I STILL HAVE the 50p poster from the gig. It was a great night and my first ever gig. I had actually been a Queen fan after hearing them on the *Old Grey Whistle Test*. Their first single, 'Keep Yourself Alive', was played and my brother bought the album. I went to quite a few gigs after that and still have some of the tickets. I saw them in Edinburgh in '76 and had to sleep in the train station as I missed the last train home! I also travelled to London on the overnight train for the free Hyde Park gig in '76 and went to the old Empire Pool in Wembley, after which I slept in my car and drove back up to Glasgow the next day. The craziest thing I ever did was to travel to London for the Earls Court gig in 1977. I could only stay for 45 minutes and I had to leave because I'd miss the train back to Scotland. All the way from Glasgow to London just to see 45 minutes of Queen. Some day!

I WAS THERE: MARIA WILSON, AGE 20

MY SISTER GOT me the ticket as she was a huge fan of Freddie's and I had just had my first son and was going through the baby blues. Well, I tell you - babies and blues were completely forgotten that night. I was mesmerised and energised for ever by them. The energy in that old, falling to bits Apollo was tangible! I had seen T. Rex, The Who and the Stones there before but never ever had I felt that feeling in my heart for a band before! After the gig I remember walking down the road in the rain, singing Queen songs along with all the other fans, all going their separate ways but all with the same buzz as me. That buzz for Queen never left me.

I WAS THERE: GERRY O'DONNELL, AGE 17

I SAW QUEEN twice at the Glasgow Apollo, in 1974 and 1975. 'Bohemian Rhapsody' was at number 1 in the UK charts at the time of the 1975 gig and it's my favourite gig ever. I used to read books on myths and legends and was also into heavy metal music. When I first heard *Queen II*, which combined both of my likes, I was blown away. It's still my favourite album. When *Sheer Heart Attack* was released, I bought the album and tickets for the tour promoting it. The gig opened with 'Now

I'm Here' ('Procession' isn't really part of the set list in my opinion), with the spotlight shining on Freddie at the right hand side of the stage when he sang 'now I'm here'. When he sang 'now I'm there' the spotlight again shone on him, but he was standing at the left hand side of the stage - or someone purporting to be him was! When the band joined in with their instruments, the light show started and he was centre stage. Being an impressionable teenager, I was blown away by this entrance. I still remember it to this day.

I WAS THERE: SCOTT ARMSTRONG, AGE 15

MY BIG BROTHER and his pal took me. It was my first time in the Glasgow Apollo and I was so excited. When they played 'Now I'm Here', with Freddie being on one side of the stage and then magically appearing on the other, it was fantastic. I was blown away. The lights, the smell - the whole thing! - was wonderful.

Scott Armstrong was visiting the Apollo for the first time

GUILD HALL
10 NOVEMBER 1974, PRESTON, UK

I WAS THERE: GARRY BOOCOCK

A GROUP OF us used to run the Hibernian club in Preston and we got a lot of 'minor' acts to turn up and play (Blodwyn Pig, Keef Hartley, etc). We heard Queen as they started off and I was in the queue early in the morning on the day of the release of 'Killer Queen' at Brady's Record Store in Preston. I rushed home and played it lots. When they appeared in Preston, the buzz was electric. The Guild Hall was packed, the stage black. The opening number started and then in a blaze of light and smoke they appeared. Freddie captivated and owned the audience. Two hours disappeared in minutes. The audience was mixed ages. I remember my history teacher (Mrs Swarbrick) was there. She was about 65 at the time and I can remember dancing in the aisles with her, such was the atmosphere. Freddie looked about eight feet tall. His command of the stage was imperious. I felt he was singing to me. I am still amazed at how Freddie changed from a white suit to a black suit in a flash of light and smoke during 'Killer Queen'. How did he do that? We saw Deep Purple, The Strawbs, The Moody Blues, etc. at Preston. But nothing competed to Queen.

COLSTON HALL
12 NOVEMBER 1974, BRISTOL, UK

I WAS THERE: ANTHONY GRIFFITHS, AGE 17
I ONLY GOT into Queen when 'Seven Seas of Rhye' came out, which I thought was fabulous. I did not know much about them when we went on a coach trip with Chepstow Youth Club over the Severn Bridge to Bristol. I think my sister Liz was there, plus friends from the youth club. I can remember the amazing guitar playing of Brian May – apparently, he used a sixpence coin as a plectrum - and Freddie Mercury in a white suit walking to the piano to play 'Killer Queen'.

GAUMONT THEATRE
14 NOVEMBER 1974, SOUTHAMPTON, UK

I WAS THERE: ANDY HUNT, AGE 20
SHEER HEART ATTACK was the album at the time. I went with a friend called Mick and we were in the upper circle. It was so loud my ears were ringing for days afterwards. It was worth it!

BRANGWYN HALL
15 NOVEMBER 1974, SWANSEA, UK

I WAS THERE: ALAN AITKEN
THIS IS THE review I wrote at the time:

Queen are indeed the new super group; any doubts on this matter were firmly settled at this concert. Queen mania has hit South Wales so all ye that mock, prepare to meet thy doom. Hustler, the group with the difficult job of supporting Queen, performed superbly throughout their short set. Highlights of the performance were 'Get out of my House' and 'The Hustler'.
  It was obvious from the start that Queen were not a group to do things by

halves and when the stage darkened and the spotlight beams gave way to a strange green glow, the audience rose as if expecting Her Majesty herself to walk on stage. They could not have been more wrong. The strange classical music from the sound system added to the mystery. Suddenly the green glow was replaced by a dazzling white spotlight and the classical music by 'Flick of the Wrist' from *Sheer Heart Attack*, the new Queen LP. Freddie Mercury prowled around looking totally evil and hateful , yielding the famous half mic stand and dressed in a stunning black-and-white cape-like top which he continually threw back over his shoulder.

'Flick of the Wrist' gave way to 'White Queen' and Mercury changed from his cape into a white suit. He reminded me of the Ajax adverts with the white tornado as he used up every millimetre of the stage. The music flowed with versions of 'Keep Yourself Alive', 'Ogre Battle', 'Lap of the Gods', 'Seven Seas of Rhye' and of course 'Son and Daughter' from *Queen I*. Throughout this time Mercury was in complete control of the enthusiastic crowd. At one point he walked to the front if the stage and asked what we would like to hear next. 'Liar', came the answer. 'Well, we're not going to do that right now' and they plunged into a track from the new LP. That's what's known as teasing.

'Liar' did come a little later and, before anyone had really noticed, dry ice began to pour off the stage and soon the hall was thick with the fog-like substance. Two huge magnesium charges went off on stage and Queen were gone. The encore was an outrageous version of 'Hey Big Spender' followed by a stunning recorded version of 'God Save The Queen' after the group had left the stage. After such a concert no Welshman could be blamed for singing 'God Save The Queen' with the vigour usually reserved for 'Men Wlad Fy Fhadau'. Perhaps one of their own songs sums everything up. It is called 'Modern Times Rock 'n' Roll'.

TOWN HALL
16 NOVEMBER 1974, BIRMINGHAM, UK

I WAS THERE: DEREK THORNTON, AGE 15

I HAD FIRST heard of Queen when they were on a Saturday evening BBC radio show called *In Concert* hosted by Pete Drummond. I was very impressed and went out a few days later and purchased *Queen II* using my paper round money. Shortly afterwards I purchased *Sheer Heart Attack* and then came the tour. It was my very first gig. Hustler were very loud.

There was no official tour programme so I bought an unofficial one outside the venue. I was still in school. I had a mock English exam the following day, and I wrote about the concert. I don't think it was what the teacher was looking for!

I WAS THERE: IAN PURVIS

MY GIRLFRIEND GOT tickets. I went along out of curiosity. What I discovered that night was a whole new way of a rock band performing! Freddie was something else and with his cultured voice and preening on stage, it allowed a new audience to enjoy a rock act. My girlfriend had already bought the *Queen II* album, which she lent me. I loved it – it was so original. I went and bought it

Ian Purvis was at Birmingham Town Hall

for myself and then had a thought: 'If this was *Queen II*, there must be a *Queen I* album out there!' There was, and so started my Queen album collection and fascination with the band. At one point I was in the fan club as, in those days, it gave you priority seats at concerts. Since then, I have also collected Queen memorabilia including a hand painted mask by Brian (for *Masks 96*, a Prince's Trust charity event). Needless to say, I am very pleased that 'my band' are as popular today as ever and the new film featuring their life was a treat to watch.

I realised that if there's a Queen II album, there must be a Queen I album!

NEW THEATRE
18 NOVEMBER 1974, OXFORD, UK

I WAS THERE: SUSAN SMITH

THEY WERE OUTSTANDING rockers. The music was amazing and Freddie was all in white, wearing a tutu and floating material, and black eyeliner and fingernails.

RAINBOW THEATRE
19 NOVEMBER 1974, LONDON, UK

I WAS THERE: PAUL STEWART

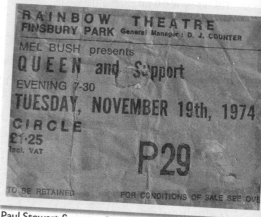

I DISCOVERED QUEEN in 1973, age 15, when 'Seven Seas of Rhye' was released. I bought the single and then subsequently their first album. Their mix of rock and pop incorporating different music styles particularly evident on some of their later albums – such as jazz, gospel, ragtime and opera - attracted me. In their early days I viewed them as a crossover between the glam rock bands and more serious rock bands of the mid Seventies. With Freddie's showmanship, they were certainly different.

Paul Stewart first saw Queen at the Rainbow in Finsbury Park

In total I saw them live seven times in different venues between 1974 and 1986. For their first UK headlining tour, at the Rainbow in Finsbury Park, I was sitting upstairs in the circle with a ticket that cost £1.25. I distinctly remember the simple stage set with lighting, which was nothing like the major productions on their later tours. They were still quite raw, but even in these early days Freddie had charisma with his movement and costumes and was honing his relationship with the crowd. One couldn't help but notice him.

My second Queen gig was at the Hammersmith Odeon in December 1975, as 'Bohemian Rhapsody' was released and a couple of weeks before the *Old Grey Whistle Test* screened their Christmas Eve concert live on TV. The venues got bigger as they became more successful and Freddie's hair became shorter whilst Brian's remained the same! At the Manchester Apollo in November 1979, I had seats upstairs and smuggled my camera in, managing to take some good photos with my telephoto lens.

I was at Birmingham NEC in December 1980. The venues and staging were starting to get bigger, and I remember four of us driving down from Manchester and then driving back for a late night curry at the notorious

Plaza at 2am. May 1982 saw them play Elland Road, Leeds on the first stadium tour. The moving lighting rigs were there but the rest of the staging was pretty basic. I remember their support act was Teardrop Explodes and the plastic water bottles that were thrown at lead singer Julian Cope mid song.

In September 1984, I saw the *Works* tour at Wembley Arena, an impressive set with stairs, backdrop and moving lighting rigs to reflect the theme of the album, and in July 1986 I was at Wembley Stadium with my girlfriend, now my wife. We sat in the stands around the half way line, a bit far away but not so far away that we missed out on the atmosphere. I remember Status Quo opening in the rain but fortunately it dried up for Queen. It was a brilliant show.

Over the years I witnessed the evolution of Freddie's performance. He really was a one off and knew how to handle a crowd. To me Queen aren't the same without him. It took me a few years to go and see the musical *We Will Rock You* as I didn't feel it was authentic enough. Yet when I did see it, I just wallowed in nostalgia. I don't fancy seeing Queen in their current incarnation. Although a great vocalist and showman, Adam's just not Freddie. And whilst Roger and Brian continue to roll out the classic hits, there is nothing new coming out which is a shame.

I WAS THERE: MICK MORGAN

I GREW UP in Borehamwood. You'd always be bumping into pop stars in the High Street because of the film studios. They would shoot all the Saturday shows – *The Des O'Connor Show* and all that sort of thing - at ABP Studios. The bands would be nipping into the shops getting their cigarettes or down the local pub. Queen filmed 'Bohemian Rhapsody' on the sound stage at ABP.

When I left work and had managed to get hold of a scooter or a car, we'd head out of Borehamwood and into London, and it was always going to see bands. We were in Dingwalls two or three times a week. We used to go up to the all-nighters in London.

My interest in Queen started in 1973 when their first album came out. I was at an all-nighter at the Lyceum in the Strand when, between the acts, they popped on 'Keep Yourself Alive' and I thought 'wow, what is that?' I'd not heard anything like that before. I immediately went out and bought that album.

The Rainbow was notorious. You couldn't get in there. You had to go up there and buy tickets and you'd be queuing round the block. It was a bloody nightmare. But I managed to get tickets for four of us. We were in the circle. That cost £1.75. We were looking down on the stage, because the circle was like a balcony overlooking the stage, and when the curtains opened there was Roger Taylor's drumkit and I'd never seen anything like it. It was an absolutely amazing pristine drum kit, glittering away before the band even came on the stage. That was my first impression of Queen. 'Look at that flippin' drum kit!'

The UK tour is followed by a 10 date continental jaunt taking in Sweden, Finland, Germany, The Netherlands, Belgium and Spain to round off 1974

TOP OF THE POPS
16 JANUARY 1975, LONDON, UK

Queen are back in the *Top of the Pops* studio performing their new single, 'Now I'm Here'.

February 1975 sees the band embark on a 38 date North American tour followed by an April visit to Japan and eight more shows.

PALACE THEATRE
7 FEBRUARY 1975, DAYTON, OHIO

I WAS THERE: DALE WALTON

QUEEN WERE RELATIVELY unknown in Cincinnati, getting no airplay from the city's rather rock-free rock station, WEBN. They were scheduled to play at Reflections Night Club, down by the University of Cincinnati, on February 6, 1975. The opening act this evening was Canadian band Mahogany Rush. My friends and I bought tickets as soon as they went on sale. We showed up early to be met at the entrance by a British guy who said he was Queen's road manager and that, after arriving at the club that morning, Queen had decided the stage was way too small to accommodate their stage show so they would not be performing. However, they would be appearing at the Palace Theatre in Dayton the next night 'and your Reflections ticket will get you in if they have room'. We'd come to see Queen but we stayed and watched Mahogany Rush.

The next night we drove to Dayton. The Palace Theatre was a converted Loews movie theatre, built in the 1900s and seating maybe 2,500 people. To the right of the theatre there was an alley that ran back along the building. My friends and I walked back there because we had to piss real bad. My friend Jerry pulled out a joint and we lit up whilst standing along the wall. We were all pissing and passing that joint when a door came open and out walked a couple of members of Kansas, who were opening that night, along with Roger Taylor and Brian May!

February being a notoriously cold month in Cincy, there was no one there. They actually put us on the platform with the lighting guy. Kansas were great and so were Queen. Mercury lost his voice or - I read later - had laryngitis and he had a hard time hitting his famous high notes. Queen's road manager may have been right about the stage at Reflections not being big enough. It was not much bigger than your average high school stage and Freddie would have had to get off the stage and run around on the floor, where they had set up a bunch of folding chairs.

By 1978, I was back in the army. Queen were a super group by then and played at the Coliseum in Oakland, California. Some friends and I drove up and watched that show. I liked the show, but it was not like the show in Dayton I'd seen in '75. That show was more up close and personal - it always is when you see a band on is way up. The ornate stage of the Palace Theatre was a perfect setting for Freddie. Sadly, the building was torn down by the end of 1975. Queen were one of the last bands to play there.

MUSIC HALL
8 FEBRUARY 1975, CLEVELAND, OHIO

I WAS THERE: LYN DAILEY

THIS WAS ONE of the best concerts I ever saw and I could not wait to see the band again. I went to go and see Queen and Freddie again in 1978 at the Richfield Coliseum, where we had second row seats. I couldn't believe what I was seeing - it was the most amazing thing ever. I saw them again the following year, an even a better show where Freddie gave everything he had. They played so well together and were so in sync it was like a theatrical magical experience. The next time we saw Queen, we had front row seats and Freddie actually engaged with us. That was one of the best nights of my life!

FORD AUDITORIUM
10 FEBRUARY 1975, DETROIT, MICHIGAN

I WAS THERE: MATT HENDERSON, AGE 16

IT WAS THE first time Queen ever played in the Motor City. I went
with the mindset of booing Kansas off stage, but they were excellent
and I've been a fan ever sense. Queen were even better. Our seats were
seventh row just left of centre stage. Queen blew us away with their
opening, playing 'Procession' and then the awesome lights to the start
of 'Now I'm Here'. I went to every show Queen played in Detroit in the
Seventies, after which I moved to Kalamazoo and never saw them again.
Until their first tour with Adam Lambert, which was not the same, but
he's the only singer that can come close to Freddie.

Adam's the only singer that comes close to Freddie

I WAS THERE: TERRY NUTT

I FIRST HEARD about Queen when they first broke in the USA and
Canada, when I was working at CJOM-FM in Windsor, Ontario in
Canada, across the river from Detroit, and we were asked to play their
album. I'm not totally sure if they had already broken in North America
with the albums prior to *Sheer Heart Attack* with 'Stone Cold Crazy' and
'Killer Queen'. I probably attended with a couple of the announcers I
worked with, and the Queen concert performance was right up there
with other bands I saw back then.

STUDENT UNION AUDITORIUM
UNIVERSITY OF TOLEDO
11 FEBRUARY 1975, TOLEDO, OHIO

I WAS THERE: RICHARD B KELLEY

QUEEN BEGAN THEIR first headlining tour of the United States in,
of all places, Ohio. It was an arduous affair that debuted in Columbus
and travelled to Cincinnati, nearby Dayton and two shows in uber-hip
Cleveland with side trips to South Bend, Indiana and Detroit, Michigan
before arriving in Toledo on an icy February Tuesday.

Queen was an early FM rock radio success story. The first album drew favourable comparisons to Led Zeppelin and appealed to the youngest of the baby-boom rockers, mostly high schoolers and young collegiates along with a healthy share of blue-collar fans. *Queen II* was even more bombastic than their debut and didn't really break any new ground. I was a high schooler working in record stores at the time. We sold a lot of both albums but our customers seemed to prefer Queen's debut.

In spring of 1974 Queen had embarked on their first tour of the US as the opening act for glam rock sensations, Mott the Hoople. Queen's participation was cut short when Brian May apparently came down with hepatitis and the band returned to England, beginning work on what was to become *Sheer Heart Attack*, initially without May who was still recovering. The album clocked in at little more than 30 minutes with not one wasted second therein. (*Queen II* had been 10 minutes longer). The album distilled the essence of what Queen was all about and the jarring cover photo assured attention in the stores when it was released in time for Christmas 1974.

The *Live at the Rainbow* album, recorded in November 1974, represents a close approximation of the show Queen took to the States a couple of months later. The big name promoters were just starting to get a foothold in the major markets, leaving small towns in the hands of college students and local promoters. One such promoter was a law student at the University of Toledo who had already presented several successful concerts including Steely Dan and Lou Reed.

I'd become friends with him because of my sales knowledge and artistic ability, which I parlayed into advertising posters, fliers and print ads for both concerts. He landed the Queen date for Toledo. He discussed the show with me and others and concluded that while Queen's popularity was beginning to soar they still weren't big enough to play the university's basketball field house, which could hold around 4,000. Instead, Queen - with opening act Kansas, also on the rise - would perform at the student union multi-purpose room at the University of Toledo. It's hard to imagine Freddie Mercury and Queen performing in a 1,200 capacity banquet hall, but they did.

The room had 20 foot ceilings and a single level linoleum floor. Concert goers sat on the floor or stood around the perimeter. The stage was less than three feet high and could be disassembled and stored if the room was being used for exams. Queen was carrying a set designed primarily for old vaudeville theatres, consisting mostly of multi-colour rear-stage lighting rigs as later seen on *Live Killers*. They were adjustable to compensate for height, and had to be collapsed to 10 to 15 feet high to fit in the student union room. Consequently, they were practically at audience eye-level, absolutely blinding – and hot!

The show had been an expensive investment for the promoter and the university so every possible ticket (and then some) had been sold. The room was jam packed, elbow to arse, with people sporting thick winter wear to offset the freezing February conditions outside. The audience also smoked. A lot. It was common for tobacco and cannabis smoke to completely fill the upper half of an arena or theatre at that time. In a room with 20 foot ceilings, the smoke was like a thick fog practically to the floor. That and the body heat of nearly 1,500 fans made the venue ghastly and uncomfortable. Nonetheless the bands soldiered on, first Kansas with nearly an hour of their overwrought Midwestern prog rock and then the main event! As if there wasn't enough smoke in the room already, Queen's crew cranked up the fog machines that had been designed for theatres with 50 foot ceilings. The cool, dry ice fog was actually refreshing but much of the audience in the tiny room could barely see the stage.

As if there wasn't enough smoke in the room already, Queen's crew cranked up the fog machines

---

Queen gave it their all. Freddie was his flamboyant self, even though he was sequestered to a minuscule portion of the stage. I'd never seen a performer use a microphone attached to top half only of the stand. Next to him, Brian May who is quite tall (and taller still when you factor in his hair), appeared awkward and oversized for the tiny stage. I assume Roger Taylor and John Deacon were there too but it was hard to tell through the blinding lights, smoke and fog. Given the conditions, no one could blame Queen if they delivered an abbreviated show, but to the best of my recollection they gave Toledo the whole ninety minutes ending with the campy encore of the Peggy Lee classic, 'Big Spender'. It was very cold when we got outside and more than a few concert goers were relieved to get out of the intense smoke and heat. I have little doubt that the evening was a major cold and flu super-spreader event!

STATE FARM SHOW ARENA
22 FEBRUARY 1975, HARRISBURG, PENNSYLVANIA

I WAS THERE: BARBARA CALDWELL SHOPF

WE LIVED IN Lancaster County, Pennsylvania, and the closest big house venues were the Hershey Park Arena and Harrisburg Farm Show Building. Both venues did a great job bringing in the best bands of the day. The arena has since closed but the Farm Show Building remains, although concerts there are a thing of the past. The one memory that is foremost in my mind is Freddie strutting across the stage in white with his arms outstretched and the wings of fabric rippling in the air, hitting notes I had never heard before and taking everyone on such a joyous ride. The drums of Roger Taylor

Barbara Caldwell Shopf remembers Freddie strutting the stage

were pretty amazing too. I'm not sure why I remember this as I am not a musician, but his sound just accentuated the music and hit my ears with such a driving force.

ERLANGER THEATRE
23 FEBRUARY 1975, PHILADELPHIA, PENNSYLVANIA

I WAS THERE: BOB PITCHNICK

THE ERLANGER WAS a beautiful old small 2,000 seat theatre in Philadelphia. Nobody really knew what to expect from Queen live and how they were going to produce all those guitar sounds from the album. I'd say 75% of the audience were local Philadelphia musicians, of which I was one at the time. We were used to seeing a guitarist set up with maybe having one or two effect pedals. But, after Kansas, Queen's tech crew came out to set up and this monster board of pedals was put in place in front of what would be Brian May's mic stand, something we had never seen before. When Freddie

Bob Pitchnick was at the Erlanger

came out on 'Now I'm Here' with the spotlight following him from each side of the stage, we were on the edge of our seats the entire show. We had never heard guitar sounds like that in our lives, harmonising guitar riffs from one person.

I WAS THERE: BRYAN PFLANZ, AGE 14

The first show I ever saw was Queen with Kansas in Philadelphia on the *Sheer Heart Attack* tour. I also saw them in 1976 on the *A Night at the Opera* tour, in 1977 at the Civic Center on the *A Day at the Races* tour and at the Spectrum for the *News of the World* tour in 1978. I went because I loved the *Sheer Heart Attack* record, because neighbourhood mates were going who had a car - and because I was dying to go to a rock concert! It was an old theatre in Philadelphia (that no longer exists) and the acoustics were fabulous! Kansas was the support and they were amazing. Queen had their work cut out for them but they didn't disappoint. They all had long hair and were dressed magnificently. I knew all the

Bryan Pflanz saw Queen in '75

tunes, and was surprised that they pulled it all off without synths. I was blown away. Queen was all that was on my turntable for the next two weeks! A year later almost to the day, they played the Tower Theatre, where the iconic Bowie LP, *David Live*, was recorded. *A Night at the Opera* had just been released, and the second tune was 'Bohemian Rhapsody' but they didn't play the whole tune. Then, after 'Flick of the Wrist' they went back to it. I was so excited. But wait - they still didn't finish it! Two songs later they did. Never have I seen anything like that, before or since.

I was hooked and they became my fave. True to form, almost one year exactly, they came back to Philadelphia to play the Civic Center, this time with Thin Lizzy as support on the *Races* tour. This one was definitely my favourite. The set list was amazing, encompassing their whole career. Freddie was just amazing. He worked the crowd like a shaman. I left there with no voice, singing every line of every song. My

God, how I loved that record! I especially loved that show because they leaned mainly on *Opera* and *Races*. The place was packed and the crowd went crazy!

Later that year, in November, they hit the big time and played the Spectrum, where all the big acts played, touring on *News*. Driving there with my mates, the anticipation was killing me. I was bouncing off the walls. This time it was just them - no support, just an LP that was on constant rotation on the radio.

Fuck's sake, they were incredible. They opened with 'We Will Rock You' and proceeded to play two hours' worth of my favourite tunes. This time, they had a real cool stage setup! And Freddie was dressed in tights as he paraded across the stage up and down, having the crowd hang on his every movement. There was not a song played that I didn't love. They even played my favourite, 'Good Old Fashioned Lover Boy'.

Every Queen gig I attended was better than the previous one

Shortly after that show, something happened to me, something life altering. I discovered punk big time! Everything changed. Even I changed. Gone was my long blonde hair, replaced by a short spiky quiff. Bands like Queen, Yes, ELP, etc. were gone from my life, replaced by Clash, Jam, Stranglers, Buzzcocks and Sham 69.

I never picked Queen up again until I heard the news of Freddie's untimely passing. It made me really sad and got me thinking about how much that band meant to me in my adolescent years, how much I loved their music and especially their live performances, and how I just abandoned them. It made me feel like a user and depressed the shite out of me! I finally made peace with myself the night of Freddie's tribute show.

At the *Races* gig, I got a black t-shirt with the album cover. I didn't have a job, so I had to save up for it. I was living with my sister and her family at the time. My nephew, who's four years younger than me, did the laundry one day and put the shirt in with white items to be bleached. I guess I don't need to go any further. I was fucking devastated.

KUTZTOWN UNIVERSITY
26 FEBRUARY 1975, KUTZTOWN, PENNSYLVANIA

THEY WEREN'T THERE: MARK MAHAL

I WAS INTRODUCED to the music of Queen between the releases of *Queen I* and *Queen II*. At that time, I was a senior in high school. I found their sound to be completely different from any of the other bands of the time. Their first local appearance was opening, along with Aerosmith, for Mott the Hoople on 1 May 1974 at the Farm Show Arena in Harrisburg, Pennsylvania. At the time they were promoting *Queen II*. There was a dispute who would take the stage first - Queen or Aerosmith. Legend has it that Brian May and Joe Perry shared an entire bottle of Jack Daniels while it was all being sorted out. In the end, Queen eventually opened the night. Brian May confessed in an interview that he was 'blind drunk and playing strictly from memory during the entire set'.

Wanting to see them do a full-on night, I was over the top to find they would be headlining in the gymnasium at Kutztown University on the *Sheer Heart Attack* tour, with both Kansas and Styx as their openings acts. We drove the 45 minutes to the show to find that Queen were a no-show. They had cancelled their concert the night before in Pittsburgh and now ours was the second of seven that had to be cancelled due to complications with Freddie's voice. As disappointed as I was to hear of this, both up-and-coming bands - Kansas and Styx - were terrific. So back to square one again where my thirst for seeing a full night of Queen was yet to be quenched.

MARY E SAWYER AUDITORIUM
5 MARCH 1975, LA CROSSE, WISCONSIN

I WAS THERE: JIM ROGERS

IN THE FALL of 1974, after closing up the gas station where we worked, me and my buddy Gary would often take a leisurely cruise in his 1970 Plymouth Road Runner around the chain of lakes in Minneapolis, Minnesota. Gary had a real kick-ass stereo in that car and one night he brought a tape of a new band I hadn't heard before, slammed it into his tape player and said 'listen to this!' The album was *Queen* by Queen. After 'Keep Yourself Alive' and 'Doing All Right', by the time we got to 'Liar' I was hooked forever. The combination of the melodic lead guitar and amazing Brian May riffs accompanied by the thumping bass, driving drum beat and a voice made in rock heaven was just too much for my young ears and I loved it!

Fast forward six months. I had moved 90 miles south to attend college in my freshman year. Gary called me on the phone one day and said, 'Hey, wanna go to a concert?' I said yes without even knowing what band or where the concert was. Gary would only tell me that he'd pick me up in two hours. I assumed it was a local concert somewhere nearby. Gary picked me up and we hit the highway, driving for nearly three hours. As we crossed the Minnesota-Wisconsin border he finally told me we were going to see Queen. I thought he was joking. We pulled into the parking lot of the Mary E Sawyer Auditorium and I still thought he was joking. There was hardly any line to get inside. The place looked like an old armoury with its squared brick block architecture.

The concert was general admission. Inside, we found the place was already pretty packed. We quickly found some seats to the right of the stage. The place, which couldn't hold more than three or four thousand people, looked like the inside of a high school gymnasium with its blank walls and bare floor. But it didn't take long for the crowd to go crazy over this new band.

I remember the members of Queen coming on stage and thinking, 'Good lord, look at that lead singer and his clothes!' Freddie had on a black jumpsuit-like outfit with his chest rather exposed by an open, plunging neckline. I was waiting to see what this Midwestern crowd would think of Queen, but by the time they'd played 'Father to Son' and 'Flick of the Wrist', the crowd really started to get into it. I remember just bathing in the sound of Brian May's guitar and being utterly mesmerised, watching Freddie be Freddie, wondering what he would do next. I thought 'who is this guy?' What a voice. And, man, could he move on stage! With all that energy I thought he looked like a cross between James Brown, David Bowie and Mick Jagger. Gary and I rocked out, taking in every note like dying men drinking water in the desert.

After several songs I was disappointed they hadn't played some of my favourite songs but I didn't have to wait much longer. The crescendos of 'Liar' and the guitar licks in 'Keep Yourself Alive' sent me over the top. Gary and I couldn't stop grinning from ear to ear at each other, which is all we could do because the sound was so loud and raw in that auditorium.

I remember thinking it was odd that Queen finished their second encore with an Elvis song, but I figured that since they were pretty new maybe they had run out of original songs. The concert went too fast and we could have listened for hours more. We had a long drive back but we were so pumped from seeing Queen that we talked about every song and every detail of the concert all the way back.

MUNICIPAL AUDITORIUM
20 MARCH 1975, SAN ANTONIO, TEXAS

I WAS THERE: JONATHAN HERBERT, AGE 15

THE FIRST REFERENCE I saw to Queen was the inner back cover of *Circus*. Living in Japan as an Air Force brat, *Circus* and *Creem* magazines were our only source of information about the music outside of Casey Kasem's weekly *American Top 40 show* on the Far East Network. There it was in purple and gold, 'In the Royal Tradition'. *Sheer Heart Attack* showed up in the BX about a week before we were packed up and shipped back to the States. The sonic power that blew through my speakers was the first I had ever heard with such a blistering sophistication. Well, I had to pack it in and ship it back to 'the World' or in this case, San Antonio, Texas.

Flash forward to Thursday, March 20, 1975. Me and my buds Dave and Pat got a ride from Dave's dad to the show at the Municipal Auditorium, paying a whopping $5 a ticket for a bill that included Al Stewart, Brownsville Station doing 'Kings of the Party' - and Queen as headliners. Our seats were second row just off centre. That equated to two hours of working at a fast food job. Ticket prices now for a show of this quality will run you several weeks' pay. There was nobody at this show. I'd stumbled on the show listed in the paper that day. It was not well promoted.

An interval followed Al Stewart and Brownsville Station. The lights went out after the break followed by a recorded version of 'Procession' and then the crunch of 'Now I'm Here' stormed through the darkness. A spotlight shone on Freddie as he sang 'Now I'm here'. The lights went out, the riff continued... 'Now I'm there' on the other side of the stage. How did he get from there to...? 'Look around...' 'but you don't see me....' Nobody could move that fast, much less in the fucking dark! Much later, I learned that one of the band's techs had dressed like Freddie and was the one everybody saw for the flash while Freddie was on the other side of the stage. Genius!

This was my first concert in the US and it blew my mind. These four guys made so much sound. The first half was in white and the second part in black, with a high contrast in sight and sound, mellow harmonies and head slamming chords.

Then came 'Brighton Rock'. Brian May, all by himself on the stage, proceeded to play the role of orchestra. Just him, his homemade guitar and

Jonathan Herbert remembers a show of high contrast - photo Jonathan Herbert

a looping device. My jaw was resting on the floor alongside a piece of chewing gum and half a nacho. That crunch. That tone. Repeated over, and over, and over… and over… and over…. 'Keep Yourself Alive' and 'Stone Cold Crazy' roared with heavy metal thunder and shook the rafters to near shattering levels.

The show finished with the classic 'Jailhouse Rock'. Queen had covered just about every style of music. Well, I don't think they did country. Thank God they didn't do country….

MCFARLIN AUDITORIUM
22 MARCH 1975, DALLAS, TEXAS

I WAS THERE: GARY DARBY, AGE 20
MY INTEREST IN the band came from a review of their first album in either *Creem* or *Circus* magazine in 1973. I was intrigued by the story of Brian's homemade guitar and the review stating his guitar playing was

Photo: Gary Darby

Freddie and Brian in action
at the McFarlin Auditorium

like a kamikaze attack. I got the first album and was very impressed with both his playing and the songs overall. I went to see them with friends that lived a couple of blocks from me. The set list was from the first two albums with a few songs from *Sheer Heart Attack*. I had nearly front row seats and got some good pictures, copies of which are posted on the Queen pages and Brian May's page.

SANTA MONICA CIVIC AUDITORIUM
29 MARCH 1975, SANTA MONICA, CALIFORNIA

I WAS THERE: ANTHONY ALONZO

I WAS BROWSING through the bins in my local record shop in 1974 looking for some artist or band that none of my classmates had ever discussed. I was intrigued by the *Queen II* album cover, so purchased the record without ever hearing the band, and fell in love on first listen. I loved the 'white and black' concept of the record. A couple of weeks later, I returned to the store to pick up the band's first album. A friend played 'Keep Yourself Alive' for me in

Anthony Alonzo saw Queen in 1975

his car. When I took the album up to the counter to pay for it, the clerk informed me that Queen had just released a new album that day. I left the store with both the first album and *Sheer Heart Attack*. Four months later I got to see Queen in concert. They did two shows at the venue that evening in Los Angeles, at 8pm and 11.30pm. I saw every Queen concert from 1975 to 1982, a total of 14 shows with Freddie. I also saw them twice with Paul Rodgers. *Bohemian Rhapsody* movie is the perfect bookend.

Queen concluded the *Sheer Heart Attack* tour
with eight shows in Japan

KOKUSAI KAIKAN
23 APRIL 1975, KOBE, JAPAN

I WAS THERE: MAYA-MIYOKO AKIYAMA

ON APRIL 17, 1975, the British rock band Queen arrived in Japan for the first time. Waiting for them at Haneda Airport were as many as 3,000 fans, the most since The Beatles in 1966. Tickets were all sold out for the initial seven shows, and the crowds were so enthusiastic that the band decided to do an additional show at the Nippon Budokan in Tokyo.

I saw them in Kobe. After 'Procession' from *Queen II* was played on tape, the show was opened by 'Now I'm Here', the last number on the A-side of the album *Sheer*

Maya-Miyoko Akiyama (left) saw Queen in Kobe, Japan

Heart Attack. As soon as the band started to play, the audience all stood up from their seats and went wild. Three quarters of the seats were occupied by very young girls like me. Since I was very short, I couldn't see the members of the band, so I stood on the seat and continued to scream and sing along with the four members until the end.

I heard that when the band returned to the hotel, next to the venue after the concert, the restaurant was already closed and the members could not eat anything. The Kobe International Conference Hall, where the concert was held, was damaged in the Great Hanshin-Awaji Earthquake of January 17, 1995 and is now rebuilt, but many other famous musicians have performed there, including David Bowie, who I also went to see.

It is now widely known that Japan was the first country in the world to pay attention to and appreciate Queen, that Freddie loved Japan so much that he even visited the country in private, and that even after his death, the other members of the band still consider Japan and Japanese fans to be special. The rock bands that had come to Japan before Queen, such as Led Zeppelin, BS&T, Chicago, Pink Floyd, Free, etc., were overwhelmingly supported by male audiences. But Queen completely stole the hearts of girls who loved ballet and classical music and had no interest in rock music. In addition, *Music Life*, a monthly magazine with a female editor-in-chief and editorial staff, published gorgeous photos of Queen and articles featuring them in every issue, attracting the attention of many female fans. And while most other foreign bands only visited Tokyo and Osaka, and rarely had a chance to see the culture of other cities, Queen tried to get to know Japan from the very beginning. They travelled to many cities, which made them even more popular in Japan.

Seeing them live was a dream-like two hours and I was completely fascinated by Freddie's clear high-tone voice and the profound but driven performance of the other three members, which wasn't inferior to the studio recordings. It was such a precious experience, seeing the four members of Queen during their freshest and most dynamic time in my home city of Kobe.

ODEON THEATRE
9 & 10 NOVEMBER 1975, BIRMINGHAM, UK

I WAS THERE: DAVID WRIGHT

I SAW QUEEN supporting Mott the Hoople at Birmingham Town Hall in November 1973. It was only the second concert I'd been to, having seen Bowie at the same venue earlier in the year. I was only 12 and my recollections of Queen are minimal, other than that Freddie Mercury wore something black. I was too wrapped up with the sheer excitement of attending another gig to be particularly interested in the support group. When 'Seven Seas of Rhye' was issued as a single a few months later, the penny dropped that I'd seen Queen and I very quickly became a big fan. Unfortunately, their next gig in Birmingham just after the single hit the charts was at Barbarella's night club, which precluded me from going because of my age. I wanted to go to three concerts at the end of 1974 but aged 13 my concert funding was very limited and I could only afford two, so I saw Sparks and Gary Glitter - and Queen missed out!

The following November Queen returned to Birmingham yet again, this time to play at the Odeon, so this time I made sure I got a ticket. They were electrifying. I was 12 rows back from the stage and bang in the middle of the row, so ideally placed. I stood mesmerised as Brian May, resplendent in what appeared to be a white cape, took centre stage a couple of minutes into 'Brighton Rock' and began a five-minute unaccompanied lead guitar workout, much longer than the studio version on Sheer Heart Attack. But something else about it was different....

Up until then all the concerts I'd been to consisted of what appeared to be a 'mono' wall of sound coming out of the speakers. This was the first time I'd heard anything in stereo, as the sound of Brian May's guitar kept travelling from one side of the stage to the other. It wasn't until seeing Bowie at Stafford Bingley Hall in June 1978 that I heard the stereo effect put to such good use again on the introduction to 'Station to Station', with a synthesizer replicating the noise of a train engine.

The *Night at the Opera* tour was to be the last time I would see Queen live, as I thought they got a little bit patchy after *A Day at the Races*, the tour of which didn't come to Birmingham. That was compounded by me morphing from a fan of glam rock to a fan of punk in 1977. Suddenly, it wasn't quite as cool to be a Queen fan. Until 13th July 1985 and Queen's 25 minute appearance at Live Aid, which remains the single most impressive bit of live footage I have ever seen by anyone to this day, despite only watching it on TV. I immediately became a big fan of Queen again until Freddie's sad demise in 1991.

The *A Night at the Opera* tour was billed as *A Night at the Opera with Queen*. The 78 show tour began in November 1975 and took in four continents, including 26 European shows that culminated in the legendary Christmas Eve show at London's Hammersmith Odeon that was broadcast live by BBC Television. The North American leg comprised 33 shows beginning in January 1976 and was followed by 11 Asian and 8 Australian shows, with the tour winding up in Brisbane, Australia on 23 April 1976.

EMPIRE THEATRE
14 & 15 NOVEMBER 1975, LIVERPOOL, UK

I WAS THERE: FRANCES REID
I WENT WITH my younger brother. I still can't believe that I saw Queen at the Empire. I remember wondering if they would do 'Bohemian Rhapsody' and what it would be like live, but it was fabulous.

I WAS THERE: PAULINE HOGAN
I WAS THREE rows back from the front row. I was lucky that my boyfriend - now my husband - worked for the *Liverpool Echo*, hence the excellent seats. The band changed costume for nearly every song. I don't think I could hear for a week afterwards. 'Bohemian Rhapsody' was just amazing. I still remember it to this day.

I WAS THERE: DEAN PRITCHARD, AGE 17

ONE OF MY cousins had been a fan since the Smile days. I heard some of that and it had a real edge to it. Then of course they changed to Queen so I started buying the singles and albums. It was like a musical journey for me. I followed the change in their styles - some good albums, some bad - but they were one of my favourite bands so that was okay. I will never forget Liverpool Empire in November 1975. I had just turned 17 and went with three mates from college. I managed to get tickets from the box office. I found out how difficult that was to become later on!

Dean Pritchard was at Wembley

COVENTRY THEATRE
16 NOVEMBER 1975, COVENTRY, UK

I WAS THERE: KEITH DEACON

I FIRST SAW Queen on BBC 2's *Old Grey Whistle Test* late one night singing 'Liar'. I went to my local record shop in Leicester called Ainsley's Records and asked if they had any records by Queen, to which they replied 'who?' This was the start of my Queen years. I started collecting magazines with their photos in plus any posters with them on, and every recording. I first saw them live at the Coventry Theatre. Me and some friends had gone there early that day, hoping to find out which hotel they were staying at. Somehow

Keith Deacon saw Queen at the Coventry Theatre

COVENTRY Theatre
HALES STREET, COVENTRY

EVENING 7.30

Sunday, 16 Nov.
STALLS

£2.50
including V.A.T.

F 9

Tickets sold cannot be
exchanged or taken back
TO BE RETAINED

we found the hotel and waited for them to come out
and when they did I had my little Kodak camera ready,
getting some good shots of them in their car. After seeing
Freddie and John get in the back and Brian in the front,
I jumped into the back of their car only to be pulled out
by the security guy, with Roger Taylor laughing out loud.

We then got to the theatre and again saw Roger Taylor coming in
and got a couple more photos. The concert was amazing. We sat in the
stalls. Freddie had everyone in the palm of his hand and it was brilliant
to be so close to them, seeing them performing.

The next time I saw them was in London at the Hammersmith Odeon
near to Christmas, and just before their Christmas concert filmed by the
BBC. This time we were seated in the upper tier, which was great, but
I wanted to get near to the stage again so I ran down the stairs, past the
security guys in the foyer and down the aisle to where some fans were
standing so I could not be found. I got some great photos and when
Freddie came to the front of the stage with a bunch of roses, I managed
to get one and I still have it pressed in a scrapbook today. You could sense
that something big was happening right in front of you.

My next concert was the Hyde Park free concert in 1976. We again got
near to the stage after getting there very early. It was a hot summer so the
weather was great and it was another amazing concert with Freddie again
commanding the stage. We stayed until the end, which made us nearly miss
our last train home to Leicester. I forgot to take my camera on this occasion!

COLSTON HALL
17 NOVEMBER 1975, BRISTOL, UK

I WAS THERE: JEFF COLLINS, AGE 15

I DIDN'T KNOW I was going until a few hours before the gig when one of my older brother's mates pulled out, allowing me to go. I loved every second of their performance and was hooked. I saw them again on 10 September 1976 at Cardiff Castle with two friends, both of whom sadly passed away as young men in their thirties. I vividly remember Brian playing the 'Brighton Rock' solo in the pouring

Jeff Collins saw Queen twice

rain, afraid he'd get electrocuted! Freddie did his usual routine of throwing single roses out to the audience and I managed to catch the stalk of one. On the bill before them were Andy Fairweather Low, Frankie Miller's Full House and Manfred Mann's Earthband. Richie Blackmore's Rainbow pulled out at the last minute. We got drenched that day and people were pointing and laughing at my face. I couldn't understand why, only then to remember that I had put my mother's mascara on the fluff above my lip to make me look older and it had run down my mouth and chin!

Now, I occasionally perform as Retro Jeff with a massive Queen/Freddie Mercury influence.

I WAS THERE: SUE SMITH, AGE 13

I WENT BY train from Swansea with two friends. The concert was utterly fabulous and I can still remember calling for 'Liar' at the end. It still remains one of my favourite Queen songs. On the return journey we sang all the way home! Such fun.

I WAS THERE: DENIS A WILLIAMS

I SAW THEM five times, including at the NEC, Wembley and Knebworth. It was total sensory escapism. Yes, Freddie was king but the whole band were performers. Roger was king of the skins, John the metronome bassist and Brian my guitar hero. I actually bought a guitar right after Freddie's death to not let the music die. I cared not that Freddie was gay, or about the tantrums, scandals and lifestyles. These guys played for me.

In the early Seventies, glam rock - real rock - was around. Then these four guys started to write good stuff. They seemed to not care, not conform to the norm. It was from the heart, with real emotion in the songs. Raw, rough sometimes, but the sheer finesse of some of the slower ballad stuff was brilliant. I remember seeing them on the *Old Grey Whistle Test* very early on. I saw an interview where they claimed to be a band for those at the back of the room. I was one of them. Their performances, their videos, were magic, visually portraying their version of rock – and fuck the rest! I got lost in their diversity. The first albums were treasured and played to destruction. Queen created their own world and I was delighted to be invited.

I remember being at Wembley and sitting just under Anita after she and Brian became official. I remember the guy with the huge guitar standing on top of the rig at Knebworth playing air guitar to the songs. But the first time I saw them live was at the Colston Hall in Bristol I went with my first proper girlfriend. I was black. I'd had to put the engine back in the car to make the trip. I wasn't sure what to expect but got blown away. We were dumbstruck. The emotion, the lights, the volume and the performance were just keys that unlocked my brain. It craved more.

At one show, they played 'Save Me' just before its' release. You never forget the dove at the end. This song later became important to me. After a bitter divorce, all I had left was my music and football. It was a very sad time and 'Save Me' was my song. The words were for me. 'A soul for sale or rent.' What a line! I can't listen to it today without tears.

CAPITOL THEATRE
19 NOVEMBER 1975, CARDIFF, UK

I WAS THERE: JEFF PERRY
WE HAD ONE record shop in the town we lived in. It wasn't a ground breaking shop for the younger budding pop music fan. In fact, we weren't encouraged to hang around in there at all. Consequently, at the age of about 10 or 11, I asked my mother in my school dinner break to go and buy me my very first record. It was

Jeff Perry first saw Queen at the Capitol in Cardiff

there waiting when I got home and was played over and over for the rest of the day. The record was 'Pretty Flamingo' by Manfred Mann.

Some three or four years later, a second record shop opened and I can honestly say I made it my second home. From the age of 15, I devoured music, propping up the counter of this newly opened shop. I became friends with the owner, Pete. I still see him from time to time to reminisce about the good old days. It was with him I saw my first live band, aptly Manfred Mann's Earth Band at the now demolished Capital Theatre in Cardiff, which held about 2,000 people.

From about 1974 to 1980 I had six glorious years of concert-going bliss. I had two stalwart companions, my two years younger sister and someone I had met in the record shop. Neither could drive so I was scout as it were, scouring the music papers for tour dates and choosing the bands and venues, and then buying the tickets. In those days before telephone and online ticket sales, you had to queue at the venue.

Getting the tickets for Queen's appearance at the Capitol in Cardiff on the *Night at the Opera* tour was a challenge in itself. They went on sale at the venue some months before on a Sunday morning, at 10am, so it was an early morning trip to Cardiff. I was there at 5am, only to see hundreds of people forming an increasingly long queue. I was slightly dismayed, thinking I'd never get any tickets. Thankfully the weather was good and the five hours passed rather quickly in a pleasant atmosphere. However, at 10am all hell broke out as what started as an orderly queue turned into a free-for-all. Everyone rushed to the doors. Fortunately, I was big enough to hold my own so in I went and at about 11.30am I walked out holding four tickets for row A in the Grand Circle. Queen, here we come.

Being a midweek concert, it was an early finish from work. We drove into Cardiff and parked up with plenty of time to spare for our usual pre-concert meal at a nice Berni Inn, not too far from the venue. The venue was buzzing with excitement, with ticket holders entering and people without tickets looking to buy some. We got to our seats with half an hour to spare to soak up the atmosphere.

A Night at the Opera was different from what I was expecting. It was a very successful album, but signalled the Queen transformation to a more folky, pop era. We still had 'The Prophet's Song' and 'Death on Two Legs' to get the volume turned up, and an attempt by Taylor with 'I'm in Love with my Car' (which I didn't like), but we were missing tracks like 'Now I'm Here', 'Killer Queen', 'Ogre Battle', 'Liar', 'Father to Son', 'Seven Seas', etc. But we did get the instant classics ''39' and 'You're My

Best Friend'. I was more than happy with the fabulous set list. A mixture of rock, pop and folk made for an unforgettable adrenaline experience. Powered by Freddie's stage persona it was truly the most accomplished feeling I'd had to date. Not bad for about £3.75 a ticket.

I WAS THERE: WENDY DAVID

I TOUCHED FREDDIE'S boot at the piano. Then the encore came and a guy grabbed my white satin scarf down the front. I elbowed him, grabbed my scarf back and he banged into another guy. Then... mayhem! The *NME* afterwards showed cinema seats knocked over and ran the story 'Riot at Queen Concert'. It was all my fault. I've still got my programme.

A NIGHT AT THE OPERA RELEASED
21 NOVEMBER 1975

Reportedly the most expensive album ever recorded at the time, A Night at the Opera was the product of work across six studios. It yielded 'Bohemian Rhapsody', which topped the UK charts for six weeks, and 'You're My Best Friend', which reached number 7 in the UK. After only reaching number 9 in the US charts on its initial release, 'Bohemian Rhapsody' reached number 2 in 1992 after being featured in the movie Wayne's World.

WINTER GARDENS
23 NOVEMBER 1975, BOURNEMOUTH, UK

I WAS THERE: CHRISTINE CLARKE, AGE 22

IT WAS THE *Night at the Opera* tour. They were absolutely brilliant, the best band I have ever seen live! The venue was packed and everyone joined in singing. I remember when they started singing 'Bohemian Rhapsody' there was complete silence in the auditorium. It was amazing.

Christine Clarke remembers complete silence for 'Bohemian Rhapsody'

I WAS THERE: DAVID HEATH

A PAL GOT me into Queen. When *Queen I* was released in July 1973, I had to buy it. Apparently, he had a friend that knew Brian May and I thought nothing of it because they were just another group and I didn't realise how big they were going to be. But I liked their music. I saw them as support to Mott the Hoople in '73 down in Bournemouth and everybody was saying 'we want Queen! We want Queen!' They got more 'we wants' than Mott the Hoople did, which I thought was amazing. They were just incredible.

I bought *Queen II* the day it was released in late '74 and absolutely adored it and my love of Queen just grew and grew. My wife and I saw them at the Winter Gardens. We had front row seats as by then I'd joined the Queen fan club. I was a fan club member for many years after. I found out later that a mate went backstage and met them all and I thought, 'Why didn't I try and do that?'

I was an underground cable jointer for Southern Electric and I had to go to Uxbridge in Middlesex to do my high voltage underground cable jointing course for nine weeks. And for the whole of that nine weeks, Queen were number 1 with 'Bohemian Rhapsody' and it was playing everywhere I went. It was absolutely amazing.

The next time I saw Queen was on December 8, 1980 at Wembley Arena, the day John Lennon died. They did Beatles and John Lennon songs in tribute to him. It was another absolutely amazing gig. Freddie was incredible. He ran from one side of the stage to the other. I took my camera with me on that day and somewhere I've got some photos of that gig. I'd put Queen on the same level as Jimi Hendrix. I'm a massive, massive fan. And the day that Freddie died, I cried.

GAUMONT THEATRE
24 NOVEMBER 1975, SOUTHAMPTON, UK

I WAS THERE: THOMAS GARSIDE

BORN IN 1956, I got into rock music aged 12, listening to people like Hendrix, Zappa, Joplin, Pink Floyd, Jefferson Airplane, Led Zeppelin, etc. My first experience of Queen was hearing 'Seven Seas of Rhye' on the radio. I sought out more of their music, which was different to today - no internet, no YouTube, so no downloading. I asked around my friends if they had any of their records, and then started to buy them myself.

I joined the Royal Navy in 1971, aged 15, and started to go to gigs at 16 when I was earning a living and paying my own way. In 1975, I was serving on HMS Dundas, based in Portsmouth, when someone found out that Queen's *A Night at the Opera* tour was playing Southampton and that the ship would be in port on that date. He asked around, organised a minibus, booked the tickets and about 10 or 12 of us went to the Gaumont Theatre. We paid for our tickets at the booking office, as you could in those days, and headed up into the gods. Luckily the seats were right at the front, and just over to the left of centre stage.

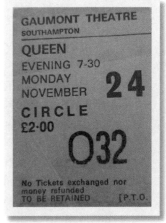

Thomas Garside was at the Gaumont in Southampton

The warm up group was Mr Big, whose set was interrupted at times by their equipment picking up calls from a local taxi firm. They had two drummers, and when they did the proverbial drum solo it was duelling banjos time.

Then we got ready for Queen. The lights were out, a low intro played and out came Freddie and the boys going straight into the opening number. I can't remember the order of the set, but they played all the fan favourites up to that date like 'Ogre Battle', 'White Queen', 'Flick of the Wrist', 'Keep Yourself Alive', 'Now I'm Here', 'Seven Seas of Rhye' and of course 'Bohemian Rhapsody', with an encore of three or four songs, finishing with 'God Save the Queen'.

We were very lucky to see Queen at an early stage in the tour, with enough dates down to polish the set, but not so far in to that they just wanted to get the tour over with. Freddie was superb. He seemed to come alive on stage, strutting up and down, using his trade mark short mic stick, and hitting every single note. He did two costume changes, one during John's drum solo and another during Brian's guitar solo - one all white, the other all black. At the end of the first or second song, he popped off and reappeared wearing a huge feather boa around his neck, glass of bubbly in hand. He walked stage front to speak with us, and his opening words were 'hello Southampton, I hope you've all been very naughty since we last met', to which we gave a thunderous 'yes!'

I have been very lucky to see quite a few bands in my time, and that night rates as one of the best, if not the best, gigs I've been to. It is no surprise to me that Queen have had such a long and successful career, the only downside being that Freddie is no longer with us.

FREE TRADE HALL
26 NOVEMBER 1975, MANCHESTER, UK

I WAS THERE: MARTIN SLADDIN, AGE 17

I WAS PERSUADED to get into Queen by a school friend who said they were 'much better than Slade'. We got the tickets for the Free Trade Hall performance long before 'Bohemian Rhapsody' was released, but it reached number 1 the weekend before the gig, so the band must have been buoyant. I heard most tracks from *A Night at the Opera* for the first time there because I didn't have the album yet. Much of the material is a challenge to perform live because of all the multi tracking, but I was particularly impressed with 'The Prophets Song'. Freddie was of course the showman he always was, and of course all of them are superb musicians. That's why they were able to pull off such a complex song as 'Bohemian Rhapsody'.

I only saw Queen live once. I haven't been to many concerts but I have definitely picked some good ones, including Pink Floyd when they did *The Wall*, Rick Wakeman and lesser known artists such as Robyn Hitchcock and John Martyn (sadly deceased), who was supported by Tracy Chapman, just before she shot to fame. And, yes, much better than Slade.

I WAS THERE: TED TUKSA

I WAS IN a harmony band. I went to see if Queen could do all these fantastic harmonies, and during the concert the harmonies were amazing. I was thinking 'Bohemian Rhapsody' would be a doddle but when it came to it, they started brilliantly and, then when it came to the main harmonies - before the head banging solo - they walked off to a taped backing. They appeared again

Ted Tuksa was at the Free Trade Hall

after the harmonies, with a glass of champagne, thanking the audience for making it number 1. That was the only part of the concert which I was disappointed with. Otherwise, seeing Queen live was one of my life highlights.

HAMMERSMITH ODEON
29 NOVEMBER – 3 DECEMBER 1975, LONDON, UK

I WAS THERE: INGRID FOAN, AGE 17

I WENT WITH a friend called Chris. I had been staying with Phil Lynott in West Hampstead. l had met him in Düsseldorf in the September (that's a whole other story) but returned to Reading and got a call from my friend asking if I would like to see a band called Queen, so I went. It was the most incredible gig. What impressed me the most was when Freddie played the piano and sang 'Bohemian Rhapsody'. His voice was awesome, completely filling the theatre and this massive sound coming from his slight frame. It was mesmerising. I have loved them ever since. Years later, I used to see

Ingrid Foan thought Freddie's voice was awesome

him in the Copacabana in Earls Court. And in the Nineties my sound engineer boyfriend used to tour with Roger Taylor.

I WAS THERE: PETE FISHER

I'D BOUGHT THE first album in 1973 after being impressed by the single 'Keep Yourself Alive', which I heard played at a local live gig between the bands. I listened to it pretty intensively that year and really liked it, even though I felt they'd borrowed rather heavily from Led Zeppelin instrumentally, and Yes vocally. I also bought *Sheer Heart Attack* around Christmas 1974, but felt they were becoming a little too commercial and

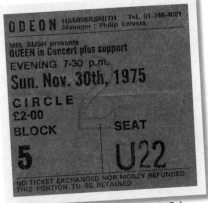

Pete Fisher was at Hammersmith Odeon

that some of the tracks were pretty weak. Towards the end of 1975, I was going out with a girl at university who was a big Queen fan, and (much to my astonishment) had never seen a real live band before. I got tickets for Hammersmith Odeon and we had a great night. I remember the band being much more rocky and down to earth than their recent recordings, and I was very impressed how well their better known songs transferred to the live stage, particularly with all the tricky, sometimes four part harmonies. Freddie was a great front man of course, and Brian May was very good at providing a backwash of guitar. I liked his Echoplex solo, but having seen Led Zeppelin twice earlier that year, he didn't blow me away. I remember the light show being pretty basic, even for back then, with a lot of simple black and white contrast. I did buy *A Night at the Opera* that Christmas, but I tired of it quite quickly and I'm afraid they lost me after that, becoming way too commercial for my taste.

I WAS THERE: DAVID BATES

I FIRST BECAME aware of Queen when 'Killer Queen' came out. It was being played on Capital Radio a lot. I bought the album *Sheer Heart Attack* in cassette format and played it to death. In December 1975, a few days before the BBC Christmas recording at the Hammersmith Odeon, I was lucky enough to get tickets to see the official tour gig. We sat on the front row of the balcony.

Mr Big were their support act, a rock band with two drummers who were very loud. However, Queen surpassed their volume, utilising banks of amplifiers each side of the stage, piled floor to ceiling and stacked up behind them on the stage. The big question in my head was, 'I wonder how they will play 'Bohemian Rhapsody' live?' Freddie went through a variety of costume changes, ending up in the white jump suit with his bare hirsute chest on display as he strutted the stage. 'Bohemian Rhapsody' began with Freddie silhouetted behind a white paper screen, singing the intro. The 'scaramouche' section was played as a backing track before Freddie burst through the paper screen onto the stage where he finished off the song whilst playing the piano.

I listened in awe as Brian May played 'Brighton Rock' with the 'Three Blind Mice' riff being sequenced through the speakers, like some surround sound effect. This was very pioneering for its time. The concert ended and the auditorium fell silent apart from the hum of conversation as the audience filed out into the cold night air. My ears were ringing, tinnitus-like. Everything was muffled.

I next saw Queen with Paul Rogers at Murcia Football ground in Spain in October 2008. Freddie was there in spirit and on stage as they played a film of him during 'Bohemian Rhapsody'. It was very cleverly done and quite emotional.

I WAS THERE: JAN RHYS WILLIAMS, AGE 25

I FIRST SAW Queen on the television doing 'Seven Seas of Rhye'. I was a massive Beatles and Motown fan but Queen were very, very different and I think that's why I liked them. I thought Freddie was incredibly handsome in a weird sort of way, and very sensual. It was him that I was really drawn to.

When I first went to see them, it was a rainy November night. I went on the train up to London with a girlfriend and I was just so excited. We had reasonably good seats and could see the stage quite clearly. The first song they played was 'Now I'm Here'. Freddie was in a white Zandra Rhodes top, with the winged sleeves that Brian tended to wear wore than Freddie. 'Now I'm Here' was in flashes. He'd be in the spotlight singing 'now I'm here' and the spotlight would go off and another spotlight would come on in a different place, and he'd be there singing 'now I'm there'. Thinking about it now all these years later takes me right back and I can remember the excitement I felt. When the show finished and we came out, I was on such a high that I couldn't breathe. I didn't want to go home and I didn't want to go anywhere. I just wanted to stand there on the pavement on a wet November night and try and drink it all in.

Jan Rhys-Williams at Garden Lodge

CIVIC HALL
7 DECEMBER 1975, WOLVERHAMPTON, UK

I WAS THERE: MARTIN ASTLEY

I REMEMBER WATCHING the support band from the balcony and then, during the interval, going downstairs and pushing my way to the very front so I was pressed up against the stage. By that time, I knew much more about Queen as they had released four albums. I certainly remember from my vantage point right at the front just how good Queen were as a live band. My one claim to fame is that during the encore Freddie Mercury threw me a red rose! I also remember at the end of the gig buying a 'silk' Queen scarf and leaving the gig covered in sweat. The cost of the ticket was about £2.25.

I WAS THERE: PAUL HAWTHORNE

I PAID THE princely sum of £2. They couldn't play 'Bohemian Rhapsody' but went off stage and played the video.

GUILDHALL
8 DECEMBER 1975, PRESTON, UK

I WAS THERE: IRENE FLACK, AGE 17

I SAW THEM when 'Bohemian Rhapsody' was at number 1, so it was mega special. I had left school and was working for a big insurance company in Lytham. I went with my fiancé, who is now my ex-husband, and his brother and girlfriend. You had to go to the Guildhall box office to get tickets. For Elton John we had to queue up overnight but I don't think we did for Queen, as they weren't quite as well known when they announced the tour. We just turned up and bought the tickets one afternoon. We were sat quite near the back on the top tier, in a corner stage left. One of the things I liked about them was that they were quite purist. They only ever wore black and white on stage and they used no synthesisers. And the light washes were quite simple. There was nothing clever. It was all about them and the music. I remember Brian May was wearing a white top with what seemed like bat wings.

I hadn't heard much of *A Night at the Opera* apart from 'Bohemian Rhapsody' – I got it for Christmas – but 'The Prophet's Song' and ''39' stuck in my mind. They did the second part of 'Bohemian Rhapsody' near the beginning of the show and the piano and the introduction part near the end. But it worked. The critics said they couldn't do it on stage and that it needed too much technology, but somehow it worked. There were no videos. It was just the four of them on the stage.

For the encore Freddie came on wearing these quite short silvery white shorts. And they did 'Johnny B Goode' and the whole place was rocking. It was quite unexpected, because we were expecting another Queen song. There were no videos, no distracting firework shows. It was just them, doing their music. And Freddie had the audience in the palm of his hand from the moment they came on stage.

I WAS THERE: GARY BOOCOCK

I WAS AMAZED when Freddie changed from a white suit to a black suit in a flash of light and smoke during 'Killer Queen'. How did he do that? I felt he was singing to me.

CITY HALL
11 DECEMBER 1975, NEWCASTLE, UK

I WAS THERE: PETER SMITH

FOR SOME CRAZY reason I didn't get tickets for the City Hall gig, but as the day of the Newcastle concert approached, I became increasingly determined to go. On the night, I turned up outside the City Hall determined to blag a ticket. Now I had done this several times, and had always managed to buy a ticket, sometimes paying a little more than face value. But this night was different. Demand had been huge, and no one was selling any tickets. No touts and no spares. A group of us were hanging around with the same idea, all desperate to get into the show. Time was passing and we could hear the support act, Mr Big, take the stage. Soon they finished their set, and things were getting desperate.

It was then that one guy spotted a ladder around the back of the venue – and an open window. He climbed up the ladder and squeezed through the open window. A couple of us followed. The window was tiny, but I managed to squeeze through, finding myself above a sink in the upstairs ladies' loo. Luckily, there was no one in the ladies and I sneaked out and found myself in the circle, just as Queen took to the stage and exploded into 'Bohemian Rhapsody'. Queen were amazing that night, although my enjoyment of the gig was hampered by my remaining in constant fear of being ejected from the venue by a steward. Luckily, everyone was standing so I stayed upstairs, standing at the side and easily blending into the crowd.

The crowd went crazy for Queen that night; Freddie's performance was simply riveting, and his vocal range outstanding. They had now actually become stars; it seemed to me that they always knew that they could, and would.

CAIRD HALL
13 DECEMBER 1975, DUNDEE, UK

I WAS THERE: BILL FINLAYSON

WHEN I BOOKED my ticket along with two others I never really knew much about the band. I think it was the album entitled *Queen* that brought them to my attention. I enjoyed the hard rock edge to the music they were writing and performing around that time. *A Night at the Opera* had just been released and I managed to grab a copy prior to the concert as I knew the set list would contain songs from the album. Of course, the main song was 'Bohemian Rhapsody'.

Bill Finlayson didn't know what to expect when he saw Queen

Come the night of the concert I remember feeling excited and not knowing what to expect. But I had a bit more respect for the band as they had just refused to do *Top of the Pops*. This was the first week 'Bohemian Rhapsody' had topped the chart and the reason given by the band for not appearing was because they were appearing in my home town of Dundee. Support act Mr Big came and went but I never really concentrated on that one. Queen were announced and entered to 'Procession'. They then went into the rock section of 'Bohemian Rhapsody'. This I found confusing as I had expected them to do the full version. However, it was still enjoyable as they did the first half of the song later in the set. The songs I wanted to hear were the more rock sounding ones such as 'Brighton Rock', 'Killer Queen', 'Seven Seas of Rhye' and 'Keep Yourself Alive' and all of these came up in the set.

I remember Freddie being his usual flamboyant self and keeping the audience enthralled. I also enjoyed Brian's amazing control of the guitar. As a group they had obviously rehearsed well and played very tight together. It was because of this I became a fan, although I never took the opportunity to go and see them again. They became more commercialised later on and I didn't fancy standing amongst a crowd of screaming females.

I had to look up the songs that were used in the encore as it was so long ago. The first song – 'Now I'm Here' – I really enjoyed and then there was a bit of fun with the group doing 'Big Spender' before leading into 'Jailhouse Rock'. Like everyone, I stood for the final track, 'God Save the Queen'. I'm not a royalist but I do still enjoy Queen's version.

I WAS THERE: JINTY MAXWELL

I FIRST REMEMBER seeing Queen on TV singing 'Killer Queen' on *Top of the Pops*. I joined the fan club at nine years old. My first albums were Queen's *Sheer Heart Attack* and The Mothers of Invention's *Absolutely Free* - I had to order that one from John Menzies in Lanark, picking it up the following week. As the youngest of six, my parents had obviously ceased to worry about the listening habits of their offspring.

I was in the first year at Lanark Grammar when I saw that the fifth and sixth year common room organised buses to gigs, and Queen at the Apollo was scheduled. The jammy thing for me was that my brother was in the fifth year, so promises from his mates that they would look after me and my wee Queen buddy meant we were allowed to go! Not like nowadays, when wee girls of seven get to see Little Mix.

Queen was my very first gig out of so many but at that age, seeing such a flamboyant and technically superb show with the relatively limited concentration of Queen catalogue at that time remains so clear in my memory!

They started with 'Now I'm Here', Freddie an early silhouette image, and went straight into 'Ogre Battle' and 'White Queen'. The running order is hazy but highlights were a medley of 'Bohemian Rhapsody', 'Killer Queen' and 'March of the Black Queen'. They did 'Brighton Rock', leaving Brian alone on stage for an eternity. I still hung on each note. I certainly don't see that lengthy guitar solo section much nowadays, albeit Ritchie Blackmore with Rainbow did that very thing at the Hydro a couple of years back. 'Keep Yourself Alive' and 'Liar' were stand outs - Freddie had black on by then!

The drama, lyrics and showmanship were what appealed to me about Queen. The gig certainly gave me that in abundance. Naturally it was the era of Freddie in white satin jumpsuit with mercury wings and Brian's Zandra Rhodes pleated angel top. Freddie had a similar one. Little bits of humour, tongue-in-cheek stuff popped in throughout the gig too, like bits of 'Three Blind Mice' from Brian at some point. They finished with 'Lap of the Gods' and Freddie chucked loads of carnations and Roger Taylor his drumsticks and tambourine out to the crowd. We were fairly close to the front in the stalls, I seriously had six inches of a carnation stem and a square inch of tambo in a wee frame for several years! I remember school the next day, my ears still ringing, telling my best friend about it in Mrs Nimmo's biology class.

HAMMERSMITH ODEON
24 DECEMBER 1975, LONDON, UK

I WAS THERE: SARAH FOX

A BOY – HUGH - who I was very keen on at the time, got us tickets to the BBC Christmas Eve concert in 1975. It was at the then Hammersmith Odeon near where we lived. That was the *Night at the Opera* concert broadcast live. The atmosphere was amazing and the impact of 'Bohemian Rhapsody', which was new, innovative, confusing and so exciting, still echoes through my mind. Watching Freddie and Brian is a memory which will not leave me. The concert was very controlled by the BBC – there were no encores at all and as an audience we were meant to respond in a way that suited the TV audience. We didn't, of course.

Afterwards Hugh and I went to the midnight Christmas service, arriving a bit late together, and as we left it snowed. Oh, to be young again. Hugh and I are still in touch and share this incredible memory which has brought us so much street cred with affection after 45 years!

I WAS THERE: JULIE CASTLEDINE

I'VE SEEN QUEEN at least once on every UK tour since Birmingham Odeon in 1974 when I was 16, and when a ticket cost £1.30. I was booked to see Queen and Adam Lambert in June 2020 for £170 – the cheap seats! I used to travel all over the country from

Julie Castledine used to record Queen shows

Leicestershire, usually hitchhiking unbeknownst to my parents. I went to Hammersmith Odeon for the Christmas Eve 1975 gig and we appear briefly in the film. I cannot believe Freddie has been absent for nearly 30 years. I have never actually met any of them, but I got up close to the stage in the early days. And I used to take a cassette recorder into gigs and still have some terrible recordings!

I WAS THERE: TIMOTHY HOPTON

AGED 16, I was working at a local pub in my home town of Castleford, a working class mining community with plenty of industry and lots of people in work, whether in engineering, tailoring, chemicals, transport, utilities or the local pits, of which there were quite a number. People worked hard and played hard. One of my colleagues at the pub, Andrew, had told me to look out for this band 'Queen'.

We all got our glimpse into the music world on a Thursday night with *Top of The Pops* on BBC1, when for a short time we were transported into the fantasy land of neon lights and glitter. One Thursday night, I was working in the bar. I always had *Top of the Pops* on and, this particular evening, Queen were on, performing 'Seven Seas of Rhye'. The thing I remember most was how different they looked from any other band. I wasn't convinced that I liked the song, but the way the band looked and performed was enough to keep my interest in them going forward. More *Top of the Pops* programmes followed and I started to like some of the singles – 'Now I'm Here' and 'Killer Queen' – so I bought *Sheer Heart Attack*.

My mate, Dave Maskill, was a year or two older than me. He had a tape of *A Night at The Opera* on in his car all the time. It was clear that Queen were changing the musical scene for the better. Dave called me and asked if I fancied going to see Queen in London around Christmas time. I didn't give it much thought at the time, but agreed to go and we managed to get a pair of tickets, which were a fiver each!

I found out that the concert we were going to would be shown live on BBC2 as a Christmas special, so I was even more excited about the upcoming trip, which was about two months away. This was to be my first proper gig.

On the day of the gig, Dave came and picked me up in his new Ford Capri, and true to type, he had plenty of good tapes for our journey, but *A Night at the Opera* was playing non-stop. We never got fed up with it, which speaks volumes about the freshness of the music. The sleevenotes said 'no synthesisers'. I didn't fully understand this at the time but it showed how talented the band were with their vocal harmonies and production values.

I was quite excited and also apprehensive when we got to Hammersmith and parked up under the flyover. The Odeon was about 60 or 70 yards straight in front of where we parked and all lit up – 'MCP presents QUEEN - A NIGHT AT THE OPERA'. We went inside for a nosey around the foyer and I couldn't believe what I saw advertised on the wall outside the ticket office - 10cc in concert, February 1976. These tickets were also a fiver, so Dave and I quickly bought a couple each, as we were sure our other two pals would be up for the return trip after Christmas. What it also told me was that there was a lack of national promotion of other acts. Or maybe I was looking in the wrong place, but I was well chuffed that I had got a ticket to see my favourite band, albeit in London.

When we eventually got inside and sat down, the atmosphere was incredible. I remember a blow up doll floating around the auditorium. Customers were obviously in the Christmas spirit. Bob Harris actually introduced the band and the place was buzzing. I remember lots of dry ice and white light, but remained slightly underwhelmed at the band's version of 'Bohemian Rhapsody', as it was only part of the song, whereas we were all spoiled by the full length video and I didn't have a full understanding at the time of editing, production and such like. I felt a bit let down, as I expected the song verbatim. But the gig was great and and whetted my appetite to see many other bands throughout my life. However, this one brings back many good memories.

I WAS THERE: JAYNE HILL

I WENT TO some Queen concerts in the Seventies and Eighties. My favourite was Christmas Eve with my dad and brother. We stood on the seats and waved tinsel about in the air like football scarves.

I WAS THERE: JOHN SPENCER

IN 1975 THEY were back in the UK with four nights at Hammersmith Odeon, and I was there all four nights. Freddie was in a fur jacket, holding the mic in one hand and talking to us - his people - while sipping champagne. Someone from up on the balcony wolf-whistled him. He looked up, threw back his head and said, 'Precocious child!' It was during these four nights that they announced Queen would be the live act for the *Old Grey Whistle Test* live on Christmas Eve. I had to go. I went to

queue up to get tickets as soon as they
were on sale. There was an alternative
option. Certain travel agents in the West
End of London would book you concert
tickets, but you had to pay a booking fee
and most fans really didn't want to pay
this, me included!

The Christmas Eve gig was totally
different. It was like a proper party.
There was a massive net up in the ceiling
full of balloons. You could see them
before the lights went down. Queen hit

John Spencer remembers a party
atmosphere at the Hammersmith Odeon

the stage and Christmas started! It was a great night. The music was
awesome as always and as it ended the balloons were released, including
a couple of inflatable women.

After the BBC switched off the cameras, out came Queen to play a few
'extra' numbers. It was a late finish, and being Christmas Eve, the tubes
and buses had finished. I can remember groups of fans heading off in all
directions walking home, singing Queen numbers as they went. You'd get
to a big junction and some would break off and go their way. I remember
it was a long, long walk all the way home to King's Cross.

I WAS THERE: DAVID MENASHY, AGE 19

IT WAS BEING shown on TV, which meant bright
lights shining into the audience that, ironically,
somewhat dimmed the experience! They wore their
famous white outfits. 'Bohemian Rhapsody' may
have been at number 1 then? I had discovered their
music in school, when I was in the sixth form. 'Seven
Seas of Rhye' was the first track of theirs to enter my
consciousness and the first album I bought was *Sheer
Heart Attack*. They were a bit noisier in those days. I
think they were a bridge between The Beatles and
Led Zeppelin. 'Killer Queen' was an indication to
me that they had a unique voice, but even so I never
imagined the impact their next single and album
would have. I never became a massive fan, preferring
The Beatles and Led Zeppelin, but I always admired
them. And poor Freddie died on my birthday....

David Menashy was at the
Christmas Eve show

I WAS THERE: NIGEL YATES

I WAS AT my mate Kev's fourteenth birthday party and *Top of the Pops* was on in the background as we were all getting into the glam rock scene. All of a sudden, a song played that literally blew our minds: 'Seven Seas of Rhye'. I became an instant lifetime fan. Purchasing tickets from Bayes Recordium in Kings Lynn, I travelled down to London with friends for the Christmas Eve show. We were 15 and 16 years old and had a hell of a time convincing our parents to let us travel alone, especially on Christmas Eve. Steve climbed out of his bedroom window because he wasn't allowed to come with us.

Nigel Yates was at Hammersmith Odeon for the famed Christmas Eve show

We left just before noon, catching the train at Kings Lynn station. Steve planned to phone his parents from Cambridge to let them know that he'd absconded. We were standing outside the phone box when he rang home and we could hear his father shouting down the phone from six feet away!

We arrived in London around 3pm. We were cold, wet and hungry. We made it to Hammersmith by 5pm. The doors didn't upon for a while so we joined the queue and got wetter and colder. It was the first concert any of us had ever attended. We weren't ready for the mad rush when the doors opened. We waited patiently inside for Queen to take to the stage and, boy, were we in for a treat. Freddie was so flamboyant, jumping around the stage. The volume of the music was unbelievable to us country yokels. What a brilliant night. A highlight was 'Now I'm Here'. The guitar of Brian May quite literally danced around the room from all directions, with the singing coming from left to right of the stage alternately. I remember Freddie doing a rock and roll melody near the end of the set. It was played as I'd never heard of rock and roll played before. It was a night we'll never forget.

After the concert we had to try and get home. The last train to Lynn had left. We tried hitchhike but by 5am on Christmas morning we'd only got as far as Cambridge and were exhausted. Luckily, we were able to raise my dad on the phone. He wasn't too pleased but, being Dad - bless him - he drove the 50 miles to Cambridge on a cold and now frosty Christmas morning. We eventually got back home at 9am. Steve was grounded for a month but, hey ho. it was bloody worth it.

The one thing that keeps me going is that I like to laugh at myself. If we were a different kind of band, with messages and political themes, then it would be different. That's why I can wear ridiculous shorts on stage and ham it up **Freddie Mercury**

1976 saw Queen set off on a world tour to promote A Night at the Opera, taking in the United States of America, Japan and Australia.

TOWER THEATRE
31 JANUARY & 1 & 2 FEBRUARY 1976, PHILADELPHIA, PENNSYLVANIA

I WAS THERE: MARK MAHAL, AGE 19

AFTER MISSING OUT on two chances to see them, a few months had passed and to my delight it was announced that Queen would be returning on a new tour promoting their new album, *A Night at the Opera*. When the tour dates were released I was ecstatic as one of the shows was scheduled for 31 January 1976 at the Tower Theater in Upper Darby, Pennsylvania, just outside of Philadelphia – the same Tower Theater at which David Bowie recorded his *David Live* album in July 1974. As the gods of rock decided. This time I was not to be denied.

Knowing the day and time that tickets went on sale I made certain to procure prime seating. We were fourth row centre and it was made extra spectacular by the bit of a catwalk added to the stage front that extended out into the centre aisle. Freddie Mercury literally strutted his stuff by me throughout the night. Having just turned 19, to say that I was in awe would be an understatement. From the moment they took the stage to the pre-recorded track of 'Procession' to their performance of 'Bohemian Rhapsody' and ending with the encores of 'Now I'm Here', 'Big Spender', 'Jailhouse Rock' and 'God Save the Queen', the night was a spectacle of sound and vision. One of pageantry, showmanship and musicality. At show's end, we sat in wonderment as the theatre emptied, wanting more and knowing that this was certainly not the end but just the beginning. We caught them once more on that tour on their return to the Convention Hall in Philadelphia on 11 February 1977 and the show was once again stellar. However, that magical night at the Tower Theater will always hold a special place in my rock 'n' roll heart.

I WAS THERE: BOBBY GILCKEN

I SAW QUEEN at the Tower theatre in Philly (where Bowie did *David Live*). The first album was played on WMMR. I went out and bought it and – wow! - we were hooked. My friends and I got seats in the front row of the balcony as there were no good seats on the floor. It was the biggest PA we'd ever seen in there. You walked in and went 'holy shit, this is going to be amazing'. And it was!

Bobby Gilcken was wowed by the size of Queen's PA

BEACON THEATER
5 FEBRUARY 1976 1976, NEW YORK, NEW YORK

I WAS THERE: ANTHONY PALUMBO

I HAVE BEEN a Queen fan since hearing the album *Queen II* in 1974. After a friend played me a bootlegged live album called *Queen Live at the Budokan*, and although the sound quality was poor, the performance really grabbed me. I said, 'I have to see these guys live'. I got my first chance at the Beacon Theater on 74th and Broadway in New York City, a relatively small and intimate venue, and I was lucky enough to score orchestra seats in the centre, right next to Queen's mixing and sound boards.

The lights went out, I heard a deep voice over the PA say, 'Ladies and gentlemen, welcome to a night at the opera' and the operatic parts of 'Bohemian Rhapsody' started playing over the sound system. With the place still dark and after the third verse of 'the devil put aside for me', there was a boom, the stage lights came on, smoke filled the stage and Freddie Mercury jumped off the drum riser and the band kicked in. It was just so electric. I was in awe.

After that they went straight into 'Ogre Battle'. When that was over, I remember Freddie saying, 'Are you ready for some

Anthony Palumbo's Beacon Theater tickets for *A Night at the Opera*

sophisticated rock and roll, New York?' We were! I don't remember the order of all the songs. I know they did a medley of songs. When they got to where they played 'Brighton Rock', Brian May said, 'We are trying something new - please forgive any mistakes.' Of course, I didn't find any and the guitar solo was awesome and the rest of the show was also great. I remember on the encore Freddie coming out in hot pants and suspenders (braces), singing 'Hey, Big Spender'. During the song, the staff at the Beacon Theater opened the side exits to show us that a foot of snow had fallen during the concert. There was no snow on the ground when we went in. It made for a fun bus ride back to New Jersey.

I WAS THERE: EDWARD GOODWIN

I SAW QUEEN live several times during the late Seventies and early Eighties. The most memorable show was during the *A Night at the Opera* tour and the venue was the Beacon Theatre. It's a small venue with approximately 3,000 seats. There's not a bad seat in the house and the acoustics are tremendous. Freddie, Brian, John and Roger were at the top of their game at that time and that show is burned into my memory forever. It was opening night of a four night stand, and they were so good several of us returned for the closing night and scalped tickets. I still have my stubs and - considering today's prices for groups of lesser talent - I paid $10 each night. I mean come on - $10 to see Freddie Mercury and Queen?

Three years ago, my son, daughter and myself went to see Queen with Adam Lambert. Freddie Mercury was a once in a lifetime talent and could never be replaced, but that kid Lambert performing with Queen was about as close as you could get. They touched my heart that night and brought back memories that brought tears to my eyes. It was something special.

Edward Goodwin saw Queen several times

TOLEDO SPORTS ARENA
15 FEBRUARY 1976, TOLEDO OHIO

I WAS THERE: RICHARD B KELLEY

QUEEN WERE NOTHING if not dedicated workaholics. Within a year they were back in the US and revisited quite a few of the smaller markets, like Toledo and Fort Wayne, whose audiences had supported them early on. The Toledo Sports Arena was a 6,000 seat hockey and boxing venue built shortly after the Second World War. Styx opened the proceedings.

My date was 16 and today would politely be described as high maintenance. She had no use for hard rock or flamboyant performers like Freddie and Queen, who she dismissed using a vulgar euphemism for homosexuals. I tested her patience with the show promising we would leave once the band played the vaunted 'Bohemian Rhapsody' which I really wanted to see performed live. About an hour into the concert, Freddie took a break from flaunting about and sat down at the piano. The opening lines of 'Bohemian Rhapsody' brought a roar from the crowd and then it happened. The lights went black. The middle segment of the mini epic was presented from a recording as green lighting barely illuminated the stage. After the complex parts were presented on tape - no digital, you could hear the hiss - the lights came up again to find Freddie still seated at the piano as the recording segued back to his live performance to end the song. 'Well, that's kind of chintzy,' I thought, but there really was no other way as the middle part of the song was simply too complex. The balance of the show apparently was similar to the previous year's presentation, but my date held me to my promise and we left soon after.

The following night I escorted the same lovely, young teen-queen to the movies to see Stanley Kubrick's *Barry Lyndon* at a suburban Toledo multiplex. The film was past its' box office prime so attendance was sparse, perhaps less than a dozen people. As we entered the theatre, who should be at the ticket counter, charming the young ladies there, but Brian May and Freddie Mercury! Instead of spending their night off in a hotel room with a bevy of groupies and a mountain of blow, they'd gone to the movies. The very tall, longhaired fellow and his shorter cohort with the huge brown eyes and bad teeth stepped aside as we arrived at the counter to buy our tickets. They bid the counter girls a good evening and strode into the theatre as we followed suit. Brian and Freddie sat about four rows in front of us. There was no one between us and them, though we did sit off to one side as Brian's height and hair was distracting.

The film included an intermission. The lights went up after the first half and audience members got up to stretch our legs. I caught Brian and Freddie's eye and nodded discreetly while my date remained oblivious. After the second half ended, we all got up and filed out. I once again caught the Queen members' attention and tried to make small talk as we exited. 'Great show!' I stammered. I was referring to their concert of the night before but for all they knew I could have just as easily been referring to Barry Lyndon. They acknowledged me politely and we all went our separate ways.

I asked my date if she recognised the two long hairs and, in her inimitable fashion, she replied, 'No! They look like (*insert vulgar synonym for homosexuals here*).' I'm pretty sure that was our last date.

CIVIC CENTER
18 FEBRUARY 1976, SAGINAW, MICHIGAN

I WAS THERE: DAVE DALTON

THE SHOW WAS full of lights and as a guitar player I was really looking forward to how Brian May was going to choose how to pick which lead guitar parts to play in the solos, given the fact the most of them were double or triple harmony parts. And then when he played one note, three came out. 'How is he doing that?' I figured it was some sort of recorded stuff the front of house guy was mixing in on cues. In any event, it was a great show in a small market that I never thought they'd come to. No back stage passes, no meet and greet, just the roar of a real rock show before they all went sterile.

It was the roar of a real rock show

AUDITORIUM THEATRE
23 FEBRUARY 1976, CHICAGO, ILLINOIS

I WAS THERE: MICHAEL NIKSIC

MY FIRST TASTE of Queen was 'Keep Yourself Alive'. Coming from the deep south side of Chicago in the middle of numerous roaring steel mills defied the odds of an openly gay singer striking a chord in an all white neighbourhood. I was 16 and starting my experimental formative drug years. Our neighborhood

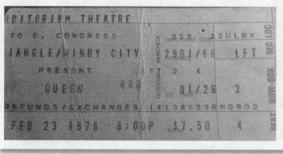

Michael Niksic saw Queen at the Auditorium Theatre in Chicago

vinyl/head shop was 12 blocks one way from our home. We did not have a car. So we walked most of the time to make our vinyl and party supplies purchases. Since our lives revolved around music and drugs, we were frequent fliers at the store. When we finally bought our first cars, we all had cassettes and Craig powerplay tape decks with Jensen tri axial speakers. If a band saw our money they were pretty damn good, ranging from Yes to Muddy Waters, Pink Floyd to The Who.

My best friend at the time formed a three piece power rock band with other friends. They'd cover Queen, Joe Satriani and the like and I ran their light board. The lead singer, Mark, was a huge Queen fan and that rubbed off on me. When Queen played at the Aragon Ballroom in '75, Mark ate his ticket as his ride never showed up and I sold mine as I had to work. In 1976 at the Auditorium Theatre, we had opera box seats. We had a tendency to buy the second best tier of seats at shows, just above ground level to prevent seat standers from blocking our view. Pablo Cruise was the warm up act. They were pretty good but not well received by a ravenous Queen audience.

We were treated to 'Bohemian Rhapsody', one of the first times they played it live. We were also partying with everyone else. Rolling joints while seated and passing them down your row was common. What fire ordinance? We also took pride in our rolling skill so it was a chance to clicit thoughts from people we didn't know about which joints were better rolled. The ride home was always listening to what we just experienced, firing up a joint and riffing on each other's rolling abilities. We did our own version of *Wayne's World's* 'Bohemian Rhapsody' driving home that night, 20 years before it was cool or a thing.

That night, Queen firmly established themselves in our minds as an all-time great band. Freddie Mercury's vocals were powerful and their stage presence unforgettable. Brian May was amongst the best of the crop of guitarists touring at the time. Queen were in their prime and rising like a NASA rocket. It wasn't by chance we picked the timing to see them in this venue. We were very experienced concert goers and never spent our money recklessly on bum bands with one good song. We all worked and $8.50 plus fees and tax and additional expenses (not including a sack of Jamaican Red) was big money. It also explained why we didn't have girlfriends in that four year stretch. None of us could afford one!

DANE COUNTY COLISEUM
28 FEBRUARY 1976, MADISON, WISCONSIN

I WAS THERE: KIM WILLIAMS

I SAW QUEEN twice in the later part of the Seventies and they were fantastic both times. Dane County Coliseum is not a large venue, but at the time it was basically 'it' in Madison, which is the capital of Wisconsin and has a large college campus. I was in 10th or 11th grade and lived 45 minutes away. I remember being so excited to go. I'm unsure what I told my parents but if it was a school night, I probably stretched the truth a

bit. It was freezing outside and parking was quite a walk from the venue. Me and my friends smoked and drank in the parking lot and pretty much floated into the concert. Queen were excellent and we sang along. I saw them again in 1977 and again they were fantastic. I was just as excited to see them as first time round and I went with the same group of friends. Once more we floated into Dane County Coliseum. We were pretty close to the stage this time, sang along to every song and had so much fun. The band rocked

Kim Williams saw Queen twice

and the entire Coliseum smelled like pot - everyone was smoking it. I have seen a lot of concerts in my day, but these Queen concerts rank in my top two!

When Freddie died, a little piece of me died with him. I cried like a baby.

MEMORIAL COLISEUM
29 FEBRUARY 1976, FORT WAYNE, INDIANA

I WAS THERE: CURTIS ALDRICH

I WASN'T QUITE sure what to expect when I got the tickets. I had been listening to *Queen II* and *Sheer Heart Attack* for over a year and was enthralled by Brian May's guitar but there was a certain something about Freddie's vocals and lyrics that I couldn't put my finger on. Leslie West and Mountain

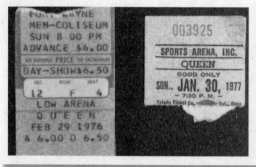

Curtis Aldrich saw Queen in Fort Wayne and the following year in Toledo

was the opening act so the show started with heavy guitars and thumping bass and drums. When the intro started for Queen, it was as if the entire mood of the arena changed. There was a huge curtain that parted but the lights were so dim we couldn't see the band members taking the stage. The next thing I heard was Brian May's lofty guitar work. From there, the intensity began to build and there was no crescendo until the final number. Then came the encore – 'Killer Queen'. Obviously, they performed the entire *Night at the Opera* album but when they mixed in 'Flick of the Wrist' and 'Now I'm Here', the crowd went wild.

My wife and recently saw Queen with Adam Lambert in Columbus, Ohio. Few singers can match Freddie's energy or stage presence but Adam Lambert did a phenomenal job. When Brian May introduced him, he said the band knew he would fit in well to which Adam replied, 'No one could ever replace Freddie Mercury and I am humbled by the opportunity to sing the music of Queen with these fabulous musicians.' Throughout the show there were images of Freddie in the big screen and, at one point, Brian played along with a video and the voice of Freddie. That was a teary-eyed moment for me.

AUDITORIUM
2 MARCH 1976, MILWAUKEE, WISCONSIN

I WAS THERE: JOHN HORA

'QUEEN WANT YOU to photograph them in Milwaukee tomorrow!'

I'm a drummer and photographer, born in 1950. I grew up in beautiful Hinsdale, Illinois near Chicago. My coming-of-age years were steeped in all the wonderful music of The Beatles, the Beach Boys and The Byrds - and that's just the Bs! I thought music died in 1970 when The Beatles broke up and other great bands disassembled and reassembled with others. The music

John Hora photographed Queen and got the ultimate compliment from Freddie

seemed to have lost something in the overproduced mix. Then I heard 'Killer Queen' on the radio and thought 'wow!' I bought the *Sheer Heart Attack* album, read all the lyrics and fell in love with Queen.

I hadn't been to a concert in years but wasn't going to miss seeing Queen live when they came to Chicago in 1976. They were masterful, and the staging and lighting were breathtaking. Queen were here for a second night; and I returned with my cameras. A faked press pass got me in. I had the run of the place and shot several rolls of colour slide film. The results were thrilling, having captured the majesty of the concert. Using special projectors, I put together a slide show dissolving one image over the other creating a slow motion effect on the screen. When played with music from *Sheer Heart Attack*, the experience was like being there. Remember, this was five years before MTV!

I reached out to Rip Pelley at Elektra Records near Chicago to see if he would be interested in seeing my slide show. Rip invited me over to his office. Along with the slide show gear, I brought a few 11 x 14 mounted colour prints from the concert. Rip asked if he could have the prints to show them to the guys. I figured it couldn't hurt for the other guys in the office to see my photos. Hopefully I could get some photo assignments from Elektra. I set up the projection and sound equipment, closed the window blinds and put on my little slide show. Rip was down to earth, really friendly, and very complimentary about my photography and thought my slide show was cool. Rip was Senior Director of National Promotion and Artist Development at Elektra/Asylum Records but I didn't know how connected he was. I wasn't sure if he really liked my photos or if he was just that nice to everyone.

A few days later, I came home and my mom told me that a guy with a thick English accent had called, left his number and wanted me to call him right back. His name was Peter Brown. I called him right away and he told me that he was with the Queen tour and that Queen wanted to hire me to photograph their concert in Milwaukee tomorrow!

I didn't need to fake a press pass. This time, I had front stage access for the entire concert. I shot several rolls of colour slide film. After the concert, I drove right to Chicago to the commercial lab I used for the film to be developed overnight, picked up the film at the lab the next day and met Rip Pelley in his suite at the Hyatt Regency Hotel in Chicago to show him the pictures.

I brought all the best images in plastic protective slide pages, 20 to a sheet. While Rip was looking at my photos, Brian May walked in, introduced himself and shook my hand, and Rip handed him one of the slide sheets. Then John Deacon walked in, introduced himself and shook my hand and Rip handed him another one of the slide sheets. Then Roger Taylor did the same and Rip handed him a third slide page. The three of them were all excitedly looking, going over each image and commenting about which ones they liked. Then Freddie Mercury walked in on all the excitement, introduced himself and shook my hand, and the guys began to show him all the pictures they liked best. Then it dawned on me that Queen were the 'guys' that Rip gave my prints to.

After looking at my photos for about 10 minutes, Freddie looked over at me and said, 'These are the best. The best we've seen.' Then he excused himself and headed out to party with some local Chicago friends. Brian looked over at me and said, 'You will join us for dinner, won't you?' I said yes. Soon I was in the elevator with the three of them and moments later we were strolling through the hotel lobby where their limousine was waiting for us at the door. I had to pinch myself a few times to be sure I wasn't dreaming.

One of the coolest parts was the drive to the restaurant. 'Bohemian Rhapsody' came on the radio and the driver blasted it right as we drove past a big record store window display filled entirely with Queen album covers. They loved it and I pinched myself again. I'd heard enough stories about how big name rockers can party really hard and, honestly, I was a bit concerned about what the evening might bring. I'm not a drinker, I don't smoke and I don't use drugs. And these guys didn't seem to fit the sex drugs and rock n' roll stereotype. Actually....

Dinner was absolutely lovely. Roger and John had just seen the movie *Close Encounters of the Third Kind* and we talked about flying saucers. Brian asked me what kind of stereo speakers I used at home and how far apart they were. I asked questions about their recording techniques, microphone types and noise reduction. Roger and John kidded Brian about gardening at midnight with a flashlight. They might have had two beers each with dinner but no more. They were perfect gentlemen and genuinely nice guys.

The story doesn't end there. Queen came back to Chicago the following year and, again, I was invited to photograph them. I had made another slide show from pictures taken the year before and transferred it to video. Queen were staying at the Whitehall Hotel this time and I brought a huge commercial video deck with me so I could show it to them on the television in their suite. Hotels in 1977 didn't make it easy to plug video players into their television sets. John Deacon and I spent half an hour trying every possible connection, cord and adaptor we could think of to make it work. Finally, it worked so that I was able to show it to everyone. After that, they let me pick a spot for lunch and we went to a trendy place in Lincoln Park not far from their hotel.

At lunch, Roger said, 'You're welcome to photograph us, but this time we're not paying you.' What!? I wasn't doing it for the money. I was doing it for the honour. He quickly explained that they had recently returned from their second trip to Japan. Photographers there had dozens of radio-controlled, motorized Nikon cameras with 100' film magazines mounted all over the stage. Queen were so famous by that time, they were surrounded by all the big magazine photographers. I was indeed honoured to be asked to photograph a group that I had so admired and then to find them to be down to earth, good-natured guys.

In 2006, I took my two sons to see Queen with Paul Rodgers in Chicago. I had left my office an hour early to get the kids ready and be there on time. What I didn't discover until the morning after is that Brian May's personal tour assistant had emailed my office from their limo on the way to the stadium inviting me and my sons to a party after the concert. Wow! Brian later emailed and said he hoped we could get together next time but that wasn't to be. Brian helped arrange photo passes for me to photograph Queen in 2010 and again in 2019, but there was no after concert meet and greet or party either time.

Though I only met Freddie the one time, I get goose bumps remembering his words, 'These are the best. The best we've seen.' Queen has all my images in their archives. Several years ago, I discovered Roger had used one of my photos of him on his super-secret YouTube page for Queen business and media videos. Brian later wrote that one of my photos of Freddie was his favourite.

When I first met Queen, it was business. They had hired me. Though star struck, I tried to say cool. I didn't ask for autographs or take pictures of them when we were out. I was working for them. I didn't think it was professional to photograph them when they weren't 'working'. We were close in age, in our late twenties. On stage they were like gods. Off stage they were regular guys, and genuinely nice guys that were fun to be with. The biggest difference I noticed between us was that they spoke with English accents and had better shoes than I did.

SANTA MONICA CIVIC AUDITORIUM
9 – 11 MARCH 1976, SANTA MONICA, CALIFORNIA

I WAS THERE: PATRICK GORE

IT WAS A very small venue. It was amazing, with pyrotechnics and huge flames coming out of the stage. They had just released *A Night at the Opera* so no one knew it yet. But I knew their music because I loved the album *Sheer Heart Attack*.

FESTIVAL HALL
4 APRIL 1976, MELBOURNE, AUSTRALIA

I WAS THERE: CAZ NE'VILLE

I FIRST HEARD of Queen when I saw them perform 'Killer Queen' on a TV show called *Countdown*. I was 14 and a fan of T. Rex and many other bands of that era. I managed to get tickets to see them at the Festival Hall in Melbourne, and my mum managed to sneak in with me as she loved Freddie. He was the ultimate showman. We were in the front row of the upstairs balcony, and it was like he was singing and playing up to us. He had everybody there in the palm of his hand. It was an amazing night that we didn't want to end. I'm so glad I got the chance to see them. I've seen quite a few bands since then, but Queen will always be number 1 as far as performance goes.

APOLLO ENTERTAINMENT CENTRE
15 APRIL 1976, ADELAIDE, AUSTRALIA

I WAS THERE: NYGEL ANDREWARTHA, AGE 15

THE FIRST TIME I heard of them was when I heard 'Killer Queen' and then saw 'Liar' on television. When they played Sunbury in Australia in January 1974, I so wanted to go but I was 12 and it was too far away. But I saw them in April 1976 at the Apollo Stadium. I crept underneath the stage with my friend Julie. She screamed at Roger as he walked in and we got kicked out. After the concert, I met Freddie at the traffic lights in his limousine while I was waiting to be picked up by a friend. Freddie wound down his window and waved - as did I!

I then saw Queen at Sydney Entertainment Centre in 1985 and at the O2 Arena with Paul Rodgers in 2008. I've also seen both tours of Australia with Adam. In 2008 I flew to the O2 Arena show and, on arriving in London, went straight to Freddie's old home at Garden Lodge. I didn't even use a road map – I just sensed where to go. As well as Freddie, I have met Brian at a press conference and Roger at the opening of *We Will Rock You*. I have met them all except John. The last time I saw Brian was at a book signing in 2018. He shook my hand and asked me what Australian song they should sing that night and I said 'Down Under', which he played that evening.

HORDERN PAVILION
17 APRIL 1976, SYDNEY, AUSTRALIA

I WAS THERE: MARY KELLAM

HAVING PLAYED THE *Sheer Heart Attack* and *A Night at the Opera* albums constantly, we were beyond excited to finally attend Queen's first concert in Sydney at the Hordern Pavilion. Freddie first appeared in silhouette behind a spot-lit screen singing the 'I see a little silhouette-o of a man' part of 'Bohemian Rhapsody' before leaping straight into the 'rock' part of the song ('So you think you can fool me...') and just

Mary Kellam's ticket for Queen's first concert in Sydney

Mary Kellam visited Zanzibar and Freddie's childhood home

exploding onto the stage. The light show, the operatic style, the invitation to *A Night at the Opera* all created the most amazing never-to-be-forgotten concert. 38 years later, I sat at a Cat Empire concert in roughly the same seats at the same venue. Telling my daughter about the Queen concert during intermission was like reliving that night.

I was travelling in Tanzania in 2017 and was determined to see Zanzibar, which is just off the coast and not that easy to get to. It's a beautiful island with interesting history and culture and it was quite easy to find Mercury House, as it is now called, in the capital, Stonetown. There was no charge or fanfare to going inside and having a look around, just an appreciation of Freddie's early history.

Queen played Sydney again in February 2020. I'd already purchased tickets for Alice Cooper before Queen announced their concert. But all was not lost! I was able to buy merchandise for both Queen and Alice Cooper that night, and the finishing times of the concerts were staggered to manage the crowds. As Alice Cooper ended and we made our way back to the station, Queen started playing 'Bohemian Rhapsody' from the open arena on a lovely Sydney summer's night. Like magic, the whole crowd walking to the station sang it in full voice to the end. It was an absolutely superb ending that made your hair stand on end.

Like magic, the whole crowd walking to the station sang 'Bohemian Rhapsody' in full voice

FESTIVAL HALL
19 & 20 APRIL 1976, MELBOURNE, AUSTRALIA

I WAS THERE: IAN MURRAY, AGE 14

IT WAS MY first concert. To say I almost wet my pants is an understatement. It was the most amazing thing I'd ever seen. During the 'Brighton Rock' solo, Bri seemed to make sounds bounce off the four walls. I also saw them four times on the rather more slick *Works* tour in Melbourne. The second and fourth concerts were the best. I ran down the front during 'Another One Bites the Dust' in the fourth show. I was about three feet from Freddie and he was giving it all.

I WAS THERE: GILDA B TURNER

I WAS QUITE young. Freddie was wearing his white jumpsuit and he had long hair. It was a superb concert and still the best concert I have ever been to, and I have been to a lot over the years. Many people are very jealous that I have actually seen Freddie Mercury and Queen in concert. I feel so fortunate.

FESTIVAL HALL
23 APRIL 1976, BRISBANE, AUSTRALIA

I WAS THERE: GARY THOMPSON

AS A TRANSPORTED Brit in Australia since 1970, I soon realised Australia was so far away from any decent music. In 1975 my parents decided to send me on holiday back home to Northern Ireland, hence the first *Top of the Pops* I saw had Queen with 'Bohemian Rhapsody' at number 1. I'd heard *Queen I* in Australia as a friend had relatives bring the LP out to him. It was

Gary Thompson saw Queen at the Festival Hall in Brisbane

something I had to get more of. On returning to Australia, in my luggage was every record Queen had recorded up to then. In 1976, Queen were on the *Opera* tour and Australia was on the agenda. Luckily my mum who is also a huge Queen fan (and now 83 years old) happened to be in Brisbane city and was passing the booking office (remember them?), saw the Queen tour poster and bought two tickets at the princely sum of $5.60 each. She then proceeded to give her ticket to my best mate Larry. The day of the gig came along and we were dropped off outside Brisbane Festival Hall, sadly no longer there. The capacity was 3,500 and it was sold out. I had already seen bands there before, T.Rex, Slade, etc. but nothing prepared us for what was coming. A local Brisbane band was support, getting maybe half an hour, and then the lights went out.

Over the PA we heard, 'Ladies and gentlemen, welcome to *A Night at the Opera* with Queen.' I think Kenny Everett did the intro. Lights, smoke, dry ice all went off, as did the crowd. 'Now I'm Here' was the opener. Queen live were one seriously heavy rock band back in the day. Tracks from earlier albums – 'Ogre Battle' and 'March of the Black Queen' - were thunderous and then you had 'In the Lap of the Gods' to bring it all down.

The band were dressed exactly as they were in the 'Bo Rap' video. I couldn't believe how thin Freddie was, while Brian was all legs and hair. For 90 minutes we were bombarded with all sorts of music. Brian's banjo/ uke made an appearance on 'Leroy Brown' and his solo spot on 'Brighton Rock' was just incredible for an aspiring guitarist like myself. 'Bohemian Rhapsody' was never played in full of course but a taste was good enough. Time rushed by and 'In the Lap' was revisited and then they were off. Larry and I just stared at each other. Other people were on their seats. Then Roger appeared with a giant set of drumsticks and proceeded to batter his kit. Brian and John appeared and started playing the intro to 'Big Spender'. On comes Freddie in a kimono and the tiniest pair of candy-striped shorts. 'Big Spender' allowed him to shed the kimono and then it was straight into the medley of old rock tunes – 'Jailhouse Rock', 'Tutti Frutti', 'Stupid Cupid', etc. The band tore it up on those old tunes. Then sadly the night did come to an end. As we exited the hall both Larry and I were speechless bar the odd 'bloody hell!' As two 15-year-olds, we had been privy to seeing one of the greatest bands ever. I know they went on to be massive as the shows did become a real spectacle, but I always think back to how I saw them just with lights and a bit of dry ice. They made me a fan for life.

With two outdoor shows planned for the end of the summer, Queen played a couple of warm up shows in Edinburgh

PLAYHOUSE THEATRE
1 & 2 SEPTEMBER 1976, EDINBURGH, UK

I WAS THERE: WALTER MCKAY
I REMEMBER FREDDIE in a black and white diamond leotard, with a plank acting as a walkway above my head.

I WAS THERE: ANDREW SPENCE
MY FIRST EVER concert. It was a great gig but I missed the encore in order to catch the last train back to Fife!

CARDIFF CASTLE
10 SEPTEMBER 1976, CARDIFF, UK

I WAS THERE: JEFF PERRY
QUEEN TOPPING THE bill at Cardiff Castle, my one and only outdoor festival. It was more memorable for the weather than anything else. I was so looking forward to this. My sister couldn't be with me because of work commitments and she was so disappointed before the concert (but glad she missed it afterwards!) so it was just me and my usual mate. We arrived in Cardiff early under grey skies, went for a bite to eat and chilled for a while before making our way to the castle. This was a wonderful setting for a concert, in glorious grounds right in the middle of the city centre. Some months earlier, 10cc had played there and someone told me how they'd heard the haunting melodies of 'I'm Not in Love' reverberating through the nearby streets.

The castle gates opened around 1pm and we were amongst the first in. As we walked through the gates it started to drizzle. The forecast wasn't great but we lived in hope. Richie Blackmore had pulled out, apparently because his signature rainbow wouldn't fit on the stage. In hindsight he may have seen the weather forecast.

Local boy Andy Fairweather Low (from the next village to me) kicked off the day. The rain kept coming. By the time Manfred Mann's Earth Band had finished I was totally soaked through. My mate had left me at our superb position close to the stage to find some cover but I stayed put. I didn't see him again for the rest of the day and we only caught up a few days later. I was wearing a knee length double-breasted wool coat, which by the time Queen made their appearance was full of water and weighed a ton!

I held my ground to the end. Queen didn't disappoint, playing everything we wanted to hear, but I couldn't really enjoy the occasion. To put the tin hat on the day, I wear glasses, although it didn't matter whether I wore them or not on the day - I couldn't see much. By the time I got home I was on my knees. The weight of my now waterlogged coat had quadrupled and it took weeks to dry out properly. That was my last open air concert for a number of years. I stuck to going to places with a roof!

HYDE PARK
18 SEPTEMBER 1976, LONDON, UK

I WAS THERE: JOY COOK

I SAW QUEEN 17 times. I'd been a fan over a year before I first saw Queen at Hammersmith Odeon. I was blown away by Freddie's stage presence. He just knew how to engage an audience. I've still got a t-shirt I bought that night. That night they announced they'd be doing a concert on Christmas Eve concert so I got tickets then and there for that one too. I was also at the free Hyde Park concert in 1976, right at the front with my sister who was seven months pregnant. The police were worried about her so they lifted her over the barrier to see the concert in safety.

Photos: Joy Cook

I also went at the fan club's invitation to two video shoots – 'We Are the Champions' and 'Friends Will Be Friends'. We always felt special at these events and were given token gifts, which I still have. I had their autographs as a prize at one of the Christmas parties. I sold them for £1,100 after holding onto them for 30 years.

You always felt part of a Queen performance. The excitement of Queen concerts stayed with you long after it was over.

Joy Cook was down front at Hyde Park

I WAS THERE: ANDY HORLOCK

FROM THE OPENING drum beat of Slade's 'Gudbuy T'Jane' I was hooked. As a 12-year-old, guitar bands were where it was at; Sweet, Mud, Bowie and the Spiders from Mars. I remember seeing them on *Top of the Pops*. From the opening bars of 'Seven Seas of Rhye' I was transfixed. I know now that they were miming, something they hated, but to a 13-year-old? Wow, they were so different. I'm not sure how I managed it, probably by borrowing money, but I bought the single and I remember sitting at the table talking endlessly about privy counsellors and titans and troubadours before finally being told to 'shut up and get on with your dinner'.

'Killer Queen' followed as a single. The words fascinated me. It was almost poetry to my young ears. I had never heard anything like this and I saved up the money to buy *Sheer Heart Attack*. I was now working on a Saturday with a massive Queen fan called Steve who'd bought *Queen II*. I thought the cover was amazing. Of course, this was the days of vinyl and to open the double sleeve and see the pictures of the band members was fabulous. The music too, with the White and the Black side.

I of course had to buy their first album, where the Led Zeppelin influences can clearly be heard. 'Liar' and 'Keep Yourself Alive' were great music then, now and always. I was 15 when I first heard and saw 'Bohemian Rhapsody' on *Top of the Pops*. There were no video recorders in those days but over the following nine weeks there was plenty of opportunity to watch this video masterpiece. This was followed by the album *A Night at the Opera*, another fine collection of music. 'I'm in Love with My Car', 'The Prophet's Song' and ''39' remain amongst my all-time favourites.

In mid-1976 it was announced that Queen were to play a concert in Hyde Park and, even better, it would be free to attend. Tickets to see the greats of the music business in Hyde Park cost hundreds of pounds these days, but we were going to see these gods stride the stage for nothing. The bill was announced. I had heard of Kiki Dee but my musical education didn't stretch as far as Steve Hillage or Supercharge.

Arriving in the middle of Hyde Park, there were thousands upon thousands of people there. It was the biggest crowd I had ever been in, before or since. I don't remember much about Steve Hillage. Supercharge's lead singer - a lad of larger proportions - was wearing a white leotard-type arrangement, perhaps in homage to Freddie. Kiki Dee had been to number 1 with Elton John with 'Don't Go Breaking My Heart' and there was a rumour that he was going to come on stage and perform it with her. In the end we had to make do with a life-sized cardboard cut-out.

Then the big moment arrived. Queen came on the stage and Freddie welcomed us to his 'Picnic by the Serpentine'. I could not begin to list the full set list from memory, but I do remember being impressed that they had been able to replicate the whole opera section from 'Bohemian Rhapsody', only finding out years later that they had just played the recorded track. Looking at the set list now, every song was one of their all-time classics - plus 'Bring Back Leroy Brown'!

Until my memory fades, the date will be forever etched in my mind. For the same reason, the date of Jimi Hendrix's death will forever be etched. Freddie, seeing a banner in the crowd, announced and paid tribute to Hendrix on the sixth anniversary of his death.

Unlike Kennedy's death, when I was only three, I remember where I was when I heard Freddie had died. I was on an eight mile run round the streets of Barking and Dagenham and heard the news from a guy who admitted he couldn't stand Freddie, the band and their music. On the other hand, he was a Cliff Richard fan and collected model buses. I saw Queen live and love being able to tell people, 'Yes, I was there'. Even now I wonder - did Freddie really sell Noddy Holder his mirrored hat in Kensington Market?

I WAS THERE: STEVE JAMES

I WAS 16 in 1974. I went round a friend's house and his brother was playing some albums. He put 10cc on and then *Sheer Heart Attack*. It was quadrophonic and loud and I thought 'that sounds pretty good'. I'd heard 'Seven Seas of Rhye' but didn't have the money to buy it. But I bought 'Killer Queen' and *Sheer Heart Attack*, and then worked backwards and bought *Queen II* and *Queen I*. My friend said, 'There's a free concert coming up at Hyde Park, shall we go?' He and I went with a third guy. It was a Saturday and it was warm. We were about halfway back, by the lights. When we got there, we had quite a good spot and then more and more people came in. In the end, I think there were about 200,000 people there. Behind me I could see burger vans 20 yards away. Next minute, they were 50 yards away. And then they were 100 yards away. The burger vans kept moving back as the crowd was coming in. There was no encore because Queen had to leave quite quickly because of the security. The police got a bit fidgety about the crowd being too big and maybe some trouble with people not getting home. It was fantastic.

After that, I saw them at the Empire Pool, Wembley on 11 May 1978, £4.25 a ticket, the *Crazy* tour at Hammersmith Odeon on Boxing Day 1979 and again at the Empire Pool in 1980, twice on the *Works* tour and at Wembley and Knebworth in '86. Hyde Park was the stand out gig out of all of those. Milton Keynes on the *Hot Space* tour was fantastic too, a great atmosphere and loud. They just played great. The vocals were great, the guitars, everything. It was just an amazing day. Knebworth was a bit too big and it lost the sound. Milton Keynes was better.

I WAS THERE: JAIMIE KELLY, AGE 14

'KILLER QUEEN' WAS on *Top of the Pops* and next day in school everyone was saying 'did you see that?' I started following them from then on. The first time I saw them was at Hammersmith Odeon in 1975, when *A Night at the Opera* came out. And then I saw them at Hyde Park, one of the best days of my life. It was a warm day. I remember having to get up early and do my paper round in Barking before I could go up to London with my mate on the train from Barking station. We wandered into Hyde Park and couldn't miss the big orange marquee, which we later found out had been used by the Rolling Stones. We must have been 120 yards from the stage, right in the middle of it. We saw the mixing desk and thought we'd position ourselves there, but when we got there, we decided it was too far away so walked forward to where the edge of the crowd was at that time and sat there.

They started with the operatic part of 'Bohemian Rhapsody' and there was more and more smoke and then all of a sudden you could just about see where they were and then the spotlight came on and Freddie came out from underneath the stage. Then the explosions went off and I got tingles up my neck. It was 'wow!' That's something I will always remember.

They only did 'You Take My Breath Away' from *A Day at the Races*, and 'You're My Best Friend' as part of a medley. When 'Lap of the Gods' finished, everyone was waiting around and waiting around in the dark, but there was no encore. We later found out that the police were going to arrest them if they went back on stage. I realised 'this isn't going to happen' so we started to make our way towards Marble Arch station, jumped the barriers and got a train home. We didn't have a ticket. When we got to Barking station, we said, 'We've just come from Mile End.'

Then the explosions went off and I got tingles up my neck

I saw them loads of times after that. The last time was at Wembley in 1986. I still go and see them but on my own now because, the price of tickets being what they are, no one wants to go with me. It's still Queen. Brian's guitar sound is unique. I've never heard a guitar sound like it. When I got married, my cousin got in touch with the fan club and all four members of Queen signed a wedding card for me. That was something special and he didn't tell me he was doing it.

I WAS THERE: ALEC MIDDLETON, AGE 16
I WATCHED THEM live in Hyde Park. We travelled from Worcestershire by coach. My overriding memory is that it poured down with rain all through, but they were fantastic and nothing could spoil the day.

I WAS THERE: BILLY WISE
I THOUGHT THEY were boring and far too camp. I watched them for about half an hour but was not impressed. Mercury's voice was very weak and flat at times – he probably wore himself out mincing about all over the stage. I saw dozens of bands live from 1971 until about five years ago and Queen would not even get in my top ten.

I WAS THERE: JAN MCEWAN, AGE 16
I ADORED THE ethereal, fairy-like theme of *Queen II*. The music was unlike anything else in the charts. My boyfriend suggested the Hyde Park concert, and it was the first time I'd ever been to one. We arrived there about 9am, and found a good spot not too close to the front so that we could get out easily enough if trouble appeared. We didn't anticipate the sheer numbers who would attend.

Jan McEwan remembers getting to Hyde Park early

I WAS THERE: JOHN SPENCER

THIS WAS A freebie! The band wanted to thank all the fans who had put
them at number 1 so they played a free concert. Obviously, they wouldn't
be on until it got dark, so there were some other acts lined up. I managed
to climb up a spotlight tower, so I had a great view of the stage to watch
the band. They had to finish by 10pm or something. I well remember
thousands of us bringing Park Lane to a grinding halt as we crossed the
road heading home. I was lucky and jumped on a bus outside Selfridges.

I WAS THERE: JAMES MCCASH

I'D SEEN THEM at the Caird Hall in Dundee, before they hit the big
time, and then went to see them at Hyde Park. I came down with my
wife and we made a weekend of it in London. We were quite far back.
From where we were they looked like stick insects.

I WAS THERE: MICHAEL WARD

IN 1974 I was 14 and lucky enough to spend my teenage years listening
to and watching Queen become one of the biggest bands of all time. I
have always been a keen vinyl collector and music fan, so with the release
of three classic Queen tracks - 'Killer Queen', 'Seven Seas of Rhye' and
'Now I'm Here' in 1974 coupled with the mesmerising performance on
the Christmas Eve *Old Grey Whistle Test* show, my love of the band in those
early years was cemented. When it was announced they would perform at
a free concert in September there was no question - I just had to be there.

I lived in Surbiton in the London suburbs and although there were
plenty of major music venues fairly close to hand this was to be my first live
concert experience. What better way to start? On a sunny late summer's
day my friends and I made our way to Hyde Park. On arriving I was
totally overawed by the sheer volume of people attending. Being young
and keen, we arrived fairly early. We took up a spot somewhere right of
the stage, probably a couple of hundred feet from the front. I don't recall
moving much all day, but I do recall a long wait for Queen to come on
stage after the last support act. But when they did come out, they were
every bit as exciting as I had imagined they would be, with flamboyant
costumes - Freddie in his white, black and harlequin leotards and Brian with
long flowing sleeves like an angel. Dry ice billowed from the stage for a lot
of the performance. Although it was quite a slow start with a number of
their quieter songs, towards the end they really let rip with all the rocking
tracks I loved so much including the epic 'Brighton Rock' (and of course

Brian's guitar solo), 'Stone Cold Crazy', 'Keep Yourself Alive' and 'Liar'. Of course, there were no large screens to relay the footage to the back of the crowd so the view wasn't great but it was good enough to know you were watching and listening to something special. Queen had received platinum discs for *A Night at the Opera* and 'Bohemian Rhapsody'. The day also marked the sixth anniversary of Jimi Hendrix's death, and I remember a couple of banners marking his passing.

I also saw them at Earls Court in June 1977 for the *Silver Jubilee* concert. My memories of this show are much vaguer, but it was my first visit to Earls Court and the show coincided with the Queen's Silver Jubilee, so everybody was in party mood as up and down the country people held street parties and celebrations with union flags flying everywhere. As with Hyde Park, Freddie was very chatty with the crowd and it was an equally explosive performance in what is a difficult venue to bring alive. A few years later I ended up living just down the road from Earls Court on Warwick Road. I was very sad to see it demolished.

I WAS THERE: MICK MORGAN

THE FREE CONCERT was extremely chaotic. It was a great atmosphere but so many people were off their faces and just staggering around, probably including myself. It was just a mass of people. We drove up there. You just parked your cars up. You could do that in those days. You couldn't do it now. Obviously, we didn't have mobile phones to contact each other – you just said, 'I'll meet you there in two hours' time.' But we were wandering all over the place. It was hard to see what was going on when they were on stage. The only thing I remember when we were down the front was Kiki Dee's set, with a cardboard cut out of Elton John for 'Don't Go Breaking My Heart'. Queen got booted off quite early because they'd overrun. I think the police pulled the plug on them. Hyde Park still has curfews now.

I WAS THERE: IAN NICHOLSON

THE FREE SHOW at Hyde Park was my third Queen gig. I didn't get there until relatively late in the day, missing most of the support acts apart from the bizarre sight of Kiki Dee duetting with a cardboard cut out of Elton John when performing 'Don't Go Breaking My Heart'! Queen debuted some material from *A Day at the Races* and there was an issue with the police when Queen tried to come back on stage to do an encore. Freddie performed in a baggy white boiler suit at the start of the show, so that was a little bit different!

I WAS THERE: JAN RHYS WILLIAMS, AGE 25

THE NEXT TIME I saw them was at Hyde Park, with my husband and the same girlfriend I went to Hammersmith with. We sat right in the middle of that massive crowd and could hardly see them, but there were screens and the atmosphere was absolutely wonderful. I remember an old man with a bicycle, who had probably walked through Hyde Park all his life. It didn't matter that there were thousands of people sitting watching a Queen concert. He was going to do exactly the same thing as he always did, and he just walked through the whole of this crowd. We felt a tiny bit let down at the end when they didn't do an encore. We were calling for them to come back on and they wanted to do an encore but they'd overrun so they weren't allowed to come back.

The next time I saw them was June 1977 at Earls Court. A massive crown came down from the ceiling all lit up with these

Jan Rhys-Williams went to Zanzibar in 2019

strobe lights and flashes and colours. It was all so dramatic. I think those kinds of effects were quite unique. I would really have loved to have seen them at Knebworth in 1986, because it's just up the road from me, but I was going through a really difficult divorce at the time and I was in a very bad place. It's one of my major regrets in life that I didn't get to see that last concert.

I haven't been to see Queen with Adam Lambert. John Deacon said that when Freddie died, Queen died. And that's how I feel. My husband is a bit younger than me and loves watching all the DVDs but I say to him, 'It's lovely to watch all this but really and truly you had to have been there, to have witnessed the atmosphere and everything that went with it.'

I'm such a fan of Freddie and Queen that I went to Zanzibar in 2019. It's pathetic really, but I stood in the street and looked at the place where he lived and just thought about how he would have been running up and down those streets and might have gone into this shop or that shop. It was just such a nice feeling.

I WAS THERE: PETER SMITH

A GROUP OF us went down to London by train on a day return ticket, returning straight after the concert on the mail train which pulled out of Kings Cross at midnight. This was a free concert, which drew a crowd of over 150,000, and was organised by Richard Branson. Kiki Dee had just been number 1 with 'Don't Go Breaking My Heart' and there were rumours that Elton John would join her on stage. Instead, she was accompanied by a life-size cardboard Elton figure and we all had to sing the Elton parts with her. Steve Hillage was great on the day, with lots of glissando guitar and amazing psychedelic trippy versions of The Beatles' 'All Too Much' and Donovan's 'Hurdy Gurdy Man'. But the day belonged to Queen.

It was a bold and brave move headlining such a major event at what was still a relatively early point in their career but they pulled it off. A powerful, energetic yet majestic set had the massive crowd captivated. The anthemic music, intense energy, vocal precision and mystical star-quality ensured that the whole audience were spell-bound. Their set was relatively short, around an hour, due to curfew and time restrictions of the time. I remember hearing that the police had prevented the band from returning for their trademark long encore. Freddie was amazing, although from where we were standing, he was a tiny white figure shining across the massive sea of people.

I WAS THERE: GARY TAVENDER, AGE 18

MY INTRODUCTION TO Queen was seeing them perform 'Killer Queen' on *Top of the Pops*. I went straight out and bought the first two albums. When I heard they were playing a free concert in Hyde Park I just had to be there. It was my first 'big' concert. I went with a friend and we were both blown away by the size of the crowd. Two things stick in my memory. Most people where we were sat were sitting down, and if anyone stood up they were pelted with cans! And the vision of Brian May, standing at the edge of the stage in a translucent white top, lit

Gary Tavender was at Hyde Park

up by the stage lights and playing the best guitar solo I had heard. To an 18-year-old from the East End of London it was magical. I've seen many, many gigs since then but, as they say, you never forget your first time!

A DAY AT THE RACES RELEASED
10 DECEMBER 1976

A DAY AT the Races reached number 1 in the UK and number 5 on the US *Billboard* chart, subsequently achieving platinum sales status. The album was promoted with the first of two North American tours that the band would undertake in 1977.

WINGS STADIUM
22 JANUARY 1977, KALAMAZOO, MICHIGAN

I WAS THERE: JEFFREY DALE JOHANSEN, AGE 15

IT WAS MY first concert. I went with a neighbour a couple years older who introduced me to them. We use to play chess and listen to albums at his house. It was cold that night. We got there a couple hours early to get good seats and waited for the doors to open about 20 feet away. It was festival seating, so there was a bit of a mad rush at the doors when they opened. I was a bit scared when everyone pushed forward. When we got close to the door, I remember being forced up against some girl. I braced myself against the door and allowed her to enter before I was forced in. Following my friend, we moved to seats to an area straight across from

Queen and Thin Lizzy toured the US together in 1977 on Queen's *Day at the Races* tour

the stage. We were about two thirds of the way up on the first tier, a great view although it would have been nice to be closer. The stadium began to fill with smoke from all the joints that were there. It was almost like a fog.

After what seemed like an eternity, the lights dropped and the warmup band came out. Thin Lizzy took the stage and played for a while. They had a couple hits and were popular enough, and they were good. But they were not who I was there to see. After what seemed another eternity, the lights went down again. It was time! 'Procession' started. The stage lights were raised as the group entered. Then all the lights went out. In the dark you could hear the Red Special kick into 'Tie Your Mother Down'. The rest of the band joined in and there were blinding lights from the steps of the drum set. I sat and stood through the set as the band went through seven costume changes and not only played music but entertained us all. The only song I didn't hear that I was hoping for was 'The Fairy Feller's Master-Stroke'. My favourite of the night was 'Brighton Rock'. It was amazing.

I saw them again at Wings Stadium on the *Jazz* tour. The music was incredible, the lights and costumes were exceptional, and the concert was unbelievable. Nobody entertained they way Queen did. Yet it did not match the incredible first concert. I have been to many concerts since, but I have never seen a better concert and been more entertained by a group than at my very first concert, by the one and only Queen. In 1984, I designed and built my own version of the Red Special. It doesn't sound like Brian's and I don't play like him, but it is a great reminder of my first concert.

I WAS THERE: RICHARD B KELLEY

COME 1977, I had moved to West Michigan for college, and Queen had produced their follow up album *A Day at the Races*. I thought the allusion to the Marx Brothers in the album titles was pretty cool, but I thought it repeated the formula of the previous record too closely and, though it yielded their biggest hit to that point, thought it was kind of boring. Queen went right back out on the road in support of it.

The Wings Stadium was a newer hockey rink than the Toledo Sports Arena, having opened just three years earlier. My date was another high maintenance although slightly older teen queen. The spoiled daughter of a nouveau riche Detroit mobster, she was used to the world revolving around her. When I arrived late to pick her up, having gotten lost trying to find her apartment, she was not amused. Wings Stadium was an hour's drive from our town so it was after 8pm when we finally arrived. I guess I should have been flattered as she was dolled up to the nines, but we had to park off site and hike through the ice and winter wind to the venue. She was in high heels with a fresh hairstyle and she was not pleased.

We finally found side stage seats as openers Thin Lizzy were ending their set. As this was my third Queen concert in less than two years, I was familiar with the gaudy live presentation of the band. Familiar songs from the earlier albums were repeated and, now a huge hit, 'Bohemian Rhapsody' was played at the beginning of the finale run which also included 'Stone Cold Crazy' and 'Keep Yourself Alive'. Once again, the middle part was presented on tape. To this day Queen performs the song the same way, as Adam Lambert disappears and the hard parts are presented using a video presentation of Freddie and the boys that harkens back to the *Queen II* album cover. A highlight of the show was Brian May's turn on ''39' but for the most part the set list, reflecting the recent albums, was a bit too heavy on the syrupy ballads and tongue-in-cheek schmaltz for my tastes, while the rockers seemed overwrought.

RICHFIELD COLISEUM
23 JANUARY 1977, CLEVELAND, OHIO

I WAS THERE: JANICE TOMASELLI STACK
I WAS INTRODUCED to Queen by my brother. He took me to every concert they played at the Coliseum from 1977 to 1982. We listened to all their albums. Queen was part of my family. We even took my mom once. My favourite song was 'You're My Best Friend'. My brother and I would sing in the car to all their hits, there wasn't a song we didn't know. The last song I sang with my brother before he passed away was 'Bohemian Rhapsody'. Queen bonded us. Those were the best days of my life.

I WAS THERE: MARCI CONNELLY
IN ADDITION TO New York and Los Angeles, Cleveland was the Midwest city where bands wanted to have huge fan support; our local fans were savvy and had been listening to the very best the genre had to offer since the 1950s going back to March 1952 and the very first rock 'n' roll concert, billed as The Moondog Coronation Ball at the Cleveland Arena, hosted by local radio DJ Alan Free. From that point on,

Cleveland became a hot spot and testing ground for new bands on the national and international music scene.

In the pre-Internet 1970s, unless the band was shooting an official video of the concert that might be televised at a later date, there was no way to see the show again or have any type of 'experience' with the band – you were there at the show in the moment and the only things left after the shows were your memories. Queen played eight shows in Cleveland on seven dates over the span of seven years. I was too young (according to my mom) to go to the shows that supported the *Sheer Heart Attack* and *Night at the Opera* albums.

Marci Connelly saw Queen four times at Richfield Coliseum

However, I did get to see Queen perform four times in three years as they toured to promote *A Day at the Races, News of the World, Jazz* and *The Game*.

The Coliseum was by no means an intimate venue. Queen had moved from playing the smaller halls like the Cleveland Music Hall (where they did two shows in one night in 1975 to accommodate the crowd) to playing the largest indoor sports arena in the area. It was a Sunday night in January of 1977 and I'm pretty sure there was not a parent from the group that was happy that four 16-year-olds were travelling about an hour in the snow to see a rock concert. But for us, we'd been listening to Queen since 1974 and this was our first opportunity to see them live and we weren't going to miss it!

Our seats weren't the best; we were seated in the lower section at the rear of the floor, a whole hockey arena away. But the advantage was that in addition to the music, we could see the light show. For the most part in the Seventies, in addition to the music the light show was really the only other part of the show. What we didn't know was that Queen planned to show their now-iconic 'Bohemian Rhapsody' video as part of the concert on the huge 'replay' screens of the arena. There were no customised video screens built into the stage or walkways built out into the audience, let alone the rigs that carry performers to the back of the venues. There was the stage, the drum platform and huge stacks of amplifiers and speakers on the stage that you hoped wouldn't block your view. It was just you, your friends and the music played live.

This was one of the few times Queen travelled with an opening act so we got to see Thin Lizzy play for about thirty minutes before the real show was due to start. Then it happened: Queen's 'Procession' could be heard and the lighting rigs were being raised so they framed the top of the stage, while the blinding lights of Roger's drum platform were on the bottom. The flash pots went off and sent a flurry of smoke into the air and Brian ripped into 'Tie Your Mother Down'. To this day, any time I hear those opening notes, I still imagine that this is the way to start a Queen concert!

The concert bounced back and forth from the fanciful tales of 'Ogre Battle', 'White Queen' and 'In the Lap of the Gods' to the touching tunes of 'You Take My Breath Away' and 'Doing All Right' into the driving force of 'Keep Yourself Alive' and 'Stone Cold Crazy'; ending nearly two hours later with 'Now I'm Here' just before encore covers of Fifties rock classics 'Big Spender' and 'Jailhouse Rock'. Then of course, like all Queen shows since the *Sheer Heart Attack* tour, the recessional was 'God Save the Queen' and they were gone from the stage and we left the arena with the music still ringing in our ears.

To say that I was blown away by the show would be a severe understatement. Queen did so much more than perform live versions of their songs and have a light show coordinated with the highs and lows and the tempo of the beats. Queen entertained every member of the audience and Freddie's charisma reached the very back of a 22,000 seat arena and made sure that everyone was experiencing the same show energy as the four band members on stage. And this happened long before Queen ever experimented with audience participation through 'We Will Rock You' or Freddie's infamous 'Ay-oh' interaction with the entire crowd.

CIVIC CENTRE
25 JANUARY 1977, OTTAWA, CANADA

I WAS THERE: LLOYD TRUSCOTT

THEY DIDN'T WANT to play the small market but the promoter, Donald K Donald Productions, told them, 'If you don't play Ottawa, you don't play Montréal or Toronto.' I can't remember a whole lot about the concert but I do remember Freddie's incredible voice. Things started at 8pm with Thin Lizzy up first for about 45 minutes and then Queen

Lloyd Truscott saw Queen in Ottawa

played until 11pm. Afterward we went to our favourite hangout, the Blind Pig at Place de Ville, a bar in the complex where we worked. The band came in around midnight and took a table not far from us. Being an ex-musician, I know I didn't like to be bothered after a performance so we ordered a round for them, raised our beer glasses and gave them a toast for their performance. Brian May came by before leaving to say thanks.

CHICAGO STADIUM
28 JANUARY 1977, CHICAGO, ILLINOIS

I WAS THERE: SUSAN P ROGOWSKI

I SAW THEM twice. I went to many concerts and Queen had the most fabulous light show I ever experienced. One memory that stands out for me is that when Freddie Mercury was on stage, he would dance across the entire stage as though he was weightless. I later read somewhere that he took ballet lessons.

I WAS THERE: TERRY KOMPERDA

I GOT MY first taste of Queen as a young teen having heard 'Killer Queen'. I then sampled various selections off *Sheer Heart Attack* and thought they sounded interesting. I then got a copy of *A Night at the Opera* and my interest in the band progressed. Things changed dramatically when my high school friend, Glenn Pradzinski, and I decided that it was time to go to see them live.

It was a brutally cold January in Chicago, and the night of their arrival was no exception. I made arrangements to meet with a ticket scalper earlier in the day, and proceeded to take a Chicago train dressed like a well-wrapped mummy to fight the frigid temperatures and make the exchange. I then headed to Glenn's house, where we listened to a brand new copy of *A Day at the Races*. I heard 'Tie Your Mother Down' and stated that they would start the show with that tune!

We travelled to the Chicago Stadium for the show and became part of the sparsely populated audience thanks to the

Terry Komperda was at a brutally cold Chicago Stadium

arctic weather. Thin Lizzy were the support band and blew the doors off of the place. Some people in attendance claimed that they blew Queen away. In my opinion, they were wrong!

Queen erupted with 'Tie Your Mother Down' and the smoke, lights and flashpots accentuated a rocking song and the start of a concert I would remember for the rest of my life. They also confirmed that they were the best band that I ever saw live, and cemented their place as my favourite band of all time. They had such energy and the ability to put across a true performance that I was hooked from that moment on. The only downside was that some idiots in the third balcony were throwing eggs and/or snowballs down onto the stage, and Brian May slipped and fell onto his guitar. An enraged Freddie threatened to end the show if the assault continued. The band instead decided to forfeit the encore songs for that night's performance.

From then on, I saw Queen every time that they came to Chicago. I also influenced many of my friends to see them live. Most notably, my friend Mike Nelson and I would always attend a Queen show together and it seemed like every time that they came to town, it was in the middle of a tough Chicago winter and we were travelling through a snowstorm to seem. I saw them seven times with Freddie, high-fived him once when I had a second row seat, and met Brian May at a record release party for his first solo album.

For all the years that I've seen the band and enjoyed their music, I regret that I didn't get to see them live the previous two times that they came to Chicago before I saw them for the first time on that brutal Chicago winter night.

SPORTS ARENA
30 JANUARY 1977, TOLEDO, OHIO

I WAS THERE: RUSSELL RAVARY, AGE 17

IT WAS A general admission show and I thought it was fantastic. The light show and such was awesome! I took my brother and a girl I had a crush on from high school. I remember them playing 'Somebody to Love' and 'Bohemian Rhapsody' and the lights and the dry ice. It was a pretty similar set to that on the album *Live Killers*. I was only disappointed that they did not do the song 'White Man' as I was into that song at the time. I recently saw Queen again with Adam Lambert. He was close to capturing Freddie's essence but not his vocal range. I doubt we will ever see someone quite like Freddie Mercury again.

MAPLE LEAF GARDENS
1 FEBRUARY 1977, TORONTO, CANADA

I WAS THERE: ELAINE SULLIVAN

I WAS 13 in 1973 when I first heard 'Liar' and 'Keep Yourself Alive'. I bought their first album as soon as I had enough pocket money. I was in high school when they first came to Toronto. I was desperate to go and a girlfriend of mine, who was rather well off compared to me, suggested we go downtown to Maple Leaf Gardens and get tickets from scalpers. I was such a mess - excited, scared shitless that we'd get arrested and worried we wouldn't get tickets! Well, we did get tickets, waaaay up in the nosebleed section, but I didn't care. I was in the same building as Freddie.

The next time I saw them was with my boyfriend (now husband), at Maple Leaf Gardens again. I was always so mesmerised by Freddie on stage that everything else around me just blurred away. I had such a huge crush on him at the time. I'm sure I wasn't the only one. It wasn't just him, though. The music, the costumes, the way their voices melded together (beautiful Roger and his falsetto!) - it was just such an experience.

I WAS THERE: ERIC BRYANT

WHAT I REMEMBER most is the unbelievable stage presence of Freddie Mercury. He was decked out in white spandex leggings, his open-chest muscle top and his chopped-style microphone pole. He would use this as a device for vocals, as well as a prop throughout the show. The fact that he chose white for his stage outfit caused most concertgoers to remain fixed and focused on him as he moved around. His piano work and vocals on 'We Are the Champions' was a highlight. Brian May is such an under-rated lead guitarist. His guitar is quite an instrument, Brian having done some custom work on the inside electronics in order to give himself that unusual and unique sound. Taylor and Deacon were very accomplished in their own right as drummer and bass player, filling in nicely in

Eric Bryant was at Maple Leaf Gardens

the background. But Freddie was the target of everybody's attention. What a show. I am so happy that I saw Queen live. I get goosebumps thinking about Freddie Mercury on stage. I saw David Bowie four times. But just seeing Queen once? It was amazing.

CIVIC CENTER
3 FEBRUARY 1977, SPRINGFIELD, MASSACHUSETTS

I WAS THERE: JACQUELINE LUX

MY MOTHER PASSED away in 1976 a few days before my 17th birthday and it was decided that I would live with my sister, who was 23, for my last year and a half of high school. We eased our grief by 'self-medicating' with cannabis and listening to some of the best music ever! My first memories of Queen are hearing them on the radio. 'Bohemian Rhapsody' was so different from the Southern rock, punk and disco that was typically being played on our local radio stations. Freddie's spectacular vocal range, the operatic style and the sounds of Brian May's guitar just made me stop whatever I was doing and say, 'Who *is* this?'

The next thing I knew my boyfriend and I were on a hunt for the 8-track tape of *A Night*

Jacqueline Lux wore out the 8-track tapes she had of two Queen albums

at the Opera and, shortly afterwards, *A Day at the Races*. We wore those 8-track tapes out, playing them at home and in my car. My sister and I knew all of the songs from by heart and sang along - as well as we could! She even announced one evening that 'Bohemian Rhapsody' would be her wedding song, someday, when she got married. Blame the cannabis!

In late 1976, I heard that Queen was going to be playing in Springfield, Massachusetts. Our local Ticketron was located at a service counter in the nearby G Fox & Co department store so off we went to get our tickets, which were about seven dollars each. My memory gets a little bit fuzzy, here, some 40 years later. Blame it on age - or perhaps that cannabis. While I am sure that we saw Queen twice in Springfield in 1977 (on February 2nd and on November 13th) the details of the two shows meld into one in my memory. I am reasonably certain, however, that it is the February Queen show that I am recalling here.

My boyfriend, my cousin, two friends from school and myself piled into my car and drove to Springfield, a 40 minute drive from our hometown of New Britain, Connecticut. It was a general admission show, so we went early and waited in line, out in the cold, for the venue's doors to open. When that moment finally arrived, there was a mad rush of boys and girls tearing through the arena for the best seats or, in our case, for the floor right in front of the stage!

Our little group was shoulder to shoulder and about eight feet from the stage. Once the show started and the crowd surged in like a wave behind us, we were even closer, but separated from each another. We were packed in so tightly I could have lifted my feet from the floor and still remained upright. One of my friends decided to leave midway through the show because she couldn't stand the squeeze or the heat any longer. Despite the discomfort, the show was nothing less than amazing. Freddie was so energetic and never stopped dancing and posing, except for his time at the piano. His voice was perfect. Brian was equally amazing and, watching him play, I marveled at how humble he seemed and how he made it all look so easy.

A highlight was Freddie appearing on stage with an armful of carnations. As he sang he seemed to take great pleasure throwing them out to his fans. I was able to catch one but, unfortunately, I got the stem end and, in a flash, it was ripped violently from my grasp. After the show, my cousin took pity on me and gave me a bud and stem from the carnation she'd caught. I won't pretend that I remember each song they played, but the hits were certainly performed as were all our favourites. Being so near to the stage, the music was thunderously loud and our ears were numb and ringing as we drove home.

We were to see Queen four more times between 1977 and 1980, three times in New Haven, Connecticut and once at the Hartford Civic Center. In November 1977 we got wedged in the spiral exit of the parking garage. The drivers behind us were not happy and were beeping and yelling. My sister finally unstuck us but was left with a large scrape on her car as a souvenir!

In December 1980, my boyfriend became my husband and in 1981 we welcomed the first of our four children. Concerts had to move to the back of the bus in our new 'adulting' life. The old 8-track tapes were replaced by cassettes and in the 1980s we bought our first CD player. Two of the first three CDs I bought were, of course, *A Night at the Opera* and *A Day at the Races*. My children, now adults themselves, all very much enjoy the music of Queen.

COLE FIELD HOUSE
UNIVERSITY OF MARYLAND
4 FEBRUARY 1977, COLLEGE PARK, MARYLAND

I WAS THERE: SHERRY CARROLL BELL

MY BEST FRIEND Nina and I started trying to get backstage at every single gig that came to the Capitol Centre to be ready for Queen to get there. We saw them for the first time at Cole Field House at George Washington University in 1977. It was just a college gig, with Thin Lizzy opening. It was our very first rock concert and just before they become wildly popular in the States. We knew all about them already, having discovered rock and roll and loved the English bands. But nothing had prepared us for the real thing - Freddie, Roger, Brian, and John in their full glory at the height of their creativity, scratching and clawing their way to be nothing less than biggest band in the world. And even though I spent quite a bit of it making out with Scott during the concert, I kept my eyes open throughout every minute of the show and the make out session (you never heard of multitasking?). It was incredible.

Nothing had prepared us for the real thing

MADISON SQUARE GARDEN
5 FEBRUARY 1977, NEW YORK, NEW YORK

I WAS THERE: JANE GARDNER

I WAS BLESSED to have been to several Queen MSG concerts. I was Freddie's waitress as well in 1981 in New York City. He lived locally part of the time. It was a lovely hour with Freddie, totally unexpected and private, and he happily signed the flip side of the table placemat for me. I also left the MSG concert in '77 with Roger's well used drumsticks from their epic set.

Jane Gardner got Freddie's autograph

At MSG, you could just linger after the concert ended and head to the stage area. We had access to everything on that stage. I was contemplating getting their set list from atop Freddie's piano, all his cups, etc... but then just asked Crystal, Roger's roadie, for the sticks. I had them for decades, but I think they were likely stolen, along with several other precious memories, by my movers during my recent move.

I WAS THERE: JUDI SPIRO WEISLO

ALL OF THEM were perfect, and Freddie Mercury's voice was so unique and powerful, with emotion. I was good friends back in the day with the bass player of Twisted Sister and he brought me to this press party where they were interviewed before a dinner at Tavern on the Green. I was standing right next to Brian May. I felt awkward, because it was more a business meeting kind of thing than social. He kept looking at me and I finally said, 'I love the way you play.' So original... He just smiled shyly. Freddie was holding court and most eyes were on him. I found him a bit pretentious. I never was quite that impressed with rock stars in a personal way, just the music. The dinner was great though!

I WAS THERE:
DEE FERRARO-BONGIORNO, AGE 17

I WAS DATING a guy aged 22. He bought the tickets. I remember enjoying the concert until the end. It was quiet and I was disappointed that they didn't perform my favourite song. Then we all heard the notes and a spotlight went on and they performed 'Bohemian Rhapsody'. It was over 40 years ago but sometimes that performance feels like yesterday.

Dee Ferraro-Bongiorno remembers the MSG show like it was yesterday

I WAS THERE: RICKY WEST

MY STORY STARTS in 1974 or '75. I'm 15 and visiting my mom in the hospital. In the next bed is another lady about her age. Her son Les, who's a lot older than me, is visiting. He and I both have long hair. I'm all glammed out because I'm influenced by bands like T.Rex, David Bowie and the New York Dolls. I looked androgynous, like I might be in a band myself. After visiting hours Les asks me if I get high. I'm a little worried about this guy - why is he talking to me? I take a chance. I want to try weed for the first time so I say, 'Sure, why not?' We're in his car, a little MGB, and he says, 'You have to hear this band.' It's a foreign bootleg of a band I have never heard of - Queen - and from the moment I hear them I am in total love.

Back then there was no Internet, no Spotify. If you needed to find the music of a band quick the only way was at your local record shop, and if they didn't have it, you were taking a trip into Manhattan where you could find anything. I lucked out. I went to a store called Looney Tunes and purchased my first, and to this day my favourite, album, *Sheer Heart Attack*. I played the fuck out of that album until my mom couldn't take it anymore!

Fast forward to me being 17 or 18. I was dating my first true love, Barbara. Many more came after her but you always remember your first. I took her to our first of many Queen

Ricky West saw Queen at MSG

concerts, at both the Nassau Coliseum and Madison Square Garden. Every time I saw Freddie Mercury sing, it was like he was singing to my very soul. I never missed a New York concert. They were the only band at the time with that special something. After I broke up with Barbara, I started dating Pam and introduced her to Queen concerts. We got to see Freddie come on stage on the shoulders of Darth Vader wearing a Superman t-shirt and short shorts. I didn't care how silly Freddie looked. He could do no wrong in my eyes. That's what I love about music - it unites us all. It doesn't matter your race, your sexual orientation or the issues you're facing in life. At that one moment, when Freddie would sing 'we are the champions', he was telling you, me and everyone there that we really are champions. We are all somebody who matters.

NASSAU COLISEUM
6 FEBRUARY 1977, UNIONDALE
LONG ISLAND, NEW YORK

I WAS THERE: ROBERT G-PA CRASTO

I WAS IN a pizza parlour when my friend played 'Killer Queen' on the jukebox. I've been a fan since then. My first concert was in February 1977. They put on a great show, and even did some of Elvis Presley's 'Jailhouse Rock' during a medley. Thin Lizzy opened and were fantastic. The second Queen show I saw was in November 1978, when *Jazz* had just come out. It was another great show. Some topless women on bicycles came out on the stage during 'Bicycle Race'.

I didn't see them live again until 2005 and 2006, when Paul Rodgers fronted them. I enjoyed the shows immensely, but it wasn't the same without Freddie. The last Queen show I was at was with Adam Lambert. They put on a very good show too.

Robert G-Pa Crasto first heard Queen in a pizza parlour

I WAS THERE: ANTHONY PALUMBO

THE SECOND TIME I saw Queen I went with my girlfriend (our first date had been the *Night at the Opera* tour) and a friend who bought his ticket late so his seat wasn't with us. We tried to find three empty seats together. Finally, we did. Although excellent, this concert was not as memorable as the first time. Queen's look had changed - haircuts, no more angel wings - but the music was still awesome. The Coliseum being a lot bigger

Anthony Palumbo saw Queen twice

than the Beacon Theatre, it had a different atmosphere but the sound was still awesome. I had always wondered what song Queen was playing when I first opened the *Day at the Races* album and saw the picture of all four members on stage with Brian May on acoustic guitar and Roger Taylor with just a bass drum and tambourine. My wonder was settled that night when they played one of my favourites, ''39', which I have sung to all my children and grandchildren as a lullaby when rocking them to sleep.

BOSTON GARDEN
9 FEBRUARY 1977, BOSTON, MASSACHUSETTS

I WAS THERE: JILL SCHALLER PAIT

I SAW THEM live more than once. The first time was with Thin Lizzy at the old Boston Garden. I was way back in the 48th row. I had a camera with me but my photos double exposed. The next time I was front and centre at the Providence Civic Center in Rhode Island. My friends convinced me to toss my white satin scarf

Jill Schaller Pait was way back in the 48th row the first time she saw Queen

onstage and Freddie picked it up and wore it for a while. The last I saw of it, he tossed it on his piano. I saw them one more time, at Hartford Civic Center in Connecticut. I have such incredible memories of Freddie and I love being able to still see Brian May. I was such a fan of his back then that I permed my hair like his! My classmates thought I was nuts! And now, after all these years, I have a tattoo of him on my left shoulder. I'm a Queen fan 'til the end!

CIVIC CENTRE
10 FEBRUARY 1977, PROVIDENCE, RHODE ISLAND

I WAS THERE: CRAIG BENNETCH

WE HEARD 'LIAR' on a progressive AM rock radio station when it was first released around '72 in the Philadelphia area and I totally got into their music from there. My favourite album is still *Queen II*. I went to school in Boston and we stayed there for 20 years so my wife and I got to see them at the Orpheum Theatre, and then when they moved into the arenas. My biggest regret is when I had tickets to see them open for Mott the Hoople and Brian May came down with hepatitis. That show never happened. I met them twice when they were still doing in store appearances in record shops. I have an autographed

Craig Bennetch was backstage and on stage for Queen in Providence

copy of *A Night at the Opera*. There were no Sharpies back then. You can still see Freddie's autograph, but only just.

The best night of my life was when we had backstage passes for Providence, Rhode Island. Thin Lizzy opened for them. I ended up on the stage, behind Brian. It was great to get the perspective of what they saw from the stage, looking out into the audience. The band were quite elusive back stage. They said their 'hellos' and that was it. But the show was tremendous.

CIVIC CENTER
11 FEBRUARY 1977, PHILADELPHIA, PENNSYLVANIA

I WAS THERE: JOE CAPRIOTTI

THE PHILLY SHOW in '77 was the best concert I ever saw. After the concert we went to a bar. It was a cold night and I stood in a car's exhaust smoke that was billowing high in the air, pretending I was a member of Queen amidst the dry ice!

I WAS THERE: HAROLD GLENN COLEMAN

IT WAS THE only time they played at that venue. I remember Thin Lizzy was the opening act. Then Queen hit the stage with a thunderous gong and 'Tie Your Mother Down'. Beyond that, all I remember is how great they were in person.

I WAS THERE: TEODORO LOPES

IT WAS GENERAL admission and tickets were $7.50. As the arena doors opened, Grant and I ran to the exact spot we wanted to be, directly in front of the sound mixing board. We almost got trampled to death taking our first 10 steps entering the place. When Grant bought these tickets, we were saying, 'Why not play at the Tower Theater or the Spectrum or even Robin Hood Dell East? Why the dreary, cold and acoustically dead Civic Center?' 'Ah man, this isn't going to be very good. Surely, this place is not any band's best friend while playing there live?' This was a 'glass half empty' scenario. Not once did we think that maybe the sheer talents of Thin Lizzy and Queen would see us all through.

But all bands are not created the same and, simply put, this was the best show I have ever attended at the Civic Center. Thin Lizzy came out and just tore the roof off the place. And I could feel a vibe that this was going to be a special show as soon as the lights dimmed and the 'Overture' kicked in. It was a cool, stylish and effective way to announce Queen's presence. From the opening tune, 'Tie Your Mother Down', to the three song encore, this was simply pure greatness in entertainment from a band in a live setting. Right off the bat these four guys looked and acted like they were all born on a stage.

Freddie and Brian both wore white satin attire, Brian some sort of folded, accordion-winged outfit. They looked like they fronted a spacey prog rock band. I thought they looked the way rock stars should. Freddie was a very impressive front man, one of the best cheerleaders, ringmasters and audience stokers I have had the pleasure of seeing and hearing, and one of the most powerful voices I have ever heard in rock.

I WAS THERE: BERNARD RIZZO

I FIRST HEARD 'Killer Queen' as a 15-year-old in 1974. I was instantly fascinated with the sound and went out and bought the *Sheer Heart Attack* record and I wore that thing out! Soon after, I bought their first two records. I became a big fan, and went to my first concert at the old Convention Hall in Philadelphia with my buddy from high school. It was magic from the first chords of 'Tie Your Mother Down'. They played most of their early hits. 'Somebody to Love' was a highlight but also 'Killer Queen', 'Love of my Life', 'The Prophet's Song', 'Spread Your Wings' and of course 'Bohemian Rhapsody'. I made sure to catch them on every subsequent tour in town - *News of the World*, *The Game* and *Hot Space*. They were always fantastic and never disappointing.

I was elated at the chance to see Queen twice with Paul Rodgers, and three times with Adam Lambert. It's still a fantastic show. Back in the Seventies and Eighties, I didn't have the means to get good seats. In 2019, as a treat to myself for my 60th birthday, I bought seventh row centre seats in Philadelphia. What a thrill - I was like a kid at Christmas! Freddie, Brian, Roger and John have been a big part of my life and helped get me through those adolescent years. I know Freddie is gone, but the best part of Brian and Roger carrying on is that my two

Photos: Bernard Rizzo

Bernard Rizzo saw Queen in
Philly in 1977 and again in 2019

sons got to hear these legends bring their wonderful music to a whole
new generation. And for that I'll always be thankful. Long live Queen!

I WAS THERE: YASHA GOLDENTYER

MY STRONGEST MEMORY is of the extremely dangerous crowding
situation outside the doors. The crowd surged forward and I had to push
against it with all my strength to protect a petite young woman from being
crushed against the wall! It was truly scary and I was always grateful that
I was able to help her survive the crush. The concert was great, but the
crush beforehand has always been my most vivid experience.

KIEL AUDITORIUM
23 FEBRUARY 1977, ST LOUIS, MISSOURI

I WAS THERE: MIKE TULLY, AGE 13

IT WAS MY very first concert. My
parents wouldn't let me go by myself
so I went with my mother and my
dad's secretary! We were in about the
thirteenth row. Thin Lizzy were the
opening act and were great. Queen
opened with the intro from *Day at the
Races* and blasted into 'Tie Your Mother
Down'. Freddie wore a karate warm up
suit for the first song but then stripped
down to tights. I still love the heavy side

Mike Tully (right, with Spike Edney)
saw Queen at the tender age of 13

of early Queen so hearing 'Ogre Battle' live was awesome! A few songs later, 'Brighton Rock' was amazing and then they slowed down and played ''39'. 'White Man' went straight into 'The Prophet's Song' which is one of their heaviest songs ever, and Freddie did his echo voice solo, harmonising with himself. 'Bohemian Rhapsody' was still in the middle of their set, and they rocked hard through 'Stone Cold Crazy', 'Keep Yourself Alive' (including the drum solo with beer - or something! - on the tom toms and flying into the air) and 'Liar'. They closed the set with 'Lap of the Gods'. For the encore they did 'Now I'm Here', starting with the call back and forth from either side of the stage, and then played a couple of covers and finished with the recording of 'God Save the Queen'. It was an amazing show by a hard rock band at the top of their game!

SAM HOUSTON COLISEUM
26 FEBRUARY 1977, HOUSTON, TEXAS

I WAS THERE: STERLING HAMILTON

THE SAM HOUSTON Coliseum was where they held shows before they built the Summit, and when I saw them on the *News of the World* tour, that was at the Summit. I went to this show with my brother, who was driving. It was amazing. They only had a few albums out then, so they didn't have a big repertoire, but they did every song that they had. They came out in the kimonos first and then Freddie changed and finished out the show in a black and white chequered leotard. I took a girl I'm still friends with, named Karen Bell, to the *News of the World* show. I saw them

Photos: Sterling Hamilton

John Deacon at the Sam Houston Coliseum

Brian May at the Sam Houston Coliseum

Freddie Mercury at the Sam Houston Coliseum

three times in total, and every time I saw Queen they never put on a bad show. They gave the audience everything and Freddie was never disappointing. These days shows are all about the light shows and the big video screens. Queen was just a performance of them themselves, achieving perfection live. They didn't have to use overdubs or tapes. If there was anything missing you didn't notice it, because everything else was that good.

Roger, John and Freddie at the Sam Houston Coliseum

FORUM
2 & 3 MARCH 1977, LOS ANGELES, CALIFORNIA

I WAS THERE: LYDIA ZAFFINI

I WAS A junior in high school in the fall of '73 when a rock song came on the radio and made an impact on me like few others. The song was 'Keep Yourself Alive' and there was something about it that made me want to learn more. No wonder that in 2008 *Rolling Stone* magazine rated that song 31st on its list of 'The 100 Greatest Guitar Songs of All Time'. I had not heard of Queen before but now rank them second only to Led Zeppelin. Thank goodness for Los Angeles radio stations like KROC, KMET and others who did not subscribe to 'formula' programming and also tutored me in Blue Oyster Cult, AC/DC, Cheap Trick, Alice Cooper and other now 'classic' rock bands.

Queen II immediately became a favourite and further cemented my love of Queen. By 1977 I was thrilled to have bought tickets to the 'Queen Lizzy' tour. As a 20-year-old attending college full time and working part time, I could only

Lydia Zaffini (left) was at the Forum in '77

afford what we fondly referred to as the 'bird' seats at the Forum. But I didn't care - it was Queen! That concert is one of the best of the hundreds I've been to over the years. Unfortunately, it was my only time to see that line up of Queen.

That concert is one of the best I've been to

Fast forward to 1985 and their incredible *Live Aid* performance, which I watched glued to my television. And fast forward again to 2018 to the award-winning film *Bohemian Rhapsody*, and what I refer to as a love letter to Freddie from Roger and Brian. I cried so many times watching that movie and, of course, sang along with all the song performances.

When I found out the *20th Century Fox Bohemian Rhapsody Road Tour* was coming to Las Vegas prior to the movie's release, I signed my friend and I up. We had a blast riding around in the specially fitted double decker bus, singing along to Queen songs with other super fans. We each received a swag bag that included a Queen stadium blanket and ear buds. What an unforgettable experience!

I WAS THERE: DARIA BROOKS

I SAW THEM IN America from 1975, on the *Sheer Heart Attack* tour, through to *The Works* tour in 1980. In March of 1977, Queen held court in the Los Angeles area during their *A Day at the Races* tour and returned in December for multiple nights on the *News of the World* tour. A consummate Queen maniac, I attended three of those concerts - one in March and two in December. I became a Queen fan in 1974, proudly numbered amongst their cult following in the US. My kid sister, Clare, and I attended their local shows on each tour beginning in 1975, screaming until we were hoarse... for days. We attended Queen concerts in a fashion comparable to going to worship, and nabbing a pass for their concerts was akin to holding Willy Wonka's Golden Ticket. We adored them: the spectacularly witty and sartorially outrageous Freddie, the mystically ethereal Brian, quiet little John and Roger, that steady heartbeat and heartthrob at the back. They were 'amazing' personified and we were completely enthralled.

I have special memories of all four of them. For John, it would be the 1977 tour, when Freddie introduced him to the audience; he was so shy and skinny he nearly fell over when the girls screamed for him. My favourite memory of Brian is from 1975 at the Santa Monica Civic. Solo on the stage, this angel with wings was standing under a single key light and spinning a web of magic from those guitar strings. For Roger, I have twin favourite memories. During the *Night/Day* tour of 1977, Freddie announced that Roger was coming to the front of the stage to sing on ''39' and we cheered so loud that he blushed beet red! He later delivered a drum solo that had all of us on our feet stomping along, to the point that I wondered if the colonnade could stand the pressure. It was like an earthquake!

For Freddie, nothing can top when, for the encore, he came to the stage barefoot in a lovely kimono and then stripped down to those crazy red and white striped shorts and the next sound was the gasp heard around the room! I have never heard another collective gasp like that in my life. It was particularly interesting to see the reaction of the many young men in the audience—and this was in Los Angeles, where we think we've seen everything! After rocking the audience to a furore, Freddie swilled champagne from a glass, looked over his shoulder at us as he prepared to leave the stage and said, 'A pleasure doing business with you.' A total 'drop the mic' moment for the ages.

I WAS THERE: JAN MARCHAND

THIS WAS THE first concert my boyfriend (now my husband of 41 years) took me to. He remembers their uniqueness and the way they managed to replicate on stage exactly what you heard on the radio.

WINTERLAND
6 MARCH 1977, SAN FRANCISCO, CALIFORNIA

I WAS THERE: JON OSTLUND

ONE OF THE first authentic live rock concerts I ever attended was
Queen at the Winterland Ballroom. The tour was supporting the album
A Day at the Races. It was the best time to be a music fan, and I got to see
all the cool bands before rock was called 'classic rock'. It was new and
fresh and we loved it. Today, much of it is even more popular than when
it first came out. You hear it everywhere, and it still sells out the arenas
and stadiums. I had become a fan of Queen a couple of years before
seeing them. My brother and I played the *Sheer Heart Attack* and *Night at
the Opera* albums all the time. When *A Day at the Races* came out, I had it
the first week. When tickets were announced in the Pink Section of the
San Francisco newspaper, we went down and got our tickets at the local
BASS tickets outlet.

The night of the show, we took our seats on the balcony and settled
in. When the house lights went down, sirens and searchlights filled the
auditorium just before the massive guitar strum of the song 'Jailbreak'.
Lizzy rocked the crowd for about 45 minutes. They were the perfect
setup for Queen.

When the lights went down the second time for Queen, the roar inside
Winterland was deafening. So was the sound system. Queen shows were
always loud, louder than anyone else. The opening bars to 'Tie Your
Mother Down' sent chills through the crowd, right back to our balcony
seats. When the spotlights hit the band, the spectacle of Queen was every
bit as thrilling as the music. Freddie Mercury (dressed in white coveralls)
owned the stage, while Brian, Roger and John made it clear that Queen
was a complete and solid band. The thrill of that moment set memories
that carried on 40 years beyond. I became a solid Queen fan that night.

The setlist included gems from all their albums. Early favourites such
as 'White Queen', 'Ogre Battle', 'Brighton Rock' and 'Now I'm Here'
were intermixed with the hits 'Killer Queen', 'You're My Best Friend'
and 'Stone Cold Crazy'. Of course, since the tour was supporting *A Day
at the Races*, a solid sampling from that album was a must and included
the current hit, 'Somebody to Love', plus 'Millionaire Waltz', 'White
Man' and 'You Take My Breath Away'. Mid show, the band moved to
the front of the stage to perform an acoustic song or two. For this night,

it was "39'. I want to believe 'Love of my Life' was also performed, but the setlist doesn't show that. It was the centrepiece for all future tours.

As the show approached the final few songs of the main set, Freddie told the crowd the band's appreciation for fans who loved 'sophisticated rock' and stated 'this one we call 'Bo Rhap'.' The piano lead to 'Bohemian Rhapsody' took the auditorium to a whole other level. The set ended with 'Keep Yourself Alive', 'Liar' and 'In the Lap of the Gods'. Of course, that was not the end. The encore stole the show - and so did Freddie when he came out in red and white striped shorts. They started with the blistering 'Now I'm Here' and just had fun with 'Big Spender' and 'Jailhouse Rock'. As always, the show ended with a recording of Brian and the band's version of 'God Save the Queen'. As with anyone who made it through a Queen show in the Seventies, we walked out with ears ringing. We thought it was a badge of honour.

After that night, every time a Queen show was announced, I was in line early Sunday morning to get the best tickets I could. I saw Queen with Freddie five times, and each time was better than the last. When they hit the road again with Adam Lambert, I was still there (four times). Make no mistake, Freddie Mercury will always be the greatest frontman there was - a mesmerising showman, a singing virtuoso, and a gifted musician and songwriter who can't be replaced. Still, we went decades without the live energy of Queen's music. Brian and Roger belong on the stage, and the music belongs in arenas. Adam Lambert is a great performer and knows his role is to give it his best and let the fans just enjoy the ride. I can't talk about Queen without at least a nod to John Deacon. His bass playing and songwriting were as essential to the music and shows and anyone else. They were a great band of four.

I WAS THERE: RON BENDORFF, AGE 17

I REMEMBER FIRST hearing 'Killer Queen' and thinking it a nice enough song, but when I heard 'Bohemian Rhapsody' for the first time in a record store I bought it immediately. It was like nothing I'd heard before. Searching out their earlier albums I discovered other gems like 'Brighton Rock', 'Keep Yourself Alive' and 'Now I'm Here'. I grew up in

Ron Bendorff had to go see Queen
when he heard they were coming

San Francisco in the 1960s and was a teen in the Seventies, so Winterland became a continual source of musical entertainment. When Queen came to town in 1977 on the heels of *A Day at the Races* we had to go. I was there with three or four of my high school friends - we had graduated in 1976 - and I was attending the University of San Francisco. It was a great night and Freddie was on top form. Brian May was also on fire. I still get goose bumps when I think of the opening to 'Tie Your Mother Down'.

PNE COLISEUM
11 MARCH 1977, VANCOUVER, CANADA

I WAS THERE: ANGIE HILLMER

MY OLDER BROTHER saw them when they backed Mott the Hoople and told me to check out this very expensive-sounding band whose sound he thought I'd love. I am forever in his debt for turning me into a Queen and especially a Freddie fan. I saw them three times with Freddie and once with Paul Rodgers. I was stunned to hear how much they all sounded like their records. I was absolutely over the moon to see Freddie sing a few feet from me. He actually sweated on me! When Brian did his guitar solo, he was standing right in front of me and I was holding onto his (very clean) shoes. It was nice to see that he didn't move but seemed to concentrate on his guitar sound. Unlike other fans at this show, I just stood there taking in a most incredible show. I knew this was something I would forever remember.

Angie Hillmer's beloved pup Mercury was named after Queen's lead singer

I got to meet John Deacon at the hotel after the second concert I attended. He was shy but very respectful and cool, a true gentleman. I was a bit surprised to see how slight he was. It was a bit daunting to talk to him. I asked him where Freddie was and he answered 'he is around here somewhere'. Alas, I never did get to meet Freddie. My girlfriend was a big fan of Brian and hung out at the hotel for the three days there were there. Brian got to know her and would say 'hello Susan' whenever he passed by. She got tons of autographs and pictures. On their last day as they were leaving, Brian went into the gift shop and bought her a rose, thanking her for being such an amazing fan. She still has it!

Years later, I got to meet Paul Rodgers and spent quite a bit of time with him and his lovely wife, Cynthia, and got a lot of inside scoop on Queen. I asked him why he ever considered taking over for - of all people - the great Freddie Mercury. He said he didn't and that he sang Queen songs as himself. I have such lovely memories of Queen. They are not only talented but so kind and decent to their fans.

I got a rescue pup a few years ago and named him Mercury. Sadly, he passed away in March.

PARAMOUNT THEATRE
12 MARCH 1977, PORTLAND, OREGON

I WAS THERE: RANDEE FIELDS

I WAS WITH a buddy and saw a bunch of our other high school friends there. We got stoned on weed and drank some beer. Thin Lizzy opened so Queen had to put on the business to top those boys - I was more interested in Lizzy at the time. Freddie had his white jump suit on. After seeing 'Bohemian Rhapsody' pulled off live I was amazed, and was thinking 'this is a toss up whether Philip or Freddie is better.' They were both at the top of their game that night.

SOUTHERN ALBERTA JUBILEE AUDITORIUM
16 & 17 MARCH 1977, CALGARY, CANADA

I WAS THERE: MARY ANNE SUZY READWIN

CALGARY IN CANADA got very little in the way of rock and roll news, but I remember hearing 'Killer Queen' as a young teen and 'Bohemian Rhapsody' totally blew my mind, so I saved enough money to buy *A Night at the Opera* and loved it so much I saved up to buy the rest. When *A Day at the Races* came out, we didn't have any big arenas so they played a 5,000 capacity auditorium. It was a huge deal.

The opening song was 'Tie Your Mother Down'. The first guitar licks in the dark, then the spotlights came up and there was Freddie in a white baggy

Mary Anne Suzy Readwin saw
Queen from the third row

jumpsuit singing and bouncing around,
just being Freddie. Brian was fascinating
to watch with his serious persona yet
amazing outfit, a white accordion
batwing type top. The other highlights
were 'You Take My Breath Away' and
an acoustic version of "39' where all the
band stood at the front of the stage and
played. The icing on the cake was 'Bohemian Rhapsody'.

The next time I saw Queen was in 2014, with Adam Lambert. They
played our now 20,000 seat arena and Brian referenced their previous
visit to Calgary some 37 years before. There weren't too many people
who'd been at that previous concert. But I was.

*After the North American tour, Queen embarked on a European jaunt in May 1977 to
promote* A Day at the Races.

PHILLIPSHALLE
16 MAY 1977, DÜSSELDORF, WEST GERMANY

I WAS THERE: DAVE COX, AGE 23

I WAS IN the RAF in Germany and not really a Queen. One day my
neighbour said he was going to see them in Dusseldorf and had a spare
ticket, so I went. I remember the crown on the stage and the terrific show.
We were at the side in the stalls and looking down I saw a guy on crutches
pick up a chair and throw it at people who were standing in front of him.
He wanted to sit down and so wanted them to do the same! The next day
I went to the NAAFI shop and bought every Queen LP they had.

AHOY SPORTSPALEIS
17 MAY 1977, ROTTERDAM, THE NETHERLANDS

I WAS THERE: FRANK PALSTRA

I SAW QUEEN live with Freddie 18 times, from 1977 through to 1986 in in The Netherlands, Belgium and Germany. I was infected with the Queen and Freddie Mercury virus in 1974 after watching 'Killer Queen' on *Top Pop* on Dutch television. My room became a Queen room filled with lots of posters. I still have them, either folded away or in scrapbooks. I got in touch with Dutch fans and also fans from abroad, first just writing, and then later swapping or buying and selling stuff with people as far afield as the USA and Australia. I built up a huge collection of videos.

The first show I went to was in Rotterdam. It got bad reviews

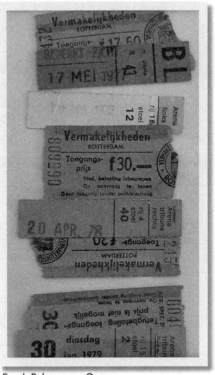

Frank Palstra saw Queen with Freddie 18 times

from the critics but the whole audience including myself loved every minute of it. It was great to see the stage, the setlist, the lighting and my heroes live for the first time! I have a towel Freddie threw into the audience in Leiden in 1986 and also a drumstick of Roger's from Forest National in 1986.

The European leg of the
A Day at the Races tour took in 19 shows

I WAS THERE: GERKO DE BLANKEN

I WENT WITH five friends. The show finished around 11pm and while we were waiting for our taxi, the members of Queen came past us in a big black limousine and waved to us! I also saw them in Leiden. The

crowd threw cans of beer at Bow Wow
Wow. That was the last day they sold
cans. I have a lot of Queen stuff like
bootlegs and picture discs as well as
the Queen box set with all the CDs.
Oh, and I have the Queen logo
tattooed on my leg.

Gerko de Blanken has Queen
tattooed on his leg

I WAS THERE: HANS SCHIPPERS, AGE 17

THEIR MUSIC CAUGHT me with 'Killer Queen'. Their first two
albums were amazing. That was music you never heard before. After my
first concert in 1977 came two in 1979, also at the Ahoy in Rotterdam.
I saw them every time they came to Holland. I'm so glad and proud I
saw Freddie performing live. I also went to the Freddie Mercury Tribute
Concert at Wembley in April 1992. What a gig that was. I'll never forget it.

HIPPODROME
23 MAY 1977, BRISTOL, UK

I WAS THERE: JEFF PERRY

IT WAS BACK to Bristol Hippodrome for
my final and most enjoyable Queen concert,
on the *Day at the Races* tour. I could now
appreciate what had come before. The first
time I'd been wound up with expectations
and excitement. The second time had been
the wash out at Cardiff Castle. This time I
could soak up and digest what was a truly
awesome experience, them playing old
favourites and, of course, the new music to
promote the album. Probably the pleasure I
got from this experience was heightened by
an addition to my little entourage, a young
lady who eventually became my wife - and
another Queen fan.

Jeff Perry's last Queen encounter
was at the Hippodrome in Bristol

GAUMONT THEATRE
26 & 27 MAY 1977, SOUTHAMPTON, UK

I WAS THERE: MATTHEW JESSUP

I PLAYED PIANO from when I could walk. My parents bought the sheet music to *Goodbye Yellow Brick Road* after I'd gone with my mum and sister to see Elton John at Southampton Gaumont in 1972, following which I started to play the songs on the piano. After a short time, I gave the book back to Mum and said, 'This is all wrong, this isn't what he's playing on the record.' I was promptly dragged, kicking and screaming, to classical piano lessons. My parents could see there was something there. But I persisted in learning by ear, which is where I discovered Queen.

I recall hearing an outlandish track that featured a very long guitar solo and both a male and female vocalist. I'd play along on my brother's drum kit. I didn't do too well, but grew fascinated with this album my brother had brought home. The track turned out to be 'Brighton Rock', the album was *Sheer Heart Attack* and the vocals, of course, turned out to be all Freddie Mercury.

There was no going back. Mum and Dad bought me my own copy of *Sheer Heart Attack* and I sat, learning all the piano parts bit by bit by ear. That album was a changing point in my musical inspiration and development. Future birthdays and Christmases brought more Queen albums. *Queen II* is one of the most genius, beautiful albums ever made, and I was just lost in Mercury's incredible and quite unique piano playing, which I had hours of fun and discovery learning to mimic. But then my brother's friend bought me *A Night at the Opera* as a birthday present. This was piano playing like I'd never heard before, and a week later I showed him how I'd learned 'Death on Two Legs', complete with that incredible piano intro.

From there I learned 'Bohemian Rhapsody', catching clips and tips from watching Freddie play it on *Top of the Pops*. My mum took me to see Queen at Southampton Gaumont in 1977. Freddie emerged in his black and white diamond leotard and, after opening with 'Tie Your Mother Down', Freddie came to the front of the stage and took a bow. He said, 'Did you like my bow, darlings? I love taking bows, Rudolph's been teaching me,' and then (and I've never forgotten it) he strutted from one side of the stage to the other like a peacock, holding his arm out and wiggling his fingers saying, 'Look everybody. How do you like my wonderful black nail varnish dears?' He was dead chuffed with his nails and wanted to show everyone. Later, I played 'Bohemian Rhapsody' at the school music festival. I won, and held the trophy for two years.

Today, 'The Prophet's Song' remains my favourite Queen work. It blows 'Bohemian Rhapsody' away and is truly brilliant songwriting, production and technique. Pure genius. Queen's first four albums are, for me, four of the greatest albums ever made and are Queen at their very best. Queen were part of my youth, and when Freddie died, part of my youth went with him. I was, and still am, gutted and I find it very hard to listen to those old albums now. 'The Show Must Go On.' Sadness surpassed by the resilience of a dying man giving the vocal take of his life. Part of my life. I was there at the beginning, and my memories of Queen will stay with me always.

I managed to get hold of the master files for 'Bohemian Rhapsody' and played along with Freddie's piano, then removed it leaving just Freddie and me, the only way I will ever get to duet with the legend himself.

NEW BINGLEY HALL
29 MAY 1977, STAFFORD, UK

I WAS THERE: NICK PARRY

I WAS 18 in 1973 and began taking an interest in music, mainly progressive rock. But I was open to any kind of rock music, which is when I began to hear songs by a group called Queen. I really enjoyed 'Keep Yourself Alive', 'Liar', 'Seven Seas of Rhye', etc. so when I started work I got *Queen I & II* and then *Sheer Heart Attack* and *A Night at the Opera* came out, which really made Queen my favourite band. I was getting into live concerts with mates, and sometimes my sister Julie would come with me. Living in the Midlands, there were a lot of venues but after the sucess of 'Bohemian Rhapsody' Queen had outgrown the medium size places. When the 1977 tour was announced, Julie, who was also now into Queen as I was always playing the albums at home, decided to go with me. We got the tickets by going to a record shop in Wolverhampton which was an agent for the promoters.

The venue, an agricultural showground used for cattle shows and exhibitions, was bigger than most other places in the Midlands and could make more money for promoters and the band. But it was located outside the town of Stafford so public transport wasn't much help. However, the show was three weeks after I passed my driving test so I could drive us there. The venue was also not much suited to rock concerts as it was a level floor. Anybody a bit on the short side wouldn't see very well, but both my sister and I are tall so we were okay.

I booked the day off work as I didn't want to arrive late and struggle to park. We arrived at the venue around 2.30pm, as did many others. We parked up in the huge car park and got ready for the show. We went to the merchandise truck and purchased a tour t-shirt, programme and tour badge. The queue was getting longer so we joined the end of it and had a great time with the fellow Queenies.

Time went quickly as we waited and we were soon heading for the gates. The excitement was building! On getting inside, our usual tactic was to go to the toilet before getting our place as we didn't want to have to try and get out and then back to our spot. We chose to stand in the middle, 10 to 12 yards from the front line, so we wouldn't be squashed in the crush at the front. With an hour to go, the atmosphere was cranking up with the crowd just looking at the stage and the roadies going about their business. Then it was show time....

When the house lights went off the noise was fantastic. The *Day at the Races* intro played and then Brian played the opening guitar break to 'Tie Your Mother Down'. It was utterly amazing to be there to see the boys in front of me playing one of my favourite songs. I was completely blown away with the sheer power and visual show that was in front of me. 'Ogre Battle' and 'White Queen' followed, with us just loving every second of it. As the songs flowed, it was easy to sing along which was something that hadn't really happened at gigs. Years later Brian said it was Stafford where it all began, so I take great pride in being one of the crowd that started it.

Halfway through the show came my highlight, 'Brighton Rock'. I love the guitar sound that Brian produces and I was standing spellbound at the sounds coming from the famous Red Special. 'Bohemian Rhapsody' was played and we all sang every word, including the operatic bits. It was just wonderful. 'Keep Yourself Alive' and 'Now I'm Here' signalled we were getting near the end. The encore was 'Liar' and then 'Jailhouse Rock'. 'God Save the Queen' meant it was all over, and after the boys had left the stage Julie and I just hugged each other and vowed we would be back for the next tour. As we all know, lots of Queen songs lend themselves to singing along so it was no surprise we both had lost our voices through singing along all night. It took ages to get out of the car park and we didn't get home until 2am but we didn't care. We had seen Queen and were very, very happy.

I WAS THERE: APRIL BOARDMAN

IT WAS 1977, the year of the Queen's Silver Jubilee, but that year stands out for me because it was my first rock concert attendance. And not just any old concert either! I was off to see Queen at New Bingley Hall in Stafford with my boyfriend and my close friend Carol and her boyfriend. The closest I had been to seeing Queen perform was on our black and white television on *Top of the Pops* in the front room of our house. It was so exciting waiting to see if they were on, performing 'Killer Queen'. I was besotted with them and their music.

Queuing up outside the venue, the atmosphere was electric. We saw Queen arrive and they waved to us as they walked through the glass corridor into the venue. I sat atop my boyfriend's shoulders waving frantically. Freddie wore satin pants and a fur jacket. Of course, when they waved back it felt like it was just to me, rather than the whole crowd. Once in the venue, I was just feet away from them. Venues were so much smaller and more intimate then, and so much better than the vast arenas where you watch from a distance and have large screens for close ups. The music was fabulous. Nobody played synthesisers then (!) and they sounded brilliant. It is a memory I will treasure always.

I was so lucky to see them in those early years. I was devastated when Freddie died and I haven't been able to tolerate seeing the band fronted by Adam Lambert. As good as he is, no one will ever replace Freddie.

I WAS THERE: ALAN CAMPBELL

I FIRST SAW Queen on *Top of the Pops* in 1974. When I heard them, they were being called the new Led Zep. I was totally blown away by what I was seeing and went straight out and bought their first two albums and, later that year, *Sheer Heart Attack*. I collected all their other albums after that, including Queen's first EP in '77.

Alan Campbell remembers 'the new Led Zep' emerging

At New Bingley Hall, Freddie burst on stage looking fabulous and burst into 'Tie Your Mother Down'. What a show! The sound, the lights, the music were all fantastic. I went with my first wife, who was five months pregnant. We went back to New Bingley Hall in May 1978 with our then eight month old daughter Louise in her pushchair for another fabulous concert, where Freddie again had the crowd in the palm of his hands. Many years later I won a competition to appear on stage at the London Dominion Theatre at a rehearsal with the cast of *We Will Rock You*. It's on YouTube under 'Mastercard Priceless Theatre *We Will Rock You*'.

I WAS THERE: YVONNE PALIN

I WAS MAD on The Glitter Band and they had a record in the charts, so they were going to be on *Top of the Pops*. Queen were on the same show. It was their first time, performing 'Seven Seas of Rhye'. It was like an electric shock. I loved it instantly and thought 'I've got to get this record' and when I did, I played it over and over and over again. That was the start of it.

Then I got their albums. I had to travel to buy those. We don't have many record shops in Shropshire. There was a little local record shop that was all singles and no albums. I bought *Sheer Heart Attack* and played it over and over and over again. I played it so many times that my poor mother went and bought me a different one so that she could have a break from *Sheer Heart Attack*. I used to listen to it every night with the arm over on the record player so that it played the same record over and over.

I saw them at New Bingley Hall in Stafford in 1977. The first song that they did was 'Now I'm Here'. It was dark and you just heard Freddie's voice and then all of a sudden, all the lights came on and it was 'oh my god'. The thrill I got from 'Seven Seas of Rhye' was nothing compared to seeing them live. I was on such a high. I was buzzing for about five days. Freddie threw flowers into the crowd. I didn't get any of them. The following year, I went to see them again at the same venue and he threw flowers again and I still didn't get any. But it was all standing and I went and picked up from the floor what was left of one of the flowers that Freddie threw. I've still got that little bag of dried carnation petals.

One of the few good things about being old is that I got the opportunity to see Queen. I've seen lots of other big names but nothing has ever affected me the way that they did, and I still listen to their music almost every day. I love 'Seven Seas of Rhye'. I love 'Princes of the Universe' because I was listening to it when I was giving birth to my son, and I love

'Nevermore' from *Queen II*. But if you get me started then it's a case of 'and I love… and… and….' When my mum passed away, we had 'You're my Best Friend' played at her funeral. My mum died when she was 92 and she loved Queen. And my older sister is a devotee too. She got it from me.

I couldn't watch a Queen video for over a year after Freddie passed, because I just cried and cried and cried. It was absolutely horrible to wake up on that Monday morning and find out that he'd gone. Other than George Michael singing 'Somebody to Love', nobody has done justice to any of Freddie's songs. He's immortal.

I WAS THERE: MARK DOBSON

I'VE GOT AN older sister, so we always had music in the house. But I was on the periphery of music until March 1974 when as a 10-year-old boy I saw Queen on *Top of the Pops* doing 'Seven Seas of Rhye'. It was like being hit in the face with a sledgehammer. The next big moment for me was Queen's Christmas concert at the Hammersmith Odeon. I literally had to beg on bended knees to get my father to let me watch it, because *Starsky & Hutch* was on the other side. My birthday falls on Christmas Day and my present that year was a tape recorder. I was given it a day early so I was able to record the concert straight from the TV.

Mark Dobson was just 13 when he saw Queen at New Bingley Hall

I was 13 when my older sister, who was at Warwick University, rang the house phone one Sunday night. She said to me, 'Put your dad on.' My dad took the phone and said, 'No, no, no, it's out of the question. No, no, no. Well, okay then, but I'm bringing him.' By this time my ears were pricking up. She'd bought tickets for Queen's *A Day at the Races* tour.

It was Whit Sunday. My dad went to church in morning and then drove us down from Yorkshire. I have vivid memories of waiting for the band to come on, of the massive gong behind the drums and of this huge sense of excitement. And this very famous thing happened at the end, where the audience wouldn't let the band come on for the encore. Roger Taylor was sat behind his drum kit and couldn't start beating the band back in because the crowd were doing football chants, singing

'You'll Never Walk Alone' and so on. I left the gig to find my dad had blagged his way in for the encore!

That Christmas, Brian and Roger were on Radio 1 chatting about the *News of the World* album. The subject of what had inspired 'We Will Rock You'/'We Are the Champions' came up. Brian said it was the Stafford Bingley Hall gig. And I was there!

I WAS THERE: STEVE LEE, AGE 18

IT WAS BRILLIANT - we were stood eight feet away from them.

Stephen Barrett and I have been mates since 1965. I was 18 and he was 16 at the time. We went down on my motorcycle. It was a really hot weekend so we just had t-shirts. I had an old aircraft flying jacket I got off a friend, and he just had a jumper. We needed both on the way home as it was wet - and cold! We got there and it was packed out everywhere. We sat down and got talking to loads of people, all of whom were

Steve Lee and Stephen Barrett saw Queen together

excited about seeing Queen. You could hear them doing their sound checks while we were outside. We thought we'd missed it until we were told 'it's just a sound check'. Panic over!

Come the time to go in, we were some of the first in so we got right near the front, about eight feet away from the stage. There were stacks of speakers either side of the stage but nothing like you would get nowadays. It was a little raw back then. They came on and - loud wasn't the word. It was awesome! They played a few songs and then they played ''39' which didn't go down well with some in the crowd. Some people started to boo. We couldn't understand why. Then, and I'm not sùre who, the tambourine was chucked at us in the crowd. People were chucking it back on. I caught it and did the same. I wish I'd kept it now. Later on, they played 'Bohemian Rhapsody' which we all ended up singing because they couldn't do live what they had done on the record and the video. They didn't have the tech then. And it finished with heads banging about, all of us. It was brilliant!

It was non-stop rain on the way home and at one point we had to stop under a motorway bridge because of it. We got home at 1.30am. I never saw Queen again after this. I wish I had.

I WAS THERE: MARK DAVIES, AGE 14

NO OTHER BAND delivered the goods in quite the same way. There was no support band on the bill and no rock music playing through the PA as at any other gig, just classical music building an air of unique excitement. The lights went down and - bang – 'We Will Rock You' thumped you with Freddie alone on the stage singing away, conducting the crowd right from the off. Every eye in the audience was on him and he loved it! Loud? Until that point, I'd never heard anything that loud! My ears rang

Mark Davies is a big Queen fan

for weeks. Blinded? I'd never seen a light show like that. I was utterly mesmerised. That's pretty much how it was for the next 10 years. I saw the band on every subsequent UK tour, including the final gig at Knebworth. I've seen some great bands in concert but none were better live than Queen. It wasn't a concert. It was an event!

I WAS THERE: PETE SMITH

I SAW QUEEN many times over the years, including when they opened the NEC concert hall and again at the NEC on the *Works* tour. They are quite the best live band I've ever seen. At New Bingley Hall, Stafford the crowd sang 'You'll Never Walk Alone' to the band, who seemed quite overcome by their reception. I met Anita Dobson at the Pavilion in Bournemouth as she was in a panto with my best mate, Jeffrey Holland aka Spike in *Hi-de-Hi!* Very soon afterwards she declared her love for Brian May.

I WAS THERE: STEVE NUTTING, AGE 16

ALTHOUGH A RENOWNED rock venue in the Seventies and Eighties, hosting acts such as The Who, Pink Floyd, David Bowie and Kiss, the hall was in the middle of the County Showground, and was basically designed for cattle auctions. Hardly your O2 or Manchester arenas. Stood outside in a field at around 5pm on a warm May afternoon, the general chatter and merchandise sales pitches fell silent as the opening chords of 'Tie Your Mother Down' ripped through the air. 'Bloody hell,' someone shouted, 'they've started without us.' 'It's the sound check, you dickhead,' another laughingly retorted.

A group of about eight of us met up in the queue, all friends who lived just a ten mile journey away. We eventually shuffled through the entrance doors, giving up our ticket stubs - a Harvey Goldsmith

Steve Nutting was at New Bingley Hall

presentation, costing just three and a half quid! This was my inaugural rock concert and I was spellbound as we walked through the foyer into the main arena, seeing the stage rigging for the first time. Jeez, how many speaker bins were there?

We took our positions in the all-standing audience, 20 yards from centre stage. Things got very tightly packed as the crowd began to fill the hall. This did not stop one of our gang producing a packeted condom, removing it from its foil, blowing it up and tying it off, for an impromptu game of 'Johnny Volleyball'!

Eventually the backing music faded, the houselights dimmed, the crowd cheered and then held its breath. The 'White Man' intro to 'Tie your Mother Down' bounced of all four walls and then – boom! - explosions, dry ice and searing lights. The masses erupted in unison as the Red Special screamed into action. Enter Freddie cavorting around in what looked like a judo outfit, Brian May 'voguing' to our right, John Deacon foot tapping to the beat on the left and Roger Meddows-Taylor with arms in a frenzy, partially hidden by cymbals and high hats, at the rear of the stage.

Freddie strutted along the width of the stage, commanding the attention and worship of the gathered disciples. Looking back, he may not have had quite the confidence and stage presence of later years, but boy, could this man entertain. Both the bass guitar and bass drum vibrated the length of the floor, as the crowd rhythmically trampolined. After a few tracks from *Queen II*, Brian stepped behind his mic for a few well chosen words, along the lines of, 'Good evening Stafford, it's great to be here, and I'm glad they managed to clean all the cow shit off the floor before we came here.' A few thousand chuckles, followed by rapturous applause was the reply.

The songs came fast and furious, with Freddie seeming to change costume for every other tune. There was a little pause in the proceedings as Deeks was called upon to sort out an electrical problem with one of the piano mics.

There were a few piano melodies followed by the guitar and vocal solos of 'Brighton Rock'/'White Man'/'Prophet's Song'. They played most of my favourites from the first four albums and a sprinkle of new tracks from *A Day at the Races*, but within no time at all came the opening piano notes of 'Lap of the Gods (Revisited)'..... 'Wow wow la la la laa...' and with a puff of dry ice it was all over.

The screams and shouts for 'more, more, encore' were deafening. And then it happened. A couple of rows in front of us several silk Queen scarves were raised and a few voices could be heard singing 'Walk on, walk on, with hope in your heart....' Pretty soon this rural cattle market turned into a football terrace as the much used football favourite from *Carousel* was belted out by the crowd for all we were worth. The band came back on for the inevitable encore. They looked at us, we looked back at them. We kept singing. Freddie looked a little uncertain what to do, while Roger, now back behind his drum kit, conducted the masses with giant drumsticks. The rest of the band looked like rabbits staring into oncoming headlights.

Eventually the singing died down and the show continued.

They looked at us, we looked back at them. We kept singing

It all ended with a fantastic rendition of 'Jailhouse Rock', followed by 'God Save the Queen'. The house lights came up, but hardly anyone moved as the ovation went on and on. I left there on such a high, and spoke about this gig to anyone who would listen - and some who didn't want to - for many weeks later.

I went back to Stafford twelve months later, to see another amazing Queen show.

I went on to see Queen another couple of times, with my last Queen concert, and unfortunately Freddie's last, being at Knebworth Park in 1986. I have since seen the *Live Aid* set and Wembley '86 DVDs many times. Queen became the perfect, faultless live band, but I question if this was better than the gigs of the late Seventies. Freddie's voice had obviously got stronger and coped with the long two hour sets much better, and he had undoubtedly become one of the greatest showmen ever to perform in the world of music (the greatest, in my humble opinion).

But in all honesty I prefer those gigs at Stafford. Perhaps it was the set list, the occasional forgotten lyric or mistimed intro, or perhaps am I just old school telling you all it was so much better in the 'old days'. It was not until over 20 years later that I discovered that the inspiration to the writing of the track 'We Will Rock You' was my first ever gig at Stafford Bingley Hall. 42 years on, I still await my royalty cheque, Dr May!

APOLLO
30 & 31 MAY 1977, GLASGOW, UK

I WAS THERE: COLIN HUNTER, AGE 16

MY FIRST CONCERT. I didn't know what to expect. There was no support group, which made the excitement build even more. The lights went down, the *Day at the Races* intro started, the smoke bombs went off and they started playing 'Tie Your Mother Down'. An amazing start and the best start to a concert I ever saw. They were at their best then. I still smile when I think about it. They knew how to put on a show.

I WAS THERE: SHEILA HARVEY

I'D SEEN QUEEN in Edinburgh in 1976 but in 1977 I met the band after one of their Glasgow concerts. After a bit of snooping – I phoned the hotel and said I needed to leave a message for one of the band! I knew where they were staying and so I booked myself and my friend Gill into the same one. It cost a bloody fortune. We met Roger and John before the concert and sat with Brian for several hours in hotel bar afterwards. Roger and John were there too, along with the crew. We got a 'hello darling' from

Sheila Harvey booked herself into the same hotel as Queen

Freddie as he waltzed out of the hotel with a couple of chaps... bodyguards maybe? He was off to a gay nightclub. Most of the others in the bar left one by one to go to bed. That left me with Brian. About 5am, I said I needed to grab a couple of hours sleep as I had to catch an early train home. I was living in Inverness at the time. Brian took me up in the lift and walked me to my bedroom, bent down and gave me a kiss saying it was a pleasure to have spent time with me and maybe we would meet again. It was a fabulous night that I will treasure forever.

I WAS THERE: JANICE MEIKLEHAM

I WENT WITH my pal Jenny and this was our first live concert so we didn't know what to expect. We arrived to see a big queue outside and it was obvious everyone was excited. When we got in, we found ourselves in the second row. We didn't know the first few rows had been removed the year before to let people have a better view.

They burst on to the stage at bang on 8pm and played 'Tie Your Mother Down'. The audience went wild. Freddie was a true performer and

Janice Meikleham was at the second night at the Apollo

we lapped it up. He strutted his stuff in a skin tight leotard while Brian showed his guitar skills wearing a beautiful white top with batwing sleeves which I believe Zandra Rhodes designed. John played quietly along on bass whilst Roger gave it his all on drums. I was in seventh heaven!

One of the highlights was 'Bohemian Rhapsody' of course, with Freddie tickling the ivories and which ended with Roger banging the large gong behind him. Brian got his chance to take lead on vocals on '39' with acoustic guitar sitting on a stool. They played for at least two hours, only going off for a couple of minutes to change costume. Before the end Freddie threw roses into the crowd and the guy in front of me caught one and turned round and gave it to me!

When it was all over, I floated out the door clutching my rose and waited at the side door to see them leave. I only got a quick glimpse of Roger before they were whisked away to their hotel. I remember getting on the bus with a crowd of excited teenagers and chatting non-stop. That concert will always be the best concert for me.

EMPIRE THEATRE
2 JUNE 1977, LIVERPOOL, UK

I WAS THERE: SHARI A HELLYER

IN 1977 I left school, fell in love, lost a grandparent and saw Queen twice, the most memorable year of my life so far. I had only been in the fan club for just over a year and had been given priority information about their forthcoming 1977 European tour. 'The first two rows are reserved especially for fan club members,' said Therese when I phoned up to enquire. I chose tickets for Liverpool Empire, and pleaded with my dad to pay for and take me and my younger sister to see Queen. Knowing how much it meant to me, he shelled out £3.50 for two top price tickets.

Shari Hellyer was at Liverpool Empire in 1977

My dad shelled out £3.50 for two top price tickets

I'd converted the whole family to Queen by now. My mum adored the dark good looks of Freddie, while my dad liked the lighter side of Queen, ''39' and 'Good Company'. My sister? Well, she had to like them. Because I loved them so much, everyone in the whole house had to. Many a night we would go to bed and I would test my sister on her Queen knowledge, asking her questions about them. She remembers two answers vividly to this day. Veronica and three. (What is John's wife's name? And how many children does he have?).

I'd gone from the teeny bop idols of Donny Osmond to The Hollies, Bay City Rollers, Slade, then Sweet and finally Queen. Since I was 14, I've grown up with these four guys, who – though I'd never met any of them personally – feel more like my close friends than the unattainable idols that they are. They have taught me so much in just listening to their lyrics, words like tatterdemalion, junketer, mab and harridan. On the day we arrived in Liverpool and went to look around the city. We drove past the theatre at about 5.30pm and there was hardly a queue at all.

My parents took us for pizza, which I recall was awful. We got back to the Empire at around 6.35pm. Much to my horror, there was now a huge queue. We joined it and waited about, taking in the atmosphere and chatting to some of the other fans. The Liverpool fans were loud and very funny. As we waited, we could hear Queen inside rehearsing their songs before the doors opened. I just couldn't believe that they were actually in there. One girl saw a window open on the side of the theatre and thought it was Freddie. 'Come on Freddie, show yourself,' she yelled loudly, in her Liverpool accent. It was funny. There were different age groups in the queue, but I noticed that most of the lads there were wearing denim jackets. Status Quo featured quite heavily, suggesting that if you liked Queen, you also liked Quo. But my eyes were only for Queen.

The doors opened at 7.30pm. Before we got into the auditorium, there were posters and merchandise everywhere. Seeing the gathering crowd put my sister off coming in with me. Being slightly claustrophobic, she daren't go in for fear of being squashed or trampled. I was very annoyed with her but it was decided that my mum come in with me to see the show. We dashed down to the front to find our seats, B22 and B23. Yay, second row from front centre. I couldn't believe my luck.

There were huge amplifiers on each side of the stage and Roger's drumkit presided over the whole set - 13 drums, nine cymbals and a 60 inch Paiste gong behind him. Freddie's baby grand was in place and being finely tuned by Ratty. I also saw Crystal and Nudge too. I took three pictures of the stage before Queen came on and one of the growing audience to show my sister how 'un-crushed' she would have been had she come in. There were lots of people standing at the front of the stage and we couldn't see above them which was concerning me, but one of the bouncers told me that they would be moved and that it was OK to take flash pictures.

I don't really remember Mr Big's set as I was only there to see 'my' group. They can't have been on for long as around 40 minutes later, Roger came on stage first and banged the huge gong twice, causing uproar. Then Brian came on to rapturous applause – tension mounting – then John appeared and finally Freddie thundered on to 'Tie Your Mother Down'.

At this point I shed a few tears of excitement. Freddie looked so fresh in his white baggy boiler suit. John was wearing a white short-sleeved shirt and white trousers with black waistcoat. Roger wore a baggy white shirt and black trousers. Brian was wearing a flamboyant blouson-type white shirt with leg o'mutton sleeves and black flares, and not his usual trademark clogs either. Freddie changed halfway through into a white, orange and green harlequin, low-fronted, all-in-one leotard.

During the show John looked at me several times and I caught Freddie's eye twice. Brian looked about three times but Roger only once, when he came down from the drums to play ''39'. Well, I was only 16!

The crowd was rocking and what a hell of a good show it was. I was in tears when Freddie sang 'You Take My Breath Away', because I love that song. During the show, Freddie threw out lots of pink, red and white carnations. Both my mum and I caught pink ones. Freddie at one point toasted us all with a glass of champagne. After he'd had a drink himself, he passed the glass down to the front row. They all had a drink and kept the glass! I took lots of photos during the show but only five of the 20 I took actually came out, which was such a pity as I would have got some great shots being so close to the stage.

I've never been so thrilled, and my mum too – Freddie live? He seemed very realistic and didn't show off at all. John was very relaxed, Brian seemed rather shy and Roger was just so wrapped up in his work. We met my dad and sister outside afterwards and they said they heard it all from out there. We rushed around to the stage door to join the gathering crowd for a glimpse of Queen leaving the gig, and as fast as lightning it all happened. The large, glossy black Daimlers arrived and out came Freddie, then Roger and Brian and finally John came out with the guests. My sister says she touched Roger. I managed to touch John's hair! But they sped off as soon as they got in their cars. When Brian, Freddie and Roger were driven away, only Roger turned around to wave at the fans. Or was he really waving only to me? Later, as we slowly started to make our way home, my dad noticed some Daimlers outside the Adelphi Hotel and I pleaded with him to stop. We waited around for a while but sadly saw nothing. To this day I don't know if that is where they stayed but I'd like to think it was. The whole day was wonderful and we drove home reliving every moment and singing to Queen on the car cassette player.

I WAS THERE: TIM WALKER

HOW COULD QUEEN possibly follow the huge success of 'Bohemian Rhapsody', with nine weeks at number 1 and selling more than a million copies? It was the crowning glory of *A Night at the Opera*, their fourth studio album, that moved them away from a mainly heavy rock sound into a mixed bag of rock, pop and cheeky music hall-inspired tunes. The answer was to come out with another brilliant album, *A Day at the Races*, making a matching pair with similar album artwork, both named after Marx Brothers films. Queen had emerged with a confident swagger as arguably Britain's leading rock band, embarking on world tours through the mid-Seventies to stake their claim for global recognition with their increasingly diverse set.

I was a schoolboy in Liverpool and well remember seeing the incredible video of 'Bohemian Rhapsody' on *Top of the Pops* over the Christmas period in 1975 for week after week. I had been a fan since seeing 'Killer Queen' on *Top of the Pops* and bought the *Sheer Heart Attack* album, and then their early albums. I resolved to see the band live and in June 1977 I got my chance. There was no internet in those days, so concert tickets had to be applied for by postal application, and for kids like me without bank accounts, that meant going to the post office to buy a postal order and then mailing the application, with fingers crossed, hoping for a positive result. The alternative was to queue up at the venue's box office. My school mates and I were lucky – we applied together and got our tickets in the post and waited for that special day, Saturday 3rd June 1977.

I had never been to the Empire Theatre before, so it was an extra special occasion for me. It was just before my 'O' level exams, but as I was going with friends and it was on a Saturday, my mum said I could go – great! I had secured my copy of *A Day at the Races* and had been playing it endlessly in the run up to the gig. 'Tie Your Mother Down' was a brilliant full-throttle rock song, made to be played loud, and the perfect album opener. Indeed, it was to be the concert opener, and it said, 'We're back with something just as good' – progression was assured. Oh, and one of my friends caught Freddie's tambourine.

Tim Walker's first gig was Queen at Liverpool's Empire Theatre

Despite my ears ringing for weeks afterwards, I went back for more, seeing Queen on their next visit to the Empire in December 1979, when they opened with 'We Will Rock You'/'We Are the Champions', and again the following December at Birmingham's NEC. Although distracted by punk rock and new wave, Queen remained my number 1 rock band well into the Eighties.

EARLS COURT
6 JUNE 1977, LONDON, UK

I WAS THERE: IAN NICHOLSON

MY FOURTH QUEEN show was at Earls Court for the *A Day at the Races* tour. To be honest, I cannot recall much from this show, which is remarkable, as I have looked up the set list, and it is one of the best of the five Queen shows that I attended!

I WAS THERE: RALPH CADE

AS A YOUNG child in junior school, I loved the New Seekers but when I advanced to secondary school (my junior school friends all going to different secondary schools) I realised that my musical tastes were incredibly naïve. I soon discovered the best way to make friends was to find others who shared a similar taste in music. The girls would choose between The Osmonds or the Bay City Rollers and David Cassidy or David Essex. The boys with longer hippie hair would choose progressive rock like Rick Wakeman, Genesis and Yes. Those with feathered razor cut hairdos would most likely be into glam rockers such as Elton John, Rod Stewart, Marc Bolan or Gary Glitter. The skinheads would be in to Slade and David Bowie. I had difficulty knowing what group I felt a leaning to. Having a slight artistic bent I was often asked to write the names of other pupils' favourite bands onto their exercise books in the fashionable 'bubble' writing of the time using felt tip pens.

It was whilst trying to work out how to fit 'Bay City Rollers' onto Janet Hunter's geography book that I met one of my first new school friends, Colvin Mayers. Colvin was one of two twins and stood out because of this and by having a Guyanan father and English mother. I soon discovered Colvin was colourful in more than one way. He had different musical tastes to our peers and knew of bands I had never even heard of.

Later, at his family home, he would introduce me to the delights of bands like Burlesque, Ultravox, Deaf School - and Queen.

Our group of friends dressed differently at weekends. Some had long hair, some short. We started to wear drainpipes instead of flares. I even got a pair of black velvet flares and turned them into skin tight trousers to feel like Freddie Mercury, who was fast becoming my favourite person in the world.

Colvin had introduced me to *Queen*, *Queen II* and *Sheer Heart Attack* and it was he who had heard the first play of 'Bohemian Rhapsody' on Capital Radio. We were both keen to purchase the new album *A Night at the Opera*. Suddenly, one of our favourite bands who had only appeared on *Top of the Pops* performing 'Killer Queen' would be going mainstream and we had yet to see the band perform live. We had another friend, Heather Clemenson, who knew someone that worked at the Queen fan club. She was as obsessed with Freddie as I was and she had news that Queen would be playing a huge concert at Earl's Court the next year and managed to get four tickets via her fan club contact.

We had previously missed out on the Rainbow and Hammersmith Odeon gigs so were eagerly awaiting their first 'stadium' gig. Heather was not just obsessed with Freddie, but claimed she was in love with him and would marry him one day. Through her persuasive nature, Heather somehow managed to get Freddie's home telephone number from her contact at the fan club and it was decided that myself, Colvin and Heather would phone Freddie from Colvin's home one school lunchbreak.

Heather got Freddie's home telephone number from her contact at the fan club

---

We discussed who would actually speak to Freddie first. Heather handed me the telephone number and saying she was too nervous to speak to him. Colvin was convinced the telephone number couldn't possibly be his personal number so with that thought in my mind I started to dial the number. The phone rang a few times and at this point I thought 'oh shit it is actually a real telephone number'. A person who sounded just like Freddie answered, 'Hello who's calling?' 'Oh hello, it's Ralph here. I wondered if I could speak to Freddie?' 'Hello darling, it's Freddie speaking. How can I help you dear?'

At this point I became speechless and was thinking, 'Fuck, what am I going to ask him? Why am I even calling him?' and, 'My god, I've just spoken to Freddie Mercury.' I quickly decided to try and hand the phone over to Heather, who by this point was shaking her head and refusing to take the phone from me. Colvin just had a huge smile on his face but also had no intention of taking the phone. I asked them, 'What shall I say?' Heather quickly blurted out, 'Tell Freddie I love him!' I thought, 'I can't say that to him,' but at this point Freddie asked me why had I phoned

I explained that myself and my friends were huge fans of Queen and that we wanted him to know how much we really loved him. He replied, 'That's very sweet of you dear.' He then asked if there was anything I wanted to ask him. I told him we absolutely loved the new single, 'Somebody to Love', and that we had managed to get tickets for the Earl's Court show the following year and that we were so looking forward to seeing them play live.

He then asked me how I had got hold of his personal number. I didn't want to land Heather's friend in any trouble so I simply said another fan had given it to us. He then firmly told me, 'Now listen darlings, it's very nice of you to phone me but this is a personal number and I am not sure how you have got hold of it but you must never call me on it again and please don't give it to anyone else.' I told him I was sorry to have bothered him and that we looked forward to lots more fantastic music in the future.

The Earl's Court gig seemed to take forever to come round but when it did, we were so full of anticipation it was like being in a dream. Freddie was his fantastic pompous self, camping it up and strutting around the stage. He said he had written a speech to say to the audience but in his flippant manner said, 'Sorry folks, I can't remember it now but anyway I want you all to go out and buy champagne and have it for breakfast,' at which point he raised his own glass of champagne and toasted the audience.

I will always remember Freddie in this way. He had his whole life ahead of him and I was looking forward to his future songs and the musical career that lay ahead, and how lucky I was to have such great mates and Queen in my life. I look back now with bittersweet memories, recalling Freddie's tragic death from AIDS. My friends Colvin and Heather both passed away under sad circumstances, Colvin also from AIDS and Heather from an overdose, so when I hear those old Queen songs it fills my life with joy and memories of happier times.

I WAS THERE: TRUDI HUMPHRY-RANKIN

'KEEP YOURSELF ALIVE' was my introduction to Queen back in 1973 and by the time I bought their first album I was hooked on a band that would literally change my life. Being only 13, I was not allowed to go to concerts but on 6 June 1977 my dear old dad drove three of us up to Earls Court and waited in the car outside to take us home safely. That £4 for my ticket was the best money I had ever spent. From the minute Freddie bounded on stage, he had the audience in the palm of his hand from start to finish and throughout the show they were all just visually, musically and vocally perfect.

Trudi Humphry-Rankin's first Queen show was at Earls Court

The atmosphere at a Queen concert was always electric but when the men climbed up the scaffolding and strapped themselves into the lighting rig chairs fixed with spotlights, indicating the show was due to start, the auditorium went wild. The end of the show seemed to come so quickly but you knew after several encores it was really the end when 'God Save the Queen' rang out. Hordes of very sweaty people streamed out, ears ringing but extremely happy after yet another great show which for many of us die-hard fans would be enjoying again the following nights.

Of all the bands I have seen over the years, there has never been a time when the audience virtually sang a whole song instead of the singer as in 'Love of my Life', which a Queen audience would do no matter what country they were in. Freddie was always visibly struck by this. The shows, like their albums, were so varied in genre from love songs to folk, vaudeville and even disco. Queen did it all, but when they rocked no one could touch them!

Travelling the UK and Europe to see Queen, my friends and I planned trips even further afield but Knebworth 1986 was the last time we saw Queen together and the rest as they say is history. So many years and concerts, being in videos, watching them rehearse and going backstage, amazing memories and experiences which really were wonderful times.

The Freddie Mercury Tribute Concert was a sad event and at the end, when his image was shown with his crown and cloak, there was not a dry eye in the place. Truly the end of an era. I was persuaded to see 'Queen' when they toured with Paul Rodgers and although it was great to see Brian and Roger, with no John and especially without Freddie, it just made me sad and I

Trudi Humphry-Rankin with Brian May in 1982

realised it was all over for me. Queen brought so much more than just music to thousands and thankfully have left a huge legacy for fans old and new, but I feel for anyone who never saw Freddie on stage. He truly is an irreplaceable presence with huge shoes to fill.

I WAS THERE: ANN CHIVERTON

HAVING HEARD ON the radio that Queen tickets were on sale, my husband queued at Earls Court but they were sold out. His cousin was coming over from America so when we heard there were some extra tickets going, again he rushed to Earls Court. We did get the tickets this time and - surprise - were right up front as the stage was not as big as expected. These were production tickets they'd managed to squeeze in because the stage wasn't as big as they'd planned for. What a bonus. What an experience! Queen were at their best on this day. The whole experience was incredible, Freddie with his beautiful voice and the audience going wild.

Ann Chiverton was at Earls Court

I WAS THERE: JOHN SPENCER

1977 WAS THE Queen's Jubilee year, and when Queen played Earls Court it was billed as the Jubilee concert. They had those terrible fold up seats and my mate nearly broke his leg when he was standing on his chair and it folded up. Freddie came on stage in a harlequin outfit. He always made me smile, looking at some of his outfits. They were on the record album and then tour thing by now. As a fan I'd read the *NME* cover to cover, trying to find out as much as possible. There was no internet. You'd see a tiny article that they were in a studio here or there working on tracks, and then eventually a release date, and then a trip to the record shop to get your hands on whatever single or album came out first.

TOP OF THE POPS
16 JUNE 1977, LONDON, UK

Queen perform 'Good Old Fashioned Lover Boy'.

NEWS OF THE WORLD RELEASED
28 OCTOBER 1977

Queen went back to basics with an album that had more of a live feel and relied less heavily on overdubs. It also produced two stone cold classics in 'We Will Rock You' and 'We Are the Champions', which double-sided single reached number 2 in the UK charts and number 4 on the *Billboard* Hot 100. *News of the World* reached number 3 in the US and number 4 on the British album charts.

TOP OF THE POPS
3 NOVEMBER 1977, LONDON, UK

THE BBC BROADCAST a promo for 'We Are the Champions', Queen's new single. It's an alternate take to the official promo video.

The North American leg of the *News of the World* tour comprised 26 shows, starting on 11 November 1977 in Portland, Oregon and concluding on 22 December 1977 at the LA Forum in Inglewood, California.

CIVIC CENTER
11 NOVEMBER 1977, PORTLAND, OREGON

I WAS THERE: SUE MORGAN

MY HUSBAND AND I knew we liked them but at the concert we both thought, 'Wow, I didn't know they sang all those hits!' We had pretty good seats off to the side of the stage. I'm so glad we were able to go. I remember, when they got to 'Bohemian Rhapsody', looking forward to the difficult part of the song, and at that point all the lights were turned off and you only heard the music. A little bit of magic, I guess.

Sue Morgan remembers the magic of 'Bohemian Rhapsody'

PROVIDENCE CIVIC CENTER
15 NOVEMBER 1977, PROVIDENCE, RHODE ISLAND

I WAS THERE: RICK STOCKHAUS

I WAS A Queen fan from first hearing *A Night at the Opera* and *A Day at the Races*. I finally got to see them a couple years later at the Providence Civic Center, still to this day it was the best show that I have ever seen. The lighting console wasn't working and so the massive array of 1,000 watt par lights were on full bright for the entire show. Freddie stopped at one point and exclaimed 'the light board is fucked!' They went on to perform all of their songs in grand fashion. For ''39', a smaller stage came down from above with minimal equipment on it. Freddie took a break during that number. The show ended with

Rick Stockhaus remembers the lighting console failing – and Freddie's reaction

'Bohemian Rhapsody', which they only performed the non-operatic parts of live. Even with the operatic parts pre-recorded it was amazing.

The encore was spectacular. The arena went completely black and everyone had their lighters out and were shouting for more. Suddenly out of the darkness we heard the thunderous boom of Roger playing the famous beat to start 'We Will Rock You'. Soon all 10,000 fans were stamping their feet and clapping their hands in time with Roger. A single spot light came on, on centre stage, only showing Freddie singing. Next another spot came on showing Brian as he started playing. While Brian played the ending of 'We Will Rock You', the light on Freddie went out and everything faded to black as the song ended. Suddenly a single small spot came on aimed at stage right where the grand piano was, and Freddie was seated there playing and singing the intro to 'We Are the Champions'. The energy only built up from there, becoming so huge and powerful and ending with a massive display of showmanship from all of the members of the band. We came away thinking that we had just witnessed history in the making.

VETERANS MEMORIAL COLISEUM
16 NOVEMBER 1977, NEW HAVEN, CONNECTICUT

I WAS THERE: LESLIE ODELL LIMOGES, AGE 20

THE FIRST QUEEN song I remember hearing was 'Bohemian Rhapsody'. I was a senior in high school, working at a local bank in the afternoons after my morning at school. One of my co workers was a girl named Bina, 10 or more years older than I, who was of Italian descent. She latched onto 'Bo Rhap' at first because of the 'mama mia' and 'magnifico', etc. She sang that song every day at work for weeks and I became hooked too. I stunned my mom when I brought home the *A Night at the Opera* album, because I am a classically trained violinist and rarely listened to rock, pop or any modern music. Queen and

Leslie Odell Limoges saw Queen in New Haven

their music turned me. I listened to that album until I wore it out!

In the fall of 1975, I went off to college but when I learned Queen would be in the US in 1977 and in Connecticut too, I reconnected with Bina and made plans to meet her at the concert. One beautiful week night in 1977, I drove to Connecticut alone despite the desperate warning from my mother, who foresaw 'nothing good coming from going to a rock concert - and out of state too'. Bina and I were in the very last row, with our backs against the wall, but we were breathing the same air as Queen! In a flash of smoke, Freddie came onstage in one of his harlequin black and white spandex jumpsuits and I was transfixed. Of course, I had bought and worn out the other Queen albums apart from *A Night at the Opera* and therefore knew (and sang at the top of my lungs) every word to every song.

It was so very different from other concerts I had attended. I felt drawn in by the entire band, as if the concert wouldn't be complete unless I joined. Each of the band connected with each one in the audience as if each of us were the only one there - I drove back home that night, voiceless from the singing, but sated.

I followed Queen throughout the years but never had the opportunity to see them live again. I graduated college, got a job teaching music, married and had children. Like all Queen fans, Freddie's death devastated me, particularly because I had lost my lifelong friend to the same disease in 1989.

Fast forward to 2017. For my 60th birthday, my husband bought tickets for my brother, sister and me to see Queen+Adam Lambert in Brooklyn. My siblings and I all live in different states, but we gathered for this! The three of us took the train to NYC and stood on line with fans of all ages - some as young as I was when I first discovered Queen, and some even more ancient than I was at that point. Once again, our seats were in the nosebleed section, and once again, I sang every word to every song at the top of my lungs. My siblings were amazed at my stamina - and at my memory. I don't compare the original Queen with the band with Adam. Freddie is gone from this world, but never from my memory. I was over the moon to have been able to see them all in 1977, but I was equally delighted to see Brian and Roger with Adam in 2017. Never comparing, just thankful to be able to relive a bit of my youth and rock out with the new generation who are experiencing the magic of Queen.

COBO HALL
18 & 19 NOVEMBER 1977, DETROIT, MICHIGAN

I WAS THERE: RANDY APCZYNSKI

MY CO-WORKERS WHO I hung with outside of work would go to different concert venues. My twentieth birthday was coming up and my buddy said, 'Hey, I got an extra ticket.' I already had tickets for myself and my girlfriend for the first night, which turned out to be our first date, so I ended up seeing them both nights. First night we were in the first level of seats about a quarter of the way back, about 20 rows back from the main floor, so we had a great view. What really stands out in the memory is Freddie wearing that black and white jump suit throughout the whole show. He was just a master on stage. It was the *News of the World* tour and hearing 'We Will Rock You' and 'We Are the Champions' live and right in front of you was really cool. For ''39', all four of them were standing at the front of the stage. Roger Taylor just had the bass drum, the tambourine and the mic and Brian May and John Deacon were playing guitar and Freddie was joining in. They all sang that song acoustically and acapella. It was the highlight of the concert.

I WAS THERE: ANTHONY KACZYNSKI, AGE 18

I WENT WITH my then girlfriend, a woman named Dawn who was an obsessive Queen fan, as was I. What I remember most was Freddie's outrageous harlequin outfit and his way of handling the mic stand. And the voice, and the nearly tactile sound of Brian May's guitar in the live setting. I'd become a fan of the first album after hearing 'Keep Yourself Alive' on WABX in Detroit. *Queen II* and *Sheer Heart Attack* really clinched the deal. I wore those records out.

Dawn and I lived together for about four months at the tail end of 1977. One of the accoutrements she brought to the apartment was an enormous oil painting of Freddie Mercury, which she insisted on hanging over our bed.

SPECTRUM
23 NOVEMBER 1977, PHILADELPHIA, PENNSYLVANIA

I WAS THERE: ODD HARALD ANDREASSEN

MY FASCINATION FOR Queen started in high school in Norway around 1974. I liked the sound and the fantastic voice of Freddie Mercury. Me and my friends purchased their records from the UK via mail, read about them in *Record Mirror* and wished we could afford a trip to one of their concerts. I moved to the USA in 1977 for education and lived outside Philadelphia. Listening to FM radio we found out that Queen had a concert at the Spectrum in November 1977. This was a fantastic performance with all my favourite songs being played.

One year later, I lived in Chattanooga, Tennessee and was amazed that most of my friends did not know about Queen and that FM radio did not play them a lot. But I found out they had a concert in Nashville in November 1978, filled the car with friends and off we went. Everybody was impressed by their performance.

Odd Harald Andreassen saw Queen twice

I WAS THERE: JANELLE SCHERBIK

IN AUGUST 1977, Laura and I bought four tickets to the Queen concert at the Philadelphia Spectrum from the Music Scene record store in Quakerbridge Mall. We rode our bicycles to the local record store the day *News of the World* was released. We both bought the LP and couldn't wait to get back to her house. We listened to it five times before I had to go home.

Janelle Scherbik was in high school when she saw Queen

The day of the show, we left school early and got a ride to the show from Trenton, New Jersey. Our seats were on the floor, in the 19th row. We sat there awhile and I stood up on my chair and noticed four seats near the stage that no one was sitting in. I said, 'Laura, no one is in those seats.'

Queen did not come on at 8pm. I said, 'They're late. What's going on?' Laura was going to secretly tape the concert with the recorder under her seat. At 8.15pm I said, 'Where are they, why aren't they on stage yet? They are late.' People were now chanting 'Queen, Queen....' At 8.19pm, the arena lights went out, a smoky haze filled the darkness of the Spectrum and there was the tick, tick, tick of the drum... then - bam! - the lights atop the crown went on and there they were - John to my left, Brian to my right, Freddie somewhere in between and the time keeper behind the drums.

The opening number was 'We Will Rock You'. The crowd was in uproar and Laura and I could not believe they were right there in the flesh. I was crying already, and screaming. After 'We Will Rock You' I said, 'Laura, those seats are still there. Let's go.' We made our way through the standing crowd and rows of people – 'excuse me, they're our seats, excuse me' – until we reached those fourth row seats. We made it, Laura with her recorder in tow.

'Brighton Rock' was the next song, and I proceeded to stand and jump around on the seats, screaming the entire time. Laura kept pulling on my jeans: 'Shhh... you're gonna ruin the recording.' I continued screaming and carrying on through 'Somebody to Love' until I heard behind me 'sit down'. Between 'Somebody to Love' and 'It's Late', when it quietened down, I knew I had the opportunity to catch the band's attention through my high-pitched screaming. I waited until Freddie said something to the audience and let out those screams. All the while the crowd behind me kept yelling at me 'sit down!'. I turned around to them and yelled, 'Stand up, I didn't come here to sit down!'

Freddie would throw maracas and things to the audience back in those days. One maraca ended up two rows behind us, going over my head. I said to Laura, 'Do you think he's trying to knock me out?' She said, 'What do you think?' I was positive I had got their attention by the time they played 'I'm in Love With My Car'.

It was during 'Love of My Life', when Brian and Freddie took the stage together, that I actually sat on the edge of my seat, slumped into the chair and cried. Laura was also crying.

When they played 'Love of my Life' I cried

Then it was ''39', with Roger on tambourine and the four of them stood together on the stage. Freddie was wearing a top hat. At the line 'sailed across the milky seas', he came to the edge of the stage, looked at me and threw the hat directly to me. I caught it. I showed it to Laura. Someone in the row behind wanted to have a look at it. I said, 'You can see it, but he gave it to me, not you.' I eagerly showed it but held firmly on to it. We left the Spectrum with an adrenaline rush.

I got home and put the top hat on top of my stereo. It remained there for many years after. I still have it, and cherish it as a personal souvenir from Freddie to me.

RICHFIELD COLISEUM
27 NOVEMBER 1977, CLEVELAND, OHIO

I WAS THERE: MARCI CONNELLY

LESS THAN A year later, there was yet another snowstorm on yet another Sunday night – and Queen were in Cleveland again, this time promoting *News of the World*. We set out early because we couldn't be late - Queen would be playing the entire show! I still remember walking up to the 'will call' ticket window and asking for our order. I peeked inside the small envelope and the ticket manager had filled our order with front row seats. I was there with two girlfriends and my boyfriend; I tried so hard to be cool and contain my excitement until we stopped in the ladies' room, where the three of us screamed like crazy teenage girls (oh, wait we were teenagers!). We all felt a certain elation as we walked down the stairs to the entrance of the floor seating and then all the way down the centre aisle to the front row.

We sat filled with anticipation. We knew we'd miss the vastness of the light show but we would feel every note because the stacks of speakers were only about 20 feet away, we would hear the music before it ever hit the amps and we would see the faces of the band that we had only seen on album sleeves or in music magazines.

We were so close to the stage we would hear the music before it ever hit the amps

---

Then it started, the boom-boom crack of the drums as huge lighting rigs rose above the stage and flashed in time with the beat. We felt the pure rush of the crowd as we all joined in with the stomp-stomp clap of 'We Will Rock You'. The audio played and the crowd was in a frenzy as the studio recording of the song played loudly and then the flash pots blew and Queen were on stage playing their uptempo version of the song.

After nearly five years of touring the world Queen were masterful at carrying their audience, from the hard rock songs like 'Brighton Rock' and 'Liar' into the softer lines of 'Love of My Life' and 'You're My Best Friend'. Freddie was completely at ease on the stage – nothing seemed rehearsed, yet every step and every note was beautifully deliberate. His vocals were flawless and so natural; more significantly Queen were really having fun on stage. One of my favourite parts of the show was when Freddie sat at the piano to perform the unlikely trio of 'Death on Two Legs', 'Killer Queen' and 'Good Old-Fashioned Lover Boy'. As the keys responded to his touch, his manner was pure playfulness and fun.

But don't think Freddie was the only one having fun. At one point, Brian was at the very front of the stage and looking down into the audience. He caught my eye and said, 'God I love this!'… and it was evident that he and the other band members truly loved what they were doing, no matter how crazy the schedule.

CAPITAL CENTRE
29 NOVEMBER 1977, LANDOVER, MARYLAND

I WAS THERE: SHERRY CARROLL BELL

THE *DAY OF the Races* tour was continuing, growing to stadium size and starting to set records. We only caught a glimpse of them in their limos as they drove past us into the backstage area but by then we had learned a thing or two so we left the gig early and were waiting in the car when their limos rushed out, following them all the way into downtown DC, giggling and screaming. They did their best to lose us until they got to some Japanese restaurant and we refused to budge from out front until they came out again so we could follow them to the hotel. But Queen turned out to be creatures of habit and once we knew where they were staying, we could head straight for the hotel every time and, if we were lucky, beat them there and always get to see them pass through the lobby.

I WAS THERE: GREG PHILLIPS

MY BEST FRIEND in high school first exposed me to the music of Queen. We listened to *A Night at the Opera* I don't know how many times. I fell in love with the intricacies of the music and the vocal harmonies. It was the kind of music that filled your soul and lifted you up into the heavens. My first Queen concert was on the *News of the World* tour. To this day, I have never seen anyone who could hold an audience

Greg Phillips was introduced to Queen by his best friend in high school

in the palm of their hand like Freddie, with the soaring vocals and the lyrics which told a wonderful story and begged you to come along for the ride. Brian May played his guitar more like it was a part of his own body than something separate. All the boys had so much fun on stage. It was like I got to spend two hours in Nirvana.

I WAS THERE: GODFREY WHITESTONE

MUSICALLY THERE ARE moments in your life that you remember forever, and throughout my life I have had many of those moments. But the first and most memorable was the Queen concert I went to at the Capital Centre. I was a high school senior and liked several Queen songs but that was about it. A friend invited me to join him and a couple of buddies at the concert. I lived in a mostly rural farming community in Maryland and figured what's not to like about the opportunity to do something other than watch the corn grow? Considering it was November and there wasn't much corn growing happening, I said yes. It was a 90 minute drive one way in the back of my friend's pick-up truck, and it was cold - no heat in the bed of a truck - but to this day I still reach out to that friend every year and thank him for the invite.

The Capital Centre was a huge venue, like 18,000 people big, and for Queen it was full. Our tickets put us far away from the stage, in the upper levels of the arena but we didn't care. We were in the building. It was the perfect way to experience the kind of performance Queen put on, and our seats gave us a panoramic view of everyone else rocking out which added to the fun.

The opening was 'We Will Rock You'. I remember the foot stomps in the stands when this was played at our high school football games. It was a thousand times more intense at a Queen concert. From the very first 'stomp-stomp-clap' to the last, it was gorgeously deafening, and I honestly thought the arena might collapse, but none of us cared. It was an amazing experience to feel so many tons of steel and concrete absolutely shaking under the collective foot stomps and claps of the 18,000 plus people that accompanied that tune. There was genius in the simplicity of a three beat rhythm that invites everyone to join in. And join in we did.

After such a dramatic and powerful opening, the atmosphere in the arena was electric. We were instantly best friends with the people around us. From that opening song to the end of 'God Save the Queen', everyone was on their feet grooving and dancing.

Freddie was such an amazing talent. His keyboard skills, his perfect pitch, his flamboyant costumes and stage presence…he was the total package. Although it was a large venue, the format mostly worked for the show Queen put on. It is only in hindsight that I realise how magical it was. The energy of the band and the audience was all so organic and authentic. There was none of the artificial hype you get from many of today's groups. Of the tunes they performed, the ones that stick in my mind from that night are 'We Will Rock You', 'We Are the Champions', 'Killer Queen' and my personal favourite, 'Keep Yourself Alive'. But 'Bohemian Rhapsody' fell flat in that arena environment. I think it was just too big of a song for the venue and the format of that particular show. A few months later, a different set of friends and I rocked out to 'Bohemian Rhapsody' of all places in an AMC Pacer fully a decade before *Wayne's World*. When I saw that scene from the movie, I laughed so hard I cried because it was so us! Except in this case the Pacer was a putrid lime green colour.

That concert in 1977 and everything Queen did after it made such an impression on me that I shared my love of Freddie and the lads with my son when he was a teen in the Nineties. He's now an adult and has passed that appreciation along to his own son. It is a wonderful thing for me in 2020 to hear my five year old grandson enthusiastically belting out the lyrics to 'Radio Ga Ga' at the top of his lungs. Of course, my son and I are careful to keep his exposure limited to age appropriate lyrics. No 'Fat Bottomed Girls' for him yet!

MADISON SQUARE GARDEN
1 DECEMBER 1977, NEW YORK, NEW YORK

I WAS THERE: FRANCESCA MARTELLO WHELAN

WHEN *A NIGHT at the Opera* came out, three of the members of Queen were signing albums at Korvettes on West 34th Street. We have all their signatures on that album apart Brian's, who was not in attendance that day, much to my friend Zowie's dismay.

In 1977 my three girlfriends, my sister and I slept out at Madison Square Garden to get tickets when they went on sale. We happened to get friendly with one of the MSG employees, who told us that we would be first in line when the next morning came to get tickets for the above-mentioned concert. We were probably the only girls there on our own;

three of us were 17 years old, one was 18 and my sister was 14 and a half. The next morning came and of course the crowd was much larger. But since we were the first ones in line and had met the man in charge, he called us from the crowd, which was by now all pushing and shoving, and had us go up the stairs towards the glass door entrances and publicly said we would be the first people to get tickets.

The crowd went wild and he wasn't then allowed to put the tickets on sale from the 7th Avenue Madison Square Garden entrances. He made an announcement that all tickets would now go on sale on 8th Avenue and 34th Street, which meant that all the people in the back would now run around the full city block and get first row seats. We were still at our same vantage point at the 7th Avenue entrance when we saw the people going in and getting tickets from entering on 8th Avenue. Various people then went up to the glass doors and broke one of them open - and by the word 'broke' I mean pulled one door off the hinges!

People started entering - my friends, sister and I included - and the cops were there in full force. One of them raised his baton to strike my sister on her back and I jumped in front of him with my face, showing him that he would have to hit me in my face which I didn't think he would do. Thankfully he did not. But instead of us getting first row like we deserved, we wound up getting third row.

On the day of the show my sister, three girlfriends and I chipped in for a bottle of Moët and Chandon and a dozen long-stemmed roses to give to Freddie - the champagne, of course, during 'Killer Queen' and the roses during 'We Are The Champions'. We did throw the roses up and they actually hit him in the face.

We threw the roses we'd bought up to Freddie and they hit him in the face

---

The people in the first row let me take the bottle of champagne up to the stage. I was trying to get Freddie's attention during the song, but to no avail, and finally I just banged the champagne bottle on his shin once or twice. That certainly got his attention! Initially, he was not too happy when he looked down but when he saw what it was, he stopped the song and raised the champagne bottle up over his head to the roaring crowd. He then went to the right and left sides of the stage, raising the bottle for everyone to see, and even went and showed the people seated behind the stage. Then they restarted the song and finished it up.

I WAS THERE: REGINA TAYAR CIOFFI

WHEN I WAS four years old I heard a song in church that had my name, Regina, in it. I was just learning to read, and I knew what my name looked like spelled out. After the Mass ended, my mom explained that Regina meant queen in Latin. All my four year old ears and brain heard was that I was a queen, a joke I continued with friends as I grew up.

One day around Thanksgiving in 1974, my friend Russ called me up and told me to listen to the local rock radio station, WNEW, and the *Things From England* show with a DJ named Scott Muni as he would be playing a song called 'Killer Queen'. Crouching under my covers, the radio on its lowest volume so as not to awaken my sisters, I heard 'Killer Queen' for the first time. That song changed my life. I was immediately hooked on Queen.

Growing up in Brooklyn in the 1970s, most people had a nickname or a street name. You needed to inform people what your nickname was before they had a chance to bestow an unflattering one on you, so I decided my nickname was Killer Queen #1 (for my close friends, this was shortened to KQ#1). The song is great. At my tender age, I somehow already knew that Moët & Chandon was a fancy champagne. But I didn't realise the song was about a high-priced call girl. I just thought that she was a very cool chick who drank champers and hung out with Khruschev and Kennedy. I also didn't realise she played for both teams ('…anyway, incidentally, if you're that way inclined…'). Yeah, so with the nickname I gave myself, I was basically calling myself a hooker and a lesbian. Oops!

I saw Queen at Madison Square Garden on December 1 and 2, 1977. It wasn't common for bands to do two nights at MSG, so this was a sign of Queen's appeal. I took the subway to Penn Plaza. The wind was freezing and buffeted me on the Plaza while I waited for Russ, who had got the tickets for both nights. The first night our seats were good. The second night we were way up in the nosebleed seats, but I had a set of binoculars to try and follow the show. Both nights were great.

Freddie wore the black and white harlequin outfit, starting with a leather jacket that he shed at some point. My eyes were glued to him the whole time - he was mesmerising! He did a costume change and came out with the sparkly one piece leotard. Eventually, he was so hot he took off the sleeves and tied them around his waist. All night, he kept up a banter with the audience, calling us 'darlings' as he introduced some of the songs.

They started the show with a fast version of 'We Will Rock You' that melted your face off. From there it was one great song after the next. One highlight was ''39', with Roger on a kick drum and tambourine, and all the band lined up at the front of the stage. Brian's guitar work on 'Brighton Rock' was a revelation. I was dying to see how they would pull off 'Bohemian Rhapsody' live - I was so young and naive! After the first part, they ran the famous video and left the stage for a costume change. I was so disappointed because I honestly thought they would do the entire song, including the opera section, live. But they blasted back after the opera section to melt our faces yet again with deafening bombast. After 'Bo Rhap' they continued to rock with 'Keep Yourself Alive', 'Tie Your Mother Down', 'We Will Rock You'/'We Are the Champions' and then blasted out 'Sheer Heart Attack' to leave us deafened and reeling. They finished with 'Jailhouse Rock', which surprised me, but I later learned they had done that a lot previously. And finally they took their bows to 'God Save the Queen'. Indeed!

The first night I was a total naif. Someone set off a firecracker that scared me, and I didn't have a lighter for the encore. But the second night I was a pro with binoculars and a lighter. Now I was a fan for life.

I WAS THERE PHILIP NATALE

I WAS LIVING on Long Island. I used to play basketball with my neighbour, who was four years older. We'd play in front of my house with a homemade backboard and rim and he'd play music on an 8-track tape for us to listen to. The first song I heard was 'Liar', and I said 'that guy's got some voice'. Then I heard the introduction to 'Keep Yourself Alive' with 30 seconds of drums and guitar before they started singing and thought, 'Wow, this is definitely different.' I started buying the albums. I had my own room with my own stereo system and the whole nine yards, and as a teenager I had my mom knocking on my door saying 'turn that shit down!'

I went to see them with four people from my high school. We took a train into Manhattan. The train station is underneath Madison Square Garden so you walk up, you're seeing other people with their t-shirts on and you know where they're going and you're getting all excited. You're hearing all these guys scalping – 'Got tickets? Sell tickets?'

Most bands play other bands' music before they come on, but Queen were playing what sounded like circus music. And the big thing at concerts was beach balls being banged around by the crowd, until the ushers would stop them. Then all of a sudden the music stops, the lights go off and you're getting all excited. It was like an out of body experience, watching them play on stage. The light show was just over the top. They never ever put less money into a tour just to make more money in their own pockets. They wanted to make sure they put on the best show possible so they could say, 'You know what? We left it all out there on the stage.'

You can look at YouTube all you want. But seeing anybody live, and especially Queen, is just on a complete other level. If Brian played a solo, it wasn't for 45 minutes where you forgot what song they were playing. When Brian played a solo, it would be in most of the keys of the song. And Freddie made you feel that, even if you were in the last seat on the last row, he was singing to you and you alone.

Freddie made you feel that he was singing to you and you alone

---

I saw them three more times at the Garden plus twice at the Nassau Coliseum. In the Eighties they decided they didn't want to tour America any more after the 'I Want to Break Free' video ban. A lot of industry people were turned off by the video. And I saw Queen with Paul Rodgers, who's a great singer. He's got the bluesy voice. It was okay, but I went just to see Brian and Roger play. Adam Lambert has a great voice but it's still never going to be the same. I give him credit for being out there. At the Garden, one of the first things he said was, 'Okay, let's get this out of the way. Yeah, no shit, that's not Freddie Mercury.' You do have a lot of die-hard fans that don't want to give an inch. But Brian and Roger still want to play. They have the right to still play their music.

Freddie died the week before my birthday. I was driving to work. I heard the news and I was 'wait a second, let me turn it up. Let me put another station on.' I was in disbelief. Then I heard it again and I just had to pull over. I couldn't drive for like 15 minutes. It was like losing a family member. I've broken down many times since then.

At the first showing of *Bohemian Rhapsody*, I went to the theatre by myself because I knew if I went with family and friends, they would start asking me, 'Phil, is that true?' and I'd be saying, 'Shut up, I want to watch the movie.' Next day I went and watched it with my wife, and she asked me questions. All the big fans know that songs weren't played in the right place in the film, and they didn't do this or that and so on, but, overall, they did a fantastic job of the movie.

I truly feel sorry for those people who never got to see Freddie live. They'll never get to see the greatest entertainer of all time.

UNIVERSTY OF DAYTON ARENA
4 DECEMBER 1977, DAYTON, OHIO

I WAS THERE: JON BAKER

I SAW A fantastic Queen concert in Dayton, Ohio which myself and some of my friends loved. I then saw them almost a year later down in Cincinnati at the Riverfront Coliseum, the day after Thanksgiving. The crowd was too full of turkey and kinda dead, but the concert was excellent. I remember Freddie Mercury trying to get the crowd into it. Both shows were sold out or very close to it. One of my older brothers saw Queen in downtown Dayton back in 1975 at a theatre that is no longer around. My brother was one of the workers who set the stage up for them. Freddie loved to interact with the crowd and to get the crowd into it. They were a great group to see in concert. I lucked out getting to see them twice.

CHICAGO STADIUM
5 DECEMBER 1977, CHICAGO ILLINOIS

I WAS THERE: NEIL GERARDO

THE PERFORMANCE WAS nothing short of incredible. Freddie was beyond dynamic, a genuine crooner in any music genre and from any generation. I was actually there to listen to Brian May's guitar work, having learned to play guitar at a young age and living a few blocks north of Duane and Gregg Allman in Daytona Beach. Allan Jenkins, the tuba player in the London Symphony Orchestra, privately taught me music theory. I knew Brian May was a physicist, which added to my interest.

I was living and working out of Chicago at the time and found out

Neil Gerardo saw Queen in Chicago in 1977

about it during a visit with my mother in Daytona. Brian May's guitar execution was brilliant and exciting, his unique use of an Echoplex was original. His guitar work was perfection in every aspect. I listened intently for the slightest imperfection but there were none.

Queen ended the show with 'Bohemian Rhapsody' and I left that concert with a new and wonderful perspective. I had been forever changed, overcome by both the music and the distinctive visual performance of Freddie Mercury's amazing vocal talent and stage presence. I walked out of the auditorium realising I had just witnessed greatness.

The day Freddie died I could not hold back the tears

The day Freddie Mercury died I could not hold back the tears. I still can't. The exceptionally gifted talent that was innately bestowed on him as a singer and as a stage presence extraordinaire is an event that comes around once in a lifetime if we are very, very lucky. 'Under Pressure' came on my car radio recently and I had to pull over. The emotional heights I experienced watching Queen perform in Chicago all came back. I found myself smiling and yet my eyes were filled with tears. Once again, I was listening to Brian May's guitar work while Freddie Mercury took complete command of the stage and the audience, the band electrifying everyone with a striking and stunning, jaw-dropping performance to end all performances.

OMNI
8 DECEMBER 1977, ATLANTA, GEORGIA

I WAS THERE: DARLENE SKIPPER COLE, AGE 19

I WENT WITH my my brother, Arnie Cain. Freddie was wearing a tights outfit. He was flipping and swinging from an acrobat's rope. He was amazing. I found out later he was in a circus when he was young. And you could tell. He was in the air. What an amazing show. I wish I had pictures of that evening. But it was a last minute invite and I didn't think to take a camera. I really wish I had.

INGLEWOOD FORUM
22 DECEMBER 1977, LOS ANGELES, CALIFORNIA

I WAS THERE: JEFFREY LAYNE

I SAW THEM three times with Freddie and twice with Adam Lambert. Even with Adam they raised the bar. I had Queen's first album and followed them religiously throughout their career. The *News of the World* tour was the best. They were at the top of their career at that time and just rocked. It was a great stage show and the setlist was all my favourites. They opened with blinding lights to the fast version of 'We Will Rock You' and closed with 'God Save the Queen'. The electricity in the place was second to none. Brian May's guitar was flawless, John Deacon was just laid back and Roger Taylor was hidden by the drums. The stage show was incredible. The jam at the end of 'Bohemian Rhapsody' was spectacular and the rotating light with all the dry ice was awesome. Freddie wore six different outfits, starting out in leather and ending up in tiny little shorts. It was without doubt the best concert live ever. My wife said that of seeing them with Adam. I've been to over 500 concerts and there truly is no one better live than Queen.

I WAS THERE: CAROL PETERSON

THE FIRST SONG I heard of theirs was 'Killer Queen'. It forever left an imprint on my young 14-year-old mind. After much nagging my older sister took my friend Ladonna and I to the Los Angeles Forum when we were around age 15 in 1975. The concert left me speechless, as I had only been to one other concert prior to that. That Christmas my sister bought me the *Night at the Opera* album which just increased my interest in this band. When Ladonna and I started driving, we made sure we saw every live show when they returned to Los Angeles between 1976 and 1978.

Carol Peterson queued for Queen tickets

In 1977 I was a junior in high school and Led Zeppelin seemed to rule the radio but Ladonna and I were loyal to Queen, driving around on cruise nights blasting 'Bohemian Rhapsody'. We saw them in concert in 1977 and again in 1978 for the *News of the World* tour. That year was especially fun because I spent the night in the LA Forum parking lot with another friend, Tina, to purchase tickets for that tour. In our minds we risked our lives sleeping in my car, brushing our teeth at a gas station with some scary looking people, but looking back it was worth it. We were amongst the first 50 people in line. We bought tickets to see them three nights in a row. At $18.50 apiece it seemed crazy and expensive but experiencing 'We Will Rock You' at this sold out venue was amazing. I'll never forget the feeling of stomping our feet and clapping our hands while Freddie pranced around on stage. It was magical. I can still see him at the piano during the 'Bohemian Rhapsody' ballad. They put on a hell of a show every time we saw them.

In 1979 I met my husband and life took us on an adventure across the USA, finally settling down in Colorado. Queen always held a special place in my heart and I was very saddened at the news of Freddie's death in 1991. My husband and I enjoyed seeing Queen with Adam Lambert a few years ago in Denver. I always thought Adam Lambert sounded a lot like Freddie on *American Idol* and he put on a fantastic show. It was like reliving the old Queen days 40 years ago. Adam will never replace Freddie, nor does he try to, but it was still fun to see Brian May and Roger Taylor again. I am very happy there is renewed interest in this band with younger people due to the *Bohemian Rhapsody* movie. Freddie would be very happy knowing he still leaves such an impact and is forever a legend.

I WAS THERE: SCARLET DENISE RUSSO

I WAS A belly dancer, solo and with a group. Diane Webber was the director and a twice *Playboy* centrefold. A ballerina and belly dancer, she got a call for some dancers to dance at an after party for Queen following a Long Beach Arena show. She sent me and five other dancers and three musicians. The after party was for a Long Beach Arena show in 1977. As I was getting ready to leave the party, Freddie came over to me and started a conversation with me. We had a little chat. He was friendly and... well, nice. Brian said something to me in passing but I could only make out my name. The conversation with Freddie was wonderful. He was very open.

One of the dancers then dated Roger and was invited to dance at the

Forum show. She called me and another girl at the request of Brian to also dance at the concert. I remember the lighting in the Forum was done so I could see everything on stage but the audience was voided out. It looked like black space out there, until they turned the lights on and I could see thousands of people! I think I gasped. There were too many people out there. But I had a great time and will never forget it. At the time I saw it as a dance gig but I later realised how lucky I was to get to experience it.

Scarlet Russo got to dance onstage with Queen

The European leg of the *News of the World* tour encompassed 20 shows in the spring of 1978

ERNST-MERCK HALLE
14 APRIL 1978, HAMBURG, GERMANY

I WAS THERE: MONIKA BACIULIS, AGE 18

MY FIRST EVER concert and it was awesome. They performed in their tight black and white costumes and the music was breathtaking. 'You Take My Breath Away' was one of the songs they performed. Brian played a 30 minute solo – wow! Since then, he's my favourite guitarist of all time. At the end of the concert, they threw the drumsticks into the crowd and we tried to catch one but failed. Nearly 30 years later, I experienced a Queen concert in Hamburg again, this time with Paul Rodgers. It wasn't the same without Freddie. RIP.

Monika Baciulis remembers Brian's 30 minute solo

FOREST NATIONAL
16 APRIL 1978, BRUSSELS, BELGIUM

I WAS THERE: GEERT ROTTIERS, AGE 15

IT WAS THE *News of the World* tour, and while I was sitting in my classroom at the Sint Norbertus College in Antwerp, Belgium a couple of days before the concert, the huge robot that's on the album sleeve came by, being towed by a truck. Everybody at school talked about that robot. The two Brussels shows sold out immediately so a third show was added, also selling out. I attended all three. One night, when the concert started there was a big problem with the huge crown. The right side was going up but the left side stayed down. The band members were a bit confused and it was clear they were afraid that it might fall down again so they didn't stand under it while they were

Geert Rottiers was at Forest National for Queen

performing the fast version of 'We Will Rock You'. Freddie apologised for the technical problems and promised to set this right by playing an extra long concert. Which they did!

HALLENSTADION
30 APRIL 1978, ZURICH, SWITZERLAND

I WAS THERE: KURT BICKEL

THE SHOW WAS fantastic, with a great light show and a marvellous Freddie Mercury. The songs at this time were very dynamic with great rhythm. 'Bohemian Rhapsody' is the best song ever written. Queen were at their best.

NEW BINGLEY HALL
7 MAY 1978, STAFFORD, UK

I WAS THERE: DAVID HALL

SEEING THE HAMMERSMITH Odeon
Christmas Eve show on BBC television
in 1975 made me eager to see them live.
I had to wait until May 1978 to achieve
my dream. Having worked out how to get
to New Bingley Hall by several trains and
buses, we were finally standing in the hall
waiting for the greatest band on earth. After
what seemed an eternity, the lights dimmed
and the crownless (the crown wouldn't fit
into the hall) light rig rose above the stage in
a cloud of dry ice. Suddenly, a strange yet

David Hall saw Queen
seven times in total

familiar guitar riff burst through the hall. 'What was it?' we wondered
and then realised. It was an as-yet-unheard fast version of 'We Will Rock
You'. The senses worked overtime as we strived to see the band and then,
suddenly, there he was at the end of a catwalk - my hero, the one and
only Freddie Mercury.

Gone were the Zandra Rhodes outfits and cat suits, although Brian would
wear his legendary cape for the encore, and an all-new Freddie was belting
out the lyrics at rapid pace. He was now transformed into a shiny leather
biker, with red stripes on his trousers and New York motifs on his jacket, all
topped off by a peaked biker's cap. What followed was a concert of amazing
quality, showcasing the new album *News of the World* and their back catalogue
of hits, topped by the stunning medley of 'White Man'/'The Prophet's
Song'. If I hadn't been hooked before, two hours later I certainly was.

I WAS THERE: BILLY HARRISON

THE EXPLOSION OF sound was incredible.
Live music cannot be beaten! The earth woke
up to some incredible music produced by four
incredibly intelligent song writers. Freddie
was an incredible human being, his vision for
combining art into the stage productions was
beyond anything anyone had seen before.

Billy Harrison was at New Bingley Hall

I WAS THERE: JACKY HAMILTON

I WAS SIX months pregnant with my first child when my husband Stewart and I went to see Queen in 1978. It was the first gig I went to. I was taking everything in - 'Seven Seas of Rhye' blasting everywhere, Freddie strutting like a rooster, Brian making his guitar strum out the most wonderful guitar riffs ever… that man's a genius. The drums were magnificent and Freddie on the piano was like the leader of his orchestra. I thought he was as mad as a box of frogs but I was a firm Queen fan from then on. That night I felt on top of the world.

Jacky Hamilton was not long married when she saw Queen

I WAS THERE: PAUL EVANS, AGE 17

I WENT WITH my best mate Gary. Having waited in the very long queue for what seemed like an age we made our way into the huge barn. Because I'm tall and Gary isn't I said, 'Let's get to the front.' We managed to sidle our way to the right side of the stage, where we had a great view even if we were a little close to the mighty PA stack. We did not care. We could see the huge crown of lights over the stage.

Then - boom – the lights went out, there was a massive drum sound and the band came on. Hysteria followed. Freddie was prancing around all superb, lapping it up. Gary by this time was in faint mode due to the crush at the front. I had to withdraw to the side for a few minutes and find a lovely St John's medic who revived him. Back in we went, bouncing along and singing our hearts out, soaked with sweat.

I cannot remember the whole set list, but I do remember the dry ice of 'Now I'm Here'. Freddie was one side and then - lights out - Freddie was on the opposite side of the stage. Very clever! And – boom - Freddie was right there in our faces through the dry ice, just feet away. What a blast.

They must have played well over two hours. I was completely shattered. Once the last chords were struck, it was bye bye Queen. My ears ringing, my whole body shaking with excitement and sweat, the lights came on. My first experience of Queen was the best I saw them. I could not afford a t-shirt but went to buy a programme. For some reason they had run out, but still had the '77 programme. Being a big fan, I bought one. It was cheaper!

I WASN'T THERE: PAUL WHITEHEAD

I USED TO spend a lot of time with a friend of mine. In the dining room was one of those record player cabinets which many had at the time. He had a small collection of LPs. One of his sister's albums sounded brilliant to me and we played it regularly. It was *A Night at the Opera*. I'd just become a lifelong Queen fan! Previously my main interest was The Sweet, Slade and Mud.

I had joined the Queen Fan Club in 1977 and bought tickets to see Queen in Stafford in May 1978. But in 1978 I joined the RAF and I had a weekend between basic training and trade training. At 16, I did not know where Stafford was. Rather than see Queen I chose to spend the weekend visiting my parents.

In 1979, I went to Germany. My room was covered in Queen posters. I was known as a Queen fan because of the music coming from my room. In 1980, I got tickets for Dusseldorf and went with a friend. It was a spectacular show, considering the early days. Concert stages would improve year after year. Freddie was obviously the star, but each member was involved. Even John. However, with Roger's drum solo with kettle drums and Brian's 'Brighton Rock', and both of them singing, they had a higher profile than John.

In 1982 I went with different friends and saw them in Dortmund. The stage moved around. The lights had improved. Queen were a show. I often sat at the back to get a good view. During the performance they got together at the front of the stage and sang the likes of 'Jailhouse Rock'. Freddie got everyone involved.

I WAS THERE: ROB HARVEY-DUFFIELD

ME AND A girl I was in the Sixth Form with queued all night outside the original Virgin Records in Birmingham for tickets. The local newspaper rocked up and photographed us. Next day, we were in the Birmingham *Evening News* complete with a photo. We caught hell off the headmaster afterwards for wagging

Rob Harvey-Duffield was caught out by the *Birmingham Evening News*

school, but it was worth it!

Mercury was resplendent in a harlequin leotard and opera mask, throwing flash bomb-type fireworks over the heads of the crowd. It wouldn't be allowed today. They opened with the fast version of 'We Will Rock You' that no one had heard before and he was throwing these flash bombs. They blew us away – almost literally!

Me, my mate Paul and his little sister Karen were jammed against the barrier at the front for the second year of those Stafford shows. We had queued outside since about 11am but it was worth it. Freddie fucked up the lyrics to 'Love of my Life', slamming the piano shut and saying he would have to start it again. The whole crowd sang it to him and for once he just stood there speechless, his mouth open. It was really a special moment. Did I say the place reeked of cowshit? Not quite so special, that....

EMPIRE POOL
11 MAY 1978, LONDON, UK

I WAS THERE: MICK MORGAN

THE NEXT TIME I saw them was at the Empire Pool. I took a camera with me even though you weren't really supposed to take cameras or recording devices in. The seats we had were about three quarters of the way back from the stage. It was a good set and it was a good stage display, with a big canopy like a crown with Queen on it. I said to my wife, 'I'm going to pop down to go to the loo and see if I can get some pictures down the front', and I went down the front, pointed to a steward up by the side of the stage, pointed at my camera and pointed to indicate where I wanted to stand and he said, 'Yeah, come up and stand there, take your pictures and then bugger off.' And Freddie actually came over and stood there and posed for me.

I WAS THERE: LESLIE LANE

I WAS 13 when I heard 'Killer Queen' on the radio in 1974. Down came the Suzi Quatro posters in my bedroom and up went white wallpaper and painted black skirting boards in homage to 'my' band. All the boys were into Bowie, Roxy Music or Slade and the girls mainly The Bay City Rollers or David Cassidy. Only a very small handful were into Queen. Knowing I was a Queen fan, the girls in my class would give me their

Jackie magazines when they were done with them, and photos of or interviews with Queen went into my scrapbook.

The 1975 Christmas Eve show at Hammersmith Odeon concert was shown on television and I sat there recording every minute, replaying the tape over and over again and longing for the day that I could get to see Queen myself in concert. That day came in 1978 for the *News of the World* tour.

I went to that first concert with my mate Alan James. His brother Andy co-owned a merchandise company called Concessions who had the selling rights for

Leslie Lane took down his Suzi Quatro posters for Queen

all merchandise sold at Wembley Stadium and Wembley Arena, and it was Andy who us the tickets.

The stage looked huge and before we knew it the house lights were turned off and the show was to begin. Loads of dry ice billowed across the stage as the magnificent crown lighting rig slowly rose up into the air. Seconds after, Queen came into view as they went into the opening number, 'We Will Rock You'. This was a completely new version of the song. It was very fast and it rocked! Roger's drum kit looked huge and he used every drum as he played out the end to the song, going into a brief solo.

Hearing all these songs live was fabulous. We were hearing some in their infancy, before they went on to become the mainstay classics that everybody loves. The first thing I noticed was how loud they were. They played for a good two and a half hours, including seven songs from *News of the World*. When the show came to an end, I left thinking, 'Wow, what a concert. I've got to see them again.' My mate's brother, Andy, had somehow managed to fall asleep during the show.

I WAS THERE: MARK W FAULKNER

AS A TEENAGER, I was musically influenced by my elder brother. We shared a room. He was into blues, Ten Years After and John Mayall. I left school in '74 and was earning an apprenticeship wage, which also meant freedom from my brother's taste in music. My first real taste of Queen was on an 8-track player when I heard 'Bring Back That Leroy Brown'. Wow, I was sold. These were stranger sounds than what I had been brainwashed with. I thought that with my first pay packet I must buy this. Unfortunately, there were no copies of *Sheer Heart Attack* in the shops so I went blind and bought their first album. Playing this on my brother's single suitcase turnstile did not do it justice so through a catalogue I purchased my first record player, a Décor with four speakers, thinking 'that should work'. It sure did, much to my parents' annoyance.

Mark Faulkner was mistaken for Freddie when he visited Rome in the Nineties

Queen soon became *Queen II* as I bought the albums in sequence. I got goosebumps learning the lyrics and joined the fan club. My mates soon started calling me Freddie. I had the teeth and similar looks so I didn't mind. Queen were my life, as was my football team West Ham (oh dear). My parents' annoyance started to change when *News of the World* came out, with the thud of 'We Will Rock You' vibrating along my bedroom floorboards to the living room while they watched *Coronation Street*. Unknowingly, they would be tapping to the beat.

I used to help my mate with a disco, touring around and sometimes hosting Radio 1 disc jockeys, and supporting bands who came from the TV show, *New Faces*. Queen were not much of a dancing band, one had to listen. When 'Bohemian Rhapsody' was released, blimey, it changed the world. My mate got a copy before the shops and he played it at a disco. The dance floor just emptied and people returned to their seats. 'Oh fuck,' said my mate. My reply was, 'Hold on, wait for it to sink in.' That night the song was requested and played ten times. Each time the crowd either sat or just stood, listening.

I was fortunate to see them live three times, on the *News of the World* tour at Wembley Arena, on the *Hot Space* tour at Milton Keynes Bowl and lastly at Knebworth, their last performance live with Freddie. It was incredible to be there amongst 250,000 fans. My love and admiration for the band was unimaginable.

In the Nineties I went to Rome for a holiday and people were stopping and pointing at me! Freddie still looked like me. It was a weird experience, but humbling. I have five grown children now and all are Queen nutters. They've all visited Logan Place to see Freddie's last home.

I WAS THERE: CRAIG WOOD, AGE 16
MY PARENTS BOUGHT me *News of the World* for Christmas. I went to this show with my aunt and uncle, who are also massive music fans. We were in a prime spot overlooking the stage. That was when you could send a postal order to the value of the ticket to Harvey Goldsmith entertainments, the promoter. It all seems a blur now in my 58th year, but what is not is the feeling that I was in the presence of greatness. The lights, hidden by a huge canvas black crown, took off and the band all appeared as they blasted into the fast version of 'We Will Rock You'. They blew me away. Or, as Freddie said, 'we're gonna murder you lot tonight'.

Craig Wood got *News of the World* for Christmas

I thumbed my way through that tour programme for weeks after the event, reliving every note and every beat. I remember many of the tour songs then, much different to the ones now. Freddie excited the hell out of me, Brian was that masterful guitar god making my ears almost burst when he hit those high notes. Roger was hitting those drums and John in white trousers nonchalantly played bass at the back. Then it was over. Three hours that changed my life!

The 35 date North American Jazz tour kicked off in Dallas, Texas and wound up with three nights at the Inglewood Forum in Los Angeles.

CONVENTION CENTER
28 OCTOBER 1978, DALLAS, TEXAS

I WAS THERE: JEFF RANDALL
THIS WAS THE first show of the *Jazz* tour, so I was in the first live audience to hear 'Fat Bottomed Girls', 'Bicycle Race' and others from the new album performed. Freddie sang 'Dreamer's Ball' reading from a lyric sheet! It was not the cleanest of shows. They struggled to a halt at one point when Roger started a song out of order ('Sheer Heart Attack' instead of 'Fat Bottomed Girls'), and Freddie adlibbed while Brian and Roger worked out which song they were playing. It was the first concert

with the new 'pizza oven' lighting rig. I had my reservations about the new lighting going into the show, as it was not as impressive under the house lights as the 'crown' rig it had replaced. I had second row seats, so I can attest to the heat factor of the lighting rig. When that huge board tilted towards the audience from behind the stage, it generated a tremendous amount of energy in light and heat. It's hard to believe the boys were mere feet from the source of all that light.

CAPITOL CENTRE
6 NOVEMBER 1978, LANDOVER, MARYLAND

I WAS THERE: SHERRY CARROLL BELL

THEY WERE COMING back, and on my 18th birthday! We knew where they were staying, we had a ride and crazily enough we got backstage passes. Crystal (Chris Taylor, Roger's drum tech) loved my black and white striped leotard, black mini skater skirt and black and white striped over the knee leg warmers and said he 'couldn't leave you outside in that fabulous outfit'. He gave us all passes to get in to the outer edges of the backstage. Things could not have been more perfect and it felt like the luckiest night of my life, right up until this moron friend of ours, who had promised to chauffeur us around all night, told about three hundred little girls all wearing 'I Love Roger Taylor' buttons (while we were indoors backstage and he had to sit in the parking lot waiting) the one thing we knew that nobody else did - what hotel they were staying at.

We didn't slip out of the show early, hoping to see the band while they were inside the arena, where no one else could get at them. Now the secret was out and was spreading like wildfire but they were just too well guarded for that. I handed a bodyguard a few pics we'd taken of Freddie and were especially proud of into the dressing room. He came out with two words from her highness: 'not bad'. A bit rude, but - what the hell, we would take it.

The crowd of girls that our ride John had shown off to beat us to the hotel, packing the hotel lobby full to bursting. When I saw the throng, I knew any chance of a moment or two to connect with Roger was now impossible. As the band entered, he was surrounded. I dejectedly started to walk away. All of a sudden, I heard a familiar voice shouting above the din of dozens of squealing girls.

'Roger!' screamed Nina. 'Roger Taylor! Turn around right now and look at me! I said now!' The entire hotel was staring open mouthed at

Nina, pointing her finger at my departing back. She said, 'My best friend Sherry loves you more than anything in the world and it's her birthday and you are going to talk to her!' The 'or else' was a given.

By now even I had to turn around - there was no other option - to see every eye in the place gawking at me. Roger said graciously, 'Why of course, come here Sherry,' wiggling a finger at me like dangling tuna at a frightened kitten. An aisle started to open in a direct line between Roger and I, like the parting of the Red Sea. My hopes of having a private moment when our eyes would meet and we'd fall madly in love were hopelessly dashed by this point, and this was the last place in the world I wanted to be now. But I began slowly walking towards him, eyes downcast, like an obedient little peasant girl. I stood in front of him, eyes still downcast, and he put his hands on his knees and bent over to look me in the face. In the voice of a clown talking to a timid three year old at a loud birthday celebration surprise, he said, 'So it's your birthday is it? And just how old is it you are then today?' 'Eighteen,' I mumbled, absolutely humiliated and terrified he was going to pat me on the head before this whole ordeal was over.

'Well, happy birthday to you!' and he stuck his hand out, with his elbow bent like you would to a kindergartner at graduation. I took it, shook it and ran for my life. Once again, the crowd of girls started squealing and giggling as they closed back in on him while he signed autographs. But by then I was halfway to the car. I will never be able to thank Nina enough. We laughed hysterically the whole ride home!

I WAS THERE: EMANUEL MANNY STAMATHIS

I WAS IN eleventh grade. I went with five of my high school friends. I remember the 'We Will Rock You' opening and how they stepped back out of the spotlight and let pre-recorded audio and video play for the middle of 'Bohemian Rhapsody' live. Seeing the movie *Bohemian Rhapsody* made me realise just how talented they were. They were different from any other band in terms of sound, vocals and style. No one could ever try to copy them. I didn't drink or take any drugs in my youth so I saw and heard this with all my senses in order!

Manny Stamathis now realises just how 'truly great' Queen were

COBO ARENA
9 & 10 NOVEMBER 1978, DETROIT, MICHIGAN

I WAS THERE: CARL MAKI

IT WAS MY first concert – the 'Fat Bottomed Girls' tour. Our seats were in the rafters, and our backs were against the wall in tier C. The stage was tiny from where we were sat but the sound was massive.

Carl Maki (right) was at the Cobo Arena with his pal Andy

NASSAU COLISEUM
19 NOVEMBER 1978, UNIONDALE
LONG ISLAND, NEW YORK

I WAS THERE: BILL MARINO, AGE 20

I THINK THEY had the girls on the bicycles on stage. And they played a great acoustic set. Of course, Freddie and Brian and the whole band were great.

I WAS THERE: RICHARD HENN

I WAS 14 when I first heard 'Bohemian Rhapsody'. I made my father take me to the record department in TSS department store where I purchased *A Night at the Opera*. After listening to that there was no looking back. My first Queen concert was for the *Jazz* tour at the Nassau Coliseum and I was just blown away. My next Queen concert was in '82 for the *Hot Space* tour at Madison Square Garden. It took a while for me to appreciate that album but, again, the concert blew me away.

Richard Henn was at the Nassau Coliseum

It's funny how we take things for granted because my next Queen concert was 2005 in New Jersey and it was Queen and Paul Rodgers. It just wasn't the same. But I was five rows away from the end of the catwalk stage, and it was the first time in my life I ever said these words to another man. I screamed at the top of my lungs, 'I love you, Brian!' I believe he smiled.

I WAS THERE: TERRY PARRETT, AGE 16

I WAS 14 in 1976. I kept hearing 'Bohemian Rhapsody' on the radio. I asked around to find out who this band was, bought *A Night at the Opera* and just fell in love with it. I played it to death. I liked the variety of music styles they had. It wasn't just one type, like Kiss, there was always something different to take in. I started buying the back catalogue and, by the time *Jazz* came out, I was at the store on the day of its release. I thought it was terrific.

Nassau Coliseum was a B level venue and a very popular concert venue for bands that weren't able to sell out the Garden. For kids on Long Island, it was much easier than trekking all the way into Manhattan. You could drive there, hang out in the parking lot, have some beers and get ready for the concert. Parents were much more likely to let you go there than Manhattan.

Queen were fabulous. It was one of those things where you can't believe what you're seeing. They were that good. I saw them again at the Garden in '80 and at the Meadowlands in '82 on the *Hot Space* tour. That was the one that killed them in the States, because that album was not well received at all. But it was a good tour and, as always with Freddie, a great show. You couldn't keep your eyes off the guy.

Terry Parrett first saw Queen on Long Island

197

THE SPECTRUM
20 NOVEMBER 1978, PHILADELPHIA, PENNSYLVANIA

I WAS THERE: TEODORO LOPES

I WAS ADJACENT to the sound board, 60 or 70 rows back. Tickets were $8.50. As good as they had sounded in February at the Civic Center when I last saw them, they sounded even better at the Spectrum. Their sound crew were a very talented bunch. By the end of their first song, 'We Will Rock You', the sound was distinctive, crystal clear and at a perfect volume.

Freddie Mercury came running out onto the stage dressed all in black with dark sunglasses on. You could tell within a minute of looking at him that this guy was a rock star. His voice was so massive and powerful. Although he missed a few notes here and there, he still could be the most talented singer I have ever seen live in concert and in my top two or three front men.

Brian May had a tremendous presence on stage, recreating his guitar parts just as he played them in the studio. John didn't do much on stage apart from stand there, but that's all he has to do. He did his job by laying down perfect, powerful beats for each and every song while Freddie entertained the crowd. And Roger, like John, just kept everything going perfectly and smoothly, seemingly without much effort. A talented drummer, I found myself watching him pounding the skins as much as I did watching Freddie.

Freddie and Brian didn't dress like prog rock wizards with capes on, like they had before. They just wore basic jeans and nice t-shirts. Although they played very few songs from their first two albums, the set list was still great, the crowd was great, the atmosphere was great and the band was great!

CHECKERDOME
23 NOVEMBER 1978, ST LOUIS, MISSOURI

I WAS THERE: LIZ KRINSKY, AGE 16

IT WAS THE *Jazz* tour. There was no opening act. We paid $8.50 for our seats. We drove to the box office at the venue. This was long before Ticketmaster days. I was a junior in high school and my best friend Darrin went with me. We were huge Queen fans. We once got into a knock-down drag-out fight at our local K-Mart over the one copy of *Sheer Heart Attack*. This show was the first time Darrin and I had been around so many fellow Queen fans. Queen were not popular in our school in 1978. My school was big on southern rock and Led Zep, and being a Queen fan meant you'd get your ass kicked. My *News of the World* album got thrown down the stairwell by the cafeteria and smashed. Darrin got beat up and his Queen t-shirt was literally torn off of him. Now it seems all my classmates were big fans and at that show. They were not!

My dad drove us to the show in his 1967 Camaro. We had no idea at that time how cool that car was. We got it new in 1967 for Mom to take me to school and then Dad used it to drive to work because Mom bitched that it didn't have power steering! We lived in Illinois, across the river from St Louis. We had to drive old Route 111 to get to Route 40 (now I-64) to go to St. Louis. It was about a 23 mile drive. Jimmy Carter was president and despite our excitement about the show, the news on the radio was sombre. It was only a few days after the members of Jim Jones' cult, The Peoples Temple had killed themselves in a shocking mass suicide. It was all over the news.

Man oh man, we were so excited. The Checkerdome was a huge old place that was nicknamed The Barn. You would take the Hampton Avenue exit off of Route 40 and exit right on to Oakland Avenue. On all of the surrounding corners around the huge parking lot were stands for the unofficial band merchandise. All the official stuff and programs, etc. were sold inside the venue. Queen was the first big rock concert that we went to without the parents. The arena was the official home of the St Louis Blues hockey team. If you had floor seats during the hockey season, the ice was under the temporary flooring and your feet froze. We didn't have to worry about that because we were on the mezzanine level. Queen had the pizza oven lighting rig that slowly lifted up to reveal the stage, and on the band came. Oh my god, they were fabulous.

But what a show it was. It went by in a colourful blur. After the show we went to see them leave in their limos. We were right by the rails, right in front looking down. I had a pair of really tall platform clogs and somehow in all of the excitement, I lost one and it landed with a clunk on the hood of the limo. I was embarrassed. Then Brian May stepped out and very politely handed it back to me.

Darrin died of AIDS, just like poor Freddie. His birthday was in September, also like Freddie.

RICHFIELD COLISEUM
25 NOVEMBER 1978, CLEVELAND, OHIO

I WAS THERE: MARCI CONNELLY

FAST FORWARD TO one year later (almost to the day) and Queen were back at the Coliseum with an all-new show promoting their latest release, *Jazz*. The album had a slightly different feel and the concert did as well. Don't get me wrong, Queen were fabulous and they were still rocking the crowd so hard that they wouldn't sit down the entire show. However, this show seemed a bit more scripted - in a good way. The first half of the show featured several new songs from *Jazz* and

Marci Connelly was back at the Coliseum in 1978 for her third Queen show

for the first time, they played an acoustic set featuring 'Dreamer's Ball', 'Love of My Life' and ''39'. This was also the first concert that featured Brian May's infamous guitar solo as part of 'Brighton Rock' - which is probably as intense as you can get at a Queen show. He was unstoppable and his solo was nothing less than wild perfection.

Queen finished the second half of the concert with 'Fat Bottomed Girls' from *Jazz* and then a bombardment of some of their hardest rocking songs featuring an alternate arrangement of 'Keep Yourself Alive', 'Tie Your Mother Down', 'Bohemian Rhapsody', 'Sheer Heart Attack' and 'We Will Rock You/We Are the Champions'. The energy in the arena was incredible. Queen didn't play 'Don't Stop Me Now' on this night, and played it at fewer than half of the *Jazz* shows.

Leaving the *Jazz* show felt different, almost as different as the concert itself. Queen had reinvented themselves and we watched this unfold on stage. They were more than a great band playing their songs to a live audience and having fun doing it. If *News of the World* was the peak of their concerts, *Jazz* was the beginning of their full-scale shows. They had become not only designers but masters of their whole production. Musically, the instrumentation was tight and their harmonies were increasingly more intricate and impressive; but a live performance by Queen was now a complete musical and visual experience.

WAR MEMORIAL AUDITORIUM
28 NOVEMBER 1978

I WAS THERE: JJ MOON

THE BLIZZARD OF 1977 in Buffalo, New York was a nasty snow storm. People were stranded in their homes for days, and I found a copy of *News of the World* in the shop I worked at part time making waterbeds. It was the only album in the shop so out of boredom I began to play it. I'd heard 'We Will Rock You' before but not listened to it like this. Brian's guitar playing blew me away. I made eight bed frames that day, double what I would normally make. Queen gave me that much energy.

JJ Moon's productivity at work was boosted by listening to Queen

Freddie had the ability to make you part of the song. He drew you in, and in my mind I was part of the music. I could actually feel the emotions of the songs. Most of my buddies at that time were listening to Foghat and Aerosmith. I was only able to get one of my buds to get into Queen. It was in the spring of 1978 that John and I became true Queen fans. We bought 8-tracks for our cars and we played Queen. Oh, and a Johnny Cash 8-track.

One day I overheard a customer talking about going to a concert at the Memorial Auditorium. I was only making $2.10 an hour and between fuel and the basic necessities I just didn't have that kind of extra money. They wanted $8.50 for a seat. That meant we had to raise $17.00. It would take me three weeks or more to try and save that money. I began walking to work to save on gas, and we offered to do yard work and whatever we could to make extra money.

I told my grandmother John and I were going to see Queen. She said, 'You'd better dress appropriately and be on your best behaviour.' She thought we were going to meet *the* queen of England! She ended up sneaking me the money so my grandfather wouldn't find out. He was old school and only listened to classical music. Everything else was the devil's seed – the man had no culture, and he did and ate the same thing every day until his death.

Anyways, we now had $20 plus what I saved. The weeks before the concert were the worst – the anticipation, the excitement ran through us both. We knew that we would have to take the bus downtown, and the weather wasn't cooperating at all. The cold and the wet snow didn't stop us. We arrived four hours early, thinking we'd be the first in line and thus better seats. We never looked at the tickets and didn't realise they were assigned seats....

MAPLE LEAF GARDENS
4 DECEMBER 1978, TORONTO, CANADA

I WAS THERE: MARTIN DOCHERTY, AGE 17

THE CONCERT WAS very memorable, starting with the stage being covered with curtains. As the stage was filling up with smoke, here they came with the clapping of the hands on 'We Will Rock You'. Suddenly the curtains opened and there they were, bigger than life and pounding it out loud and clear. We were fifth row, dead centre on the floor of the concert bowl as it was called back then. They were as entertaining as any band I had seen at that time. They really were fucking incredible, and I always refer to that Queen concert as one of my best ever.

DANE COUNTY COLISEUM
6 DECEMBER 1978, MADISON, WISCONSIN

I WAS THERE: PAM HARNACK

MY FAVOURITE CONCERT ever. Freddie had tight leotard-type pants on with white boots and wings on the boots. There was a big screen in the back of the stage showing the band members close up, singing as a group. It sounded just like the album and he played piano beautifully. I loved it!

CHICAGO STADIUM
7 DECEMBER 1978, CHICAGO, ILLINOIS

I WAS THERE: JOHN DAMRATH

AS A KID IN Houston, Texas in 1975, I built model rockets, railroads and airplanes. I often listened to the radio and was familiar with songs such as 'Killer Queen', 'You're My Best Friend' and 'Bohemian

Rhapsody'. But I didn't know the names of those songs, or the group. I didn't really care. I just recall being intrigued by the sound. It wasn't until 1978, after moving to Chicago, that a high school friend had me over to his home after school where he played Queen albums and told me to focus on what in his opinion was the greatest rock band ever. He played everything from 'Doing All Right' to 'It's Late' and I was drawn in.

I read about the group and immediately realised they were different. They seemed unafraid and scared to death at the same time. I could relate. Who couldn't? Risk takers who cared. Queen didn't care what anyone thought, but cared what everyone thought. I could relate. They paid attention to every detail and exhausted things until they got it right. I could relate, but I doubt they realised what an impact they had on people like myself. They were one of the driving forces in my life and I hoped to one day meet them.

As a junior in high school, I got up enough courage to ask a girl to join me at the Queen concert. She agreed. I recall I had a hockey game prior. She attended my game and I didn't play well. We won, but I recall worrying during the game about getting to the concert in time! Immediately after the game, we raced down to Chicago Stadium to see Queen. It was the *Jazz* tour and I was absolutely hooked on the greatest band ever! From 'Let Me Entertain You' to 'Don't Stop Me Now', Chicago Stadium got a treat. As an athlete, I remember thinking how exhausting it must have been for them doing show after show and I appreciated the effort and energy they gave us in Chicago.

KEMPER ARENA
8 DECEMBER 1978, KANSAS CITY, MISSOURI

I WAS THERE: BARRY GENTRY

THE SUMMER AFTER my eighth grade school year, I heard the brand new song 'Bohemian Rhapsody'. It was completely different from anything I had ever heard previously. I immediately went out and purchased the LP. I immersed myself in the whole album, really enjoying every song so much that I purchased the entire Queen back catalogue. I was officially a Queen freak! Queen were popular in Topeka, Kansas but not like Kiss and Rush and other bands. Having listened to every song many times, I knew what a lot of my peers didn't know – that Queen rocked hard if you let them. I went into high school 100 per cent a

Queen freak, with every Queen album on vinyl and various albums on 8 track tape. I was famous at my school for being the weirdo that had every Queen album in my backpack every day!

Somewhere along in there, *Live Killers* came out and that was spectacular. *Midnight Special* and other weekend music television shows featured the ubiquitous Queen videos of the era, all pre-MTV by a couple of years. Other bands played live on these shows, but Queen must have thought they had too much production or whatever and they sent tapes. But after hearing *Live Killers*, I knew I had to see them live.

Barry Gentry was viewed as a weirdo for carrying his Queen albums with him

I remember the first time I heard 'Somebody to Love' on a Sunday morning in my bedroom as I was waking up and then later, on a boy scout winter camp out, I heard 'Tie Your Mother Down'. At that point, I was squarely positioned in the Brian May camp and really went back through all the albums, figuring out the authors of the various songs. I realised what a great song writer John Deacon really was, and that Roger was the guy singing the really high stuff and his songs were great too. They all had their own personality, yet they were unarguably a band.

In my senior year, Queen toured the States for the first time since before I knew them. Myself and a neighbour got our $17 tickets, hopped into my 1973 Oldsmobile Cutlass and made the 60 mile pilgrimage to Kemper Arena in Kansas City for what I still consider to be the best live concert I've ever seen.

Fate brought my friend Dana Myzer and myself back together two years later for the next tour. Although not quite the same calibre, it was still stunning. In college, my interests in Queen somewhat faltered, but I still bought all the albums. *The Game* was probably the last album I was really into. Myself and my late wife enjoyed *Live Aid* on TV, and I suffered through the tragic loss of Freddie and, later, the tragic loss of my wife. But Queen live on. I have four sons - all musicians – and they had no idea Queen could full on hold their own with Led Zeppelin or Metallica! I will always love Queen.

PACIFIC COLISEUM
14 DECEMBER 1978, VANCOUVER, CANADA

I WAS THERE: CURT PALME

IT WAS MY second concert. My first was Renaissance. (How did a 13-year-old Vancouver kid get turned onto the UK band Renaissance? I can't remember!) I went to Queen with my best friend and his younger sister. Their mom drove us in their station wagon. On the way my friend's sister said 'I can't believe we're going to see Queen'. My friend and I both laughed and said, 'Of course we're going to see Queen, who did you think we were going to see?' She explained that the band seemed larger than life, as we'd hear the music on the radio and on records, and read about them in rock magazines. For some reason the sentiment stuck with me all these years.

Curt Palme took time out from selling VCRs to go see Queen

We had floor seats towards the back of the venue, but Freddie's energy penetrated to the far corners of the building. It was the first time I'd ever seen motorised lighting, and a manned follow spot on some sort of arm followed Brian May to the floor during 'Get Down, Make Love', with lots of guitar effects and tons of smoke machines. It seemed a bit surreal. As an audio and video geek even back then, I also noticed that one of the moving lighting trusses had a loose cable, and a few of the lights went out part way through the show.

Freddie's energy penetrated to the far corners of the building

---

OAKLAND COLISEUM
16 DECEMBER 1978, OAKLAND, CALIFORNIA

I WAS THERE: DON MURPHY

AS A TEEN starting high school, I was in marching band and everyone there was a Queen fan and that got me into it. I joined a mail order record club (Columbia Record Club) where you received 12 or so records for a penny and bought *A Night at the Opera, A Day at the Races* and *News of the World*.

Queen were noticeably louder than anything I had seen, including Kiss. It was exciting to hear the fast version of 'We Will Rock You'. 'Now I'm Here' and 'Brighton Rock' were fantastic.

Don Murphy remembers Queen being louder than any other band he saw

The concert was closely mirrored on the *Live Killers* album in terms of play order and song length. Freddie's interaction with the audience was excellent and he exhorted us to clap along, sing along, etc. I was learning to play guitar at the time and Brian's loud solo's and use of the echo during 'Brighton Rock' were very inspiring. I was blown away. I wasn't a huge Queen fan but this concert changed my viewpoint.

I WAS THERE: SCOTT MOSHER, AGE 13

I WAS BARELY a teenager at the time. I won tickets from KFRC radio in San Francisco. My neighbour drove me since I was too young. The concert was sold out. The smell of marijuana was everywhere, you could not escape it. But although the weed was thick the show itself was stellar. Freddie was always himself, dancing around the stage. At the time he has his long hair. There was nothing

Scott Mosher's ticket for the Oakland Coliseum gig

fake about any of it. I didn't know any songs but it was the thrill of going to a concert. I remember being showered with confetti after the last song and the band taking a bow. As a little boy I would do chores around the house and would earn money from my parents so I could go out and buy what I needed or wanted at the time. I still have the concert shirt I bought with my allowance, at home on my mom's cedar chest. I bought the concert shirt with my chore money.

THE FORUM
19 DECEMBER 1978, INGLEWOOD, CALIFORNIA

I WAS THERE: LARRY WILLIAMS, AGE 19

HAVING BEEN RAISED on all sorts of British rock I was quick to embrace Queen's debut album. After being unable to get tickets for their earlier US tours, I was finally able to snag a couple of nosebleed seats for their *Jazz* tour at the Fabulous Forum in Inglewood, California. My seats were literally at the very back of the arena, the second row from the top. As the arena filled up, my date and I walked around the inside of the arena to get a closer look at the stage. Then, as fate would have it, I ran into a friend from high school who was an usher at the venue. He was responsible for verifying tickets before allowing people to enter the floor area. He told me to come back after Queen started and said he would try to let me down to the floor level if there were any empty seats. My date and I retreated to our nosebleed seats to watch the first two opening acts. About 10 minutes into Queen taking the stage, we went down to the area where my friend was working as an usher. He said, 'There are two seats in the fourth row right in front of Freddie's piano. Sit there and act like you belong there. If someone comes up with tickets, you will have to move.' I was practically bouncing out of my skin. There we were, sitting fourth row in front of Freddie Mercury's piano, watching Queen perform all of their hits. I was close enough to see them sweat. It was unreal.

Queen's Live Killers *tour took place between January and May 1979, taking in Europe and Japan. A double live album, recorded during the tour, was released on 22 June 1979 and reached number 3 in the UK album charts and number 16 in America.*

STADTHALLE
20 JANUARY 1979, BREMEN, GERMANY

I WAS THERE: KARIN DESCZKA, AGE 12

I SAW QUEEN three times. My first ever rock concert was the *Live Killers* tour. They opened with 'We Will Rock You'. The second time was again at the Stadthalle on *The Game* tour, and I saw them with Paul Rodgers. I moved on to punk rock, but Freddie is the greatest and most charismatic performer I ever came across.

Karin Desczka saw the *Live Killers* tour

AHOY HALL
29 JANUARY 1979, ROTTERDAM, THE NETHERLANDS

I WAS THERE: PATRICIA VAN GROOTEL

I WAS NINE when 'Bohemian Rhapsody' entered the Dutch charts. The voice, piano, choirs and heavy guitar, the length of it and the videoclip caught me the first time I heard it. My dad, who always listened to the radio in his photo studio that we lived above and went enthusiastically on about something fantastic he had heard. I replied, 'It's Queen, right?'

Dad gave me the money to buy *A Night at the Opera* and my friend and I went to a record shop for the first time ever. Misled by Mick Rock's classic image on its cover, we bought *Queen II*. Only afterwards did we realise this album did not contain the song with the difficult name we could not pronounce, so we bought the seven inch 45 as well. My dad was annoyed, but I was hooked. Everything Queen released became my daily life, my oxygen.

Being only 12 in 1978, I could not go alone so my mom took me. I remember what I was wearing, how we took a wrong exit, how we stressfully got in in time, how we had seats quite close to the stage and how I stood there for two hours, completely mesmerised. The stage was rather simple, dominated by the huge lights above it in red, green and yellow. The drum kit had the *Jazz* logo, Freddie had his black leather outfit and it was the best night ever.

In the summer of 1979, we were at our holiday address and music was played all the time. One morning I awoke to the noise of an audience, cracking fireworks and… 'We Will Rock You' (the other version) blasted through the house. My dad had bought me *Live Killers*. By then he, and actually the whole family, was sold on Queen. He promised to take me to the next gig they played in the Netherlands.

FESTHALLE
2 FEBRUARY 1979, FRANKFURT, GERMANY

I WAS THERE: GREG BRUCE, AGE 18

I WAS IN the US Army in Frankfurt, Germany. It was the tour with the album with naked bicycle riders and songs like 'We Will Rock You' and 'We Are the Champions'. It was my first true rock concert and I was blown away. Brian May was a wizard on guitar. Freddie Mercury wore a leather biker's outfit with leather coat, pants and hat. There were red, green and white lights above the stage, flashing in sequence to the music. It was a very good time.

Greg Bruce was in the US Army

I WAS THERE: IAN WAITES

I SAW THEM on the *Live Killers* tour in Frankfurt and more recently in Adelaide, with Adam. Both shows were fantastic. There's only one Freddie but Adam did them proud. I am a musician. Queen was my band and Brian May my hero guitarist. Their ability to write music is equal to the great composers from the past. They - and Freddie – were, and are, truly one of a kind in the music world. Their music will live on forever.

The *Live Killers* tour also took in 15 Japanese shows

NIPPON BUDOKAN
13 & 14 APRIL 1979, TOKYO, JAPAN

I WAS THERE: HIDEO OGAWA

I SAW QUEEN live five times between 1979 and 1985 and once with Paul Rodgers and twice with Adam Lambert. I still love them! I was 11 years old the first time I heard them on the radio. It was 'Ogre Battle' and it knocked me out. I've been a fan ever since, even when their musicality changed and Freddie grew a moustache. Seeing them live, I couldn't sing loud because I was a shy Japanese boy. I remember Freddie fell over on stage!

MAKOMANI ICE ARENA
5 & 6 MAY 1979, SAPPORO, JAPAN

I WAS THERE: YUKIKO OYAKE, AGE 15

THE CONCERT WAS held at Makomanai Ice Arena in Sapporo where figure skating game was held for the Sapporo Olympics in 1972. I went there with my friend. The opening song was 'We Will Rock You'.

Yukiko Oyake's ticket for the Queen show in Sapporo

The *Crazy* tour encapsulated 20 shows around Britain and Ireland, culminating in seven London shows at different venues in the space of under two weeks, with a day off for Christmas.

RDS SIMMONS HALL
22 NOVEMBER 1979, DUBLIN, IRELAND

I WAS THERE: LINDA O'GORMAN

'SEVEN SEAS OF Rhye' introduced me to Queen. I fell in love straight away with their harmonising sound. I thought Freddie's voice was amazing and loved everything about him, from his flamboyant moves to his cheeky grin and of course his unique style. My older sister always bought the weekly girlie magazines which were filled with all the pop stars, so I quickly collected a number of amazing pictures of the band all over my bedroom wall. My true love was Roger. I had pictures stuck inside my geometry box, pencil cases and wherever I could without teachers ever spotting them. Roger and his super sexy eyes got me through some difficult times.

Linda O'Gorman was at the RDS

I didn't get my first album, *Sheer Heart Attack*, until I started work in 1978. *Queen I* and *II* quickly followed and I played them continuously in the house. I recall my mum (now deceased) falling in love with what she called 'Freddie and the Queeny boys'. I'd listen to the harmonising and at one point I even tried to sing all the parts. One day I'd be Freddie, another day Roger, and I'd air drum to all the tracks. I only have to hear some of the earlier Queen songs today and my hands are up in the air, playing my drums as I sing along.

When I heard the band were coming to Dublin in 1979 I was so happy. I counted down the days, hours and minutes for that night to come. I persuaded my older sister and girlfriend to come with me. I was super excited. I had dreamt about this day and this gig for what seemed like years.

It was a cold November night but off we trundled to the RDS. I had been to a few small gigs in Dublin but nothing on this scale. As we entered the venue, it seemed enormous. There were quite a lot of people rushing to get to the front. We managed to get an ace spot not far from the front. We were surrounded by a lot of older people, mostly men, and to be honest I was a bit afraid. But that fear very quickly left as the smoke came from the stage and I heard the sound of the drums. 'Let Me

Entertain You' was the first song. Wow, I was here, going to see the best band in the world. I think I died and went to heaven that night.

From the very first song to the last, we sang along, screamed and clapped and jumped up and down. Freddie was a superstar, a true performer, and Roger, Brian and John were pretty awesome too. I felt I could reach out and touch them. In my mind they were there performing just for me. When we left the venue, it was miserable and raining heavily. But my heart was skipping.

I WAS THERE: ALAN KEARNEY
MY FIRST 45 was The Beatles' 'Hello, Goodbye'. As the Sixties turned into the Seventies I loved the Sweet singles, which weren't too far away from the sound of Queen. 'Bohemian Rhapsody' blew my mind and I wanted to know who these lads were. I remember seeing Freddie Mercury on *Top of the Pops* and thought he looked completely different. When I heard 'Now I'm Here' they became 'my' band.

Dublin in '79 was my first ever gig. Milton Keynes in '82 was brilliant, as seen in the *On Fire* DVD. I saw them again in Dublin in '84 and at Slane in '86, where they were rubbish really. They weren't media darlings, especially with the *NME*, and it's great to see that they are now bigger than ever. I love them. I always got them.

NATIONAL EXHIBITION CENTRE
24 NOVEMBER 1979, BIRMINGHAM, UK
I WAS THERE: ALAN SHARP, AGE 15

I WAS 10 and into Bowie, Alice Cooper and Mott the Hoople. They kind of fitted into that. I remember 'Killer Queen' on *Top of the Pops* and then the video for 'Bohemian Rhapsody'. The NEC show was my first ever gig. I went with my cousin and a couple of friends, catching the train from Gloucester up to Birmingham Airport and then walked across a bridge and straight into the NEC. They were just in one of the halls, with a makeshift stage stuck up at one side.

They were using the same stage show as appears on the cover of *Live Killers*. At the start of the show, Freddie came onto the stage in the leather hat

Alan Sharp caught Freddie's tambourine, but didn't get to hang on to it

and with the big moustache, sat on the shoulders of a man dressed as Superman. At one point Freddie threw a tambourine into the audience. I caught it at the same time as someone standing behind me and it was yanked out of my hand and then it was gone. They played 'Save Me' and said this was the first time they'd played it live.

I saw them again at Knebworth. We were a long way away, but I remember Freddie was wearing a yellow outfit. I drove everybody there. There was a murder at the show and the police were stopping everybody on the way out to question them, so it took longer than usual to get out of the car park. We didn't get to leave until 6am.

I WAS THERE: MARTIN BAGGOTT, AGE 16

THE WHOLE SCHOOL was buzzing with excitement after the first time we saw the 'Bohemian Rhapsody' video on the previous night's *Top of the Pops*. Everyone sang it on the coach on the way to school that Friday morning. The tour was advertised in either *Melody Maker* or the *NME*. There was always

Martin Baggott saw Queen on their *Crazy* tour

a copy of one or the other in the sixth form common room. I begged my parents to send a cheque in the post and a while later the tickets arrived. Myself and a school friend went by train. It was our first concert. We got there early and there was a bit of a panic as we could all hear the band playing so everyone started running. It turned out to be a soundcheck!

Live Killers had been released earlier that year so we knew what to expect. The thing that got me was how loud they were. We were pretty close to the front at first but getting crushed. Security were trying to create a barrier and thankfully we managed to slip back a bit. It was November so we had dressed accordingly but it was intensely hot and I remember feeling the sweat running down my forehead. In the loft I still have the programme. On the night, I carefully slipped it between my jumper and my leather jacket to avoid creasing it.

I WAS THERE: DAVE BALL

THE NEC WAS an all standing venue then and there must have been 15,000 crammed in. The atmosphere was, as usual for a Queen concert, electric. Freddie the master showman was on top form.

Dave Ball remembers Freddie being on top form

I WAS THERE: PAUL HANSON, AGE 18

I TRAVELLED FROM Huddersfield to Birmingham in my mate's Morris 1300. It was my first ever concert. I had a ticket to watch the Sex Pistols' last ever UK gig at Ivanhoe's Club in Huddersfield on Christmas Day 1977 but chose to visit my grandma and grandad instead. Me and my mates were seated fifth row from the front. What a fantastic day!

Paul Hanson passed on seeing the Sex Pistols but was there for the Crazy tour

APOLLO
26 & 27 NOVEMBER 1979, MANCHESTER, UK

I WAS THERE: MARTIN GALTREY

FREDDIE CAME ON stage sitting on Superman's shoulders. Great opener....

I WAS THERE: GILL MARSHALL

WE SAT ON the front row of the circle and I swear you could feel it bouncing. It was fabulous. They sounded as good live as they did on record.

I WAS THERE: ANDY FETHERS

I WENT TO a lot of gigs in those days - living in Macclesfield we used to get the train down to Manchester

Andy Fethers' ticket for the Manchester show

and most of the bands played the Apollo. It was the only time I saw them play live. The lights were amazing. The whole show was amazing.

APOLLO THEATRE
30 NOVEMBER & 1 DECEMBER 1979, GLASGOW, UK

I WAS THERE: FRANK MURPHY

MY MOTHER BOUGHT me a camera when I was eight and I thought, 'Why didn't I get a pair of football boots?' But it paid dividends, as I ended up working as a freelance music photographer, covering most of the events at the Apollo in Glasgow and pushing

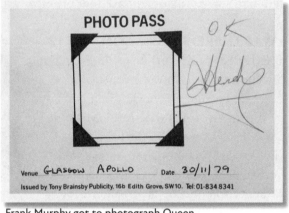

Frank Murphy got to photograph Queen

photographs to the likes of *NME*, *Sounds* and *Melody Maker*. The first gig I covered was Alice Cooper in 1972. I photographed Queen twice, and saw them five times in total. The first time they were a support act for Mott the Hoople. I was lucky enough to get the approval to photograph their first headline gig. It might be the Glaswegian in me but I remember thinking, 'These guys are a bit too posh and well educated to be rockers.' But the place was bouncing. Bands would often start or end their tours at the Apollo because it had such a great reputation.

There was always something about Queen. Their shows were a bit more creative and better choreographed, both in terms of their music but also their costumes and their sets. They used to have huge banks of white lighting behind them, which with the dry ice made it difficult from a photographic point of view. One time at the Apollo Freddie had this white outfit on and technically it was quite difficult to photograph. But their costumes were amazing and their musicianship was outstanding. I always remember them being great gigs to go to, hence my sometimes going just as a fan as opposed to as a photographer so that I could enjoy the whole gig.

The rule still to this day is that you get three songs and then you have to stop taking photographs and just watch, or move to a different part of the auditorium, although as you get more involved with particular bands you get more leeway. The promoters and the management teams used to be quite strict. The rule is three numbers, no flash and out. It used to be quite good to get home and into the dark room and find out whether you'd caught the shots you hoped you'd got. I was taking pictures of Jackson Browne and I had 36 exposures on the one frame because the film had stuck. You don't have that problem with digital.

I WAS THERE: JIM LAWSON, AGE 15

I SKIPPED SCHOOL to go and stand in line for my ticket. It was my first concert ever and I went on my own. I remember getting to my seat and being in awe that I was just six rows from the front, just right of centre. I thought the stage was very small in height. But it was the bank of lights from the *Live Killers* album cover, and when the band were about to take the

Jim Lawson was at the Apollo

stage, they began to stand up like a huge door opening up from the floor. Some of the lights were flashing and when the band came on, all the lights shone brightly. I can remember looking around and everything was lit up. The Apollo looked so cool. What a show they put on.

I WAS THERE: JOHN GRAHAM

THAT WINTER IN Scotland was particularly cold. My friend and I stood outside the Apollo from 4pm, both frozen but first in the queue. Everyone else started turning up around 6.30pm. Around 6pm, a van stopped outside and two of the crew jumped out, opened the back door and took out a huge hamper. It was the band's stage costumes. Once inside the venue, we ran upstairs where there were tables laden with merchandise such as programmes, posters, badges and scarves.

We took our seats and the place started filling up. I can't remember what time the band came on, but chart music was playing over the PA system and suddenly it stopped, the lights were put out and we knew we were seconds away from them coming on. Everyone was cheering and whistling and the noise was deafening, like thunder rumbling in the distance. The stage filled with dry ice and the rumble just got louder and louder as the lighting rig swung into action. The lights were bright, the noise was reaching a climax and just when you thought it couldn't get any louder, the whole stage exploded as the band emerged from the dry ice. The volume of noise was unbelievable - and they were on!

Freddie liked to talk to us a lot, throw water over us and swear at us, but we loved it and everything he did got a huge cheer! After running around the stage and finishing either 'Somebody to Love' or 'Don't Stop Me Now', he climbed exhausted onto the top of the piano, lay on his back with his legs in the air and said 'I've been shagged'. He got a huge cheer for that!

Brian was not happy about something with his sound and was having a heated exchange with the crew at the side. Roger stood up to drum during 'Let Me Entertain You', John constantly danced over his side of the stage and up on the drum riser, and Freddie, in black leathers and red knee pads, just amazed everyone with his antics everywhere. The light show was fantastic. The bass drum had the *Jazz* album cover on it.

John Graham's scarf from the Crazy tour

WAS THERE: DAVID YOUNG, AGE 16

WE GOT THE 6.30am bus into Glasgow to queue for tickets. It was so cold they allowed us to form a loop in the box office before it opened. I'd already read that they were going to leave the stage during the operatic bit of 'Bohemian Rhapsody' but when Brian burst on for the solo it was gobsmacking. For 'Crazy Little Thing', Freddie came on with his fingers

APOLLO THEATRE, GLASGOW

Harvey Goldsmith Entertainments presents

QUEEN

IN CONCERT

Saturday, 1st December, 1979
at 8 p.m.

STALLS

No 36 T

TICKET £4.75
TO BE RETAINED
TICKETS CANNOT BE EXCHANGED

David Young's Glasgow Apollo ticket

placed in a D shape on the acoustic ready for him to play the intro. I remember Roger having beer in his skins for his solo so that it sprayed everywhere. I've seen hundreds of bands and Queen are still in my top three. I recently got a bootleg of this gig. All the hairs in the back of my neck went up when I listened to it.

I WAS THERE: JO SEGARRA

I FIRST SAW Queen on *Top of the Pops* singing 'Seven Seas of Rhye'. It wasn't just a great song - there was something about Freddie. He was so charismatic with his offbeat good looks. I was nine years old at the time. They kept my interest with subsequent excellent singles.

I befriended Caroline in 1979; she was a few years older than me and disabled, with cerebral palsy and partially sighted. I was an experienced babysitter by that time, and her parents needed someone to be with

her if they went out. She was a big music lover with really good taste, and Queen was her favourite. That December they were coming to Glasgow to play the Apollo and Caroline's mother asked me, if she bought the tickets, would I 'mind' accompanying Caroline to the show? Would I mind? My parents were extremely strict and not fans of modern music, and they would never have let me go under any other circumstance!

On the day of the show, 'Crazy Little Thing Called Love' was riding high in the charts. When the curtain went up, there was Freddie striding across the stage in his black leather cap and jacket; it was like a dream come true and I will never forget that image in my whole life. The whole show was amazing but for me the highlights were 'Crazy Little Thing', with everyone singing and clapping along,

Joe McSwiggan roadied for Queen after first seeing them as a fan

and "39', with the band all sitting in a row at the front of the stage with acoustic guitars and Roger with a tambourine.

But if the show was terrific, the best was yet to come. We met Caroline's mother at the side entrance as agreed, to avoid a crush, and she told us that she had had a word with one of the security staff. She explained that her daughter was visually impaired and would love the chance to view the stage up close so would it be possible for her to take a closer look once everyone had left the area? The guy said he would see what he could do. He came back and told her that this was a more than reasonable request, since they usually had to deal with people saying they wanted to go backstage and meet the band, so they sent a stage manager to escort Caroline and myself up to the stage, with all the instruments and equipment still there! We each got to sit at Freddie's piano and touch his sweaty towel, and I pointed out to Caroline the big gong at the back that Roger strikes at the end of 'Bohemian Rhapsody'. She was ecstatic, and so was I.

This was such a kindness on behalf of the Apollo staff and no doubt people who worked for the band as well. After 42 years, this still stands up as one of the best nights of my life. Losing Freddie so young was very sad and made the memory all the more cherished. Queen is still a favourite on YouTube and my children, not born then, know who they are and admire them too!

I WAS THERE: JOE MCSWIGGAN

I MET ALL the band in 1979 on the *Crazy* tour when they were playing two nights at the Apollo. They were all going back to the Albany Hotel and headed out to Saints and Sinners in St Vincent Street, which is now King Tut's Wah Wah Hut. They were all great and had time to speak to everyone. They signed my programme, although sadly I have not got it any more. But years later I worked as a local roadie and production runner at the SECC, the Hydro and other Glasgow venues and so worked with Queen+Paul Rodgers and Queen and Adam Lambert.

I WAS THERE: TOMMY WEIR

I WAS INTRODUCED to them by an older friend who had seen them support Mott the Hoople at the Apollo and then in their own right. What caught my attention was his collection of memorabilia, including album covers torn from display stands, a drumstick from Roger and a tambourine Freddie had launched from the stage. Said friend bought me a ticket for my 16th birthday in October 1979 for the second of two nights gigs at the Glasgow Apollo. The only problem was the gig wasn't until December, a tortuous two months away. It couldn't come quick enough.

On the night, we travelled to Glasgow with huge excitement building up inside of me at the prospect of seeing my favourites in the flesh at long last. Inside the Apollo, the scene was one of darkness and a musty odour from the years of neglect but, boy, did that place crackle with atmosphere on a gig night, especially if it was sold out, as this was. I was a teenager trying to soak it all in, what the history of this place was, the bands who had played there before – and, more importantly, what I was about to experience. I was determined to get some memories to keep and decided to smuggle my small Kodak instamatic camera down my trousers to get it past the infamous Apollo bouncers... mission accomplished.

We got to our seats, although seats were never really used in this place as everyone stood and stretched their necks to see their heroes, the Apollo stage famously being 15 feet high. As the lights went down, the noise from the crowd was unbelievable. I've heard loud crowds at football matches, but this was much more intense and definitely more atmospheric. The thunder began, the dry ice started to meander its way from the stage and over the crowd, and this place was going crazy. And not a note had been played!

Then the pizza oven lighting rig (as on the *Live Killers* album cover) began to rise from the stage and there they were, my idols, blasting out their faster version of 'We Will Rock You'. Me? I was just standing on my seat, mouth wide open and trying to make sense of the whole thing, seeing my idols amidst a mass of frenzied Glaswegians screaming and shouting and singing along. It was surreal but hugely exciting, and beyond any dreams or expectations I had beforehand.

The crowd roared approval at, and sang along with, every song. It was amazing as they flew from one song to the next. 'Somebody to Love', one of my favourites, became a huge hand clapping singalong and it was great to join in! Up next was 'Mustapha', a song I've never really liked much, and then into 'Death on Two Legs', a dark and aggressive rocker which I love. Then Roger got to sing 'I'm in Love With my Car', and I only found out later that Roger forgot the words to it!

'You're My Best Friend' was next, the first Queen single I ever bought, and then 'Save Me', Freddie announcing it was the first time it had been played live. It was also the first time I had seen Freddie with a guitar when he played 'Crazy Little Thing Called Love'. All the familiar tunes were there, all with audience participation, and then they went into the small acoustic session, singing ''39' and 'Love of my Life'. Well, they didn't really sing that one as the audience completely took over it. It was my first experience of the Glasgow Apollo choir, 3,000 manic Glaswegians all singing in unison... magical.

I remember trying to get a good photo of when they blasted back on stage after the operatic part of 'Bohemian Rhapsody', the stage exploding in smoke and all different colours. After that, the place was even more manic but went up a level again when they played 'Tie Your Mother Down' and 'Sheer Heart Attack'.

I knew we were nearing the end of the show and was still trying to take in what I had witnessed. It was just an incredible night, topped off with the encore of 'We Will Rock You' and 'We Are the Champions' and the obligatory 'God Save the Queen.' We filed out of this bear pit of a place, and made a mad dash down to the city centre to catch the late bus home.

CITY HALL
3 DECEMBER 1979, NEWCASTLE, UK

I WAS THERE: BRIDGET DAVICO, AGE 14

IT WAS MY 14th birthday. My Queen fan club pen pal, Janet, had bought me a ticket to see Queen. I was really excited to meet her and to see Queen, and travelled by coach to Newcastle where Janet's mum picked me up and took me to her house to await Janet's arrival home from school.

We set off to City Hall to wait backstage for Queen to arrive. We were very giddy. It seemed like ages but they arrived and, oh my God, I saw Freddie first. I called out his name and he heard

Bridget's 14th birthday present was meeting Queen backstage

me, came over and gave me a hug. I couldn't believe it! Janet was after Roger, her favourite member. It happened so quickly and everyone was congratulating me. One lady said that Freddie loved his young fans. I was reeling, I couldn't believe it. I thought, 'I'm never going to wash the arm that went around him ever again!'

Janet got Roger's autograph. She was really happy and smiling ear to ear. So was I.

The concert was amazing, we had the best time. Queen were phenomenal. I've never forgotten how I washed my hair with my left hand for a long time after. It was just the best time.

I WAS THERE: PETER SMITH

I DIDN'T THINK that I would ever see Queen back in the City Hall again. By 1979 they were a massive band more used to playing arenas and stadiums than provincial concert halls. But the *Crazy* tour included two nights at Newcastle City Hall. I made sure that we got tickets - no more hanging around outside trying to blag my way in and no climbing through a window this time.

As soon as we entered the venue it was very clear just how big a band Queen now were, and how much of a 'show' we were about to witness. A massive extended stage seemed to take up almost half of the stalls, complete with a walkway for Freddie to come out into the crowd. A mass of lights surrounded the stage set up, and the drum kit stood majestically on a massive, raised platform. This was very different from the early days.

The show itself was ultra-professional, and in parts very staged, at times a little too much. The Queen I saw from 1979 on was majestic, pomp rock, a true spectacle. I must also admit to missing some of the raw rock 'n' roll that the early band were so good at. And at each concert, Freddie seemed to have grown a little more in confidence, craziness and stature; he began to truly command the audience, and his vocal strength also seemed to grow alongside his presence. This was the last time I was to see Queen in such an intimate setting. After this, I would watch them from the pitch or stands of a football stadium. It was inevitable that their career would progress that way; their anthems and Freddie's stage presence were made for the rousing singalongs of the terraces.

The City Hall show that night saw Queen take us through all their classics in a long and very impressive set. It was almost as it they were marking their territory as one of the UK's and the world's major bands. We left the hall that night, feeling privileged to have seen something truly legendary, unique and spectacular.

I WAS THERE: JANET KAMAL

I NEVER REALLY noticed Queen until the video of 'Bohemian Rhapsody' on Christmas Day *Top of the Pops* in 1975. I was 10 years old and absolutely spellbound watching Freddie with his eyeliner and amazing features. I thought he was like a real life pharaoh from ancient Egypt, and I was captivated by the harmonies and the now famous operatic section of the song. I couldn't wait for the Sunday night Top 20 show on the radio, so I could record it onto a cassette player and then listen to it whenever I wanted to. God only knows what words I made up singing along, but they weren't 'Bismillah' or 'monstrosity'.

I used all my pocket money on the £3.75 needed to buy *A Day at the Races* from Presto supermarket on its release. which I then listened to obsessively until I could afford to buy *News of the World*! I would lie on the floor looking at the inside of the *Day at the Races* sleeve, wondering what it would be like to see them live. My chance came in December 1979 and I bought tickets to see them at Newcastle City Hall, both nights.

When the day came, I couldn't really believe it. We waited outside the backstage door as soon as we got into town to try and get autographs, but they were bundled in the hall by security. I managed to get a photo of John and Brian, and one of Roger's back! Freddie was flanked by security.

When the lights went out and the intro started, all the hair on the back of my neck and arms stood on end. It was real! Obviously, the gig was amazing. I remember hearing 'Save Me' for the first time, as *The Game* hadn't yet been released, and absolutely loving it. I couldn't wait for the next night as I had wonderful tickets, front row balcony near to the stage. That was amazing for such a near and clear view, which really spoilt me for later years. I remember the bomb that used to go off after the operatic section of 'Bohemian Rhapsody'. I was so close I could smell it!

EMPIRE THEATRE
6 & 7 DECEMBER 1979, LIVERPOOL, UK

I WAS THERE: KEVIN BAREFOOT

IT WAS IN a music class that our music teacher played *A Night at the Opera* and I was immediately hooked by 'Death on Two Legs'. The lyrics and the music opened up a whole new world. I quickly saved up and bought the first three albums and from then onwards bought every album and more or less every single. I have great memories of rushing to the nearest music shop when a single was released just so that I could buy the single with a picture sleeve. These were proudly displayed in my bedroom whilst the singles were placed in bright new record sleeves, titles carefully hand written.

I was a young lad from Rotherham in South Yorkshire with hardly any money but in 1979 a friend and I managed to get over to Liverpool Empire with no tickets and bought one each outside. Wow, just wow. We were six or seven rows from the front and the band were everything I'd hoped for and more. I had taken some old sixpenny pieces with me to give to Brian but that never happened. Security was very tight as we all had to remain in our seats or where we were standing. I recall Freddie orchestrating the audience and us all singing 'Love of My Life' with him. Had he wanted it, we would still have been there singing it today. The encore saw Freddie come on stage in a sequined ballet outfit on Superman's shoulders. Only he could do that! At some point he launched his tambourine into the crowd where obviously everyone tried to grab it. Unbelievably it fell at my feet and to this day I can see the slow motion in my head as I leaned down to pick up the prize, only for the person next to me to snatch it before I could. Imagine having that as a Queen fan (sad face now!).

I never saw them again with Freddie. I remember the day they announced his death. I was driving to work and the radio presenter said Freddie had passed and then played 'You're My Best Friend'. I had to stop the car and I cried like a baby. Even now I still feel that emotion - how strange.

The radio presenter said Freddie had passed and then played 'You're My Best Friend'. I stopped the car and cried like a baby

---

When Brian and Roger announced the tribute concert, I was in and what a wonderfully bitter sweet event it was. My wife and I travelled to London, excitedly queued on Wembley Way and saw bands we would not normally have seen perform during the day. I recall the hysteria of Axl Rose passing us in a Rolls-Royce whilst queuing, but it was nothing compared to the glory of Queen performing with these guys. They did Freddie proud. My wife and I still laugh about the hand clapping on

'Radio Ga Ga'. Her timing was awful but enthusiastic to say the least. Leaving Wembley with thousands of loyal excited fans and talking about the experience was in some strange way quite cathartic. We all loved Freddie and still do.

Since then, I've seen Brian and Roger with both artists (twice with Adam) and whilst both are impressive singers, there can be only one, eh? Adam does Freddie proud, and I firmly believe he would approve. Of course, the love never ends and as soon as *Bohemian Rhapsody* hit the screens, I was there on day one at the local IMAX to get the immersive experience.

44 years on from that music lesson and 'Death on Two Legs', Queen gave me the greatest music, the biggest smiles, the most awesome memories and of course the saddest moments too. Thanks, guys.

HIPPODROME
9 DECEMBER 1979, BRISTOL, UK

I WAS THERE: DAVE HOLLAND

I HAD BEEN to the *Day at the Races* tour at the Bristol Hippodrome, having finally persuaded a bunch of my friends that Queen were the real deal live, and my parents that as a 16-year-old I was responsible enough to mingle with scary rock fans and not come home smoking a joint and calling everybody 'maaan'. That first gig had been an oral and visual assault that still burned inside me, and the culmination of years of vinyl collecting, music paper hoarding and hero worshipping on a grand scale. I had finally got to witness the explosion in a music shop window that was the live Queen experience.

Having become the huge band they were always destined to be, Queen had decided to go back to basics and stage a *Crazy* tour of the provincial theatres that had given them the leg up to superstardom in the first place. The Bristol Hippodrome was on the schedule.

If you wanted to go to a gig, you either threw yourself on the mercy of the UK postal system - risking your fevered request being stuck in a postal strike - or presented yourself in person at the venue's box office. The tickets for Queen's *Crazy* tour went on sale at 9am on a Friday morning. Those same bunch of friends who had attended the '77 gig were now almost as desperate to go as me. How desperate? Well, me and Colin 'Dog' Gardner decided that there was nothing for it but to camp out all night. We finished work at 5.30pm, met at the steps of the

Hippodrome with a sleeping bag and a wad of cash, and made ourselves uncomfortable for the night.

We got a lot of sympathetic looks and plenty of small change from the theatre-going crowd attending a performance of *Swan Lake* by the Russian State Ballet, having been mistaken for a couple of homeless urchins. By about 2am we had been joined by a further 20 rabid Queen fans and spent the rest of the night singing, napping and fielding questions from curious coppers who, once we explained what we were up to, nodded appreciatively and let us carry on.

Amongst the 20 or so of us were a couple of local Italian lads who promised us all 'a treat'. They didn't disappoint. At some point after midnight a very nice limo purred up. 'It's Freddie!' somebody exclaimed hopefully. It wasn't, but it was the next best thing – the father of one of the Italian lads was a local restaurant owner, bearing boxes of pizzas for the lot of us. At 9am, Dog and myself were at the front of a by now very large queue and bagged front row tickets.

On 9th December 1979 there we were in the front row, so close you could see the sweat pouring off them, and close enough to occasionally think you had caught Freddie's eye. The performance was phenomenal and we caught the full force of the energy Queen always whipped up on stage.

There was a scary moment. Roger Taylor kicked off the intro beat to 'Sheer Heart Attack' as they always did live. He didn't always kick it off quite this fast, though. It was like a through train thundering past and, being a drummer myself and not averse to a bit of punk rock, even I thought it was a bit pacey. It seems that John Deacon agreed with me as he began to struggle to keep up. After plenty of glowering at the blurry drummer, he made it to the end of the song (just), unshouldered his bass and hurled it full force at the forest of cymbals that adorned the left side of Mr Taylor's kit.

The lights did a 1970s blackout and the band sprinted off. We all looked at each other in amazement. Was this part of the show? I hadn't read about it being a feature of the *Crazy* tour, although it looked pretty crazy to me. Had we just witnessed the end of Queen? The PA began playing music to cover up the shouting backstage and the stage was suddenly invaded by fireflies. Well, it was actually roadies bearing torches frantically rebuilding the drums. 'They must be coming back on then', my punk rocker brother pointed out sagely.

And they did, as if nothing had happened. We got several encores and the pizza oven light show tilted backwards for 'We Will Rock You' and 'We are the Champions' and made me feel light-headed from the front row with the almost unbearable heat of it. God knows how Roger Taylor coped with it being just behind him.

I was lucky enough to see the band on several other occasions, including Milton Keynes and the now legendary Saturday Wembley 1986 *Magic* tour show. All have been special and unique in their way. And I think that also sums up Queen for me.

I WAS THERE: EMILY LEWIS

I WAS SIX years old and Queen were my favourite band. I had grown up listening to them as my mum and dad had *A Night at the Opera* and *Sheer Heart Attack* - my favourite. I treasured my own seven inch copy of 'Tie your Mother Down' and, having an old record player in my bedroom, would blast it out on maximum volume when I woke in the mornings - about 6am!

Emily Lewis went to the Hippodrome for the Crazy tour but didn't stay

My parents had obviously heard that Queen were doing a tour of small venues and had done their best to keep the fact from me. Money was short and there was no way they could have afforded to buy tickets. At the time, my dad's sister and her husband ran a small entertainment-booking agency in Bristol and were given two tickets for the concert. Originally for members of the press, my aunt had been told that she could use the tickets herself or give them to whoever she wished. She and my uncle had a baby, so she very kindly gave the tickets to my parents. I still can't believe that they decided to give one of the tickets to me, rather than go themselves and ship me out to a babysitter, but there you go.

Armed with my recently purchased copy of *Live Killers* (in the hope of getting it signed at the stage door after the show - hindsight tells me this probably wouldn't have happened as Queen liked to 'take the money and run', a quote from a Freddie biography), Dad and I got into the Ford Escort and off we went. We parked up just round the corner from the Bristol Hippodrome. My dad was disabled - he had haemophilia and couldn't walk or stand for long periods - so parking was never an issue with his trusty blue badge, and in we went.

There was no support act. The safety curtain slowly rose and through the fog of dry ice, a bank of lights appeared, much like a scaled-down version of the front of my *Live Killers* LP. I was so excited… and then, there they were. My idols!

It quickly became apparent that my six-year-old eardrums were not seasoned to loud music. Those maximum volume renditions of 'Tie Your Mother Down' at six in the morning had done little to prepare me for how loud they would be. Dad had the foresight to bring cotton wool, which I stuffed into my ears, but it was too little too late. A lady behind us offered a handkerchief. (Huh?! Maybe it was offered by way of a gag, to shut up the kid in front complaining that it was too loud).

Barely six songs in, and with me crying and holding my ears in distress, my dad graciously admitted defeat and we left. We weren't allowed to wait in the foyer, so went home. Dad could have dropped me home and gone back, but he decided that he'd already have missed too much. I didn't think much of his sacrifice but as the years ticked by, I increasingly felt guilty at denying Dad the chance to see a full Queen concert live. He never complained about our early departure or told me off but he must have been gutted. He always marvelled at how brilliant Queen had been, even in just the short time we'd been there, and talked about the concert with much fondness.

I will never forget sitting down in front of the TV with him to watch Queen perform at *Live Aid*. That was a really special shared experience. Dad also loved David Bowie and who else but he could have followed Queen on that day? Fantastic. I resolved that one day I would treat Dad to tickets to a Queen concert. I started my first job in August 1991. On Sunday 24th November that year, just after 7pm, Freddie passed away. I remember hearing the news on Simon Mayo's Radio 1 *Breakfast Show* followed by him playing 'Radio Ga Ga'. I went into work that morning fighting to hold back the tears.

My eldest daughter was born in 2002 on Sunday 24th November, just after 7pm – coincidence? My other daughter was born on my grandad's birthday. My grandad's name? Freddie. The very thought of having to leave a concert early due to my child finding it too loud are unthinkable. Whether because of that experience, or *Live Aid*, or just my love of their music, I have felt a bond with Queen my entire life. I genuinely look upon Brian as a 'kindly uncle' and have meant many times to write to him and Roger, but never have.

And lastly, my lovely, patient dad passed away in March this year. The chance for him and I to see Queen together in any form (with Paul Rodgers or Adam Lambert) has gone. Maybe, just maybe, he's up there telling Freddie about that fateful night in December 1979 and they are having a right old laugh about it.

TIFFANY'S
17 DECEMBER 1979, PURLEY, UK

I WAS THERE: DEREK COLLINSON

I WAS LUCKY to see Queen at Tiffany's, a nightclub in Purley, Surrey that only held a few hundred people. It was a birthday present from the same friend that took me to see Led Zeppelin in 1975 (what a great mate he was). This was their *Crazy* tour, where they played small venues promoting the new single, 'Crazy Little Thing Called Love'. I remember walking in with my friend and across the dance floor to the bar to get a pint. We went to the front of the floor, to the left of the stage, only about a foot away from the stage. After a couple more beers, the lights started to dim and entry music started to play and to our right we could just see Brian May, Roger Taylor and John Deacon coming onto the stage in the darkness, but there was no sign of Freddie. They then started playing 'Jailhouse Rock' but there was still no sign of Freddie. But we could hear him humming his trademark 'ooohhhh!'.

The next thing we saw was a large man dressed as Superman coming onto the stage just to my left. He stood in front of my friend and I, with his hands on his hips and his legs apart, and we could then hear Freddie's voice. All I could see was these bright red Superman pants in front of me, but I then noticed feet either side of his hips and - lo and behold - there was Freddie, sitting on Superman's shoulders. I raised my glass to him and shouted out 'alright Freddie' and I am sure he winked at me. It was a truly crazy concert but what an evening, with no hassle from bouncers or idiots. I'm so glad I saw this as it felt very personal. Alas I no longer have the ticket but I do still have the programme, tucked up safely inside my copy of *Live Killers*.

LEWISHAM ODEON
20 DECEMBER 1979, LONDON, UK

I WAS THERE: CRAIG WOOD

BACK THEN AS a kid I only had pocket money so I had to save up
for my next concert, which turned out to be the *Crazy* tour of London.
I went with a school friend. Lewisham Odeon was a pokey little place,
and a much smaller affair than the grandeur of Wembley Empire Pool,
but it was local and I could get a bus. Me and my mate were standing
up at the back waving our scarves and singing with great gusto, while
the rest of the audience were sitting on their arses in front of us. I was
thinking, 'Get up, you boring people.' By the end they were! Another
thing I remember from this concert is the 'Overture' at the start. A silent
hum which grew and grew and then thunder and lights and smoke as the
smaller lighting rig took off, revealing the stage immersed in light. New
songs on this tour were the tracks from *Jazz* including 'Fat Bottomed
Girls', 'If You Can't Beat Them' and 'Don't Stop Me Now'.

I WAS THERE: ROB PALLADINO

AS A SPRIGHTLY 10-year-old in London's East End. I recall hearing
'Killer Queen' and 'Now I'm Here' and getting my head turned from
the chart pop of the time. The moment I bit was the first viewing of the
video for 'Bohemian Rhapsody.' In time I bought the single, with 'I'm
in Love with My Car' on the B-side, and it was rarely, if ever, off the
turntable. My mother never got to hear her small collection of Dean
Martin songs again. Then, for Christmas of '75, she bought me a copy
of *A Night at the Opera* and my life was changed forever.

The faded-in piano at the start of 'Death on Two Legs', still one of my
all-time favourite Queen songs, amazed and intrigued me, as did the rest
of that now legendary album. 'The Prophet's Song' really caught my
imagination and began my lifelong love of progressive rock/metal. I had
entered a new world and I wanted more. I bought *Sheer Heart Attack*, *Queen
II* and the debut album in short order. I loved them all but *Queen II* was
my favourite.

I first saw Queen play live on the *Crazy Tour of London* at the long since
demolished Lewisham Odeon. I managed to get one of the last tickets
standing way at the back of the circle. From what I could see, it was a
great show even if the sound up there in the gods left something to be

murky and muggy. I next saw Queen at the Hammersmith Odeon six days later on December 26th. It was the final show of the *Crazy* tour and part of the *Concerts for the People of Kampuchea* staged to raise money for the victims of war-torn Cambodia. The night Queen played was, and still ranks, as one of the finest live performances I've seen to this day by anyone. From the cheesy opening of 'Jailhouse Rock' through to 'Champions' they were as perfect as any band could be.

The last time I ever saw them was the next year on *The Game* tour at Wembley Arena. It was a freezing cold December evening. They were superb and I was still a fan, but I felt they were going through a songwriting block. From the debut album through to *News of the World* they hardly put a foot wrong but with *Jazz* it sounded like the band were starting to struggle for half decent material. *The Game* followed and then the disaster that is *Hot Space*, which is perhaps the least liked album in the Queen catalogue. Half-arsed disco was never my thing. They made a couple of decent albums in *The Works* and the wonderful swansong, *Innuendo*, but all too often early to mid-Eighties Queen sounded like they were no longer capable of delivering albums that had cohesion, direction or passion.

With Adam Lambert, they are simply a cash cow. To be honest the band finished when Freddie died and was further weakened by John Deacon's decision to retire. This version is really nothing more than a cynical cash-grab and has sullied the name of one of the truly innovative and talented bands I've ever heard.

ALEXANDRA PALACE
22 DECEMBER 1979, LONDON, UK

I WAS THERE: ADRIAN GRANT
I SAW QUEEN many times in the Seventies, including once at Alexandra Palace. Freddie opened with the line, 'Welcome to this shit hole!'

I WAS THERE: DAVID HALL
THE *CRAZY* TOUR of 1979 would see me at three of their concerts, starting at the new Birmingham NEC and then a few days later Manchester Apollo. Then an additional concert was announced. The new gig was at London's Alexandra Palace. This was a truly awesome gig. Whilst waiting for the doors to open we caught a fleeting glimpse of the band as they arrived. We then stood in the cold for several hours,

cheered only by the sound of the soundcheck within the hall - 'one two, one two' - and then the guitar strains of 'The Hero'. Suddenly the doors opened and a huge surge ensued as we entered the hall and were thrust like champagne corks to the front, finding ourselves on the right hand side of the central catwalk. More tense waiting ensued and then to a burst of light and smoke the frenetic sound of 'Jailhouse Rock' swept across the hall and there, towering above us and resplendent in black and red leather was the greatest front man of all time, the legend that is - and was - Freddie Mercury.

A concert filled with many highlights followed. Freddie dropping his microphone into the crowd, to be eagerly grabbed by myself and my friend alongside me, so we could sing live during the vocal extravaganza section of 'Get Down, Make Love' will long live in my memory. 'Bohemian Rhapsody' also stands out as it was delayed by what seemed like four or five minutes as the crowd continued singing 'Crazy Little Thing Called Love', eventually compelling the band to join them - a truly magical moment. It was also the first time I heard their then new single, 'Save Me', for which the video was filmed during the concert. If only the original footage could be released, as I would surely be visible singing along in the crowd below Freddie. This was a truly great gig by the greatest band of all time and at what is my favourite phase in the band's history.

I would go on to see them again at Birmingham in 1980 and Leeds and Milton Keynes in 1982. All great gigs but nothing could surpass the night at Ally Pally. I have since seen them play both with Paul Rogers and the amazing Adam Lambert. The technology on their 2017 tour was out of this world, making the pyrotechnics and lighting of the Seventies and Eighties seem tame in comparison. However, no one could hold an audience in the palm of his hand for a thrilling two hours better than the great Freddie Mercury.

I WAS THERE: LESLIE LANE

WITH QUEEN PLAYING smaller venues, tickets were going to be hard to get. I decided that Alexandra Palace, as one of the bigger venues and holding around 5,000, was our best hope of success. Four of us would be going - my mate Alan James and two others, John McGuigan (a soul fan) and Tony Heath (a Mod who was into The Jam). I was all set to send off our postal applications and hope for the best. Just before I did, Alan phoned to say his concession-owning brother Andy would get tickets for us. Rather nervously, I agreed and then waited weeks with no news. All Andy would say was 'don't worry'.

Come the day of the show, and with still no news or tickets, we met at Alan's house. Their mum said she knew Andy was having trouble getting hold of tickets as the show was sold out. I was thinking that we weren't going to the show and that I should have booked them myself. Just then, Andy turned up in his big Jag and said 'jump in lads, let's get up to this gig'. He said nothing else.

When we arrived, the queue for this all standing gig was huge. The venue only had one big entrance, so the first in would be at the front and the rest would fill in towards the back. I was thinking, 'We are going to be right at the back,' when Andy said to the security guy 'where is the front door?'. The security guy pointed the way and Andy told us to follow him. Loads of people were looking at us as if to say 'where do you think you are going?'

We arrived at the entrance and, lo and behold, the guy on the door was an old friend of Andy's. Andy said, 'I'm taking four lads in to see Queen. Where's the special guest list for Queen?' So Andy hadn't been able to get tickets but had somehow managed to get us onto Queen's guest list. The four of us were in before the doors had even opened and we went straight to the stage edge with a few other guests of Queen. I couldn't believe it. I would be almost within touching distance of my heroes.

The crown lighting rig had been replaced by the pizza oven, a huge bank of lights that covered the whole stage. Like the crown rig, it started off quite close to the floor of the stage and rose up into place, but this rig shone down onto the crowd as well as the band.

As in the 'Crazy Little Thing Called Love' video, Freddie came out on stage all in leather including a leather cap. John was now sporting a new crew cut/skinhead style haircut, Roger was just Roger, as cool as ever, and Brian had his long curly hair, the same hairstyle he still has to this day! Roger's drum kit was huge and he still had the massive gong behind him that he would only use once during the show, at the end of 'Bohemian Rhapsody'.

They played four songs from *Jazz*. 'Let Me Entertain You' was perfect to follow on from 'We Will Rock You'. 'Crazy Little Thing' went down very well. Strangely, at some point during the show a bicycle chain was thrown onto the stage aimed at Freddie. Luckily, it missed him and I don't think he even noticed. Queen played a brand new song, 'Save Me', which was going to be the new single and Freddie informed us that they were filming the song's chorus for the video and for us to really get into the song, and to wave our arms and sing along. Sure enough, the live section of the video they released was from our gig.

It was great to see Queen so close up. And my two mates? The soul fan said he quite enjoyed the show and that Queen were 'quite good'. The Mod said that Queen were good but 'not as good live' as The Jam. But in the years since, both have quite proudly told people that they saw Queen!

HAMMERSMITH ODEON
26 DECEMBER 1979, LONDON, UK

I WAS THERE: PAUL PHILLIPS, AGE 14

A FRIEND PLAYED the *Sheer Heart Attack* album to me. I quickly purchased it and then *Jazz* and *Live Killers*, which is when I realised that groups played live to their fans. I had previously thought that rock music was a purely studio recording affair. How naive was I? Being allowed to go to the Hammersmith gig required permission from my parents. A double plea as it was on a traditional 'family day', Boxing Day. They reluctantly gave their consent, which was fortunate as I had already forked out my £4.50. Me and the friend who had opened my world to Queen arrived at Hammersmith Odeon, my first ever gig, and were amazed at the army of denim and leather clad rock fans everywhere – in the long gone Britannia pub, milling around outside and in the foyer of the theatre. The venue reeked of tobacco and weed.

I recall the merchandise stand with its t-shirts, badges, patches, sweatshirts, scarves and programmes. I bought a scarf with the *Crazy Tour*-styled Queen logo on it and two programmes. We entered the downstairs stalls and found our seats, two rows from the back. I was amazed by the buzzing atmosphere. The auditorium was semi-lit. Smoke hung over the thick atmosphere. Queen's crown lighting rig was hovering horizontally just about Roger Taylor's black drum kit. The kit glistened in the half light. Either side of the stage were huge towers of Marshall speakers. I was in awe.

The show was supposed to start at 8pm, but rock bands weren't punctual as I was about to find out. The delay just added to the anticipation, drama and atmosphere. The dry ice began to emerge on stage, the lights dimmed and then blacked out to a huge roars from the crowd and Queen burst onto the stage to a fast version of 'Jailhouse

Rock', as the crown lighting rig elevated and burst into white light. My heart was beating out of my chest to the rhythm of the drum beat. I had never heard anything so loud and powerful before.

The first song choice concerned me as their hit single, 'Crazy Little Thing Called Love', was true rock 'n' roll, but I needn't have worried as they moved into a marvellous set mirroring much of the *Live Killers* album. I could not take my eyes off Freddie Mercury, clad in red leather trousers and blue knee pads. He was so alive and energetic. The band had such a tight sound and the mix was incredible. The red, white and green crown lights overhead and the lights on the drum riser burnt into my memory. Highlights of the gig included 'Somebody to Love', which I had never heard before, a new song, 'Save Me', with Brian on piano, Roger's drum solo and 'Get Down, Make Love'. Freddie surprised us all by donning his 'I can only play three shitty little chords' guitar for 'Crazy Little Thing Called Love.'

The encores were incredible, with Freddie upending some of the Marshall speakers, standing on them and smashing them with his short microphone stand. He emerged for the slow version of 'We Will Rock You' on the shoulders of Superman! The gig ended with Roger Taylor kicking over his drum kit, nearly taking Freddie out with it. My ears were ringing, my heart was pounding and I was hooked. I couldn't sleep when I got home, so spent the early hours adorning my bedroom wall with pictures from one of the two programmes I had purchased.

THE GAME RELEASED
30 JUNE 1980

The only Queen album to top the US charts, spawning 45s that also made number 1 in America with 'Crazy Little Thing Called Love' and 'Another One Bites the Dust'. It also reached the number 1 spot in the UK as well as Canada, The Netherlands and Argentina.

The North American tour to promote
The Game included 44 shows

COLISEUM
1 JULY 1980, SEATTLE, WASHINGTON

I WAS THERE: MIKE STREBY, AGE 18

I HAD JUST graduated from high school. My friend Don Taylor and I made the 140 drive to Seattle from Yakima, leaving early in the morning so we could amongst the first in line. It worked, as we were among the first thousand or so people in the door. It was all general admission so we were right up against the railing that protects the stage. This was *The Game* tour and the show was awesome, and still to this day Queen with Freddie, Brian, Roger and John remains the concert I judge all other performances against. No one has ever come close.

I kick myself in the ass for this, but about five years ago Queen with Adam Lambert came to Tacoma, Washington and I didn't go. What a fucking idiot!

INGLEWOOD FORUM
8, 9, 11 & 12 JULY 1980, LOS ANGELES, CALIFORNIA

I WAS THERE: ALAIN VINZON

WE WENT ON the third night. They opened the show with 'Jailhouse Rock'.

I WAS THERE: GEOFFREY POWER, AGE 14

MY COUSIN DAVID lived a few towns over in Downey, California. I was 12 and he was 15. David was older, cooler and always given permission to listen to edgier music. During Christmas dinner that year, he took me to his room and opened this new album he had just gotten for Christmas, *News of the World*. I had just opened mine - *Born Late* by Shaun Cassidy. My parents were obviously abusive and satanic! David sat me down and we listened to most of the tracks.

Geoffrey Power got into Queen via *News of the World*

His favourite was 'Get Down, Make Love' (obviously, because he was 15) but every track on that album sent alarms off in my head. I had already heard some tracks on the radio but this was music I could listen to until I died. The following week I used the money I had received for Christmas to purchase my own copy of *News of the World*.

My birthday gift was my own stereo system and I blew $30 on headphones with a real long, curly extension cord so that I wouldn't disturb my younger brother as I went to sleep listening to Queen, Kiss, Aerosmith and The Beatles. I listened to *News of the World* hundreds of times in my room.

Due to budget cuts, in 1978 my Los Angeles area school district combined junior high schools with high schools and so I began attending high school as an eighth grader. I was adopted by a group of much older students who knew my older sister. They were die-hard Queen fans and introduced me to the 'real' Queen. I bought all the older albums and found myself listening to music that made my parents question my sanity – 'The Fairy Feller's Master-Stroke', 'Seven Seas of Rhye', 'Fat Bottomed Girls' and 'Tie Your Mother Down' all seemed to come out of opposing musical corners. This music tied together my music with my Lord of the Rings habit, which I got from the same group of older kids.

By the time I got to see Queen live I knew all of their songs by heart. One of the older friends bought a ticket for me and one summer afternoon called me to say, 'We will pick you up for the concert in 20 minutes.' I had forgotten. I had forgotten to give my buddy the money. I had forgotten to tell my parents. I had forgotten to ask my parents. I was 14 years old and had never been to a concert before. Heck, my parents rarely let me go to the movies with my same age friends.

After somehow getting permission I showered, jumped into a Volkswagen bug and cruised with four other guys to the Forum. Queen played a pretty wide variety of their best songs. I bought a concert t-shirt which became my badge of honour and my prized possession that summer until my buddy Jeff Thompson fell out of the back of a pickup truck on the way home from Huntington Beach wearing that shirt and had to have it cut off his 'road-rashed' body by the doctor. Unfortunately, my shirt died. Also unfortunately, Jeff didn't!

Two songs left an impression with me from that concert: 'Get Down, Make Love', which was the first song I remembered hearing with my cousin David a few years earlier, and 'Bohemian Rhapsody'. I had wondered if they could pull that one off live with all the voice tracks. I sang along with nearly every song. We all did in my group.

I never owned a Queen album released after *The Game*. I was also disappointed that Mercury was blatantly gay at that point. It was hard for me to grasp, but it did mean the lyrics to 'Get Down, Make Love' made more sense. Overall, the concert at the Forum was the turning point for me as a young man and as a music lover. It brought the sounds that lived in my head every night to life. Later, MTV made that same transformation for the next few generations, but that summer in 1980 Queen took me to the next level. God bless them.

I made all six of my children listen to various Queen tracks so they could understand that music doesn't have to be basic songs but can be a feeling, a vibe, a movement, a statement, a disappointment and - for me - a declaration of manhood. I'm not sure my kids ever bought into it, but at least I tried to bring them closer to what I believe is the greatest transitional band of the Seventies.

OAKLAND COLISEUM ARENA
13 JULY 1980, OAKLAND, CALIFORNIA

I WAS THERE: MICHAEL GARNER

MY OLDER BROTHER always took me to see Queen whenever they came to the San Francisco Bay Area. The third time we saw them was at the Oakland Coliseum Arena. Somehow Jim managed to get tickets in the 15th row. After playing 'We Will Rock You', Freddie flung the tambourine into the crowd, right at my brother. I had a hand on it, but Jim wouldn't let go. It was a fantastic moment for us and our always close relationship. He passed way too young, and I inherited the tambourine.

I WAS THERE: RICK SALADO

MY OLDER BROTHER and I have been to hundreds of live shows over the past 40 plus years. Visiting him in Arizona four years ago, he asked me. 'What was the best live performance you have ever seen?' Without hesitation, I said Queen. He asked why and I

Rick Salado still rates Queen as the best show he ever saw

told him, 'They were all excellent musicians and they were really tight, but it was their live sound more than anything. Freddie's voice and the entire band sounded great live, plus Freddie was a great entertainer.' I've seen a lot of great bands, but none were as good live as Queen.

RIVERSIDE CENTROPLEX ARENA
6 AUGUST 1980, BATON ROUGE, LOUISIANA

I WAS THERE: ELIOT THERIOT

IT WAS MY first concert experience. The stage was huge and the musicians seemed larger-than-life. I remember Freddie coming out on stage - after they had taken a break – dressed all in white and sitting behind a white grand piano to play 'Bohemian Rhapsody'. He sang intensely and with an emotion that made each audience member feel as though he were directing a semblance of gratitude to each of them personally. The entire stage area seemed to glow in a blazing white aura as the band played. The crowd surged and exploded with delight as the band nailed the performance perfectly. Freddie, ever the showman, was shirtless with solid white trousers and sporting white suspenders.

I remember the t-shirt I bought from the show had orange sleeves and a scantily-clad, large-breasted woman standing tall on a cloud. Her arm was raised up in victory and her fist was clenched tightly and filled with lightning bolts. Her flowing blonde hair seemed to be lilting in the air on the still shirt. Most of the audience were speckled with the familiar 'baseball jersey' shirts that seemed to be the norm in concert t-shirt sales during the early 80s. And there were a lot of feathered haircuts back in those days!

CIVIC CENTRE
20 AUGUST 1980, HARTFORD, CONNECTICUT

I WAS THERE: JOHN FURA

THEY STARTED WITH 'Jailhouse Rock'. Maybe Freddie was bisexual, but out of the 35 concerts I've been to over the years it was the only concert where, when he went to the edge of the stage, I saw 50 girls jump out of their seats and go running up to the edge of the stage to gaze at him. And right before they did 'Fat Bottomed Girls' Freddie said, 'I like girls with big tits and big asses'.

THE SPECTRUM
22 AUGUST 1980, PHILADELPHIA, PENNSYLVANIA

I WAS THERE: ANDY CASTELLANO

I SAW QUEEN live several times, firstly on the *Day at the Races* tour.
I met Brian May after the *News of the World* concert in New York
City and he was an absolute British gentleman. And I met Freddie
Mercury outside a Philadelphia hotel after a concert on the *Game* tour.
A friend and I had snuck into the hotel but were escorted out by a gruff
Englishman who was clearly not amused. As we were leaving, a limo
pulled up and Freddie got out, alone. My friend and myself almost
choked. He was very relaxed and cool, smoking a cigarette. He signed
my programme, which I still have, chatted a bit and went inside. I was
blown away, and was a bit surprised how 'normal' he was, with no 'dears
and darlings' or campness. Dare I say it, a regular bloke!

CIVIC CENTRE
24 AUGUST 1980, PITTSBURGH, PENNSYLVANIA

I WAS THERE: BILL PARKISON, AGE 17

IT WAS AN excellent show. *Queen II* is incredible, and 'March of the
Black Queen' one of their best rockers; awesome.

I WAS THERE: JOHN M BOYLE

I REMEMBER FISHING by the side
of a lake with a friend. 'Bohemian
Rhapsody' came on the little portable
radio and we looked at each other
like, 'What the hell was that?' We
were metalheads and didn't like
anything we heard on AM radio. But
deep down I was hooked. I bought
A Night at the Opera, opened it up and
was hooked on every note, on every
song. From there my obsession grew.
When you bought a Queen album it

John Boyle (right) saw Queen at the Civic Arena

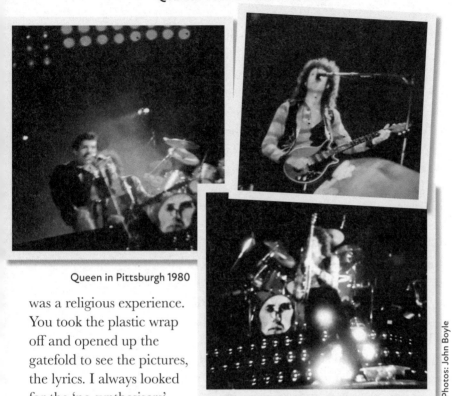

Queen in Pittsburgh 1980

Photos: John Boyle

was a religious experience. You took the plastic wrap off and opened up the gatefold to see the pictures, the lyrics. I always looked for the 'no synthesisers' message. My heart was broken the first time that wasn't there.

In Pittsburgh on *The Game* tour in 1980, I was on the front row, Brian's side. It was an amazing concert and Brian gave me a little wink and a smile. And I now have a 15 year old daughter who is as obsessed with Queen as I was at 15.

FORUM
29 AUGUST 1980, MONTREAL, CANADA

I WAS THERE: MARIE CLAUDE DESCHÊNES

I WAS 14 years old and it was just before Christmas 1975 when I first listened to 'Bohemian Rhapsody'. This was the beginning of my love affair with Queen. I listened to the album on a loop. I spent nights listening to all the albums and singing Queen songs with my friends. In Québec we speak French and we didn't know English. But because the lyrics came with the albums I knew the words by heart.

In the summer before I moved to Montréal for university, I heard a song on the radio. It was 'Play the Game' by Queen. I saw them in

August 1980. I attended this concert with my then lover, David. It was one of the most beautiful days of my life. I remember everything about the concert I attended. All my senses were on alert.

When I heard the radio commercial for *Flash Gordon*, which Queen wrote the soundtrack for, I was there at the premiere with my brother, Paul André. And when two Queen concerts were announced in Montréal in November 1981, I went. Tickets were not expensive at the time and I was there with my friend Giselle and my brother Paul André. His ticket was on the floor, in row H on the left side of the stage, where there was another stage where Freddie came to sing. My brother let me use his seat for 30 minutes and I was so happy to have Freddie in front of me. What I didn't know was that they filmed the concert and that there was an album too, *Queen Rock Montreal*. I was there!

I saw them again in 1982 at the Montréal Forum. This time my seat was on the floor. I took some photos with a disposable camera but, unfortunately, I gave them away. This was the last concert I attended with Freddie, Brian, Roger and John.

In 2017, Queen and Adam Lambert played Montréal. I live in Québec City, a six hour return trip. I had to go as it could be my last chance to see them. I had a seat upstairs. I was dizzy and alone, but I was offered a seat near the stage. It was a chance to be close to Brian and Roger. I cried.

Queen will be with me until the end, no matter how old I am. I told myself that if I get married, 'Love of my Life' would play in church. That's something that never happened. But I'll have Queen played at my funeral.

MAPLE LEAF GARDENS
30 AUGUST 1980, TORONTO, CANADA

I WAS THERE: PATRICIA BLYTHE

IN 1973, MY best friend Lyle had just received their self-titled debut album as a gift. He came bounding through the door of a mutual friend's place and promptly put it on the turntable. Six or seven of us huddled around the stereo listening with rapt attention. 'Keep Yourself Alive' had all of us at the first guitar riff. Great discussion ensued after the first play and it was determined we needed to hear it at least one more time. I lost count the number of times that album was on repeat. Everyone fell in love with the music and Queen has been my favourite band these last 47 years. I raised my two sons on Queen's music and today they both still listen to it. It has become tradition for the three of us to attend any Queen concert or theatre production together.

After that initial introduction, I promptly joined the Queen Fan Club, collected memorabilia, saved concert tickets. I managed to see them in Canada, with Freddie, five times. I have a whole box of Queen 'stuff' I'm not quite sure what to do with. To see Queen live for the first time was spellbinding. After listening to them on vinyl for so long, to hear Freddie's voice and watch them all come to life was actually quite surreal and almost overwhelming. I had to keep pinching myself. Roger's drums were just thundering and Brian's guitar....? Well the show was damn near note-for-note off the albums. I remember Freddie bounding around on stage, disappearing and reappearing in another location, while 'White Queen' took me to a different place. It was a concert you couldn't get enough of. None of them were. I was totally awestruck.

Many years after that first concert, I took my eldest son to the *Freddie Mercury Tribute Concert* at Wembley in 1992. Lyle, my friend who had introduced me to Queen's music, joined us in England. It was both magical and wonderful to experience Queen's music together, albeit without Freddie. The three of us also met up with another group of friends, one of whom is Freddie's cousin and is the spitting image of Freddie. Al and I have also been very close friends for over 30 years. (Al's mom and Freddie's mom were sisters). I came close but unfortunately never met Freddie in person.

Queen's music has touched every corner of my life and although their show is quite the spectacle today with Adam Lambert, there will never be anything quite as spine-tingling and thrilling as seeing Freddie perform live, 20 feet away from your seat. He left us a magnificent legacy and a fabulous catalogue of music.

I WAS THERE: DEB HENRY

MUSIC HAS ALWAYS soothed my soul, and rock 'n' roll has got me through many tough times. I always looked up to my older brother, who introduced his annoying little sister to rock music. Queen mesmerised me and Freddie Mercury stole my heart from the start.

I was 15 or 16 when we went to Maple Leaf Gardens. Our tickets were $10 or $15 and they were great seats. I remember the excitement. I was with my brother and a couple of his friends. We all took the streetcar. I was just a tagalong but I did not care – we were all pumped for the event. We got off at the Gardens, where the area was crawling with teenagers and young adults, every one of them going to the Queen concert.

The arena was absolutely packed and the anticipation and the marijuana smoke were both thick in the air. I was pretty young so I wasn't a seasoned partier but I recall having a bit of a glow, which assisted in the Queen concert experience. It only grew my passion for Freddie Mercury. I could feel his presence and his energy. I have been to many concerts over the years, but this one will always be my most memorable and inspirational. My love and addiction for Freddie Mercury and Queen became an important part of me and my life.

CHECKERDOME
17 SEPTEMBER 1980, ST LOUIS, MISSOURI

I WAS THERE: JOHN DAMRATH

AFTER OUR FAMILY moved again, to St Louis, I remained in touch with what Queen was doing. When *The Game* came out in 1980, I made sure I had the concert schedule and ended up going to see them in Milwaukee, St Louis and Chicago. In St Louis, I went to the rear of the Checkerdome very early in hopes of catching the band as they arrived. A couple of girls were there hoping to do the same. They told me Queen were staying at the Sheraton Hotel and that I should leave the concert during the encore if I wanted to meet Queen because they would be in their limos and on their way to the hotel before 'God Save the Queen' had finished!

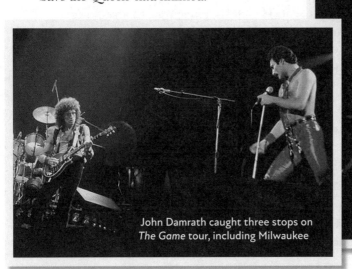

John Damrath caught three stops on *The Game* tour, including Milwaukee

I took their advice and headed to the Sheraton during 'We Will Rock You'. After all, I'd seen it just one week earlier. I got to the hotel and wandered around, pacing the lobby. I didn't see any activity and decided to get in the elevator. When the door opened, I got in and found myself sharing it with two girls and a guy. The guy was John Deacon! I rode up in the elevator with them. I was so nervous I didn't know what to say and I didn't want to make a scene. John said 'hello' and I said 'hi'. The elevator stopped and I got out, telling John 'nice show'. He said 'thanks!' I went back to the lobby and stuck around for a while, but didn't see anyone. No Freddie. No Brian. No

Photos: John Damrath

Roger. I thought I'd blown it, but I really didn't want to intrude either. I just hoped to meet them.

I went home that night and didn't sleep a wink. I'd been training with the St Louis Blues for my upcoming hockey season at Ohio State, who started school a month later than most schools, so I was able to go back to the hotel in the morning to try to meet the band. I went there early and awaiting around. I knew they were heading to Chicago next and thought they may be leaving in the morning. To my surprise, the lobby elevator opened and out walked Freddie, Brian, Roger and John! After blowing it the night before, I wasn't going to be denied, so I ran up to Freddie with my *Game* album cover and asked him to sign it. He agreed. I then got Brian, John and Roger to sign it. I said, 'This is so stud' to Roger. He asked, 'Stud?' I explained 'cool' and then thanked them all. They hurried out the front door into a limo, presumably to the airport. That was it. I was stunned, relieved and happy I'd actually spoken to each of them.

Guys like this don't come along very often. I can't begin to describe how they influenced my life. They didn't take 'no' for an answer and I learned from that. Because of Queen, I am a very tenacious person and I am forever grateful. Those guys may think their influence was their music, but it was much, much more.

I WAS THERE: JIM KREMER, AGE 17

I SAW THEM on *The Game* tour. Queen were always my favourite. I wore out *Live Killers* on LP. The concert was brilliant! I absolutely loved it - the lights, the sound and the songs. I feel fortunate I was able to see them live.

JOE LOUIS ARENA
20 SEPTEMBER 1980, DETROIT, MICHIGAN

I WAS THERE: PETER LUCAS

I DIDN'T KNOW who they were. My dad had picked my brother and I up and took us to the concert. I only realised it was Queen about a week later and I heard 'Another One Bites the Dust' on the radio and then I was like 'that's who we saw!'.

RICHFIELD COLISEUM
21 SEPTEMBER 1980, CLEVELAND, OHIO

I WAS THERE: MARCI CONNELLY

QUEEN HAD PLAYED three concerts at the Coliseum in only 23 months and promoted three different albums, so…. after waiting nearly two years, as the band had played consecutive tours in the UK, Japan and Europe during 1979 and then managed a short break from touring to work on recording *The Game*, Queen were back on a full world tour of the United Kingdom, Japan, South America and North America.

When they finally played Cleveland in September of 1980, I was interning with *Scene* magazine, Cleveland's weekly music and entertainment publication that covered everything from the local music/bar scene to rock concerts. Since I covered hard rock, Queen was my assignment and I wrote the review for the show. Little did I know then that the 1982 censoring of 'Body Language' and the subsequent 1984 banning of the video 'I Want to Break Free' by cable stations such as MTV would result in Queen's refusal to tour the US. This would be the last time I would see Queen until 2014.

I had been given floor passes from *Scene*, but not assigned seats as the show was a sell out. We found ourselves at the back of the floor near the sound/light control boards and having more fun dancing and just getting into the music with the masses. Queen had always put on a great show, but they had doubled down and now they were performing at a new level of excellence. Queen had clearly grown exponentially in the three years since my first time seeing them in 1977. Freddie's voice was stronger than ever and his presence was now as powerful as his voice; he had more control of the stage and the audience. As much as I had loved seeing Queen from the front row, it was remarkable to feel the full effect of his persona and their music all the way at the back of the floor.

They opened with 'Jailhouse Rock', a song that had previously been used as an encore number and it wound the crowd into an immediate frenzy. They followed the Elvis classic with their up-tempo version of 'We Will Rock You' and then 'Let Me Entertain You' from *Jazz*. When Freddie sat down and began hitting the opening notes of 'Play the Game', it was easy to see that Queen was going to take us all on a musical journey and they were calling all the shots. They moved easily from their classic songs into the newly released tracks and it became obvious that their days of experimenting with sound were far from over. Brian and Freddie had an amazing time playing off of each other using the unique sounds of the 'Red Special' and Mercury's vocal acrobatics.

With *The Game*, Queen ventured into new musical experimentation, but like all of their previous albums and shows, there was a very wide variety of sound from hard and driving rock to funk and a little pop and their signature ballads. Plus, on the album and of course on stage, for the first time, Queen used the effect of synthesisers in their music which added an all-new dimension. Just imagine sliding from 'Save Me' into 'Now I'm Here', 'Dragon Attack' and then 'Fat Bottomed Girls' followed by 'Love of my Life'. Queen had truly mastered taking their audience on a musical roller coaster for the senses.

This show, like *Jazz*, was a definitive precursor for the vast stadium shows that we are familiar with and can now enjoy on numerous video recordings. For example, 'Love of my Life' was again done acoustically and the audience sang the entire time. Both Brian and Roger had extensive solos; and for the first time that I saw, Freddie did his 'sing back' with the audience. It wasn't the 'ay-oh' vocalisations that we see in later tours – it was much simpler and was embedded in 'Now I'm Here'. He sang works like 'okay', 'alright' and 'yeah' and the audience was quick to repeat whatever words Freddie sang. His control of the audience, the pace of the show and the entire experience was continuing to develop, strengthen and evolve - although it was still a few years away from its peak.

I've been a follower of Queen since 1974 when I first heard 'Killer Queen' and 'Tie Your Mother Down'. I loved their hits and many of the lesser-known songs. I feel so fortunate that I had the experience of seeing Queen in concert during such a significant time in their careers as musicians and performers. I only wish that I had been a little older or maybe a little wiser and could have truly appreciated the sheer genius and talent of their musicianship. Instead, I was a fairly typical teenage fan that wanted to live in the moment of the music and become engulfed by the experience of the show – and take home a memory and a rose!

GROENOORDHALLEN
27 NOVEMBER 1980, LEIDEN, THE NETHERLANDS

I WAS THERE: ILSE VAN VONDEREN

I WENT WITH my dad. Roger played the drums so well that my dad instantly became a fan. It was amazing, and a great light show. I was thrilled that my dad and I had a great time together. It's a wonderful memory, and I never forget the show.

Ilse van Vonderen went to see Queen with her dad

I WAS THERE: JAAP REKVELT, AGE 14

WHEN I HEARD 'Bohemian Rhapsody' on the radio for the first time in 1975 I asked my mother if I could buy the single from my pocket money. At home I played it endlessly. I bought *A Night at the Opera* and soon knew all the songs by heart. I had never heard anything like it. My Queen fever had started and I bought everything they had released to date. Before the release of a new LP, I went to the record store every day to ask if the new album had already arrived. I also bought all the singles and later also the bootlegs and their first EP. Soon I was a member of the Queen fan club and I got the English club magazine. On fan club days I bought cassettes with illegally recorded concerts.

They came to the Netherlands and it was fantastic. Two years later they played the Groenoordhallen again and I tried to record the concert illegally on cassette. The pictures I took weren't of good quality, but I cherished them. I knew (and still know) all of Queen's songs by heart, studying the lyrics. My entire room was full of posters of my heroes.

In 1986 Queen were guests at the hotel where I was working at the time. They had eaten in the coffee shop and entered the lobby. I was amazed to see my hero Freddie Mercury walk just two metres from me. I was so surprised I was only able to say 'Brian!' before they passed by. He turned around and gave me a hand. What a moment!

Freddie died two months before my mother. I said to a close friend, 'my childhood is over.' 'Made in Heaven' and 'Too Much Love Will Kill You' have often brought me to tears. With the birth of my three sons, my life became busier and Queen moved a little to the background but every now and then I played their music. My children heard it and when they became young teenagers, they started to play old Queen songs. I went to the Dutch premiere of *Bohemian Rhapsody* with my oldest son: it was fantastic and the goosebumps and emotions during the film were indescribable. I immediately thought, 'Rami Malek will win an Oscar for his role!' For my 51st birthday, my 15 year old son studied 'Bo Rhap' on the piano and my 11-year-old dressed as Freddie and sang the lyrics to the song for me with passion. It was unforgettable. The circle is complete!

I was amazed to see Freddie walk just two metres from me

I WAS THERE: PATRICIA VAN GROOTEL
THIS TIME MY father was happy to join me and he loved it. However, he did not understand how Brian could do a wonderful solo and why the audience was screaming and applauding but hardly listening. I told him, 'Yeah Dad, we're not here to listen, we're here to worship! Listening is what we can do at home. This is where we can show how much we love them!' A lot of fans, including me, were not too fond of the introduction of synths, and there were a lot of banners on the subject.

DEUTSCHLANDHALLE
30 NOVEMBER 1980, BERLIN, GERMANY

I WAS THERE: MICHAEL BEHRENDT, AGE 14
FANS CLIMBED ONTO the lamps to get a good view. I remember the thousands of fans singing the songs together and an unbelievable and charismatic show from Freddie. He understood how to inspire all of the people. It was so cool when the songs started that all of these different people sang together in a huge choir.

NATIONAL EXHIBITION CENTRE
5 & 6 DECEMBER 1980, BIRMINGHAM, UK

I WAS THERE: ANDREA RHODES, AGE 19

I WAS THERE with a mate. I'd seen the band a few times but she had never been to a rock concert before. As we were walking out after the most incredible night, we were approached by a roadie and invited to an aftershow party backstage. Of course, we went and there they all were! It was amazing – drinking, laughing, chatting. The biggest shock was how tiny Freddie was. We were there for hours and it was hilarious afterwards, walking across a completely deserted car park at 4am to a solitary little Mini with its crooklock on. It took me ages to convince my mate that this didn't happen every time you go to a Queen concert. She thought it would!

Andrea Rhodes went to the NEC afterparty

WEMBLEY ARENA
8 – 10 DECEMBER 1980, LONDON, UK

I WAS THERE: PAUL PHILLIPS

BY NOW I'D joined the fan club and each month bought another album to complete my collection. Through the fan club I managed to secure a second row ticket. The stage set had changed, with a black drum riser stand and lighting rig for Roger. Blue and yellow colours added to the lights above the band. Another change of direction had seen Queen just release the soundtrack to *Flash Gordon*. They retained the slightly late on stage build up and the dry ice and high ampage opening 20 minutes.

Freddie was moustachioed and clad in white, buzzing as ever. I was on the left hand side so spent a lot of the time watching the cool, calm John Deacon and Freddie at the piano. Highlights of this gig were new songs 'Play the Game', 'Dragon Attack' and a far rockier version of 'Another One Bites the Dust'. I now realised that at a Queen concert they didn't give you the LP versions of songs; the group adapted them. Sometimes I didn't know what the next song was going to be from the intro they had devised. I have never heard another live band like this. I was collected from the show by my dad. Whilst he was waiting for the show to end, he had been invited into the auditorium by a security staff member, and saw 'We Are the Champions' and 'We Will Rock You'. Dad said he had never seen anything like it and was amazed. He now understood some of my obsession.

I WAS THERE: WILLIAM MARTIN

I HAD NEVER seen Queen before. As we set off for the concert, we were recovering from the shock news that John Lennon had been shot the day before. We had good seats at the side of Wembley Arena and the lights and sound were fantastic. As a tribute to Lennon, they did an acoustic version of 'Imagine' halfway through the set. I will never forget that moment.

I WAS THERE: IAN NICHOLSON

MY FIFTH AND final Queen gig was at the Empire Pool, Wembley. The day started with the awful breaking news that John Lennon had been shot dead in New York. It was a very sombre journey up to Wembley that day. Queen paid tribute to John that night, playing 'Imagine' with Freddie reading the lyrics from a piece of paper, and the audience joining in. It was a moving moment, and one of those special memories that stand out in nearly 50 years of gig going.

I WAS THERE: MARGARET DENMARK

I WAS IN my late twenties and my husband was two years older. We both looked young for our age and wore appropriate clothing but in those days the audience was pretty young, while we - as parents of a young family - found it was great for us to park our children with grandparents and have an evening for ourselves. I have to admit though, that we felt as if we were verging on the geriatric. Fans are very much more widely spaced in age these days.

Margaret Denmark's body was palpably humming when she left the arena

   The arena was pitch dark when the concert started. The 'We Will Rock You' rhythm thundered out, vibrating almost violently through our bodies. The lights then came on and the concert took off. It was totally absorbing, a physical thing. They were fabulous and there were no weak link songs. We were familiar with all the music because we'd been buying the LPs throughout the Seventies and played them repeatedly, but seeing them live was spectacular. We'd followed them from the beginning of their recording careers and already gone through the state of slight shock one felt on hearing various tracks for the first time and were able to relate to them as familiar friends. They were similar to people like Prokofiev and Shostakovich in that they were so different from what had come before.

On the first hearing one has to familiarise yourself with the new unexpected sounds but after that one can savour them. They had us both and everyone else in the arena in the palm of their hands throughout the entire evening. Freddie Mercury was utterly magnetic. His stage presence cannot be overstated. It was only when we left the arena at the end of the evening that we both realised that we were almost completely deaf and our bodies were still palpably humming from the reverberations that shook the arena for the entire concert. It took a couple of days for the buzz to fade and an entire week for our hearing to gradually return to normal.

After five February shows in Tokyo, Japan on the Flash! tour, Queen moved on to the South America Bites the Dust tour, with five shows in Argentina and two in Brazil.

The *South America Bites the Dust* tour took in five Argentinian and two Brazilian shows. The first Sao Paulo concert was attended by 131,000 fans, a world record at that time

---

ESTADIO JOSÉ MARÍA MINELLA
4 MARCH 1981, MAR DEL PLATA, ARGENTINA

I WAS THERE: MARCELO VALES GARBO

I SAW QUEEN at the local soccer stadium in Mar del Plata, a very popular vacation city because of its beautiful beaches. Or at least they were beautiful at that time, in the south east of Buenos Aires province in Argentina. I was with my sister, her boyfriend and a few friends from my

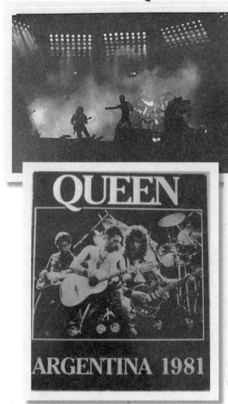

Marcelo Vales Garbo saw Queen in Argentina

hometown in Buenos Aires. It was a cool night going to cold. It was the first show I ever went to where an international famous band like Queen was playing. Actually, it was the first time I ever went to a live show, and it was nothing less than my favourite group! We paid for tickets in the best place, on the field just a few feet away from the stage. No chairs, no security bothering us, no drugs, no violence. Nobody was there with anything in mind but to listen to the band and enjoy their great music. I guess those times will never return....

I recall Freddie singing on stage, the band playing my favourite songs and the warm environment coming from everybody around us. We were singing the parts of the songs we knew and jumping and screaming, 'Idols! We love you' with all the power of our lungs. Roger on the drums was perfect all night, as was John playing the bass and Brian with his exquisite guitar sounds. It was perfect in every way.

I don't recall much of the concert. It's over 40 years ago already, but I do remember Freddie's energy and him hitting a speaker in the heat of the moment. We were so happy at the end of the concert. We couldn't believe we were there.

ESTADIO JOSÉ AMALFITANI DE VELEZ SARSFIELD
8 MARCH 1981, BUENOS AIRES, ARGENTINA

I WAS THERE: MARIA FERNANDA CASTELLARI

I FIRST HEARD Queen at a friend's house. It was 1978 and we were 14. Her brother brought home *Jazz* and the first thing I heard by them was 'Mustapha'. I instantly became a fan. And I saw them in a football stadium!

ESTÁDIO DO MORUMBI
20 & 21 MARCH 1981, SÃO PAULO, BRAZIL

I WAS THERE: MIRIAM RODRIGUES, AGE 17

I WAS A member of Brazil's official Queen fan club. I had just woken up and turned on Rádio Cidade, a famous radio station in São Paulo. They announced that Freddie Mercury would be there at 2pm for an interview. I thought, 'I can't miss this.' It was an opportunity to see Freddie Mercury right before my very eyes so I took my purse and camera and left for Paulista Avenue. I arrived at 1pm, took the elevator to where the radio station was and found there were more young people there. After 45 minutes, a guy said we had to leave because Freddie was coming. But the porter told us to hide and return when the interview had started. After the interview, a man came to call the elevator. I was sat in front of one of the elevators and it was my elevator that Freddie came to. I saw Freddie, took a photo and said 'hallo' to him. He answered back and of course I almost passed out!

Miriam Rodrigues saw Queen in Brazil

At the concert I was interviewed by Band TV. I was so nervous all of my body was shaking and, when the reporter asked what my favourite song was, I said 'Rapsodia Bohemia'. And then Freddie surprised me by announcing the name of the song in the same way I'd said it. I felt loved by Freddie.

On the Sunday I went to the Hilton Hotel in São Paulo where Queen were staying. I met my new friends from Radio Cidade and the team who worked for Queen gave us a lot of souvenirs like photos of *The Game* album and stickers for the Japan and Brazil tour. I didn't see Freddie again but Roger and Brian gave me their autographs and Brian hugged me too. It was amazing!

I WAS THERE: FERNANDO LANDULFO

I WAS A teenager. One of the first songs they played was 'Play the Game' as they were promoting that album. The second concert I saw was Rock in Rio in 1985. To get to Rio, I escaped from my home and lied to my mother about where I was going. I ended up in the third row from the stage, no more than 20 metres away from Freddie. The sensation of watching them live was incredible.

Fernando Landulfo saw Queen twice

I WAS THERE: CARLOS EDUARDO BASTIDA DOS SANTOS, AGE 12

I'M A QUEEN fan since 1978, when my dad gave me the *News of the World* album. I saw them in 1981, in 2008 with Paul Rodgers in Sao Paulo and Rock in Rio in 2016 with Adam Lambert. That was nothing compared to 1981!

The second leg of the South American tour was badged as the Gluttons for Punishment *tour. Two of the eight planned shows were cancelled.*

ESTADIO DE BEISBOL IGNACIO ZARAGOZA
17 OCTOBER 1981, PUEBLA, MEXICO

I WAS THERE: ENRIQUE RODRIGUEZ, AGE 17

AT 9AM, ME and three of my closest friends were in a 1977 VW Beetle, heading east on the highway to Puebla, 130 kilometres from my hometown of Mexico City. We arrived in Puebla and found the Zaragoza Stadium around noon, with lots of cars and lots of people). We were allowed into the stadium at 6.50pm and chose a spot on the left side of the field. I could see only about two thirds of the drums but I was able to see the rest.

The show started at 8.30pm. I'm still impressed by the power of the PA Queen had (150,000 watts, I later learned) and still today I have not heard a band that sounded so powerful. It was my first time at a major rock show and the images and sound of that special day are still in my memory as if it was yesterday. Unfortunately, there was a security problem and a few assholes amongst the crowd of 80,000 were throwing shoes, stones and batteries at the band.

During 'Now I'm Here', a guy climbed onto the stage but the bodyguard sent him flying with only a little push. And during Brian's 'Brighton Rock' solo, he got a pantyhose full of sand and got dirty. But the group - as professionals - performed as planned. At the end, when 'God Save the Queen' was playing, Roger was so pissed off that he took one of the cymbals to throw it away but turned back and threw it at the drum riser. Freddie said 'muchas gracias Mexico', 'take your shoes' (the ones some people threw to the stage), 'adios amigos, you motherfuckers' and 'goodbye, ciao'.

Too bad they never came back, but for the 80,000 people that were there this was the best audio visual experience ever, to be part of something with the greatest band on the face of the earth.

THE FORUM
24 & 25 NOVEMBER 1981, MONTREAL, CANADA

I WAS THERE: FATIMA GUERREIRO

I WAS IN Montreal for a vacation. My Canadian friends knew I was a big Queen fan so bought the tickets as a surprise. It was the time of my life.

I was very impressed with Freddie Mercury. I was near the stage staring at him and, because of the lights and the smoke they used, I don't remember much about the others. But Freddie was great. For part of the show, he was singing near the audience and spoke a lot to us. Sometimes, and I know it seems stupid now, I felt like he was looking at me and singing to

Fatima Guerreiro saw one of the shows filmed for *Queen Rock Montreal*

me. He was a giant on stage and it was a mesmerising concert that I cherish deeply in my heart. Someone started to shout nasty things to Freddie, calling him some bad words, but the people near that guy shut him up and then a policeman came and took him out of the arena. Freddie didn't stop the show but carried on as though nothing had happened.

The 30 date European Hot Space *tour began in April 1982. The accompanying album was released on 21 May 1982, reaching number 4 in Britain and number 22 in the United States.*

SPORTHALLE
6 & 7 MAY 1982, KÖLN, GERMANY

I WAS THERE: PATRICIA VAN GROOTEL

I SAW THEM in Leiden in 1982 on the *Hot Space* tour. One of my relatives had some friends at Mojo Concerts. In return for a free ticket for the driver and three friends, I got a lift. When we got at the ticket booth, there were tickets reserved for me but we had to pay for them. I ended going alone with my friend. The guys were too cheap to pay. Then my uncle in Köln in Germany phoned me and said, 'I got you Queen tickets'. It was not their best tour but it was wonderful to see them twice in such a short time.

CARL-DIEM-HALLE
9 MAY 1982, WÜRZBURG, GERMANY

I WAS THERE: DAVID ESCAMILLA

WHAT GOT MY attention was seeing the audience sing along to all their songs from start to finish. One of the best shows I have ever seen.

It was one of the best shows I have ever seen

ELLAND ROAD FOOTBALL STADIUM
29 MAY 1982, LEEDS, UK

I WAS THERE: ALAN RUTHERFORD

I WAS CLASSICALLY trained in music, attending York Minster School, the choir, etc. Life was wrapped up in a choral bubble. In 1974, when I left the choir aged 13, I saw 'Killer Queen' on *Top of the Pops* being performed by this extraordinary singer in a fur bolero jacket and wearing black nail varnish. 'Killer Queen' is so classical in construction as a song and I imagine that's one of the reasons it grabbed me. It was electric and I bought every song they ever released after! 'Bohemian Rhapsody' was an awesome gift for school kids - that middle bit, the operatic section. We used to sit and fire lines at each other until that last 'for meeeeeee'!

I went to Elland Road with my girlfriend, Jenny. They were incredibly tight and introduced the new sounds (*Hot Space* wasn't a popular album for many Queen fans, as part of it bordered on funk) with a rockier twist. I remember being unbelievably excited as Freddie climbed a little way up the scaffolding during one song.

And I went to Knebworth with a mate called Paul Hilton, who now works at BBC Radio London. I remember seeing the band arrive in a white helicopter as Big Country performed - rock 'n' roll! Queen closed the event in front of 130,000 people. During 'Who Wants to Live Forever?' Brian May sat at his DX 70 keyboard with his guitar on his lap. As night fell, the fag lighters lit the event.

I WAS THERE: MARK DOBSON

THERE WAS A bit of a cloud over Elland Road in the build up to the gig. It had absolutely hammered it down with rain all week. But the day of the concert was beautifully warm. Leeds United had just been relegated, so there was another cloud over Elland Road. And Queen were playing this show off the back of *Hot Space*, which is probably their dodgiest album. Freddie Mercury had been staying at the old Dragonara Hotel and security was enormous. We'd all been down the night before to try and blag autographs, and failed miserably.

They started with the 'thump-thump-thump' intro from 'Flash' and you just got the impression something good was going to happen. The gig was unbelievably powerful. They played a selection of tunes from *Hot Space*, but they played an absolutely red shot show, as though they had something to prove. I think they knew the album wasn't great, but stuff like 'Staying Power' really came to life played live. Brian May has since said that Elland Road was one of the best nights they ever played. It was so tight.

I saw them on the *Works* tour two years later and they were back on track musically, but the live performances weren't as good as Elland Road. They were literally on fire that night, and they played Milton Keynes Bowl a week later. If you watch the DVD, you can see that they were as tight as when they played Hammersmith back in 1975.

Queen used to get the most diabolical reviews back in the day. Now Queen fans are having the last laugh.

I WAS THERE: JULIAN THOMAS

I WAS 11 years old in 1973 and I played 'Killer Queen' to death on the youth club record player. I was a young man who had posters of the band on my bedroom wall at my parents' house. I wish I'd seen them before 1982 but I was too young. I'd love to have seen them around 1974. I first saw them at Elland Road. I drove up to Leeds and stopped at the ground. They were rehearsing so I waited for them to come out. I saw Freddie, Brian and Roger - not John – and got their autographs on an album cover. I followed them back to the Dragonara hotel and I checked in and met them and the crew at the bar. This was the evening before the show. I remember following their limos down the motorway in my Renault 12! The hotel cost me £75 a night even then, so it was expensive but it was worth every penny for the memory.

It was a warm day. I remember wearing just my Queen t-shirt from the fan club. They opened with 'Flash' and then 'The Hero'. It was all so unbelievable and I'd never seen anything like it - the lights, the sound, the crowd. I was in awe and finally watching my heroes. I also saw them at Wembley Arena, Wembley Stadium twice, Bristol and Knebworth. I was a Queen fanatic and still am but I'm not fussed on Adam Lambert at all. I understand what Brian and Roger are doing but they toured Cardiff a few years ago and I didn't want to watch them. With Freddie, I would have sold my house for a ticket.

INGLISTON SHOWGROUND
1 JUNE 1982, EDINBURGH, UK

I WAS THERE: GEORGE HOGG

I SAW THEM in '79 on the *Crazy* tour at Glasgow Apollo and again in '82 on the *Hot Space* tour. In '82 the Teardrop Explodes were supporting them and didn't go down too well with the crowd as they were a fairly new band on the scene at the time and a Scottish crowd don't hold back. For the first four songs the crowd just chanted 'shite, shite, shite' repeatedly! Then they played 'Reward' and the crowd cheered and sang along. Julian Cope must have thought at that point that they had won us over. Nope, straight back to the chant for the rest of their set. They were pretty shite, right enough.

George Hogg remembers the Teardrops getting a traditional Scottish welcome

I WAS THERE: JOHN GRAHAM

WE LEFT OUR town of Elgin on a five hour coach trip that the local music store had organised down to Edinburgh. We got there at 6pm and went straight inside after buying a programme. Queen were due on at 8.30pm. The support band were Heart, but while they were okay nobody was really interested in them.

Once they left the stage the roadies were busy setting up for Queen. Chart music was playing out of the PA system, then it came to an abrupt end and the large hall was plunged into darkness. The opening intro of 'Flash' started and the dry ice filled the stage as the noise built up to a deafening level. Then Brian emerged first to the opening 'The Hero' as Roger and John moved into place and then some 30 seconds later Freddie came running through the clouds of dry ice to a huge cheer and they were on. I was right at the front of the stage on Brian's side with only a moat between me and the stage so I was only 10 feet away from the band. The stand out moment was when Freddie came to the edge of the stage. I can't remember what he was singing, but for a brief second he looked me straight in the eye. I can still see him now!

The road crew had hung a bright yellow rubber duck on a very thin wire from the lighting rig. When Freddie was near the front of the stage, the crew would lower the duck to a few feet above him. The crowd would then point and laugh and cheer. As Freddie turned round the duck was quickly hoisted back up, so he would see nothing! This happened a few times to our great amusement, and obviously Freddie was in on the joke and played along, but it showed they all had a sense of humour. As Brian sat at the piano playing the intro to 'Save Me', Freddie stood at the side of the piano bent over it like a snooker player, with his mic stand pretending to take a shot at one of his drinks as if he was going to knock it over Brian. They both started laughing and smiling at each other. It was such a lovely moment.

At the end of the show as the band took the applause before walking off, Roger threw his sticks into the crowd. They hit one of my friends on top of his head but as he tried to grab them someone behind him got one of them. The band left the stage. Roger was behind Freddie and jumped on Freddie's back until they were out of sight and the house lights came on. With us being at the front, the crew were handing out cups of water off the top of Freddie's piano. I managed to get to the coach with my plastic pint pot but my friend sat on it before we got out of the car park!

I WAS THERE: KERR DAVID BRAND

WE WERE FAIRLY close to the stage. After Heart, the stage went black and you could hear smoke being pumped into the area. Then the loud beat to the start of 'Flash Gordon'. Spot lights on gantries came on and swung out over our heads. Beams penetrated the smoke before the stage lights came on fully to the sound of 'Flash'. Freddie was a true entertainer and one of a kind. I've never seen anyone take control of the stage the way he did.

I WAS THERE: TOMMY WEIR

THE HALL ITSELF was a huge hangar-type building and it was all standing. The start of Queen shows were always dramatic, with their vast lighting rigs and effects and this was no different. The pumping bass line of Flash Gordon' lent itself to the sections of the rig moving around and flashing in unison, raising the levels of crowd roars and then Brian May burst out centre stage and blasted out the opening riff to 'The Hero', swiftly followed by Freddie behind him, launching full force into the song with the crowd going crazy as usual.

Then it was into the faster version of 'We Will Rock You', the same as on the *Crazy* tour, and then a newbie from the *Hot Space* album called 'Action This Day'. They then alternated between the classics and new tunes – 'Play the Game', 'Staying Power' - with the crowd singing along with Freddie on 'Somebody to Love'. In the small acoustic section of the show, "39', 'Love of my Life' and 'Save Me' had the crowd all singing at the top of their voices.

I remember it being hot and sticky and it went up a notch when 'Under Pressure' was rolled out. Freddie nailed it like it was his own and not a shared tune. We then got a treble of crowd favourites in 'Fat Bottomed Girls', 'Crazy Little Thing Called Love' and 'Bohemian Rhapsody' and just for good measure they ended with 'Tie Your Mother Down' and sent the crowd into a wild, bouncing and throbbing frenzy. For the encore, the band returned with 'Another One Bites The Dust', the John Deacon bass line making it a stand out for the crowd, 'Sheer Heart Attack' and then the traditional one- two of 'We Will Rock You' and 'We Are the Champions'.

Another tour, another venue and another great experience. Queen were quite simply the best live band on the planet.

MILTON KEYNES BOWL
5 JUNE 1982, MILTON KEYNES, UK

I WAS THERE: JAMES HAYES

HAVING TAKEN MY 'A' levels I was in need of a release, so when one of my school friends said his older brother had obtained tickets to see Queen I blurted out that I would have a ticket even though I couldn't call myself a massive Queen fan. Racing home I had to ask my parents for the cost of the ticket, a huge commitment for them, but they said yes. I had never been to a gig before.

James Hayes, here with his puppy Freddie, thinks Mercury is the best performer he ever saw

My recollection of the day itself is a little hazy. I do remember thinking that being a famous singer was maybe more of an attractive option than my dream of playing for Arsenal! I had never seen so many people in one place before and remember how hot it was. We also had to park in a field which after the gig led to a two hour search for our transport home.

When people mention the best group I have ever seen, I reply that the best performer I ever saw was Freddie Mercury. What a showman. All these later, if I close my eyes, I can still hear the roar of the crowd and Freddie's soaring voice.

I WAS THERE: FREDDIE KEHOE

I STARTED LISTENING to Queen in 1974. I was 12. I saw them in 1977 and 1978 at Stafford's New Bingley Hall, and again in 1982 at Milton Keynes Bowl on the *Hot Space* tour. I waited nine hours at the Bowl to see them. It was a very hot day. I've seen them with Adam too. I received a letter from Brian in 1979 and I still remember opening it. I got married on Freddie's birthday, and 'Bohemian Rhapsody' was playing in the registry office. Fantastic memories.

Freddie Kehoe waited nine hours to see Queen at the Bowl

I WAS THERE: LESLIE LANE

SOME 60,000 PEOPLE attended. Because I was ill with a type of glandular fever, my best mate Ian (Nobby) Burns and I sat on the hill towards the back of the venue. As usual, the Queen roadies were beavering away getting the stage ready and soon enough the usual dry ice started to waft across the stage as the taped intro to 'Flash' played through the speakers. Then after what seemed like forever, Brian May ran through the dry ice and went blasting into 'The Hero'. The crowd roared and then Freddie was there, singing the song. The fast version of 'We Will Rock You' followed and then 'Action This Day' and 'Play the Game'. Freddie then announced to the crowd, 'As you may know, we have a new record out and we'd now like to play a song in the black funk category.' There were a few groans and boos from the crowd and Freddie replied, 'People need to calm down. It's only a record. It doesn't mean we have lost our rockier side.' They then played 'Staying Power' and I found myself preferring the live version to the recorded version. In fact, most of the songs played from the *Hot Space* album sound so much better live.

Next Freddie was sitting at the piano going through the keys when suddenly he slammed down on them and said 'let's try and get a little Aretha Franklin vibe going here'. He sang a very slow intro to 'Somebody to Love' and just before getting into the song proper, he said, 'Are you ready brothers and sisters?' Queen then played the best version of 'Somebody to Love' I ever heard. 'Under Pressure' started up with that familiar bass line and I was certain David Bowie was going to walk on stage. Sadly, he didn't....

I WAS THERE: PAUL PHILLIPS

THIS WAS MY first outdoor gig, and my largest crowd so far: 40,000 people. My mate and I secured a place about five yards from the stage. There was no drinking of anything as there was no way you'd have found that spot again if you needed a pee. I wore my Under Pressure t-shirt. I used to buy subtle Queen t-shirts, as having the word 'Queen' on your chest in those days could cause a bit of aggro.

The support acts were Bow Wow Wow, The Teardrop Explodes, Joan Jett and The Black Hearts and Heart. Needless to say, the first two acts didn't go down too well, although I thought Julian Cope and his combo were great. A degree of nervousness emanated from the audience around us, as Queen had just released *Hot Space*, with its funk/disco-based A side. What would they do on stage? Another strength of this group was to keep the audience guessing. We needn't have worried.

In the half light of the sunset, we saw the lighting crew climb into pilot seats hanging just below each section of the lighting rig to aim multi-coloured spotlights at the band members. Smoke rose and the band exploded onto the stage to 'Hero' from the *Flash* soundtrack. It was a phenomenal gig, Freddie doing a great sing-a-long with the crowd, cavorting over the scaffolding and unleashing great versions of 'Somebody to Love', a 'Now I'm Here'/'Dragon Attack' medley and 'Play the Game'. The funkier songs from *Hot Space* were dismissed as 'it's only a bloody album' by Freddie. Queen rocked them up, especially the marvellous 'Staying Power'. I recall a rocking Brian May guitar solo that went silent midway through as he managed to unplug the lead to his guitar as he traversed the huge stage.

I WAS THERE: DON MURPHY

DAD WAS IN the US Air Force and got us stationed to England again in 1980. I finished my schooling in England and asked for Queen tickets as a graduation present. I was a crazy Queen fan, had all of their albums and had obtained a few bootleg concert tapes of their shows. I was looking forward to the show and had money saved for souvenirs, etc.

Don Murphy got Queen tickets as a graduation present

The opening act roster was the most extravagant I'd ever seen with Joan Jett, Teardrop Explodes and Heart keeping everyone entertained. Joan especially was on top of her game. Heart were pre-MTV superstardom and were excellent.

The helicopter flew over and we all realised Queen were inside it and started cheering loudly. The concert started with 'Flash' coming over the speakers. 'The Hero' was one of my favourite songs and I was blown away that they did a chunk of that to open. The guys were loud as hell and every note carried through the air. Everything was perfect. Freddie was on top of the world and danced and waved, punching the air. It was a top of the line performance from the master.

The only glitch occurred during Brian's solo where he walked to the end of the catwalk and got too far and unplugged himself. He laughed, we all laughed and then he proceeded to plug back in and changed the solo by adding some really excellent pieces.

The press of the day was largely rock and they slammed the album. I was a die-hard Queen fan and was going to buy the album anyway. I didn't initially like the dance-y feel but the tracks came alive onstage, especially 'Staying Power'". Roger's drum solos were fantastic and the version of 'Now I'm Here' they played was over the top and the best version I've heard. John's bass was the punchiest and most powerful I've ever heard. Normally he got drowned out but on that day, he ruled. It was the best performance of Queen's entire career.

I WAS THERE: PHILIP GAMMAGE

I FIRST HEARD of Queen in 1974 when they did their Christmas TV concert at Hammersmith Odeon. I went to see them at Milton Keynes Bowl with my school friend, Derek Hughes. I still live in Milton Keynes and do a weekly music show on CRMK in Newport Pagnell on Monday mornings.

TOP OF THE POPS
17 JUNE 1982, LONDON, UK

In their last in person appearance on Top of the Pops, Queen perform 'Las Palabras De Amor'.

Starting on 21 July 1982, the world leg of the *Hot Space* tour took in 39 concerts in North America and Japan

---

CAPITAL CENTRE
25 JULY 1982, LANDOVER, MARYLAND

I WAS THERE: MARGARET BATES

I HAVE BEEN a Queen fan since the first album in the early Seventies when my brother Mike said, 'You have to hear this band!' I was hooked. I was lucky enough to go backstage, but missed meeting them. I have listened to Queen every day since their first album came out. Seeing and hearing them live and getting to take pictures of them was definitely a highlight of my life! Their music has touched my life. Even my Facebook page says Queen fan. It doesn't matter how bad my life goes, Freddie's voice can always make me feel better.

Margaret Bates took a few shots of Queen in action

BOSTON GARDEN
23 JULY 1982, BOSTON, MASSACHUSETTS

I WAS THERE: RICHARD JAMES

I WENT TO see the opening act and figured I wouldn't mind sitting through Queen. By the end of the concert I was blown away. Everything about them was tops, Freddie was Amazing. The opener – Billy Squier - didn't have the benefit of the lights, theatrics or even the audiences attention and was just okay!

SPECTRUM
24 JULY 1982, PHILADELPHIA, PENNSYLVANIA

I WAS THERE: DAVID PELTON

IT WAS A great show. I remember someone throwing a beer on stage and Freddie shouting, 'Now I know why they call this place Filthy-delphia!'

CIVIC CENTER
25 JULY 1982, LANDOVER, MARYLAND

I WAS THERE: SHERRY CARROLL BELL

I HAD A ticket and a ride arranged for the show in 1980, but the friend didn't arrive. That was the last time I ever spoke to her. I had to wait two years for the next show.

Myself and my friend Shari were only happy if we got inside every single show that came into town free. We made friends with every crew we could at every gig on every tour, finding out when and with what band they would come back to town. We would get the names of their friends on other tours to watch out for, and know to ask for them personally. We flirted unmercifully with every person working every door, and every goon operating security at every local event. We made friends with every union stagehand and every truck driver, t-shirt man, gaffer, rigger and roadie in sight, cosying up to every limo driver and every regular hotel employee at all the hotels the bands were always booked into. We made sure we knew everyone and made sure we were known and appreciated by every promoter as well behaved and worth having around, not sleazy, low-class troublemakers. To find out where the best parties were going to be, we did detective work that would have made Phillip Marlowe proud. We learned to contact the band's A&R person at the label in New York or LA in advance to see if we could sweet talk our way onto 'the list'.

They soon learned there was never any hope of us doing sexual favours for passes for any show, like some of those girls at the back door, but you could always count on us to show up at 10am, bringing fresh baked cookies or a homemade meatloaf for lunch in order to keep the bored, exhausted boys on the bus entertained on a long, hard day and night out here in the middle of suburban nowhere. We truly cared just as much or more about our friendships with the roadies as we did about meeting the bands. That was what made all the difference, made us special. We had a genuine desire to get to know them because they were much more interesting than the local boys our age could ever be, and we really wanted them to have a nice time while they came to town.

It was still a shock when we scored VIP passes and got into the show! And before it was over we had the golden ticket, getting invited upstairs to party at the band's hotel. Unfortunately, when we got there it was only the crew, and even though we made sure to get names and make friends with the people closest to the band and able to get us passes forever after, little did we know that there would be no more next times in DC.

MAPLE LEAF GARDENS
2 & 3 AUGUST 1982, TORONTO, CANADA

I WAS THERE: LUCIA FRACASSI

I SAW QUEEN with Freddie six times in Toronto, and went to *Rock in Rio* in Brazil. In February 1977, I had front row floor seats slightly to the right of stage for the *Day at the Races* tour. I saw them both nights on the *Jazz* tour in December 1978, with front row floor seats to the left of the stage. For the *Game* tour, at CNE Stadium in August 1980, we had second row centre floor seats, and for the *Hot Space* tour at Maple Leaf Gardens we had front row centre floor seats both nights. Freddie threw white roses into the crowd both nights and I caught the roses at the 2 August show. Freddie actually commented 'good catch, lovely'. I kept those roses for many, many years but sadly they got lost in a house move.

BRENDAN BYRNE ARENA
9 AUGUST 1982, EAST RUTHERFORD, NEW JERSEY

I WAS THERE: MARYANNE CHRISTIANO-MISTRETTA

AGED 12, I went to school wearing black nail polish on my left hand to be like Freddie. I was too young to go to concerts (my mother wouldn't let me). But I collected all the photos from magazines - *Creem, Circus, Hit Parader* - and had a few posters. Back then it was hard to collect stuff. I finally saw them in 1982. It was unbelievable seeing them live. I feel blessed to have seen them with Freddie.

After I read *Mercury and Me* by Jim Hutton, I reached out to his publishing company to let him know how much I enjoyed the book. This was in the mid-1990s and people still sent snail mail as opposed to email. Well, Jim Hutton himself wrote back to me. At the time he had HIV but was negative and still in good health. He sent me a Christmas card with a picture of his new kitten in a Christmas tree.

POPLAR CREEK MUSIC THEATER
13 AUGUST 1982, HOFFMAN ESTATES, ILLINOIS

I WAS THERE: MIKE ARMSTRONG, AGE 15

ONE OF MY friends had a Queen record and I borrowed a Queen record from the library. I remember listening to 'Bicycle Race' over and over again. My friend Frank Stack and I saw that they were coming to Poplar Creek and he said, 'Hey, my mom can drive us.' She drove us to this outdoor venue that was in the suburbs. It's gone now. Lawn seats were five or seven dollars, which was crazy cheap. To this day, I think it's one of the best shows I've ever seen. They had a lot of smoke, and on each side of the stage they had these weird spotlights on what looked like the mechanism for a bucket truck, big arms that kind of looked like spaceships. Each one was operated by a guy and they moved them around and up and down through the smoke. That was right around the time that *Flash Gordon* came out so they were probably playing up that whole space angle. There was so much smoke….

I WAS THERE: LAUREL NIXON

'BOHEMIAN RHAPSODY' IS the first Queen song I remember hearing. It was different enough that it was compelling... rock and classical rolled into one. I think I was driving in the car and it came on the radio. Freddie Mercury's voice was amazing. I'm not sure how to describe it, but I think almost everyone would agree it was a great one.

I'm not sure how we bought tickets for this show but it was from a legit vendor, not scalped. I went with my fiancé. Billy Squier was the opening act. He was very good and very loud. I knew we'd be in trouble when they brought out more huge speakers for Queen's performance. I honestly remember not hearing because it was so loud, so very loud. I'm sure my hearing was damaged. Our seats were in the middle of the pack. It might have been smarter to have listened from outside of the venue. I'm pretty sure that it could have been heard from blocks away. My fiancé's younger cousin was sitting in the row ahead of us. He wasn't old enough and wasn't supposed to be there, so we were sworn to secrecy. I guess almost 40 years later, it's okay to share.

I remember George Michael was able to come close to Freddie's voice. And now Adam does very well, but as Paul McCartney once said, 'You can't reheat the soufflé.'

MISSISSIPPI COAST COLISEUM
19 AUGUST 1982, BILOXI, MISSISSIPPI

I WAS THERE: RUSS SSCANNAVINO

MY FRIEND TURNED me on to them when I was 14. I bought their first album and it was almost regular rock and roll. The following albums were typical Queen music. They sounded just like their albums, and were the only band I saw out of many that did. I don't know how they did that but they were great, especially Freddie.

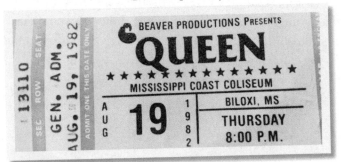

Russ Sscannavino saw Queen in Mississippi

THE SUMMIT
20 AUGUST 1982, HOUSTON, TEXAS

I WAS THERE: CRAIG SCHLICHER

I FIRST HEARD 'Crazy Little Thing Called Love' when I was a senior in high school. My next significant memory is after my first year of college. I was taking two years off from school and was working in a factory building control panels. The factory was in Houston, Texas and not very far from the new venue, The Summit - now Lakewood Church, a megachurch. I recall leaving work and standing in line to get four tickets for me and some of my friends. I scored some seats stage left, up in the stadium seating about halfway up from the floor. It was an amazing show! At one point one of my friends who had brought a frisbee with him threw it towards the stage and it landed stage centre and skidded to a stop, back stage right. Freddie watched it fly in as he held the mic. He was singing and, never skipping a beat, he picked it up and threw it out straight over the crowd where it landed near the back of the arena. The crowd went wild.

The artistry of albums such as *A Day at the Races* just amazed me. When *News of the World* came out, and this was the only time I recall doing this, I took it straight to a friend's house and put it on the turntable. He had not heard of Queen, but 'We Will Rock You' made him an instant fan.

MCNICHOLS ARENA
30 AUGUST 1982, DENVER, COLORADO

I WAS THERE: MICHAEL NESSETH

BILLY SQUIER OPENED for them. I loved the lights and Freddie was amazing. My best memory is the vocal improvisation. There were many roses tossed at the end.

I loved the lights and Freddie was amazing

LA FORUM
14 SEPTEMBER 1982, LOS ANGELES, CALIFORNIA

I WAS THERE: IRA KNOPF

I was at their 1982 concert, for the final night of that tour at the LA Forum. The opening act was Billy Squier and Queen's set list from that night was:

We Will Rock You (fast version)
Tie Your Mother Down
Flash
The Hero
Action This Day
Play The Game
Staying Power
Somebody To Love
Now I'm Here
Dragon Attack
Now I'm Here (reprise)
Love of My Life
Save Me
Back Chat
Get Down Make Love
Under Pressure
Fat Bottom Girls
Crazy Little Thing Called Love
Bohemian Rhapsody
Sheer Heart Attack

Encore:
We Will Rock You
We Are the Champions
God Save The Queen

I WAS THERE: SUE DURIS

I'VE BEEN A Queen fan since 1974 when I feel in love with 'Killer Queen'. I didn't start going to Queen gigs until the *Jazz* tour. Previously, my parents told me I was too young. Seeing Roger in his 'tigerskin' trousers on the *Jazz* tour was well worth the wait. I was never too young to buy albums and read about them – as much as I could get, that is –

in my favourite music magazines, *Creem* and *Circus*. Ironically, the most Queen coverage in the US came in the likes of *16* and *Tiger Beat* magazines. I didn't know about the import magazines like *Music Life* in Japan and *Sounds*, *Melody Maker*, etc. in the UK until years later. I loved the pre-Internet age when the phone, writing letters to pen pals and going down to your local record store to find out about and to buy records of your favourite artists and buy concert tickets was life.

Sue Duris saw Queen's last ever American show

I've been fortunate to see Queen a plethora of times, including in several countries. I was fortunate to be at Queen's last concert in the US with the original line up. I was bummed too because the US lost them after that show.

Some things stood out for me at that show - Billy Squier, Roger and his beautiful chrome kit, the Freddie vocals and the strut, Freddie and Roger volleying back and forth on 'Action This Day', Brian playing magic on that Red Special. And who could miss John's dancing? I absolutely loved 'We Will Rock You' - the fast version - live in the arena and it was fab, something I'll never see again. That was made for one Freddie Mercury. All of this combined with a stellar light show - what could be better? It was also fab to hear some great songs from the catalogue like 'Dragon Attack', 'Save Me', 'Action This Day', 'Now I'm Here', 'Tie Your Mother Down' and - a regular favourite - 'Jailhouse Rock', which Billy Squier came back on stage for.

Even though not a sell out, the show was high energy, the band was really hot and quite energetic on stage and everyone was upbeat for the show, and that excitement showed throughout the arena. I remember the Forum really shaking! It's a night I won't forget, not just for the being part of history part, but to be part of a great concert experience with four blokes known as Queen. Queen is one of the few artists that have been able to last throughout time. Queen has been able to navigate a changing musical landscape and an evolving music industry, and come out victorious. They had a plan, they stuck to it, and wouldn't let anyone put them in a box.

Freddie used to say Queen was a form of escapism for people to be entertained. I couldn't agree more. Two months prior to the show, my dad died. His life and death had a profound influence on my life. To this day, I listen to my huge Queen – and other band member projects – collection to reminisce, when a certain feeling hits me, and to enjoy really great music that will never die. Some people don't ever go to rock concerts and live through Queen's music – whether that's audio, video or a combination. I count myself as one of the lucky ones.

I WAS THERE: MATTHEW DI PIERO

I DISCOVERED QUEEN in 1978ish via KMET and KLOS. I saw them twice at the LA Forum. The second time I was close to the stage. Billy Squier was the warm up act and the dude was loud. He had the biggest speakers I've ever seen, reaching to the ceiling. Amps stacked on top of amps. And the stage lights - hundreds of them. You could literally feel the lights.

After Billy Squier it was pretty dark and we waited for the show for what seemed to be an hour but in reality was probably 30 minutes. Then Freddie came out, stage left, on Superman's shoulders....

THE WORKS RELEASED 27 FEBRUARY 1984

Spawning four singles, including 'Radio Ga Ga' which reached number 1 in 19 countries, number 2 in Britain and number 16 on the Billboard Hot 100, *The Works reached number 2 in the British album charts and number 3 in the USA.*

The Works *tour kicked off in Belgium in August 1984 to promote the album of the same name.*

FOREST NATIONAL
24 AUGUST 1984, BRUSSELS, BELGUIM

I WAS THERE: ELS VAN DER SYPT, AGE 17

IT WAS SUNDAY morning. I woke up and realised I hadn't dreamed. All the events of the previous day played around in my head, just like a movie. Tears ran down my face but I didn't know why. Strange emotions swept through my body. It was probably the after effect of an overdose of adrenaline the day before....

Two days earlier, Queen had started their concert tour *The Works* with a big bang. Chaperoned by my four years older brother, my mum had allowed me to attend the show. We travelled the four miles from our quiet suburb town to Antwerp Central train station on his rattling Honda Amigo moped, where we took the train to Brussels South station. We walked the last few miles to the venue. It had been a whole journey and my butt hurt from

Els Van Der Sypt caught one of Freddie's plastic earrings that he threw into the audience

sitting on the uncomfortable metal back seat, but it was worth it.

My brother had been to Forest National many times before so he knew the place. After the show, he took me down to the artist exit where a group of fans was already waiting for Freddie, Brian, John and Roger to emerge. We were tired, hoarse and sweaty with whistling ears. In those days there was no legal decibel limit in concert halls. Hannie and Anja from the Dutch Queen fan club were there as well. Suddenly there was a commotion and the boys appeared! Shielded from view by oversized bodyguards, they were quickly ushered to their waiting limos. Freddie passed right in front of me and I remember thinking he was much shorter than I had imagined. At five feet 11, I was probably a tall girl, but still. The limos drove off and that was it. Or so I thought.

Then Hannie walked over to us and casually asked if we wanted to participate in the recording of the 'Hammer to Fall' video which was to be shot in the empty concert hall the next day. The video would represent a live performance interlaced with general audience shots from the concert night, and they wanted some extras to act as fans standing near the stage for the close up shots. I thought I had died and gone to heaven.... The next morning, I dragged my brother out of bed to accompany me once again on the long journey to Brussels. He had no choice. I'd rather die than miss this opportunity.

Around noon, about 20 fans were waiting outside the closed doors of Forest National. Around 2 pm the first black limo pulled up, carrying John I think – it was hard to tell through the tinted windows. After a while a second limo appeared, probably Roger. Half an hour later Brian arrived – I clearly recognized the hairdo. Last but not least Freddie's limo pulled up. All four of them had finally arrived!

A security agent walked up to us and led us inside. His instructions were strict. We were to remain seated. We weren't allowed to make any noise and under no circumstances were we to approach any of the band members or we'd be promptly removed from the hall. I had never been in an empty concert hall before, and the prevailing silence was in sharp contrast with the hot, smoky and deafening atmosphere of the previous night. The central area near the stage, where I was struggling for a shoulder width of space the night before, was now packed with cameras and recording gear. There were busy crew members everywhere but they didn't seem to notice us. We sat down on the first row of seats and I felt a bit lost in the empty hall. The stage was the only place that still looked the same as the night before. Soon those big cog wheels would start rotating again.

Suddenly I spotted Brian amongst the crew a few yards away, casually wearing a pair of tiny white shorts and sneakers. My breath choked. I could hear him talk, I actually heard his own, unamplified voice! 'Hammer to Fall' was written by him so he was the director and gave instructions to the crew. I was mesmerised and watched everything in a daze. I couldn't believe this was truly happening....

Brian disappeared and a little while later he walked onto stage, along with the other band members, all dressed in last night's outfits. Silently, the light engineer ran a last check of the stage lights and the cog wheels started turning. Through a set of metallic sounding speakers, we suddenly heard the guitar ripping the intro of 'Hammer to Fall'. The sound was barely audible compared to the volume of the night before, but it was loud enough for Freddie, John, Roger and Brian to create a very convincing 'live' playback act, which ended with a series of fiery explosions along the edge of the stage.

A cameraman followed every move. After each take there was a break. Brian discussed technical details with the crew, lights were adjusted, camera positions changed. Freddie smoked a cigarette and cracked a few jokes with the crew. We could hear him talk and we laughed as well. It was so surreal.... Roger sipped a beer and chatted with John. A fresh series of fireworks was put in place on stage and they continued. Over and over again the whole song was being repeated. The boys worked themselves in a genuine sweat for hours on end. Distant shots of the whole stage, close ups of Roger on drums, Brian strumming the chords, John fingering the bass, Freddie's tireless moves... every detail was meticulously caught on camera. If you watch the official video, you can tell Freddie hated playback. At times he's pointing the microphone away while he continues to sing.

During one of the breaks Brian suddenly walked over to us, apologised for the delay and asked if we were not bored. My voice was hoarse, I choked up and barely managed to whisper 'not at all'. He explained that not enough people had turned up to actually fill the first couple of rows so they were going to go ahead without close up shots of fans near the stage. I just couldn't care less at that point. My heart was racing, I wiped my sweaty hands on my jeans. Brian was standing just a few feet away. My hero, the man who moves me with his incredibly sensitive guitar sound. I saw his hands, those beautiful, precious guitar hands. I had never before stood face-to-face with an idol. This was simply surreal. Then he asked us if we were hungry. Suddenly I realised we hadn't gotten up from our chairs for hours and I hadn't eaten anything the whole day. I was starving. It was 8 pm already, time had flown by.

Brian talked to a crew member while he pointed at us. Half an hour later the man came back holding a cardboard box full of Big Mac menus and distributed them to us. I couldn't believe it. Such an unexpected and considerate gesture. Brian is a rock star, but without the antics. A caring, humble man who often takes the time to spend a few appreciated moments with his fans.

During the whole trip back home with my brother I was mute, in a daze. I had a turmoil of impressions and emotions to digest. 'Hammer to Fall' played non-stop in my head. The next morning, I woke up and realised I hadn't dreamed. I had experienced something fantastic and unique, and I wept.

RDS SIMMONS HALL
28 & 29 AUGUST 1984, DUBLIN, IRELAND

I WAS THERE: LINDA O'GORMAN

IN 1984, THEY came back to see me in Dublin. Everything was as good as my first experience. The only difference was the catalogue of songs had grown, so more fantastic tracks were played and I sang along with each and every one. I remember being hoarse and had a sore throat from all the singing and screaming, which wasn't ideal for me as I was getting married the following week so I obviously needed my voice. I felt so happy having seen my boys again.

NATIONAL EXHIBITION CENTRE
31 AUGUST – 2 SEPTEMBER 1984, BIRMINGHAM, UK

I WAS THERE: DAVID HYNER

MYSELF AND MY two friends had managed to get tickets. We had recently been wowed by Genesis on their *Mama* tour, but were like kids in a sweet shop waiting for Queen's support act to get off stage (so memorable that I can't even recall who it was) and be replaced by Freddie, Brian, Roger and John. Fourteen and a half thousand fans were noisy and expectant, and were not disappointed.

David Hyner saw Queen transform their audience into part of the band

A cacophony of industrial machine sound greeted the band on stage and the crowd went crazy. I have never heard a room rock like the NEC did that night. There seemed to be every cross section of life in the concert hall that night and yet, like a rock choir, we all sang every word to every song with Freddie, who responded by giving us his most flamboyant and emotional vocal to both the *Works* album tracks and the classics we all knew and loved.

There were magical moments when the crowd sang along and if by chance you caught the eye of another fan, you would give a knowing nod in their direction in a mutual acceptance that we were all in a moment of time where we were witnessing something special. It was as if the fans were performing to the band at times. It really was that magical.

I was not (at the time) a huge fan of 'Radio Ga Ga' but when you have been part of a huge crowd performing the song, complete with the obligatory hand clapping above head, you have a memory that stays with you for ever. I owned a very cool *News of the World* t-shirt that my dad had washed into an insipid pink colour. I was too embarrassed to wear it out, apart from that night. One guy even asked where I had the shirt from.

Our throats sore from singing loudly, our pockets empty from the overpriced food, drink and merchandise, we sat in silence on the train home with other fans, all wearing huge grins that we believed would never wear off. I have never witnessed a singer and band perform with such passion and love of their art that it transformed the audience into part of the band.

I WAS THERE: PAULIE LEADBETTER

I THINK I was 16 when I first really heard of Queen, outside of 'We Will Rock You'. I was living in the US and walked into choir class where two of my classmates were playing the opening strains of 'Bohemian Rhapsody'. I moved back to the UK in 1983, at the start of Queen's real resurgence. I went to see the *Works* tour at the NEC. I remember being disappointed that Freddie didn't come out in his *Coronation Street* drag outfit for 'I

Paulie Leadbetter was disappointed Freddie wasn't in drag

Want to Break Free'. I saw them again at *Live Aid*. Freddie's 'day-oh' is on YouTube but it's nothing like it was being there. He was positively feeding off the energy, and we gladly gave it to him.

I WAS THERE: IAN BALDWIN, AGE 18

IN 1981 MY older brother began playing Status Quo. I was 15 and I thought, 'I need to find a band I like.' I went on a school trip, ended up in a record shop and bought

A Night at the Opera. I took it home and played it over and over on my parents' Panasonic stack system. I was hooked. I couldn't believe I had the LP with 'Bohemian Rhapsody' on it. I proceeded to got to Bedworths record shop and buy all the Queen LPs.

My friends and I heard about Queen coming to play at the NEC. We thought we would go and just try to get a t-shirt or something from outside. We set off in my 1975 Ford Capri, with Queen blasting out on cassette. As we were walking around outside, looking at the crowds, somebody

Ian Baldwin got in to the NEC on the toss of a coin

walked past and said 'tickets.' Tickets? We couldn't believe our ears. The man said, 'I want £20 per ticket.' We went through our pockets and we had just over £18 between us. The man said 'that will do' so we tossed a coin and I won! I gave my car keys to my friends and in I went. I found my seat about 50 yards away from the stage. I couldn't believe I was going to breathe the same air as Freddie.

A couple by me asked how much did I pay for the ticket. '£20,' I said. 'Wow,' they replied, 'we sold it for £10.' I wasn't bothered. I was going to see Queen live.

The smoke machine started and everyone was getting on their feet. Slowly Roger Taylor's drum skin was gone, the first notes of 'Tie Your Mother Down' nearly made me deaf and on came Freddie in leather jacket and skin tight red and black Lycra trousers, flashing his teeth. It's an image that will live with me forever. I can't remember much more, except that Freddie came out for the encore with a great big black wig on his head, the one from the 'It's a Hard Life' video. As the end came and Freddie and Co waved, I'm sure he looked at me.

The arena emptied and I started to reluctantly move down the row of seats. I spotted a programme and, no hesitation, it was straight up my t-shirt and down my pants! As I came out of the arena I thought, 'Where's my mates? How do I get home?' Straightaway, they were in front of me. Thank you, I thought. I told them about the concert but they were excited as me. The security had let them in for the encore so we were all over the moon. We managed to find my car and sped off back to our normal life at home.

The next couple of days my Capri didn't seem the same. I found out that my friends, one of whom I still hang out with, was doing wheel spins everywhere and my rear tyres were totally wrecked! I had to buy two rally remoulds. But that night lives with me forever.

I WAS THERE: ANDY BARNES

I WAS 8 years old when Queen went to number 1 with 'Bohemian Rhapsody' and were on *Top of the Pops*. To this day it's the greatest song ever written in my opinion. My older sister had introduced me to them. She bought a few Queen albums off King front man Paul King, who she worked with at Rolls-Royce in Coventry. (He hadn't become a musician at that stage). Bit by bit, I started to listen to Queen more and more, buying albums and singles with the little money I had. My sister went to see them a few times in the Seventies and early Eighties. I didn't see them until 1984, on the *Works* tour at the NEC, and they were incredible.

It's hard to put into words how brilliant they were - Freddie's vocals, Brian's guitar riffs, John's brilliant bass beats and Roger's brilliant drumming - but it was nothing compared to the Wembley show in 1986 and the *Magic* tour. Everything about the show was incredible - the inflatables, the set list, the support bands - and you could see famous people watching in the stands, including Mick Jagger.

We then went to the extra Knebworth date and I was right at the front, bouncing around to 'Tie Your Mother Down' with Freddie standing right in front of me. That's a memory that will live with me forever. I have seen more than 100 concerts including all the greats – Prince, Madonna, Elton John, Billy Joel, Neil Diamond, Paul Simon. No one comes close to Queen live.

Andy Barnes thought Queen were incredible

I WAS THERE: MARGARET BILLS

I SAW QUEEN with Freddie on the *Works* tour at the NEC and at Knebworth on the *Magic* tour. I still have my programmes from those concerts. When Freddie died, I made a scrapbook of all the newspaper cuttings from then, which I still have. Since Adam Lambert took over the lead singing role, I have seen them twice and am planning to see the *Rhapsody* tour. The band themselves now can just connect with anyone, whatever their taste in music. Queen remain my all time favourite band and my daughters and granddaughter are all massive fans to this day.

Margaret Bills kept a scrapbook of press cuttings about Freddie

I WAS THERE: TOMMY WEIR

I TRAVELLED DOWN with a friend to Birmingham from Glasgow on the train and spent the hours wandering around the city centre to pass some time, before travelling out by train to the Exhibition Centre for the concert. When we arrived at the huge complex, all huge hangar-like buildings and each individually numbered, we discovered that not only were there loads of Queen fans milling around but also that Birmingham's up-and-coming pretty boys Duran Duran were in the adjacent arena, filming the video for their single 'Wild Boys'.

This was a gig I was really looking forward to, especially after seeing the 'Hammer to Fall' video which had been filmed in Brussels at the Forest National and which displayed the lighting rig to great effect. The support act was another mismatched group. General Public played and went off to a lukewarm reaction.

We hadn't managed to secure standing tickets and were seated about a quarter way back in this huge arena. The lights went down and the usual thunderous roar ensued, the stage billowed with dry ice and the lights started flashing as the rig slowly came to life and began to raise and split and bend into its shape as 'machines'. Its electronic sounds cranked the levels up even more, with two massive cogs appearing at the back of the stage to add to the mechanical nature of the show's beginning.

Then the band appeared from the smoke and dry ice and stormed into a double dose of 'Tear It Up' and 'Tie Your Mother Down' and the place was rocking, the crowd lapping it all up like ravenous lions baying for blood at the Coliseum in times gone by, a sea of bobbing, bouncing heads and hands all raised in unison and tribal triumphancy.

'Under Pressure' followed, with no let up on the effortless ease with which they just went from one song to the next, onto 'Somebody to Love' and 'Killer Queen'. What followed was an absolute thrill for me as they belted into three in a row of my all time favourite tunes – 'Seven Seas of Rhye' with its tinkling keyboard riff, 'Keep Yourself Alive' and its chugging guitar, and then into 'Liar', a huge fave of mine and one which they didn't play enough live for my liking. That night, I was in my element. I looked at my friend, who was attending his first Queen gig, and he looked as pleased as I did at my first back in 1979.

Things slowed down a little with 'It's a Hard Life', not one of my faves, and then into the disco funk of 'Staying Power'. The funky theme continued with 'Dragon Attack' and then took off again with

'Now I'm Here', the bright and colourful lighting rig seemingly having a mind of its own as spotlights followed Freddie all over the place with pinpoint accuracy.

They allowed the audience to calm down and catch a breath as they introduced a new song, 'Is This the World We Created?', and combined it with the traditional Queen singalong, 'Love of my Life', where Freddie caught his breath as the crowd serenaded him as always. Then they sprang a little surprise by going back in time and playing two songs I'd never heard live before, 'Stone Cold Crazy' from *Sheer Heart Attack* and 'Great King Rat' from their first album. A nice treat.

After Roger's drum (and timpani) solo, a keyboard solo from Spike Edney and Brian on his own 'Brighton Rock' extravaganza ,where all sorts of sounds and echo effects swirled around the arena during his solo, we were treated to 'Hammer to Fall', a really rip-roaring rocker where everything was on full tilt - the lights, the rig, the band. It was magnificent to see.

We then paid a visit to John Deacon's classic 'Another One Bites the Dust' with its disco themed bass before Freddie strapped on his guitar for a little bit of 'Crazy Little Thing Called Love'. They ended the main part of the show with the epic 'Bohemian Rhapsody' and, when the operatic section ended, they didn't disappoint, exploding onto the stage again behind vast smoke bombs and lights, the crowd going into a new level of frenzy. The passion of a Queen audience was something else.

This was followed by another new song, 'Radio Ga Ga', where the crowd hand clapping was done in unison as it is in the promo video. It was a sight to behold as Freddie conducted them. There was a small break in the proceedings for us to catch our breath, and back they came with 'I Want to Break Free', which got a bit of a singalong, before launching into the frenzy of 'Sheer Heart Attack' and then 'We Will Rock You' with the hand clapping going again and the ritual chanting back at Freddie. The show closed with the standard 'We Are the Champions' and the absolute closure of the show with 'God Save the Queen'. We made our way back into Birmingham and, as our train wasn't until the morning, we bunked down in a quiet corner of the station and slummed it until the morning, sleeping with one eye open until our train could take us back to Glasgow.

WEMBLEY ARENA
4, 5, 7 & 8 SEPTEMBER 1984, LONDON, UK

I WAS THERE: MICK MORGAN

I SAW THEM again at what was then Wembley Arena, on the *Works* tour. That was really peculiar, because I didn't really relate to the *Works* album and the stage set was so distracting. They had all these huge cogs on stage and really weird-looking stuff (the set was based on a scene from Fritz Lang's *Metropolis*) and you couldn't really see the band. But they did a good set and they were good to see live again.

I WAS THERE: LESLIE LANE

QUEEN WOULD BE playing four nights at Wembley Arena and thanks to my mate's brother Andy I got tickets for all four shows. Tickets through the fan club would only get me a ticket for one show. I wanted to see all four! I was told to be at the main door of the venue for 6pm. My mate Alan was working at the venue and he popped his head out and gave me that night's ticket. My seat was close to the stage but slightly to the side, good enough for me to get a perfect view of Roger (my favourite) on the drums. The stage set was inspired by the 'Radio Ga Ga' video which featured Fritz Lang's *Metropolis* movie, resembling a city-type backdrop whilst the front of the stage had large cogs and wheels.

This complemented Queen's opening number, 'Machines (Or Back to Humans)' from The Works, which was quickly followed by another new song, 'Tear It Up', and then 'Tie Your Mother Down', 'Under Pressure', 'Somebody to Love' and 'Killer Queen'. They were firing on all cylinders and this was the best I had ever seen them perform indoors. A great first night.

The second night I was in the exact same seat. The guy showing me to my seat gave me a look of recognition but said nothing. It was Freddie's birthday. Once again, Queen were on fire, playing the songs brilliantly and loud. 20 minutes in, Freddie sat at the piano, fluffed the intro to a song, turned to the audience and said, 'Fuck it. This show was perfect up until I messed up, and on my birthday too.' To which the crowd suddenly burst into 'Happy Birthday'.

They played 'Liar', 'It's a Hard Life', 'Is This the World We Created?', 'Hammer to Fall', 'I Want to Break Free' and a great segment of Elton John's 'Saturday Night's Alright for Fighting', leading nicely into 'Bohemian Rhapsody'. Two shows down. Two to go....

The third night the guy showing me to my (same seat) said, 'Haven't you been to the other two nights?' This show was exactly like the previous two, with no changes to the setlist. At the end of the show, Roger suddenly exploded out of his seat and wrecked his drum kit just as the stage lights briefly went off. When they come back on, the drums were all over the place and poor old John was sitting on his arse, having been knocked off the drum riser. Roger turned my way to take the accolades from the crowd. I was standing there pointing at Roger with my thumbs up and he returned my thumbs up pose, pointing back at me.... or was it me?

On the final night I had asked for two tickets as I wanted to take a girlfriend. As we approached our seats, a young guy came over to check our tickets when my old friend the other security guy said, 'No need to tell him where his seat is. He has been here every night.' It was my friend's first time seeing Queen. She loved the show and I loved looking at her during certain parts of the show (when I knew what was coming) to see her reaction. The *Works* tour was over and what great shows they were.

I WAS THERE: NIGEL YATES

THIS WAS THE second time I saw them. I was now married with kids and working for NACRO as a multi skills trainer, teaching the long termed unemployed to fit security fittings in pensioners' homes. The job was enjoyable but the pay was crap. There was no way I could afford to go see Queen. Then a stroke of luck. A training course for fitting a new type of lock came up in Deptford. I managed to persuade my boss to let me go. It would mean three days in London with travel, hotel and expenses paid for, and it was within a bus ride of Wembley. The day I left I was given £100 to cover additional expenses. I was now determined to get to the concert.

I tried all the local outlets around Deptford but everywhere was sold out. Some of the others on the courses were interested in coming with me so we decided to chance our luck and find a tout. We got to the Arena and the place was crawling. There were people everywhere and quite a few police officers around. We thought that was it and started wandering around aimlessly, wondering what else we could do. Out of nowhere this tall African-looking man tapped me on the shoulder. 'Hey dude, you boys looking for tickets?' We couldn't believe our luck. We took four tickets off him for £45 each. Expensive, but we paid. Looking around, we started to see dodgy character everywhere. We started walking in, with me thinking 'are these tickets genuine?'. Luckily, they were.

It was standing room only. The lights went down and the synthesiser struck up. It seemed to last for ever but in the dark we saw movement on the stage. We guessed they were taking position. The lights came up and 'One Vision' blasted from the speakers. Freddie bounded on from the right hand side and the show began.

What a show. From the latest hits to earlier classics, including one of the best versions I ever saw them play of 'In the Lap of the Gods (Revisited)' and Brian giving a blinding solo halfway through that had us all mesmerised. 'Bohemian Rhapsody' was brilliant and as I remember it there were two encores.

By the end we were exhausted. God knows how Freddie and the boys felt. We all filed out. What an amazing atmosphere. Everyone was happy and there were no trouble makers. We made our way back to the hotel in Deptford and got roaring drunk. Fantastic.

I WAS THERE: PAUL PHILLIPS

I WAS BACK at the Arena, but further back this time as the ticket was really difficult to come by. The set had moved on, with mechanical wheels and the *Metro*polis film backdrop from the 'Radio Ga Ga' video. Freddie had gone a bit retro, wearing a leotard with a black lightning bolt emblazoned on it. The band were back into their rock mode. Powerful versions of 'Tear It Up', 'Crazy Little Thing Called Love' and the stunning synchronised crowd clapping and chanting for 'Radio Ga Ga'. It was another 10 out 10 evening.

I WAS THERE: RICHARD ROGERS

I ENTERED A Queen competition in the *Daily Mirror Rock & Pop Club* and won a runner's up prize of concert tickets and a copy of *The Works* so I went with my girlfriend to see them at Wembley Arena. I was a bit unsure how they were going to reproduce songs like 'Radio Ga Ga' on stage but they did it perfectly. The hairs stood up on the back of my neck. It was just so powerful.

Richard Rogers won Queen tickets via a newspaper competition

Experiencing Freddie Mercury's voice and some of the random things he was doing in between the songs just showed off his operatic voice. He could reach to the back of the arena and barely needed a microphone.

I WAS THERE: JOHN SPENCER

5TH SEPTEMBER 1984 was Freddie's birthday. We stopped the concert five times just by singing 'Happy Birthday'. You could see he was shocked, pleased and humbled by this. Some nearer the front threw cards and presents onto the stage, which he gladly picked up. The atmosphere that night was brilliant.

It was about now that the press decided it was 'pick on Queen' time. They were a massive success, so lots of stories about them splitting up were being published, always blaming this band member or that member wanting to give up. Luckily, nothing ever happened.

WESTFALENHALLEN
11 SEPTEMBER 1984, DORTMUND, GERMANY

I WAS THERE: SASHA SPADES

I STARTED LISTENING to Queen in the late Seventies. A friend's parents had a very high tech record player. And I heard them via sleepovers with my older cousin, when we would stay up late listening to music. In 1980, aged 10, I bought my first single and my first album. The single was 'Another One Bites the Dust' and the album was *Live Killers*. I got a huge blue Sony Walkman for Christmas and a tape of Queen's *Greatest Hits*. Driving down to Spain or Austria for vacation, I'd listen to that tape until the batteries ran out. I started buying the albums. They had the lyrics inside and soon I knew half of their songs by heart and spoke better English than my English teacher!

In 1984 Queen played Dortmund. I was squeezing through the crowd to get as close to the stage as possible. I was hardly able to breathe but I was screaming my lungs out! I saw them again in 1986 at the football stadium in Cologne. I will never forget 'Radio Ga Ga' live in that football stadium.

I had heard about Freddie's disease around 1988 from a friend's father who worked in the music business, so the news of his death came as no surprise. I still cried.

SPORTS PALACE
14 SEPTEMBER 1984, MILAN, ITALY

I WAS THERE: ALEXANDER MACINANTE

MY OLDER BROTHER introduced me to Queen when I was 8 (he's 10 years older than me), feeding me with *Greatest Hits* and *Live Killers*. When *The Works* came out and we saw them on TV at the San Remo Festival, he promised me that if Queen came to play in Italy he would take me to see them. When in late summer news spread about Queen playing Milan, we were in heaven.

I remember the full day queuing under the sun, the fans chatting, the atmosphere. There were also bad episodes - a long delay before the opening of the doors caused some fights and made people very pushy. But when we entered and got our spot in the front all was forgotten. There was no support band. After a bit the lights went down, the 'Machines' tape started and the band came on stage through the dry ice. I clearly remember watching Freddie singing just two metres away from me. It was unbelievable. We managed to stay at the front until 'Killer Queen' and then we moved backwards as the crowd was far too pushy. But we enjoyed every second.

I have fabulous memories of us clapping along to 'Radio Ga Ga' and of Freddie sporting a pair of tits and wearing a wig when they encored with 'I Want to Break Free'. I was enchanted by the lights and by the *Metropolis* stage. Strangely enough, the concert was far from being sold out and one third of the Sportspalace was empty. Can you imagine that today?

GROENOORDHALLEN
20 SEPTEMBER 1984, LEIDEN, THE NETHERLANDS

I WAS THERE: MARCEL PAULUSSEN

THIS WAS THE first time I saw Freddie live and it was amazing. I went on to see them five more times. Without Freddie, I preferred Adam Lambert to Paul Rodgers. Adam stays Adam, and doesn't pretend he is Freddie!

FOREST NATIONAL
21 SEPTEMBER 1984, BRUSSELS, BELGIUM

I WAS THERE: SJON NOORDHOEK

ALTHOUGH I BEEN fan since 1976, it took me until 1984 to get to a concert, and it was a birthday present. I saw them on *The Works* tour in Belgium and then in Leiden in 1986. Of course, the band was great, and there's a bootleg of the Belgian concert called *King's Favourite*. The Dutch concert was a family thing and we took my then 13-year-old nephew with us. Brian shook his hand and my nephew still talks about it.

1984 saw the band play nine shows in Sun City in Bophuthatswana, South Africa, controversially breaking the cultural embargo on South Africa that was in place to bring added pressure on the government there to end its apartheid policy.

SUN CITY
5 – 7, 12 – 14, 18 – 20 OCTOBER 1984, BOPHUTHATSWANA, SOUTH AFRICA

I WAS THERE: KAY BATEMAN

I SAW QUEEN in Bophuthatswana. They were amazing. There were three generations of people there. The lighting was fantastic. Obviously, they had to apologise for going to South Africa when they got back to the UK. But I remember as they got on stage Freddie shouted, 'Hello, you arseholes,' and the place just erupted.

Queen began 1985 with a two show visit to Brazil, on 11 and 18 January

---

ROCK IN RIO, BARRA DA TIJUCA
11 & 18 JANUARY 1985, RIO DE JAINERO, BRAZIL

I WAS THERE: FÁBIO RUIZ, AGE 18

WHEN THE LINE up for *Rock in Rio* was unveiled with Queen scheduled to play on two days, I knew I had to be there for both shows.

Tickets were sold at banks, because it was the first time a show of that magnitude had taken place in Rio or in Brazil, indeed probably in South America. I got a ticket for the opening night, which was easy because Iron Maiden and Whitesnake were playing and not a lot of people were heavy metal fans, while the Brazilian attractions were not appealing to a wide public. On the 18th, both The B-52's and The Go-Go's would be playing, along with some Brazilian artists that were popular at the time among teenagers, especially female. Our parents were not used to an event of that size and were unwillingly to let their kids go. The girls' parents were even harder to convince, but a softer programme without 'metal' bands was more appealing to them. Even so, some insisted on accompanying their kids. Not mine, thankfully. Having got my ticket for the opening night, a high school friend tipped me off that they were selling five day passes to the last five days of *Rock in Rio*. I bought one so I could attend Queen's second show.

January 11th was a beautifully sunny summer's afternoon and not excessively hot. The City of Rock was on the west side of Rio, a relatively new neighbourhood with a lot of space for an event like that. It took my friends and I almost an hour to arrive there by bus, but when we did, we understood the extent of what we were getting ourselves into. It was like a huge rounded stadium, surrounded by a rounded 'street' with stores on each side selling food, clothing and an assortment of merchandise. We went straight to the already half full grass field and waited for the shows to start.

It was an eclectic night. The Brazilian attractions were Baby Consuelo and Pepeu Gomes, Erasmo Carlos and Ney Matogrosso. The international ones were Whitesnake, Iron Maiden and Queen, a controversial line up because of the different styles. After Iron Maiden left the stage, they started remodelling it for Queen's show. It was late and it took at least a couple of hours for them to prepare it. We were all anxious. When we heard the first notes from the technicians testing the sound, it was a relief and soon enough the moment we were all waiting was there in front of us. The stage looked like the cover of Queen's latest album, *The Works*. I had already bought it, even though it would take at least six months after its release in the US and England to hit our stores, and I had all of them. We were tired, hungry and thirsty but no one would leave their spot. Nobody wanted to miss a thing.

It was in the early hours of January 12th that Queen hit the stage. It was a dream come true. They started with 'Tie Your Mother Down'.

It was magical, the lighting so colourful through the fog. It was worth waiting for - Freddie, Brian, John and Roger singing for us. When Brian played the first notes of 'Love of My Life' on the guitar, we knew that would be a 'wow' moment, and it was. Some 300,000 people sang it for them. I don't think they expected that, or if they ever had a bigger audience, and it was a moment to cherish forever.

The last song was 'Hammer to Fall'. When we left, there was no more grass on the ground. It was almost four in the morning, and we still had a bus to catch. The sun was rising at Leblon beach when I got off the bus. I walked on the sand and into the water, thankful for that experience.

A week later, I saw Queen again. Queen repeated their performance flawlessly but this show was not as good as the first for me, because the anticipation and anxiety were lost, and it was challenging to attend an event with two feet of mud beneath your feet. Many lost their shoes and sneakers in the mud, but it was all good fun.

I WAS THERE: SÉRGIO LUÍS ANTUNES, AGE 20

INTERNATIONAL CONCERTS IN Brazil were very rare until the Eighties. Queen were one of the first to play here, packing the Morumbi Stadium on a historic night in 1981. I was too young to go, but watched the highlights on TV. When the first *Rock in Rio* Festival was announced, I decided to go. It would be 10 days with the best rock bands in the world. The first day was the greatest for me. Three Brazilian artists followed by Whitesnake, Iron Maiden and Queen. I was working as programmer and had to miss four days from work to go to the festival. My bus left São Paulo at 11pm

Sérgio Luís Antunes was at Rock in Rio

to take the 600 kilometre journey to Rio de Jaineiro, arriving at 7am on the opening day of the festival.

Can you imagine a bus full of excited rockers, travelling to the most important rock festival until that moment in Brazil? No one slept during the trip. I arrived in Rio and started searching for a room in a cheaper hotel. The hotel I stayed in was not rated by stars, but crosses. It was really bad. But it didn't matter. I was in Rio and would be seeing my idols up close.

The gates opened at 2pm and I got a spot in front of stage, under that summer sun all afternoon. The first Brazilian artist, Ney Matogrosso, started his show at 6pm, but I was very tired after no sleep on the bus and being in the sun for four hours. I held on until the third Brazilian artist, Pepeu Gomes, before falling asleep. It felt like I was in my bed. I didn't see or hear anything else.

I woke up with a scream. It was David Coverdale from Whitesnake. Finally, the authentic rock and roll sound had made its debut at the festival. Then it was time for Iron Maiden. And then there was another interminable interval of two hours to dismantling and setting up the stage. But the time had come for the headline act - Queen!

Can you imagine the speed my heart was beating at? I got as close as I could to the stage. I didn't want to miss any detail. When the intro began I though my heart would stop. Then Freddie, Brian, John, and Roger walked on stage, all in white, and began playing 'Tear It Up'. I took a big jump - and fell on top of the guy in front of me!

'Under Pressure' showed Freddie's versatility, because the record in the album is sung by him and Bowie, but live he did both voices. Incredible. Then he went to the piano and started 'Somebody to 'Love', one of my favourite songs. Queen were promoting *The Works* and played a lot of songs from it. The highlights were 'Radio Ga Ga', when the crowd of almost 200,000 people followed the choreography of the video, and 'Is This the World We Created…?' followed by 'Love of My Life'. Both songs were sung by the crowd with Freddie, who sometimes stopped singing to admire the audience. It was a magic moment. Another great moment was 'I Want to Break Free', when Freddie wore the same outfit as in the video.

The show was heading towards its end. The band came back for the encore, 'We Will Rock You' and 'We Are the Champions', and the crowd sang along with Freddie. I had almost lost my voice but tried – and failed - to keep up with him.

Then it was time for the grand finale, with Freddie wearing a crown and a Union Jack on his back as they came on to the sound of 'God Save the Queen'. Brian Helped Freddie open the flag to reveal that it was attached to the Brazilian flag, to the delight of the audience. Everybody was screaming and applauding in an extreme frenzy.

The band said goodbye to everyone and left the stage. I just stood there astonished, thinking, 'What was that? I was only able to move because the crowd around me started pushing me to get out. I was completely numb, and I confess I don't remember how I got back to the hotel. I woke up the next day thinking, 'Was it a dream?' No, it was true. I got to see the best band ever live. The memories of that historic show remain clear in my mind to this day.

I WAS THERE: LUCIA FRACASSI

IT WAS A great concert but the venue was way too big. It was very messy as it rained quite a bit for the entire 10 days of the concert, but I had a great time regardless as I was able to meet all the members of Queen. Roger and John were staying at the Rio Palace along with some of the crew and I got to speak to them both on a couple of occasions. While we were having lunch in the hotel restaurant, Roger recognised us and sent over drinks. He was very personable. John seemed to be very shy but Roger was great. He even directed us to the Copacabana Hotel where Freddie and Brian were staying, and I had the pleasure of meeting Brian and his family by the pool. We had a very lengthy conversation.

That same evening, we met Freddie. Although heavily escorted, he stopped to chat. Again, both Freddie and Brian were very personable. After I mentioned to Freddie we were from Toronto and that I was a huge, huge fan, he provided us with passes to a party at the Copacabana later that evening where I got to meet many artists such as Rod Stewart. I spoke to Freddie again that evening. He was a super nice person.

I WAS THERE: CLAUDIA CARNEIRO DE PAULA, AGE 22

WHEN I HEARD that Queen were going to play at *Rock in Rio* it was a dream come true. I arranged to travel the 1,200 kilometres from Brasilia to Rio, talked to my boss and worked a lot of overtime to cover the days I needed to go. On Thursday 17th January I got on a bus. It was a 17 hour journey but my biggest dream was coming true so I travelled happy! It was raining in Rio de Janeiro that night but who cared? Queen topped a bill which featured Brazilian and international acts and the crowd was anxiously waiting for the moment when Freddie Mercury and company would take the stage. Nobody cared about the storm that was falling.

Claudia saw Queen at Rock in Rio

I was already dressed in big garbage bags and my tennis shoes were pure mud. And did I care? I was the embodiment of happiness! People held up their cigarette lighters to light up the audience, hoping the band would be able to see us.

Peace reigned. It is difficult to explain so many years later, trying to convey that feeling. I don't believe Queen knew how much they were loved in Brazil. Today, reviewing old photos and filming, the impression I have is that they were really surprised. Or at least, that's what I want to believe. One thing I'm sure of is that they were there, singing to me. And I will never forget it.

I WAS THERE: ANNA CRISTINA ANANIAS, AGE 16

I WAS AT *Rock in Rio* 1 in 1985 and again in 2015, when they came with Adam. Both were amazing. In 1985, it was raining a lot. There was mud everywhere. I lost my shoes in the mud. My parents had forbidden me to go. I lied to them and went with my friends. When they started singing 'Love of my Life', Freddie let us sing almost all the music alone. He was totally overwhelmed. In

Anna Cristina Ananias saw Queen in Rio

2015, I wasn't expecting a show as amazing as 1985, but it was fantastic. Adam never tried to be like Freddie. Everyone who was there loved it. People are always complaining about Adam, but whoever sees him live loves his performance.

I WAS THERE: ROGER DASILVA

I WAS RIGHT up front, near the stage. If you watch the lame ass *Queen Live in Rio* video release, you'll hear me in the crowd during 'Love of my Life', when the people around me finally joined me in screaming 'Brian, Brian, Brian' during the song's bridge where Brian plays alone. I say this with pride, because I spent the whole show screaming 'BRIAN!' between the songs, and the people around me were all older than me and they were like 'dude, you're annoying'. But then they joined me. I was very surprised that it came out in the audio of the show.

I WAS THERE: FÁBIO FRANCA

I WENT TO the show with friends. I stood right in front of the stage and Freddie Mercury threw water at me.

Fabio Franca was down front at Rock in Rio

I WAS THERE: ROGERIO FRANCO, AGE 21

I SAW THEM three times in Brazil. The first time was in Morumbi Stadium. I was very far away and using binoculars. The second and third times were in 1985 at *Rock in Rio 1* and I was close to them, on the right side both times. During the first three or four songs it looked like they were preparing the voice, instruments, getting the concentration levels right and feeling the mood of the fans, etc. After that we were on a journey of feelings and emotions, led through this fantastic music by Freddie Mercury. When Freddie started singing 'Love of my Life', he gave us his microphone and we, more than 200,000 people, started singing the song. And when I say singing, I mean singing all the music and not just part of it. I guess it was a surprise even for him.

Rogerio saw Queen three times in Brazil

More than 200,000 people started singing 'Love of my Life'

I WAS THERE: ANTÔNIO HENRIQUE SELIGMAN

I SAW QUEEN in São Paulo at the Morumbi Stadium in March 1981 and at *Rock in Rio* in January 1985. I still have a piece of a tissue where Freddie cleaned his sweat at Morumbi. On both occasions – '81 and '85 - I imagine that people at the back only saw distant stage lights because there were none of the screens that are common today.

Antonio Henrique Seligman met Brian at his hotel

But I got there early and took good places on both occasions. In 1985, me and my wife Liane (she was my girlfriend then) saw Roger in front of his hotel and we met Brian at the beach in front of his. We were about five metres from the stage at *Rock in Rio*, and looking back from that position we saw a sea of 250,000 people!

I WAS THERE: NELSON MESSERE FILHO, AGE 20

THE WEATHER PROMISED rain at any moment but it didn't take away the vibe of the almost 250,000 people who were there. When the rain came it wasn't possible to have a glass of beer. The rain was so heavy it turned the floor into pure mud. But the crowd were jumping and singing along with the shows. Freddie Mercury later described the performance of the song 'Love of My Life' as the best ever made by the band. With our feet buried in the mud of so much rain, we sang the chorus with all our strength and wept with happiness that we were part of that historic day. Sometimes I go on YouTube to watch the video of that song and it still makes me emotional.

After the show was over, I went home and changed as I knew there would be a private party at a club called SOTÃO in Copacabana. The nightclub was packed with celebrities like James Taylor, Nina Hagen, The B-52s and Al Jarreau. One of my friends told me to look over and see who was dancing on my right side. It was Freddie, dancing and smiling next to me. I went over and thanked him for playing the concert and for being there at the party with us. He smiled, said thanks, asked my name and gave me a hug. The DJ called him onto the small stage and asked him to sing a song for us. He toasted us with an acapella version of 'We Will Rock You'. The audience was delighted, so he called Nina Hagen onto the stage and together they sang 'New York, New York' with everyone joining in on the chorus. It was an unforgettable night.

Freddie was dancing and smiling next to me

MOUNT SMART STADIUM
13 APRIL 1985, AUCKLAND, NEW ZEALAND

I WAS THERE: ANGELA ROBERTS, AGE 17

I FIRST DISCOVERED Queen around 1977 when I was 10 years old and living here in Tauranga, New Zealand. My sister is eight years older than me and she was given a record player for her birthday. Because we had to share a room, I had to listen to what she did. The first record I remember her playing over and over was a 45 with 'Bohemian

Angela Roberts (left) saw Queen in Auckland with Marlise Hughes and Paula Baxter

Rhapsody' on one side and 'I'm in Love With my Car' on the other. She headed off to London when I was 13, leaving all her albums behind, including *A Night at the Opera*, *A Day at the Races* and *News of the World*. That's when I really started to love them. When I started high school, I met two girls who had moved here from out of town and we formed a great friendship. We discovered that we were all Queen fans and had many fun times at each others' houses listening to their music.

In 1984 we found out that Queen were going to be performing *The Works* tour in Auckland. We all decided that we had to go, and as we all had after school jobs at one of the local supermarkets, we saved up and bought tickets. Back then our favourite radio station would do concert deals where you paid a set price that covered the show ticket as well as going up and back in the concert bus provided by the station. The venue, Mount Smart Stadium, was a six hour return trip and as we were all only 17, we - and more so our parents - decided it was the best option.

The countdown was on! Every day we would say to each other '100 days until Freddie' and '50 days until Freddie' until, eventually, it was, 'We are going to see Freddie today!' I remember us being so excited, as it was the first concert we were ever going to see.

The bus ride up to Auckland was so much fun, a bus full of about 100 teenagers all hyped up, and the music playing through the bus was of course Queen. We piled into the stadium and, because we got there just as the gates were opening, we managed to get places right up by the stage. Only the security guys were closer than we were. We had made an agreement that if we got separated at any time, we would meet up at the gate afterwards.

The support act came on and unfortunately didn't get a very good reception as it was obvious that the 40,000 plus fans were there for one reason... Queen! I can still remember the crowd surge when 'Tear It Up' started playing. That's when I got separated so I spent the entire concert apart from my friends who were nowhere in my sight, but I really wasn't worried. Some of the highlights of the show were Freddie throwing his fake boobs into the crowd after they finished 'I Want to Break Free' and when Freddie sang 'Love of my Life', which my friends and I still talk and laugh about. This song had never actually been released as a single here in New Zealand, so when Freddie was silent leaving the crowd to sing you could hear a pin drop and Freddie yelled out 'fucking sing!' I guess they should have been pre-warned that no one really knew it unless they were huge Queen fans like us.

On tour with Queen was Tony Hadley from Spandau Ballet, and he and Freddie did a duet on 'Jailhouse Rock', which went down really well. The most poignant part was when Freddie sang 'Is This the World We Created?' I think there were a few tears amongst the crowd, including mine. It's such a thought provoking song which still stands true today. Freddie had the crowd in the palm of his hand the whole time.

After the concert, I met up with my friends and we headed back to the bus. On the way home the majority of people wanted to sleep (as it was close to 1am) including my friends, but there was one guy who stayed awake and ended up coming to sit next to me and we talked and sang all the way home. He ended up being my first love and we dated for four years but went our own ways when he moved overseas for work. I have Queen to thank for us meeting.

When *Live Aid* was broadcast later that year my friends and I set up camp in the lounge and stayed up all night just to see Queen, as we had no idea when they would be on stage. When I say stay up all night, I mean drinking way too many cocktails and being sick, passing out and then waking up just in time to see them.

My friends and I reunited when *Bohemian Rhapsody* the movie came out and we all sat together in the front row and sang every word to every song and the memories came back. I still listen to Queen every day and at the moment I have my 8 year old grandson staying with me. As soon as we get in the car he always says, 'Nana can you play 'We Will Rock You' and then 'Don't Stop Me Now'?' He got this love of Queen from me.

I WAS THERE: CRAIG TAYLOR

QUEEN WERE ONE of the most outstanding bands I ever saw. We got centre front row and Freddie was passing drinks down to me, because I was standing on a pile of old Coke cans and, being tall, I was about a foot higher than everyone else. Coke cans were really strong back then and made of steel rather than aluminium. I've still got a couple of them, along with two cups that Freddie passed down!

I managed to sneak into the launch party for *We Will Rock You* in Australia. I found out you could get tickets through the fan club so I joined the fan club and ended up on the front row at the media launch. Afterwards, I noticed that everyone was going to what looked like a party next door. A few people were walking off as if they were going home and I said 'if you don't want to go to the party, I'm really keen' and they gave me their tickets. All the food was free and all the cocktails were named after Queen songs. Ben Elton got really drunk and was singing funny cowboy songs. Even though all the press and celebs were there, Brian and Roger still came over and talked to us, which was pretty nice.

SYDNEY ENTERTAINMENT CENTRE
25, 26, 28 & 29 APRIL 1985

I WAS THERE: JEAN BURDEN

I SAW QUEEN five times. The Entertainment Centre in Sydney was an amazing place to see these artists and I saw so many there, but Queen were amazing. My daughter always came with me, and we always sat in Row F on the side of the stage. No one has a voice like Freddie's and I am sure there are so many people who miss him. Queen were brilliant on stage. There was nobody like them.

Jean Burden saw Queen five times

I WAS THERE: LEE LEVERINGTON

IT WAS THE summer of 1984. I was 14 and watching *Countdown*, an iconic Australian music TV show, with my wonderful mother when the host, Molly Meldrum, introduced the song, 'Radio Ga Ga'. I was very naïve, as my mum had a massive crush on Freddie and then pointed out to me that, disappointingly, he was very much homosexual. I was impressed by the video clip and started researching this fascinating band. I was amazed at just how diverse their music was. I borrowed my cousin's *Greatest Hits* album on vinyl before buying *The Works*. It wasn't long before I had listened to all their albums. Queen took this country boy on a journey of musical discovery.

I was so excited that Queen were touring Australia once again. Mum was almost as excited. We had tickets to the Sunday night show. The night of the anticipated concert, we ventured into Chinatown and had some delightful Asian food. We arrived at the Sydney Entertainment Centre, only a short stroll from Chinatown and found our seats. We were four rows from the front. Mum had done a great job of getting us such an excellent view of the stage, which was inspired by Fritz Lang's *Metropolis*. After the truly awful local support band there was a 20 minute wait for Queen. The sound of 'Machines (or Back to Humans)' started and it was only a matter of time before Freddie, Brian, Roger and John hit the stage. The concert itself was non-stop. Freddie's voice was in fine form that night, as was his sense of humour. The vocal impromptu he did leading up to 'It's a Hard Life' was haunting. The stage setting, lights and performance by all four members was spectacular.

I left the show on the biggest natural high, and couldn't sleep for well over 24 hours. My ears were ringing and the whole Sydney Entertainment Centre crowd were satisfied. When they performed 'We are the Champions', everyone was waving their hands. We all left the concert that night winners. That concert is now more special to me, as my mother passed away in February 2019. Over the years, we always reminisced about the night we saw them. Thinking about that concert and the happiness it bought the both of us always picks me up.

NIPPON BUDOKAN
8, 9 & 11 MAY 1985, TOKYO, JAPAN

I WAS THERE: STEPHANIE HOJIN

I SAW QUEEN in Tokyo when I lived there. They were amazing. Freddie Mercury was so energetic. The crowd loved him. I remember him singing 'We are the Champions'. I went with my Japanese boyfriend, who I later married. He didn't know them then, but became a fan too. Freddie Mercury was very popular in Japan. He used to visit the country privately.

Stephanie Hojin saw Queen at the Budokan

On 13 July 1985, Wembley Stadium in London hosted the British segment of Live Aid. *Allotted a short time slot, as were all the performers, Queen's performance is generally acclaimed as the highlight of the day and was witnessed by an estimated global TV audience of 1.9 billion people.*

LIVE AID
WEMBLEY STADIUM
13 JULY 1985, LONDON, UK

I WAS THERE: NICK PARRY

WE HAD ALL seen the harrowing news footage of the famine in Ethiopia in November 1984, and when Band Aid released 'Do They Know It's Christmas?', we purchased it to do our bit to raise money for the cause. Sadly, that hadn't solved the famine crisis so Bob Geldof and Midge Ure came up with the idea of *Live Aid*, a 'global juke box' concert. My sister Julie and I said we would go if we could get tickets. Queen were one of the many acts on the bill. I bought the *New Musical Express* back then, so eagerly awaited the announcement of how to get tickets.

When the details were announced, I booked a day off work. Tickets were going on sale at 9am at Birmingham Odeon, where Queen had played some years earlier. I lived 13 miles from Birmingham so had to get up at 5am and walk to catch the bus to the railway station at Stourbridge, where I caught the train to the city centre. I arrived at the Odeon at around 7.30am. I was worried that there would be a massive queue, but thankfully it wasn't that big. A security guy showed me to the end of the queue and asked how many tickets I was buying. I said 'just two' and he said I would get them as my position in the queue meant I was well inside the number of tickets they had for sale. The hour and a half went by quickly, as everybody was in great spirits and high excitement, looking forward to the gig. 9am came, the doors opened and I walked into the warm. Within 15 minutes I had my two tickets. Excited wasn't the word. I went home and told Julie how easy it was to get the tickets. Just imagine if a concert of that magnitude was announced today. The web site would surely crash.

Our excitement grew as the date neared, with the line up getting better and better. We lived 110 miles from London so train tickets were purchased for the Friday morning before the show. Our plan was to arrive mid-afternoon on the Friday and queue overnight to get our preferred place between the mixing desk and the stage. We decided it would be the best sound there and we wouldn't be crushed right up by the stage.

On the way into London on the Friday the train passed Wembley Stadium. We then had to get the Underground out to Wembley and it was then that we realised that many others were also planning to queue overnight. The walk up to Wembley from the Tube station just heightened the excitement, despite the continuous harassment from ticket touts wanting to buy our tickets. We were continually saying 'no chance', or something a little stronger, all the way to the stadium.

The atmosphere that night was amazing. We had a great time with very little sleep but we didn't care, the adrenalin would get us through. More and more fans arrived overnight and once the Underground started up again in the early morning, the queues lengthened quickly. The turnstiles opened around 9.30am. We made a quick visit to the toilet and then took up our position around 15 yards from the mixing desk and 25 yards from the stage.

12 noon arrived and the show started with Status Quo. The roar was simply amazing. What a day it was going to be. The bands came thick and fast and it was a whirlwind of superstars. The Style Council, Phil Collins, Sting, Dire Straits, Paul Young and U2 all did their 20 minutes or so. When George Thorogood had finished in America, we knew it was Queen time.

I can't put into words the thrill at seeing the boys appear on the stage

I can't put into words the thrill at seeing the boys appear on the stage that day as they prepared to play a sensational set of what Bob Geldof said was the whole premise of the show, all the hits they could cram into their allotted time. Before they played a note you could see that they were up for it. When Freddie walked to his piano, there was a smile so wide on his face. He knew it was a one off and was determined to give it everything. 'Bohemian Rhapsody' got some of the non-Queen fans in the audience up and singing so they already had the stadium in their hands. 'Radio Ga Ga' is one of Queen's best audience participation songs and it seemed everyone joined in, a truly amazing sight. Then Freddie did the 'ay-ohs' and the response was just brilliant. The volume of all the audience joining in was stunning.

'Hammer to Fall' is a great rock song and went down well. Then Freddie dedicated the next song to 'all the beautiful people here tonight, that's all of you', which was a nice touch, and they played 'Crazy Little Thing Called Love'. Queen have a few great singalong songs and perhaps the two best were played at the end, 'We Will Rock You' and 'We are the Champions', a very personal, heartfelt song by Freddie that again got everyone singing.

All too soon Queen had finished. My sister and I just looked at each other and said 'we just witnessed something special there!'. It took some time for it to sink in but the bands kept coming, with three not-too-bad acts in David Bowie, The Who and Elton John. It really was a dream to see it all. Brian and Freddie then came back to do 'Is This the World We Created?' and it was so brilliant to see them hold the world's attention with such a stunning song. I was so proud to be there. Queen stole the show and blew everybody away with 20 minutes of brilliance.

The walk to Wembley station was like walking on air, we were so high from the experience of the day. Luckily a train for Wolverhampton stopped at Wembley so we didn't have to go back into London, and we both slept for the two hour journey back to Wolverhampton and then got a taxi home through a terrific thunderstorm.

I still have my ticket, t-shirt and programme and would never part with them. They are treasured possessions. I sometimes go on too much about *Live Aid* but it was a highlight of my life. So why not?

I WAS THERE: NIGEL BARTMAN, AGE 17

I WAS 17 in the summer of '85. I know, it does sound like a Bryan Adams lyric. I had got to the age where I could just about afford to get from Billericay to London and go to concerts thanks to my Saturday job at International Supermarkets. Tears for Fears at the Royal Albert Hall was my first gig. 'Shout' was in the charts and the magic of live music had been discovered that night and has stayed with me through the hundreds of gigs since.

Nigel Bartman's Live Aid ticket

I had diverse musical tastes for an Eighties sixth former – Ultravox, The Boomtown Rats, Queen, Bruce Springsteen, Simple Minds and The Teardrop Explodes. Apparently, this wasn't quite what the rest of my sixth form friends though was cool. The Smiths and the Cult were. When the rumours of the *Live Aid* gig started, I thought it would be a great chance to see a few of these bands I liked. But how could I get a ticket? Digging round the local *Yellow Advertiser*, I saw a coach and concert ticket company advertising tickets and phoned to see what the deal was. They said if I brought over £40 straight away, they would put me on their list. I persuaded my Mum to drive me and a friend over so we could buy two tickets. I had a receipt for £80, and hope.

I woke up on 13 July to a sunny day and a sense of excitement, but not really knowing what the day would bring. We boarded the coach in Basildon at 10am and arrived at Wembley at 11.30am. On the way into the stadium, I noticed a tout was trying to sell tickets for £5. The reality was that on the day no one turned up without a ticket. Fans didn't expect there to be any for sale. I managed to get a programme as we dashed in but sadly the t-shirts were already sold out. We nudged our way to a spot in front of the sound desk, to the left looking onto the stage, as the concert started. And there we stayed for the day in the boiling sun, with sweaty sandwiches and a litre bottle of Coke each. Very rock 'n' roll! Status Quo's 'Rockin' All Over the World' was the perfect song to kick off an expectant Wembley Stadium.

I don't think the stadium was filled with Queen fans that day. There were plenty of U2 flags around, which to me makes what happened when the band came on all the more remarkable. I remember seeing Freddie bounce on stage, and I just knew as he sat on the piano stool and felt the keys that this would be special. I don't think people were expecting 'Bohemian Rhapsody', which was way too complicated and long, but Queen had worked out a 20 minute set that will never be rivalled. The moment Freddie started singing 'Bohemian Rhapsody' he had already won the audience over, and although I don't think he was lacking any confidence, he was already feeding off us.

I don't think the stadium was filled with Queen fans that day

---

Then came 'Radio Ga Ga' and the double hand clap and two hand salute which every music fan had seen on the video. It was like Queen had planned this long ago. It made the show more intimate. Everyone was now converted to Queen and involved, which is not easy to achieve at Wembley Stadium. The sea of hands around me was mesmerising. The 'day-o' section that followed just broke the barriers down more and by the time we echoed his 'all right!', we were all part of the show itself. Freddie was having a ball as 'Hammer to Fall' kicked in. I remember Freddie then putting on his white guitar and starting to strum the intro to 'Crazy Little Thing Called Love' and saying 'thanks for coming along and making this a great occasion.'

'We Will Rock You' and We are the Champions' were perfect back-to-back stadium songs, but as I looked at Freddie during the last song, the words stuck with me, 'And bad mistakes I made a few,' and 'you brought me fame and fortune and everything that goes with it, I thank you all.' As I looked at the big screen, there was a glint in his eyes. Freddie knew this was his moment.

Freddie and Brian came back on stage later for an understated acoustic version of 'Is this the World we Created?' The words to the song were pertinent to the event - 'just look at all those hungry mouths we have to feed' and 'you know that every day a helpless child is born'. It certainly had the attention of everyone around me.

The day after *Live Aid* was also memorable. Being at the event meant that you had not realised how big the event had become. The whole country had stopped and watched it on TV. I was lucky to have all of *Live Aid* recorded on VHS, which I started to watch. Seeing the audience clapping to 'Radio Ga Ga' is one of the most powerful things I have seen in music. It was an honour to be there.

I WAS THERE: PAULIE LEADBETTER

I WAS 16 when I first really heard of Queen, outside of 'We Will Rock You'. I was living in the US and walked into choir class where two of my classmates were playing the opening strains of 'Bohemian Rhapsody'. My family moved back to the UK in 1983 at the start of Queen's real resurgence. I went to see them in 1984, during the *Works* tour at the Birmingham NEC. I remember the only disappointing thing was Freddie didn't come out in his Corrie drag outfit for 'I Want to Break Free'!

I saw them again at *Live Aid*. Freddie's 'day-o' was fabulous. You can see it on YouTube but it was nothing like actually being there. He was positively feeding off the energy, and we gladly gave it to him.

I WAS THERE: WILLIAM MARTIN

I ONLY MANAGED to get one ticket, a day before the concert, so it was a very early train from Ipswich station at about 6am. My ticket was for the opposite end of the stage, about halfway up, so I had a perfect view of the concert. Queen, as we have all seen since on video, were superb from start to finish. How I arrived home I don't really know, but I arrived back at Ipswich station in the early hours of Sunday morning. What a day.

I WAS THERE: MARTIN NOKE

WE DECIDED TO go because we wanted to see The Who. We were travelling up from Wiltshire so we drove up the M4 and stopped at Heston Services to buy a copy of *The Sun*. Only then did we realise how many bands were going to be there. Bands were being announced at the last moment and added to the bill. My first memory is that Status Quo came on and the whole place started jumping when they went into 'Rockin' All Over the World'. And I remember Elvis Costello coming on and saying 'here's a northern folk song' and playing 'All You Need is Love'. That was great. But then it did drag on a bit in the afternoon and you had bands we weren't that much into – your New Romantics and Spandau Ballet. Howard Jones was a good time to go for a piss.

Howard Jones was a good time to go for a piss

Then we got U2 and then Queen came on, and they were brilliant and so professional. They were really slick on the changeovers, going from one song to the next with no messing about. The whole place just jumped up because Freddie loved his audience so much, and they loved him. When he sang 'you brought me fame, fortune and everything that goes with it, I thank you all' in 'We Are the Champions', he held his hand up to the audience. He knew he owed it to them, and he didn't forget that he owed it to them.

They were very good at Wembley in '86 too. It was the way he pranced out to the front – 'Wha-hey, it's Freddie' – and did that 'dayo' thing. The crowd responded to it. He had them in the palm of his hand. I've always said there are three brilliant front men – Mick Jagger, Steven Tyler and Freddie. He was the greatest.

I WAS THERE: RICHARD ROGERS

WHEN *LIVE AID* was being discussed, there was talk of Paul McCartney appearing and as a huge Beatles fan I thought, 'I must try and get tickets' because Paul hadn't toured and I hadn't had the chance to see him live. My dear old mum was taking the bus to bingo and it was her who saw a poster advertising a *Live Aid* coach trip and concert ticket package being put on by the local bus company. I managed to get a couple of tickets.

I thought we should try and get seats rather than stand all day. You could sit wherever you wanted, so we got seats near the Royal Box, where we had a great view of the whole thing. At various points during the day we'd go down to try and get a drink or a programme, and there was a big passageway for anyone going from the Royal Box to the stage, so you'd see the artists walking by, such as Elton John with George Michael, and Sting and Bob Geldof. So I then spent a lot of the time downstairs seeing who was coming in and out. And I saw Brian May with John Deacon and got them to autograph my programme.

Before Queen came on, I was telling people what a fantastic band they were and saying 'this is gonna be great'. I knew that when they started playing 'Radio Ga Ga', the audience was going to have to get up and start doing all the hand gestures. They were absolutely fantastic. If I watch the video of it now, it still gives me goosebumps. But it was ten times better being there.

I WAS THERE: PETER SMITH

I MISSED OUT on tickets to *Live Aid* when they originally went on sale. The only way we could get there was to buy tickets for a coach trip from Middlesbrough, so a couple of friends and I were up at 4am on the day of the event as we had to drive from Sunderland to Middlesbrough to join the coach that was leaving for London at 5am. We arrived at Wembley well before noon, had a couple of drinks and entered the stadium, which was of course completely packed, so we found a spot in the stands right at the back. A few minutes later Status Quo took to the stage with 'Rockin' All Over the World' and the day started.

There are so many memorable moments from the day. However, Queen's performance was something particularly special and is often referred to as their greatest single live performance. Indeed, more than that, their 21 minute set is often spoken of as one of the greatest rock performances ever.

Their set was sandwiched between some great acts. U2 and Dire Straits preceded them whilst David Bowie and then The Who had the unenviable task of following their epic set. It was one of those performances where everything came together. It was the right time of day, as the momentum and magnitude of the event was building, and the crowd were ready for their stadium-filling anthems. The band were on fire, clearly ready to give it their all, realising that they were performing to a worldwide audience. Freddie was in command of us all, leading us through a few of their classic songs. He commanded the crowd that day and it propelled them to super stardom. Queen delivered the strongest performance of the event, with the press at the time reporting that the show's organisers, Bob Geldof and Midge Ure, were amongst those who agreed that Queen stole the show.

We walked out of the stadium to the coach park singing 'feed the world'. The hairs on the back of my neck stand up even now, just thinking about it. It was a highly emotional experience like nothing else I have experienced before or since. I feel truly privileged to have been part of it.

I WAS THERE: DARREN WHEELER

I DISCOVERED THEIR music from my brother who was constantly playing their early albums. At first it got on my nerves but eventually it sank in and I love their early material now. I got even more into them after their amazing *Live Aid* performance. The audience went wild. I'd had ten pints by the time they came on. I put two between my feet to clap to 'Radio Ga Ga'. When Freddie did his thing with the audience, singing 'day-o', etc, it sent shivers down my spine. *Live Aid* was an amazing day. They blew me away. I almost missed the coach that day. I had to run into town. And the coach broke down on the way home so we didn't leave Wembley until 1am, arriving

Darren Wheeler was at Live Aid for a remarkable show, and drank a remarkable ten pints

home at 5am. But it was well worth it. It was one of the best days of my life and Queen were by far the best of the bands on the day. They were unbelievable.

I WAS THERE: LINDA O'GORMAN

1985 CAME AND with it came *Live Aid*, an amazing afternoon and evening of music. I planned my day around when Queen were coming on. The house was filled with lots of cheery, happy people listening to great artists giving their time for a great cause. Of course, Queen stole the show. This event kickstarted a completely different road for them and new fans were found that day. Here we were into another decade listening to the best.

Along came 1986. I fell pregnant and, guess what, baby was due in July. So when Queen announced they were playing in Slane, I was so upset. They had to go ahead with the concert without me! I was heavily pregnant and my doctor would not allow me to go. But I was lucky to be able to see the show later on YouTube. Thank God for modern technology.

When the news came out that Freddie was sick, I was devastated. When he passed a massive hole opened in my heart. Poor Freddie. Never would we see his fab performances ever again. I also felt sad because I thought that this was the end of the band. Without Freddie fronting them, where would they go?

In 2005, Roger and Brian teamed up with Paul Rodgers and I was lucky to get to see them perform at the Point Depot in Dublin. Even though they were getting that bit older, they still could work the audience and it was another brilliant night, where more memories were made. I love the way Roger and Brian have embraced Adam Lambert. No one can ever replace Freddie, but Adam does an amazing job. There are similarities to Freddie, both in the flamboyance and cheekiness, and I think Freddie would have approved.

A KIND OF MAGIC RELEASED 2 JUNE 1986

A Kind of Magic was the last studio album Queen were to release while the band was still touring. It reached number 1 in the UK and spawned four hit singles, of which 'One Vision' reached number 7 and 'A Kind of Magic' number 3. The album reached number 46 in the United States.

The tour to promote *A Kind of Magic* again ignored North America, where Queen had toured extensively in the Seventies. Instead, it took in 26 outdoor European shows, with Queen playing to a total audience of over one million people. It was to be Queen's last tour.

RASUNDA FOTBOLLSTADION
7 JUNE 1986, STOCKHOLM, SWEDEN

I WAS THERE: PER DANIELSEN

I'VE BEEN A fan since the *Jazz* album came out, which my cousin bought. 1986 was my final year in school and I got lucky and bought two tickets for the concert in Stockholm. Of course, I took my cousin. It was pouring down that day. We used some big plastic bags to make ponchos to keep us dry. After listening to Gary Moore warm up, Queen entered the stage and Freddie greeted the audience with

Per Danielsen saw Queen in 1986

'this is typical English weather'. But for the rest of the concert, we forgot that it was raining. It was magic. When Brian tuned his 12 string and he and Freddie performed 'Love of my Life', the whole audience sang and it became the perfect singalong. It was magic. I don't think we realised what we had experienced until we sat on the bus on our way back to Oslo. I have seen many concerts since, including Pink Floyd, Dire Straits, Elton John and Sting. None of these were even close to the Queen concert. It was, and I think always will be, the greatest show I've ever been to.

My children are aged 20 and 16. After the movie *Bohemian Rhapsody*, they listen to Queen all the time. As a proud father, I can tell them about that magic evening in Stockholm way back in 1986.

Elisabeth Jakobsen remembers Freddie having the audience in the palm of his hand

I WAS THERE: ELISABETH JAKOBSEN

IT WAS RAINING but it was amazing. Freddie had the audience in his hand from the first minute.

HIPPODROME DE VINCENNES
14 JUNE 1986, PARIS, FRANCE

I WAS THERE: LESLEY GOODENOUGH

THE GIG WAS the talk of Guernsey back in 1986. Just about everyone in the hospital where I worked was going. My then fiancé (my beloved late husband Mark) took me to our local bar. He asked me to get the round in using his wallet. It had French francs in it. I turned round and he was grinning, holding the tickets in his hand. Yes, we were going to the gig!

It was organised by Summerday Tours. With my flatmates, we drove down to the ferry terminal in Mark's soft top Triumph Herald. We were checking out each other's passport pictures and Mark confessed that when completing his passport application, under distinguishing marks he wrote that he had curly hair! (He had a large scar on his forehead from a car accident).

We got an organised coach from St Malo to Paris, stopping en route at a supermarché to get wine and then later for lunch. We spent the Saturday wandering around Paris and then got picked up by coach from the hotel. We got to the Hippodrome de Vincennes in the early evening. It was really warm.

We walked down the side of the crowd. First up was Belouis Some, who were fantastic. Then Level 42, who were amazing too. The French loved Marillion but… zzzzz… until Fish finally sang 'Kayleigh'. The French sort of moved away after Marillion, so we moved closer to the front of the stage.

What can I say? Queen were absolutely fantastic. What a showman Freddie was. He was truly awesome. He had cups of water that he threw into the crowd to cool us down. We were so close that the water splashed us. It was a truly memorable moment in my life.

People are quite stunned when I say that I saw Freddie and Queen live. I also saw Queen in Cardiff with Paul Rodgers in October 2008. I couldn't believe that Paul Rodgers was playing with them, as Bad Company had been one of my favourite bands when I was growing up. I have to confess that I was screaming as the white curtain gave way to… Queen!

GROENOORDHALLEN
19 JUNE 1986, LEIDEN, THE NETHERLANDS

I WAS THERE: PATRICIA VAN GROOTEL

I SAW THEM on the *Works* tour with my sister, on Brian's side, and the stage was wonderful. In 1986 my sister and I went to Leiden again. The first two gigs were sold out before I could get a ticket but they added an extra date. In those days, you'd have to physically be there at the ticket seller, sleep in line and hope this vendor would have enough tickets to still have some left when it was your turn. Luckily, there were tickets-per-person limits on the bigger events, so even if the vendor only had 100 tickets available, you were assured of a ticket if you were number 50 in line. I was always first or second in line, and those were great nights too, sitting there with Queen fans, talking about their music and my sister bringing hot coffee in the middle of the cold night. This last concert in 1986 was the very best I'd seen. My sister and I decided that on the next tour we would go to all the dates in the Netherlands.

It never happened. It became Wembley Stadium in 1992 and the Freddie Mercury tribute concert. What a day and night that was, and it was great to be there, but how sad it was to be there without Freddie. I still listen to Queen every day. They were the absolute best band ever. But they stopped being Queen after Freddie's passing and John's departure. It was the four of them who made this magic.

MAIMARKTGELÄNDE
21 JUNE 1986, MANNHEIM, WEST GERMANY

I WAS THERE: FRANK BARING

I WENT WITH a friend. I really loved the billing - Gary Moore, Marillion and Queen, who I hadn't seen before. It was my first open air show and it was huge, with a crowd of around 75,000 people. I ran out of money because of the merch, food and drinks. The atmosphere was wonderful, even at the back of the audience. Queen's setlist was great. I loved the new songs off *A Kind of Magic* but 'We are the Champions' was the highlight of the evening. Everybody was singing along. Freddie was not only a front man, I loved the passion and expressive power. His voice didn't even dominate the song, he carried the melodies. It was just a wonderful unity.

Frank Baring's ticket for the Mannheim show

Frank Baring was at the Mannheim show

I WAS THERE: OLIVER KLING, AGE 15

THE FIRST QUEEN song I heard was 'Radio Ga Ga' in 1984, although I'd seen the cover of *News of the World* in my sister's record collection and been scared by the picture.

The day of the concert was the hottest day in Germany that year. Me and four of my friends took the train to Mannheim early in the morning. The crowd of 70,000 was the biggest ever rock festival in Germany at that point. Craaft and Level 42 were okay, Gary Moore was great and the second headliner, Marillion, were absolutely boring. They played their entire *Misplaced Childhood* album.

And then it was time for Queen. I've never seen anything like that before and after. Freddie was larger than life. He had the crowd in his hand. The one thing I didn't like was that Queen, a band with such a great repertoire of hits, played cover versions like 'Tutti Frutti', when they were joined by Fish from Marillion who sang with Freddie, 'Gimme Some Lovin'' and

Oliver Kling remembers Queen as the best concert he ever saw

'Big Spender'. I've seen hundreds of concerts since then, but this is still the best concert I have ever seen.

I WAS THERE: JENS WUNDERWALD, AGE 16

MY PARENTS ALLOWED me to go and see Queen in 1986 in Mannheim with my older brother. I took a train to Darmstadt where my brother studied and together we drove to Mannheim. It was a very hot day and absolutely unforgettable. It was the first and last time I saw Freddie, but I've seen them twice with Paul Rodgers and three times with Adam Lambert. I'm still a big fan.

Jens Wunderwald was 16 when he saw Queen

I WAS THERE: DORIS WEIGELT, AGE 21

I REMEMBER MY good friend Achim telling me one day, 'I got tickets for Queen in Mannheim – let's go!' Mannheim wasn't exactly right next to us. Our trip would have been about three hours but so many people were going to the concert that there were a lot of traffic jams. And our car broke down. It took us about six hours to get there. Because of the traffic, we were a bit late and missed most of openers Marillion. We were very far in the back and Freddie was very tiny, but I still remember the white clothing he wore. Later on, we managed to get a bit nearer. It was very hot, so the security guards splashed water on us through hoses. It was so crazy, but it was very refreshing. I couldn't believe I was actually seeing Queen and Freddie Mercury. It all seemed very surreal.

My daughter now loves classic rock. She's a bit jealous that I saw Queen, but I love telling her the story of my seeing Queen. I didn't realise how much of a big deal Queen would become, or that I was seeing a legend in Freddie. Looking back, it was one of the biggest moments of my life.

WALDBÜHNE
26 JUNE 1986, BERLIN, GERMANY

I WAS THERE: MICHAEL BEHRENDT, AGE 20

FANS WERE CLIMBING up the lights to get a better view. I remember the thousands of fans singing their songs together and the unbelievable and charismatic show from Freddie. It was so cool that people were singing together as a huge choir.

I WAS THERE: JACK PIHL PETERSEN

WE TOOK A bus from Copenhagen, the ferry from Rødby to Puttgarden and entered East Germany and drove via the transit road to Berlin. We had some trouble

Michael Behrendt was impressed by the fans all singing along

at the East German border as we had one Irish guy with us in the bus and the border control had trouble understanding what this potential spy was doing in a Danish bus. We got delayed but reached the concert just in time.

OLYMPIAHALLE
29 JUNE 1986, MUNICH, GERMANY

I WASN'T THERE: CLAUDIA STIEBLE, AGE 19

I HAD A ticket for this concert. I was in the middle of my live-in apprenticeship in a hotel about 100 kilometres south of Munich. I asked my boss for two days off. I wanted Monday off as well, since I wouldn't arrive home until the early morning. He said yes and I was a very happy almost 20-year-old (the ticket was an early birthday present to myself) getting ready for the trip. About 30 minutes before I wanted to leave, there was a knock on my door. It was my boss, telling me I had to work because the colleague who was covering my shift that day had called in sick. My boss could not do the evening rush with only one waitress. As an apprentice I could not leave knowing my colleague would be overwhelmed. If I had known this would be Queen's last ever concert in Munich, I would have told my boss to shove it.

Hindsight is 20/20 and I can't change the past, but I never thought that it would take over 30 years before I'd see Brian and Roger together on stage again. A few weeks later, I found out that my colleague had not been sick. The weather was beautiful and rather than work, she chose to spend the day at the lake, sunbathing with her fiancé.

SLANE CASTLE
5 JULY 1986, SLANE, IRELAND

I WAS THERE: JOE BURNS

I'LL NEVER FORGET the journey down in a convoy of cars and meeting others from the north of Ireland. Irrespective of religion for once and just for one weekend, we could forget the Troubles and live like normal people did. The craic on the campsite was buzzing. Tin whistle players, fiddles and even bagpipes woke us up that Saturday morning. There was a walk through the different security gates and we were very pleased with ourselves that we'd smuggled a foil bag of wine in with us. The Bangles really got the crowd buzzing, and by the time Queen came on, the atmosphere was electric. You could feel it in your chest! Even the shower of rain didn't dampen the enthusiasm of the crowd. We were caked in mud but didn't care. And when Freddie started to sing, I saw girls crying because they were so happy to be there. We were ordinary kids again, even if it was just for the weekend. Amazing.

I WAS THERE: LYNSAY NIVEN

I'VE BEEN A Queen fan since I heard them singing 'We are the Champions' on *Top of The Pops* at the age of seven. I received a record token (I'm showing my age now) for my eighth birthday a couple of weeks later and bought the seven inch double A-side single, 'We are the

Champions'/'We Will Rock You'. Fast forward to the release of Queen's *Greatest Hits* and that was my second ever vinyl purchase. I can only assume that the gap in years not buying any records was due to my age and lack of pocket money up to that point.

As I grew older and started earning pocket money and then earning money through my first part time jobs, I bought all of their albums. I loved every single song on every single album. I remember watching *Live Aid* on a very small black and white portable TV with my chum Becky in my mum and dad's kitchen. Queen were our favourite act of the whole day. My dad was a huge Queen fan too, so he joined us to sing along. He even tried to convince us that he taught Freddie to sing, and we roared with laughter.

One day at school, my best chum Fiona asked if I would like to go to Dublin to see Queen live, with her and her mum, on their *A Kind of Magic* tour. Fiona said that her and her mum were booked on the trip through our local newspaper in Aberdeen and if I wanted to go, they would add me to the booking. I was absolutely bursting with excitement. When the day arrived, we had to catch a bus from Aberdeen to Stranraer in Western Scotland and catch the ferry to take us to Larne in Ireland. Once we got there the coach took us to Dublin.

The concert was in the grounds of Slane Castle and it was the first open air concert we had ever been to. We were somewhat unprepared as it rained rather heavily all day and we had no umbrellas or anything waterproof with us. Before Queen came on, there were other bands on - The Hits, Chris Rea, The Fountainhead and The Bangles. Although they were all very talented, we couldn't wait for Queen to come on. When it was eventually Queen's turn to appear Fiona, her mum Jean and myself were absolutely bursting with excitement.

Queen hit the stage, the rain stopped, the sun came out and the whole crowd just cheered and cheered. They opened with 'One Vision', which is Fiona's favourite Queen song, and the atmosphere was electric. Then straight into 'Tie Your Mother Down' and 'In the Lap of the Gods'. When they reached the point where Freddie did his iconic 'ay-oh, way-oh' and everybody sang it back, it was all going swimmingly until he ended it with 'fuck you' and the whole of Slane Castle said it back. Except for Fiona, Jean and myself, as we couldn't possibly say such obscenities in front of Jean. But we had a good giggle about him swearing on stage.

They played hit after hit, even covering Elvis and Little Richard songs. The first encore was 'Radio Ga Ga'. To be part of 'Radio Ga Ga' was just magical, but you don't see the full impact of it until you watch it on TV and you see all the arms in the air and everyone clapping in unison. The second encore was 'We Will Rock You', 'Friends will be Friends', 'We are the Champions' and 'God Save the Queen'.

The following day we read the reviews in the local Irish newspapers before heading home and chuckled when we read that one person had been arrested for being in possession of LSD. The initials of my first name and my two middle names are LSD, so we said that Fiona must have been arrested for being with me. I wish we had kept the newspapers. It would have been something cool to look back on.

When Freddie passed away, it felt like I'd lost a friend as Queen were such a huge part of my life for so long. I stayed in bed and just cried and cried. I loved his energy, his onstage presence, the fact that he was outrageous and flamboyant. And, of course, I love their music. I never get tired of listening to Queen songs. One of my favourite moments has to be when the crowd sings 'Love of my Life' to Freddie. I always find that very powerful and moving. The closest I could ever get to mimicking Freddie's wardrobe was when I bought a pair of black and white diamond spandex leggings. Freddie had the whole black and white diamond spandex suit, I just had the leggings.

Every time I tell someone I've seen Queen live, they always say that they are very jealous and that it must have been totally amazing. It most definitely was. I still have the programme and the headband I bought at the concert although, sadly, the t-shirt is long gone. Seeing Queen live was a totally phenomenal experience I will never forget. I feel very honoured and privileged to have been lucky enough to have seen them live.

I WAS THERE: JASON THORNTON

IT POURED WITH rain and there were loads of drunk people. I remember Freddie asking the crowd to calm down. It certainly was quite a show.

I WAS THERE: KEITH CONNOLLY

THIS WAS AN amazing, thrilling, unreal gig. I knew even then that this was a special moment in time, witnessing such a forever iconic band live. The memory of their appearance at *Live Aid* was still very fresh, and changed not just my life but my whole perception of the world around me. Freddie Mercury's circus ringmaster-like performance was the high point of that day, and of all the musical acts on *Live Aid*, he undoubtedly ruled that day. I'm sure millions, nay billions, would agree.

Their Slane performance was not perfect. Outside of the many hits, played to perfection with sweat and passion, I could spot a mile away that although at the top of their game, this was just a band going through the motions for large parts of the set. Playing the hits. Pleasing the audience with crowd pleasers. The audience was already won over before Queen ever played a note. Seeing Freddie in the flesh, close up - within 30 feet at times - and looking into his eyes is what led me to see this. It's not something that can be easily spotted from a TV screen.

The Freddie I saw that day was a persona, an act, a clown. Which is fine. That's good enough for the purposes of providing mass entertainment to millions. The power of those songs, so easily sung along to, so anthemic, so epic... that's really what has stood the test of time. Freddie's part in them has been extremely well documented, but those songs are bigger than him, bigger than any performance of them, or the band. Like a lot of things of 'greatness', the songs of Queen are bigger than the sum of their parts.

I got the impression that the Slane gig was just another gig for Freddie. He was happy enough to be there, but he had played bigger and better elsewhere every other night of the week. On TV, I had seen him sing 'We are the Champions' live, and noticed how he had previously sung the line 'I thank you all!' with huge emphasis, hitting high notes for that line. The crowd went crazy, as here he was thanking them.

At the Slane gig, he spoke that line rather than sang it, with not much gusto and even less sincerity. I remember looking forward to him give us that line full blast, to perhaps indicate to us - his audience - that this Slane gig was somehow as special to him as it was to us. By that measure, it wasn't.

I was similarly disappointed when the choral mid-section of 'Bohemian Rhapsody' suddenly saw the stage plunged into darkness, with none of the band onstage, and fog and a light show was all we got. Par 64 aluminium can lights being switched on and off in sequence failed to entertain me through that bit. I really think they could've done that waaay better, somehow. If they had rolled out an actual proper choir for that bit or something, that would've been great. A DAT machine playing the music while the boys took a break... that's the stuff of pub bands, even then.

An impressive bit for me was just before they played 'Radio Ga Ga', when I noticed it was actually John Deacon playing bass for that synth-arpeggio pattern. Until then I had assumed that was a synth, to be rendered on backing track for live performance. It was played live and sounded great! Similarly, Brian May's odd-sounding guitar solo in 'I Want to Break Free' was synth-guitar, played live. I had no idea until that day that that was actually May playing guitar, albeit highly processed. This also sounded great live!

Overall, the Slane gig was closer to musical theatre in many ways, like a circus performance, rather than a gig fronted by a man who looked his audience in the eye and deeply cared for how much his audience waited on his every word. Talent and energy in abundance, but a 'show' as such, a party of fake revelry where the hosts are constantly refilling your glass, while they themselves remain the most sober ones in the room. A contrived spectacle, but a touch of 'reality' would've made it better.

I WAS THERE: PATRICIA O'LEARY

IT TURNED OUT to be the worst concert I ever attended. The band were excellent, but trouble was brewing all day, as coach loads of Northern Ireland thugs had arrived, and were causing havoc. It was the height of the troubles in Ireland, and these creatures were looking for any excuse to create havoc. The place was awash with drugs and drink. (Roger Taylor said he never saw so much alcohol consumed in his life). It was a great line up that day with The Bangles, and Chris Rea as support acts.

The weather was atrocious, and just as the show began to the strains of 'One Vision', the heavens opened and it was like a scene from the Somme. When Freddie entered the stage, he was wearing a golden crown. The place erupted and for a brief moment, the complete stage was obscured in a sea of thousands of beer bottles. They crowd went berserk and fights erupted. I was drowned in a full bottle of cider that some dick beside me poured all over me.

Whoever told Freddie to wear that crown lit the spark. The Northern scum had their excuse to kick off. Freddie did his best to keep order, saying the band would walk off if it persisted. The last straw was when Brian May was hit with a bottle. They cut the set short and beat a hasty retreat. Interestingly, in recent times the owner of Slane Castle, Lord Henry Mount Charles, said in an interview that he bumped into Brian May at a petrol station and they reminisced about that gig. I would love to know what he said.

I always think of that time, and wish it had been better. It could have been a stand out gig, and to think, it was the last time we would ever see Freddie perform.

I WAS THERE: PETER O'CONNOR, AGE 21

I WENT WITH my cousin Gerald from County Sligo. I'm from Dublin. We got to the venue by coach from Dublin on a very wet day. We weren't too far from the stage and I remember Freddie and the boys arriving by helicopter and landing just behind the castle. Some items were thrown onto the stage by some drunks whilst Queen played and they left for a short while and some audio was played whilst calm was restored. But it's the only time I ever saw Queen and it was one to remember.

I WAS THERE: ADRIAN THOMPSON, AGE 12

WHEN YOU THINK of iconic live venues around the world you think of Radio City Music Hall in New York, Wembley Stadium, Glastonbury, the Isle of Wight and the like. Slane Castle is on that list. It's situated 30 miles from Dublin with a natural amphitheatre that slopes perfectly from the historic castle on the hill down to the Boyne river, setting the scene as the backdrop behind the stage. Thin Lizzy were the first of the legendary bands to rock the famous green slopes of Slane in 1981, with a then little-known band called U2 opening for them. Over the years it has hosted various members of music royalty including the Rolling Stones, Bob Dylan and Bruce Springsteen. In July 1986, it was the turn of Queen.

Tickets priced at a mouth-watering £15 were snapped up in no time by rock fans the length and breadth of Ireland. Queen's iconic *Live Aid* performance had cemented their status as one of the world's greatest live shows and no Irish fan was going to miss the chance to witness Brian, John, Roger and Freddie and their *Live Magic* tour when it hit Irish shores. This concert was to go on to be the biggest ever at Slane Castle, the 95,000 plus crowd dwarfing that of Bruce Springsteen the previous year, and any concert since.

For me, a huge Queen fan, it was a dream come true that my idols were coming to Ireland. But, being so young, my mother wasn't in agreement with me travelling to the County Meath venue. There had been serious riots at the Bob Dylan show in 1984 and, like most parents, she was apprehensive to say the least. My two older brothers and their two mates had already secured tickets for the show but there was none for me. Nearly giving up hope on going, I gave one more full day of nagging to my mum and dad about going and it was still a firm 'no'.

I wept that night, going to bed with the thought I was going to miss the concert the next day. On Saturday morning I lay in bed and listened as my two brothers were up and buzzing around, getting ready to head off to the concert. Again, I was in tears. Then just before they were about to leave, my mum came into my bedroom and said that my eldest brother Patrick had a spare ticket and that, if I really wanted to, I could go. Before she had finished the sentence, I was out of the bed and getting dressed in my tight jeans, basketball boots and denim jacket. Off we went in a yellow Vauxhall Chevette.

It was a horribly wet day but nothing was dampening my spirits as this was my very first concert and it was Queen. What a way to start my concert going! As far as 20 miles out from Slane, traffic was down to a crawl pace with the huge volume of people making their way to the tiny village where the biggest rock band in the world today would be taking to the stage. By the time we reached the outskirts of Slane village, car parks were filling rapidly and we were forced to park about two miles from the venue. The first sight that greeted me as I stepped out of the car when we finally got parked was that of a hairy biker, stark naked and dancing to AC/DC on top of a VW van whilst sniffing glue out of a clear plastic bag. One of the older boys said to me, 'Welcome to the crazy world of live rock 'n' roll.'

We made our way as quick as possible into the village and down to the castle. This walk was like running the gauntlet, filled with tens of thousands of rain-drenched rock fans in strong singing voices and fuelled by gallons of cheap cider, the drink of choice at that time. On entering the venue, the first thing that struck me was the vast stage that was situated with its back to the Boyne river, and that infamous *Live Magic* tour stage with the white stripe sprawled across the base of the hill. And, as far as the eye could see, were people. The four boys and myself made our way down through the, by now near capacity, crowd and took up base at the bottom of the slope just below the castle itself, to the right of the stage. Chris Rea was just finishing up his set as we picked our spot on the hill.

Next up were Irish lads Fountainhead and they were followed by one of the hottest new bands that year, The Bangles. 'Manic Monday' was a huge hit in Ireland and right across the world that year and it drew the biggest response so far on the day.

The level of drunkenness on the day was very much apparent and my brother got a boot in the face by one passer-by as we sat on bags on the hill awaiting Queen's arrival. We decided to go to the toilet before Queen came on, as toilets were placed down to the right of stage and we knew we hadn't a hope in hell of making them once the band came on, as the crush down the front would be serious.

As we made the short walk down the side of the stage to the loos, a massive cheer went up and everyone was looking up to the sky. Suddenly the drone of a helicopter could be heard louder and louder over the house PA. As we looked to our right, towards the castle, the chopper was starting to drop in behind the barrier near the stage. Thousands of people rushed to the barriers and we followed. We stared in through the high wire fencing, nearly getting crushed to pieces, and then the door opened and out stepped Queen. I was in disbelief that these idols of mine, who I'd only seen on TV and in rock magazines, were standing just 20 feet from me. My heart was pumping with excitement. We saw the four lads climb the steps at the back of the stage and watched Freddie, stretching and warming up and having a laugh with the crew.

As the band disappeared behind the stage, we quickly moved back to the hill to reclaim our spot and await their eagerly anticipated entrance. As we got back near our standing space under the castle the sound from the rig changed to the keyboard sound of the entrance anthem, 'One Vision', and then with a massive cheer from the 95,000 fans, a large puff of smoke went off and Brian May ripped into the opening power chords on his infamous home-made guitar. As far as I could see back up across the rolling hills there was a sea of people with their hands in the air, a sight I will never forget.

The now legendary set was played flawlessly by the band. Minor scuffles broke out from time to time down in the pit in front of the stage, much to Freddie's dislike. He stopped at one point, after several empty cider bottles were thrown onto the stage, and asked the crowd to behave. Freddie was later quoted as saying he didn't enjoy the Slane concert due to the behaviour of some drunken fans and the hostile atmosphere at times, but for me it was a life changing experience. The week after the show, I bought my first electric guitar and a year later set up a band with my school mates.

From that day in 1986 until the present, music has become a big part of my life. Seeing Queen at the height of their fame triggered a switch in me and generated a love for rock music that will live with me for ever.

ST JAMES PARK
9 JULY 1986, NEWCASTLE, UK

I WAS THERE: MEG BARBERS, AGE 34

I CAN REMEMBER having to go to queue for tickets. It was good natured crowd in the queue. My husband Paul worked offshore – two weeks on, two weeks off – and took time off work specially to go to the concert. I was so excited.

Seating was available but we chose to stand on the pitch as there would be more atmosphere there. The music could be heard for miles around. Freddie Mercury was such a show off and a fabulous performer. He really interacted with the very enthusiastic audience. For the last song he sang, he came out in his crown and red robe. I can remember Paul lifting me into his shoulders so I could wave at Freddie. I can't see him doing that now. I'm 66 and he's 67!

I WAS THERE: CLAIRE EGAN, AGE 23

I WENT TO see them with my younger brother, I must have queued to get tickets, back in the days when they weren't the exorbitant prices they are today. It was so packed inside that it took ages to get out at the end of the concert. The atmosphere was fantastic and it was a memorable concert. Seeing the crowd all clapping in unison was just amazing. I already liked Queen, but I liked them even more so after seeing them in concert. They were so good and Freddie was an amazing performer. I used to always get the *NME* and *Melody Maker*, because I've always been into music. Back then *Top of the Pops* was how you discovered acts and that's how I discovered Queen. I also saw Queen with Adam Lambert two years ago at Newcastle Arena and that was brilliant. He pays a great tribute to the late great Freddie Mercury.

I WAS THERE: RONNIE KENNY

MY INTRODUCTION TO Queen was probably through my brother as I was more into soul music and Tamla when they first surfaced. I can remember in the mid Seventies thinking 'Bohemian Rhapsody' was a load of pretentious twaddle. But I obviously became more enamoured of them as the years went on. By 1986 I couldn't wait to see them live. Six of us girls from the office all got tickets and booked a half day holiday well in advance. We finished at 12pm and went to The Magpie, a

Newcastle United supporters private club right across the road from the football ground, on Barrack Road. There we grabbed a quick lunch and a drink before queuing to get into the ground. The atmosphere was amazing. There is something special about an open air gig.

Status Quo and INXS were the supports but INXS didn't turn up due, we were told, to 'an accident on the motorway' which stopped them from getting through. I recall that we

Ronnie Kenny, pictured here with her mum, remembers an enthusiastic Newcastle crowd

all said 'yeah, right' - or words to that effect! Status Quo basically did a double set and I have to say they were bloody good, which I really should have expected after seeing them at *Live Aid*.

But when Queen appeared… well, what can I say? If St James Park had had a roof on it, the roar that greeted them would have lifted it right off! Freddie Mercury was on top form, they all were. They were brilliant musicians led by a great showman. We didn't want the night to end. Every single person at that concert was singing and clapping along, all brought together by their love of a great band.

At the end of the night the six of us walked one of the girls to her car, which she'd parked in a residential street. Horror of horrors, it wasn't there…. We found a phone box to ring the police (there were no mobile phones in those days) but had to leave her at the phone box while we all had to run for our last buses. We only found out the next day when we all went in to work that the daft bat had been looking in the wrong street! She never lived it down.

I WAS THERE: ANDY MITCHELSON

MY MEMORY OF the day is the singalong with Freddie. The crowd kept up and he said, 'You fuckers can sing better than I can.'

Andy Mitchelson remembers Freddie praising the audience

I WAS THERE: WENDY PATTERSON, AGE 24

IT WAS AMAZING. A friend and I hung about until security let us in. I ended up on some guy's shoulders so that I could see1

I WAS THERE: BILL PROUD

I ATTENDED WITH my now ex-wife, Denise. She was pregnant and fainted before Queen performed. The following week we were confirmed as being on the way to our first and only child, Jon, who was born the following April. The evening was marred for some people by INXS not turning up, but Status Quo did an extra long stint as the warm up band and had the crowd ready for the arrival of Queen. It was the only concert I attended at St James Park, and my abiding memory is of Freddie arriving on stage wearing an ermine robe. A fabulous night.

Bill Proud remembers Freddie wearing an ermine robe

I WAS THERE: TERRY WELCH, AGE 35

I HAD LOVED their music since I was a teenager. I remember Freddie's energy and his showmanship. The crowd loved him. My husband put me on his shoulders. To me Queen's music is dateless. When I listen to it now, I am taken back to that day.

I WAS THERE: ROBIN RUMBLE

IN 1986 THE *Magic* tour was announced and my wife Margaret, who in 1973 had declined her friend's offer to go to Newcastle City Hall and see Mott the Hoople, this time got her opportunity to see the best live band in the world. On 9th July 1986 we boarded a bus that took us from Hartlepool to St James Park, Newcastle to watch Status Quo, and what should have been INXS whose van broke down on the way to the gig, to warm the crowd up before Queen put on the best performance I have seen by a band.

Who could ever forget Freddie, resplendent in his yellow jacket, going from one side of the stage to the other and whipping the 38,000 crowd into an out of tune choir on 'Love of my Life'? My wife was sat on my shoulders for that one.

We went to the Freddie Mercury Tribute Concert. What a way to spend a bank holiday Monday, celebrating Freddie's life with a memorable get together of some of the biggest names in the music world at the time, and an unforgettable version of 'Love of my Life' sung by Extreme.

WEMBLEY STADIUM
11 JULY 1986, LONDON, UK

I WAS THERE: GARY JACKSON

I WAS LOOKING for Queen tickets all over the place as I had promised my friend I'd get them. He had never seen Queen while I had, on several occasions. I had just about given up hope when another friend told me his brother Ian, who lived in London, worked at Wembley and said he would get some tickets. This he did - one for me and my friend and one for him and his wife.

We left for London on the Friday morning at 4am, arriving at my friend's brother's house at about 11am, where he showed me his *Live Aid* concert programme which had been autographed by all acts on the day.

Off we went to Wembley. We got in early, had a free tour of Wembley Stadium and were then shown to our amazing seats. We got a free programme and t-shirts and watched the full concert of course. At the end of the concert, we were led out of the stadium, elated to have seen Queen at their sublime best, and over to Wembley Arena, where we were taken to the side and up the stairs (I didn't know it had an upstairs) to the aftershow party. We were gobsmacked. Not one drink was paid for and all the food was free. The sad part was that Queen were not there but a message of appreciation was read out on the group's behalf. Of course, there were no mobile phones in those days so I don't have any pictures, but it was one of the best days of my life and will live in my heart forever.

I WAS THERE: JEREMY GOES, AGE 11

MY DAD LIVED with my beloved grandmother in Dollis Hill, two train stops from Wembley Park. I was to visit my nan and dad that weekend, so I got to the house after school at about 4pm to be greeted by Nan. My dad came home from work at 6pm, very excited. 'Jeremy, get ready. I am taking you to see Queen at Wembley!' I could not believe it. We were out the door 20 minutes later! I remember we got on the train. It was packed full of Queen fans. Status Quo were supporting them, so there were many Quo fans on the train too, singing 'Whatever You Want'. It was a great experience for this 11-year-old. We got off the train and crossed the road, walking up Wembley Way leading to the stadium. I had chills inside. I was going to see this great loud band!

We got into the stadium. Status Quo were on stage. My dad was also a big fan of theirs, so we found ourselves near the front of the stage, in the middle. The Quo set was great. Then Queen came on. I will never forget hearing that 'One Vision' opening sequence. When they came on stage, I nearly fainted! My dad picked me up and put me on his shoulders. I could see Freddie, Roger, John and Brian clearly. And Spike Edney too! I found my eyes glued to Roger Taylor. I had started playing the drums when I was six, and his sound and style as a kid was so huge. I wanted to be a drummer when I grew up.

The Friday show was filmed and finally released in 2005 on DVD. I watched it and remembered so many of those moments – Roger standing at the front right in front of me during the acoustic set, Freddie going up on the right side of the stage during 'Radio Ga Ga'. I remember that moment I was standing down there looking up at him. All captured on camera. What memories.

The next day, Dad and I walked to the stadium from our house. It was a very hot day but it started raining cats and dogs five minutes after leaving. Again, we got right to the front of the stadium. The rain had calmed down, but it was really hot in there. The second gig was even better than the previous night. Although Freddie's voice was not as strong. I remember watching Freddie running to his piano to play 'Bohemian Rhapsody'. That song sounded so powerful both nights, but Saturday's version really rocked at the end. You could feel the ground shake.

Halfway through, the rain returned and got worse. Freddie actually mentioned it. I remember that clearly. He blew his nose a few times both nights and he didn't care at all. I thought that was pure class. After the show, Dad and I waited maybe 30 minutes for the crowd to clear a bit. We decided to walk back home, rather than get the train. We walked with a group of fans and everyone was singing and cheerful, including little me!

That weekend changed my life. I became very serious about drumming from that moment and drumming has been my passion ever since then. An obsession. Why? Because I saw Roger Taylor (one of my favourite drummers) and that amazing band just two stations up the road from my house!

I WAS THERE: JOHN MARTEN

IT WAS MY brother who got me into them, around 1977. The first time I saw them was at Wembley Arena when I travelled from Suffolk to London by train with friends. Then we drove to Milton Keynes Bowl in 1982 for the *Hot Space* tour. That was my best concert. 'Somebody to Love' was fantastic. And for Wembley Stadium in 1986 we sat right at the back in the top centre of the stadium for the sound, which was fantastic. Picture yourself sitting in front of your hi-fi, but to the left and right you have two towers of speakers, both of which must be 80 feet tall. Then 60,000 fans singing, being led by Freddie. I don't think I need to say anything else.

I WAS THERE: DEAN PRITCHARD

HAVING SEEN THEM in 1973, I saw them at Wembley in '86 too, together with my now ex-wife. The atmosphere was amazing on the day. We were around 15 rows from the stage and the only annoying thing was people putting their girlfriends on their shoulders blocking the view to the stage. Queen were at their imperious best of course. Freddie owned the crowd as usual - we were putty in his hands!

I WAS THERE: PAUL PHILLIPS

MY GIRLFRIEND AND I arrived at 9.30am, queued outside and then ran to get the best unreserved seats we could when the gates opened at 1pm. We were in the stands, near the front to the right of the stage. The support acts on this sunny day were The Alarm, INXS and Status Quo. Not half bad, eh? This is a famous televised gig now, with inflatable band members floating above the audience for 'A Kind of Magic'. I remember John Deacon floating off miles above West London and Freddie being devoured by the audience as he failed to set sail fully.

Freddie wore his iconic yellow jacket and struck many a pose. His famed 'day-oh' debuted here for me. The new numbers, the aforementioned 'Magic', the opener 'One Vision' and Brian's 'Who Wants to Live Forever?', with Brian on opening vocals and synth, were stunning. The 'Love of my Life' singalong was very memorable.

The concert ending, with Freddie in crown and a king's robes, was unforgettable. The sound was epic, quite an achievement for a large outdoor gig in the Eighties.

I WAS THERE: LORETTA SHAHRABI

AS A TEENAGER in the Eighties I got into some of their later stuff like 'Las Palabras de Amor' and 'Radio Ga Ga', and then went into their back catalogue and started to get into 'Seven Seas of Rhye' and 'We Will Rock You' A friend who'd attended *Live Aid* in '85 asked me to go to Wembley and I thought, 'Okay, I'll give it a go.' We went, and it was an absolutely superb evening. It was the *A Kind of Magic* tour. They had the inflatables of themselves which they threw into the audience and we tried to catch one of them. The most memorable part was when we all clapped hands in unison to 'Radio Ga Ga' like in the video. That was quite surreal.

The atmosphere was electric. They did some early hits, their album hits and Freddie had a few costume changes. He had his yellow t-shirt which he ripped off towards the end, and of course he came on at the very end in his robes and his crown as he always did. I had liked Queen beforehand, but after seeing them live I became more of a convert. I admire Brian for what he does on opposing badger culling and protecting wildlife, but I'm not interested in seeing Queen with Adam Lambert. To me, Queen was Freddie Mercury. Going to see Queen now would be like going to see the Rolling Stones without Mick Jagger.

I WAS THERE: JOHN SPENCER

1986 WAS THE last time I saw all four of the band on stage together at Wembley Stadium. I'm not a fan of open air gigs. It always feels like some of the sound goes up rather than out at the fans. But this gig proved me wrong. There were three other bands on before them, of which Status Quo were probably the best as they got us all in the party mood. We were singing and dancing along with them. The boys were due on at 8.30pm, but as always they held back for a few minutes to get the crowd worked up. Then there they were!

I think they played for about one and a half hours but as always it went by in a flash. Freddie mentioned the press and their constant crap about the band splitting up, and said, 'They're talking from here,' bending over and pointing to his arse. That got us all cheering.

Queen were awesome. Who knew at the time that this would be the last time I'd see the four of them together? I didn't go to Knebworth. It was a massive outdoor gig, so no thanks. And I hadn't gone to *Live Aid*. I guessed they'd only be on stage for about 20 mins or so, plus I had an air show to be at that day. My in-laws had a video recorder, and recorded it for me, so I did get to see them that night. They were - as always - flawless.

I saw Queen + Paul Rodgers in Hyde Park a few years ago. I totally enjoyed that gig. Paul has a great voice and he sang the songs his way. He didn't try to emulate anyone, plus they sang some Free and Bad Company songs. And I've seen them with Adam, at Manchester Arena.

He's a funny guy, but he does have an incredible range, and Freddie is there with them. One of the sad parts for me is seeing Brian, who used to run across the stage, now just walking across. And of course, with Freddie not being there, and John Deacon too....

I met John once, many years ago when I worked at Gatwick. He was with his family so I was a bit unsure, but I went up and apologised and asked for his autograph. He was nice and polite and as he was signing my bit of paper, I asked him if he missed it. He said no! I kind of get it, constantly away from the family touring here, here and everywhere.

When I was a teenager I played them constantly. I still remember naughty Kenny Everett playing 'Bo Rap' over and over and over again.... even though he had been told not to.

I WAS THERE: DARREN WALKER

I HAVE ALWAYS been a massive Queen fan, and I managed to get a ticket to go see them in concert once, at Wembley Stadium on their *Kind of Magic* tour. It was a glorious sunny day as I waited outside for the gates to open. A few beers were consumed outside, as it would cost an arm and a leg inside, sat with the waiting crowd all in great spirits in anticipation of the forthcoming crowd pleaser!

Eventually the gates opened and I slowly made my way to my seat. Once there in I saw that I had a great view of my fellow fans and the stage. The crowd were all in good cheer and savouring the atmosphere. Turning around, I noticed something that I tended not to see at concerts. About five rows behind me was the Royal Box and there were sat Charles and Di, both looking rather out of place, as royalty tends to do when normal people are present.

While we were waiting for Queen to come on, people just started throwing random pieces of food, all good fun and no bottles or tins. It turned into a kind of game where the person that got hit by any squidgy item was expected to continue the tradition by throwing it at someone else. Perhaps failure to do so would have given them seven years' bad luck? The inevitable happened and I got hit on the head by a tomato sandwich. So, being a stickler for tradition and observing protocols, I picked it up and just lobbed it over my shoulder as hard as I could. It was only then that I remembered with increasing terror who was sat not too far behind me. With some trepidation, I turned around expecting to see a Special Branch officer laid on top of Prince Charles, having taken a sandwich for the good of the heir to the throne, and another undercover police officer heading towards me with a view to arresting me or giving me a good kicking so that the next food I touched would be hospital food.

But as I looked I was very much relieved to see that my aimless throw was well wide of the royal mark. The majestic couple still looked immaculate if a little square. I was safe! The trajectory of the food was such that it had actually hit Anita Dobson, the *Eastenders* actress and Brian May's wife. Oops! Fortunately for me, the sandwich didn't do any damage or make a mess and, bless her, she continued the tradition and randomly threw the sandwich back into the crowd. Bless you, Mrs May, you are a real sport. (I like to think Prince Charles would have done the same thing but somehow I doubt it).

And the concert itself? Queen were the best group I have ever seen live. Freddie knew how to get the crowd going and the world lost a great entertainer the day he passed away.

I WAS THERE: MARTIN ASTLEY

I REMEMBER GOING to this gig by organised coach from Wolverhampton. I possibly got the tickets from Mike Lloyd Music. A gig at Wembley was obviously different to being at the Wolves Civic. We were on the pitch to the left as you looked at the stage, about level with the mixing desk. The gig was superb but it turned out to be a very long day with the coach travel and then having to stand for several hours. There is an iconic picture of Freddie Mercury with his arm raised wearing white trousers and a yellow leather jacket, with the silhouette of Wembley's twin towers in the background. I take great pleasure in telling my three sons, 'I was there'.

I WAS THERE: LESLIE LANE

BY 1986 MY mate Alan's brother's company no longer had the selling rights to both Wembley venues and so I got my two tickets via the fan club. My mate Ian 'Izzy' White came with me. As we entered the stadium the first thing we noticed was the huge stage, which covered the whole end of the stadium.

Once Quo were off, the reliable Queen crew got to work making the final touches to the stage. The music playing over the speakers stopped and the dry ice drifted across the stage as the taped intro to 'One Vision' started. Suddenly, Brian was there playing the opening riff, the bass and drums kicked in and then Freddie was stepping out to start singing the song. 'Tie Your Mother Down' quickly followed, with the big ending to the song followed by thunder flashes going off across the stage.

After 'Another One Bites the Dust', Freddie turned to the crowd and said, 'There has been a lot of talk about a certain band called Queen, that they're gonna split up. What do you think?' The crowd, in unison, shouted 'no!' and Freddie turned his back to the audience and bent over, pointing to his backside. 'They are talking from here.' Loud cheers from the crowd. 'We are going to stay together until we fucking well die.' More cheers from the crowd. 'I keep wanting to leave,' laughed Freddie, 'but they won't let me.' They then played 'Who Wants to Live Forever?'

We are going to stay together until we fucking well die **Freddie Mercury**

After 'Love of my Life' came a medley of songs from Queen's heroes from the past, including Elvis, Ricky Nelson and Little Richard. Although it's a fun section of the show where Queen get to let their hair down, I thought we could have had another couple of Queen tracks instead. Another song started that I didn't instantly recognise and then it hit me, 'Gimme Some Lovin'' by the Spencer Davis Group. Freddie started to sing the song and after about a minute stopped, placed himself in front of his piano, the music faded out and the iconic intro to 'Bohemian Rhapsody' began.

The way the operatic section was done was pretty clever, with the tape playing all the 'mamma mias' were loudly as the huge multi-coloured lighting rig slowly came down closer to the stage while oceans of dry ice completely fogged out the stage, ready for when the band returned, Freddie seemingly coming out of nowhere to burst into 'so you think you can stone me and spit in my eye…'

I WAS THERE: STEVE VANE

I SAW THEM twice on the Magic tour and got right up front both times. Freddie had the crowd in the palm of his hand at Wembley, and considering he was already ill his voice was amazing. Knebworth was just before my 20th birthday and we did a coach trip up from Kent. The driver was selling plastic cups for a pound but you got a free beer with it!

I WAS THERE: MARGARET COLE

IT WAS MY twin Tim who took me to see Queen and I was absolutely bowled over. Tim was the one that introduced to them. And I will never ever forget the feeling I had when they were on stage. Like we lost Freddie, I sadly lost my brother George to AIDS. But we were all by his side.

Margaret Cole went to Wembley with her twin brother Tim

I WAS THERE: SIMONE VAN WOERKOM

I CAME IN contact with Queen in 1974, when I was seven, thanks to my mom who loves music in general and Queen in particular. I always used to listen to the radio and we had the albums to listen to. In 1986, I went to the post office in the middle of the night to be sure to get tickets for the announced concert, and was third in line. So, two days before my 19th birthday, I got to see my heroes live. It was the best birthday present I ever gave myself. I remember the beginning with 'One Vision'. It was the best concert I've ever seen. Freddie was fantastic! I was on the front row and saw them perform like no other band in my life. The energy coming from stage was astonishing and I loved every minute of the concert. When the DVD *Queen Live at Wembley Stadium* came out, I bought it and watch it still. And I saw *Bohemian Rhapsody* twice and loved it!

I WAS THERE: TANNER AKIF

MY SISTER USED to work for Paul McCartney and got two free tickets. I bought a brand new white cotton hooded parka jacket day before and wore it to the concert. We got right to the front, about four rows back from the stage. It was raining all day and we got soaked but we didn't care. We watched INXS and, I think, Quo but I can't remember much about them. My jacket started shrinking on me as

Tanner Akif's jacket shrank uring the concert he saw

it was drying off. It stopped raining in the early evening before Queen came on, but my size large jacket was now a small and I had to take it off as it was too tight by the time Queen came on around 8pm!

I WAS THERE: LYNNE EDWARDS

I WAS DRIP fed Queen since the early Seventies as a little kid. My brother, my three cousins and myself would go to Sunday School and then back to Grandma and Grandad's for Sunday dinner. My Uncle Ian was a teenager and would sit in his room upstairs blasting cool tunes on his record player. My cousin Kerri and I would dance outside his door, rocking out on the landing. Fast forward to the Eighties and there's that familiar sound blasting again, this time from my TV. That was it… me hooked! Luckily, Uncle Ian still had his album collection. I raided it and fell in love with Queen. I took my dad and brother along for the journey. Mum's Roy Orbison and Demis Roussos records didn't get a look in.

As a teenager, being a Queen fan was not so cool amongst my friends. They were all into Spandau Ballet, Wham, U2 and Simple Minds, etc. but my chemistry teacher was a huge Queen fan. He'd play them during lessons and I'd sing along in my head. Then, one day in class, he mentioned to my cousin Paul that Queen were going to be touring and he'd love to go. Paul is a very clever man, and as a kid was a bit of a smarty pants and a teacher's pet, especially this particular teacher! Between them, they hatched their evil plan to make it possible for Mr Crompton to arrange a school trip… a school trip to Wembley Stadium to see Queen!

So it was that a minibus full of teenagers drove from Armthorpe in South Yorkshire down to the Big Smoke! The journey was so exciting. I'd never been to a gig and, as a football fan, I'd never been to Wembley. We parked up and walked up Wembley Way. Me and my best friend Karen, arm in arm, skipping along. I cried…. hallowed turf and all that. I even lifted the edge of the boards put down to protect the grass and pinched a small handful, a present for my dad.

The support bands were fantastic, but to be fair I was just waiting... and waiting. Then the moment arrived and there they were, my favourite band right in front of me at Wembley! A bloke in front of me picked me up and put me on his shoulders. I could see over all the tops of the heads and had a clear view of the lads. At that moment, Freddie was singing to me and only me!

At that moment Freddie was singing to me and only me

I had the best day of my life. On the way home, we sang our hearts out to the Queen cassettes Mr Crompton had brought along. Wearing my tour t-shirt, I beamed the whole way home and burst through the door to my mum and dad who were waiting up for me. I gushed about what an incredible day I'd had. Dad was jealous - very jealous – so I talked him into taking me to Knebworth to see Queen again!

At Knebworth, we were miles from the stage so spent most of the gig watching the big screens. My dad, brother and myself were having a blast whilst Mum was pretty much just along for the ride. Then the moment came. The crowd roared and I cried, again. Queen on stage! In the broadest Geordie accent, and nice and loud to be heard above the music, my mum proclaimed, 'Eeee, doesn't that lead singer look like Freddie Mercury?' Muuuuuuum!! (She only knew him as a solo artist).

That has to be one of my favourite memories of my mum. That and us diving behind a bush to do a quick wee before the long trek back to the coach. Well, we thought we were behind a bush. A load of bikers revved up their engines and gave us a cheer. Mum was mortified! I met my now best friend and godfather to my kids on that coach. Mark and I spent many, many nights sitting in, listening to Queen beer in hand, reminiscing about the last night Queen performed live. What an absolute honour to have been there. We didn't know it would be their last live show at the time of course.

You know how people talk about where they were when they heard the news about JFK? Well, I know exactly where I was when the news hit about Freddie. I was sat in the living room at my parents' house with my 10 month old daughter, Caysi, sat on a white plastic garden chair feeding her Weetabix for breakfast. My dad was in the kitchen and Mum had gone to work. I sobbed my heart out. I was devastated.

I WAS THERE: CRAIG WOOD

IN 1980 I was back at Wembley Empire Pool on the *Flash* tour. It was great, although sadly I don't remember a lot about it. I was then working in Ireland, so I missed the whole *Hot Space* thing, but I had my dad tape the Milton Keynes Bowl show off *The Tube* on our new VCR. In 1984 I was at Wembley Arena to see them on the *Works* tour. They were loud as hell and Freddie's 40th birthday.

On the *Magic* tour, I waited in line for about five hours outside the stadium. When the turnstiles opened, I was running into the corridor up some stairs and down the terraces and onto the pitch. I ran down the pitch to the front of the stage, where we were told to sit down. I was sorted, front row. It rained, we had a party and we saw the mighty Quo, The Alarm and INXS. It totally knackered me out, but it was a day to remember forever. And I'm on the DVD. Brilliant!

I've many happy memories of Queen. And some sad ones, such as when we lost Freddie to AIDS. But they are such an intrinsic part of my life now. Everybody who knows me knows that! From the first beats of 'We Will Rock You' at Wembley Arena in 1978 to the dying notes of 'God Save the Queen' at Wembley Stadium in 1986, I have stayed loyal to the band. These four respected, well educated guys have certainly helped me get through life thus far.

Now 'the show must go on'. Queen continue to tread the boards and entertain many, which is fantastic for the new generation. My 17-year-old daughter is hooked on Queen, which is great for her and me. I can pass down the stories, and tell her the fun times I had at conventions, or headbanging to the closing credits of *Flash Gordon* in my local cinema. Fantastic days. Long may they continue....

MAINE ROAD
16 JULY 1986, MANCHESTER, UK

I WAS THERE: ANTHONY BENT, AGE 15

I REMEMBER GROWING up listening to Queen in my dad's car on an 8-track player. Normally it was the *Night at the Opera* album and I was obsessed by 'Bohemian Rhapsody'. The operatic bits mixed with the heavy guitar were astounding. I was probably about seven when I first heard it. Our school had some vinyl in their library and I started borrowing the Queen stuff and taping it to listen to at home, quickly knowing all the

Anthony Bent was at Maine Road

words to albums like *News of the World*, *Jazz*, *Sheer Heart Attack*, *The Works* and then their *Greatest Hits*. I was hooked by now, buying everything I could that Queen released on vinyl. I saw the 'Kind of Magic' video for the first time on TV and was blown away. Then my dad came home from work with an envelope containing two tickets for Queen's magic tour at Maine Road, Manchester, the home ground of my beloved Manchester City. I was elated and asked my next door neighbour David, also a big Queen fan and a year older than me, to come with me.

I remember walking up to the ground smelling the hot dog and burger stands, seeing all the t-shirts and scarfs on sale and being harassed by ticket touts and people asking if I would part with the tickets? Not a chance! The show began and it was magical. I remember the enormous kind of magic inflatable figures bouncing around the ground and Freddie controlling the crowd throughout the gig. It was absolutely awesome. 'Love of my Life' was a highlight for me, going acoustic and listening to the crowd singing sent shivers up my spine and when 'Radio Ga Ga' kicked in I remember the thousands of arms clapping in unity. The lights, the sound, the crowd roar - it was my first ever outdoor gig and I was hooked. I remember walking away afterwards with my ears ringing from the sound. I must have been to over 100 live gigs since then, but none have ever matched the raw emotions I felt that sunny day in July 1986.

I WAS THERE: ANDY CARTER

MY MUM LOVED Queen and was frequently blasting out 'Bohemian Rhapsody'. Only being six at the time I complained. Ironically, I turned out to be a huge fan a few years on, buying everything the band did. Then to my excitement they played *Live Aid* and I got to see them the following year at Maine Road and Knebworth. Luckily, I managed to get the boys' autographs after injuring myself at work in 1989. My mum wrote to Jacky Gunn asking if they would sign a get well card to cheer me up. I still have it!

Andy Carter received a get well card from the band

I WAS THERE: TONY BARON

I WAS GIVEN Queen's *Greatest Hits* on cassette when I was nine. I'd been in a road accident and was in hospital for 10 weeks so got a lot of presents and money. Once I had learnt to walk again, I went out and got *Queen I* and *II* on cassette. I remember seeing an Austrian advert with 'Keep Yourself Alive' on it. I love that song. My auntie was into Queen too and when I went to visit her we would always listen to their albums.

I saw the advert in our local paper that there was a coach company doing a trip to Manchester to see them. I went to their office to enquire and bought the ticket there and then. I was working on the Youth Training Scheme and the ticket was almost a week's wage. The big day came round really quick. I was on my own, but there were around 15 other people at the pickup point. When the coach from Fraser Eagles arrived, there was a few people on it already and the atmosphere was brilliant. It was the second concert I'd ever been to at the time, the first being Johnny Cash with my dad, and the atmosphere was a lot more vibrant on the Queen coach.

Arriving at Manchester City's ground, there were big queues leading to the main doors but it was a warm afternoon and a lot of the crowd were singing. We were right at the far end of the stadium but we weren't feeling deprived as we were all going to see the best band ever. They came on to 'One Vision'. Once the band started playing, we all freaked out. My first real concert and I couldn't see them from where I was, but I didn't care as the bass and noise just hit me inside. I didn't want the night to end and if felt like it wouldn't. They even did two encores. I was buzzing all night.

The coach home was mellow, with people recounting their version of the night and us all listening in case we had missed something. Once I got off the coach, I had to walk three miles home alone. I remember the walk home was quick, as all I did was remember most of the songs. Getting home I didn't stop talking for an hour. My dad was still up as he had finished work at 10pm. He sat up listening to all I had to say.

Later than year the album *Live Magic* came out, allowing me to reminisce many times since about that day.

I WAS THERE: DENISE GERRARD, AGE 33

I WAS EIGHT months pregnant with my son and went with my then husband. It was a hot sunny day with lots of supporting bands, including Status Quo. The atmosphere was absolutely unbelievable. Queen came on stage around 8.30pm and Freddie Mercury had us all in the palm of his hand. I grieved when he passed away, like he was a family member, and I am so glad I got the opportunity to watch them live.

I WAS THERE: TERRY LATHAM

THE FIRST TIME I saw them was at the NEC in Birmingham. I went with a friend. Although I knew they had good songs, I didn't know what to expect. But Freddie came on stage and he had this amazing larger than life aura about him, almost as if you were zooming in on someone optically. And he played the crowd and made everyone feel as if he was just singing to them. I then started buying the albums and the singles. *Hot Space* was the only album that didn't do anything for me.

Come 1986, I was a kitchen fitter. My girlfriend had never seen Queen, and the staff at the company I worked for clubbed together and bought us two tickets for Maine Road. When I heard that Status Quo were support I thought, 'This is great, I'd really like to see Quo.' And they were absolutely shocking. I went to the bar. But then Queen came on and, again, Freddie was larger than life.

I WAS THERE: ANDREW MAYLED

THEY FIRST CAME to my attention when 'Bohemian Rhapsody' was released. I was 11 and thought 'wow!' but it wasn't until *News of the World* came out in '77 that I really got into them. Queen was the way my school friends and my self got into 'hard rock'. It was the soundtrack of my teenage years. Then there was that boiling hot day in July '86 when I finally got to see them live. The anticipation was so intense you could taste it. The opening chord sequence of 'One Vision' blasted out of the sound

Andrew Mayled was at Maine Road in 1986

system, search lights swept the stage and there they were – incredible! All those thousands in that stadium that night, and Freddie had every one of us in the palm of his hand.

I WAS THERE: CHRIS ROBINSON

I FIRST CAME across Queen when I went round to a friend's house after school and he put on the newly released *Queen Live Killers* double live album. I was 16, and it completely blew my head off. I'd been a bit of a new wave/Gary Numan-type kid and had dabbled with punk and harder rock such as AC/DC and Deep Purple, but this album changed everything. To hear the dynamic of the band - the passion and power of Freddie's voice, the unbelievable guitar licks and tricks of Brian and the tight rhythm of Roger and John - stunned me. That they could sound so amazing live on stage made me realise, as a bit of a guitarist and keyboard player

Chris Robinson and then girlfriend Tracy met Brian at a Buckingham Palace garden party

at the time, that I had better focus on a different career! I very quickly availed myself of their back catalogue, and fell in love with the band hook, line and sinker.

It was a scorching hot day at Manchester City's old Maine Road stadium. It's now a housing estate - does whoever lives there now know that 'Bohemian Rhapsody' was belted out on that very spot? I took a friend's girlfriend, a very attractive blonde, and we decided we were a couple for the day so enjoyed ourselves. There was no hanky-panky, but she did sit on my shoulders for a while! Standing on the pitch, about 20 deep back from the stage, I eagerly awaited the band. We arrived half way through the first warm up act. I had never heard of Belouis Some but I recognised 'Imagination'. The crowd were polite and applauded, but the anticipation of what was about to come felt like nervous, almost scary energy. The second warm up act (and this speaks for itself, as they were only a warm up act) was Status Quo. They got everyone going - fast, five bar blues with all the usual Quo favourites. Now the crowd were really up for it.

Around 7.30pm, dry ice started to fill the stage, there was the low rumble of thunder and then explosions and the crowd started going crazy. It led into the familiar and spine-tingling opening synth chords to herald the start of the concert, opened by the raw open fret D by Brian, going into A, D, D, G, C, C, G, G, C, C, A, D as the band appeared to 'One Vision'. There was crazy fretwork by Brian as Freddie whipped up the crowd with his strutting and his classic pose - one arm raised, legs apart.

The next 100 minutes were some of the most memorable of my life, from the second song, 'Tie Your Mother Down', brilliantly slowed down into 'In the Lap of the Gods' through to 'Now I'm Here' (one of my all-time favourites), itself amazingly slowed right down into 'Love of my Life'... and then the crazy Presley/Pitney/Little Richard covers of 'Baby, I Don't Care', 'Hello Mary Lou' and 'Tutti Frutti'. As Freddie said, 'The things we do for money!'

Come the first encore it had to be 'Radio Ga Ga' and then 'We Will Rock You', our hands raised aloft and in unison for both, before 'Friends Will Be Friends' and the usual ending of 'We Are the Champions' and 'God Save the Queen'. It was breathtaking and exhilarating. How Freddie could have a whole stadium in the palm of his hand the instant he appeared was a sign of his true stage presence and unparalleled personality. It was an incredible day that lives in my memory for ever. When I tell people I saw Queen with Freddie, the green with envy look is always quite satisfying.

When I say I saw Queen with Freddie people are green with envy

Almost 20 years later to the day, I was lucky enough to be invited to The Prince's Trust 30th year anniversary garden party at Buckingham Palace as my then girlfriend Tracy was a Prince's Trust mentor. This was another dazzling day of weather. Dressed up to the nines, we were shoulder to shoulder with royalty, sports stars, comedians and pop stars - Rod Stewart and The Spice Girls amongst them – and all Prince's Trust ambassadors. Moving toward the roped off ambassadors' area, I spotted a tall frizzy-haired and familiar looking chap in a luminous blue suit. Yes, Brian May was walking towards me! Like a child meeting Santa, I almost dived on him. I didn't dive, but I did politely ask if it was ok to say 'hello' and shake his hand. Cue two minutes of another kind of magic as I chatted to Brian about the gig and how much of a fan I was, and still am, whilst Tracy chatted to Anita Dobson about their similar-looking spotty but beautiful frocks.

Roll on 2026 and my next Queen encounter!

MÜNGERSDORFER STADION
19 JULY 1986, KÖLN, GERMANY

I WAS THERE: VOLKER MOSTERT, AGE 15

WHEN I WAS nine my older sister and I shared a record player. She got me started on Queen. We saw Queen together in Köln. This was my first big concert and it was a breathtaking experience. Nobody had an inkling that this was going to be Freddie's last live appearance in Germany. I still love the music to this day, although I always preferred their hard rocky stuff and eventually was swept away by the New Wave of British Heavy Metal. But many of my fellow metalheads also love Queen and appreciate their sheer musicianship. I am now the lead singer of a heavy metal band and Freddie will never be surpassed as a singer and frontman.

I WAS THERE: THOMAS KRÜGER

I SAW THEM twice, at Nürnberg Zepelinfeld and at Köln, an open air show on Brian's birthday, the biggest birthday party I ever went to in my life. It was a great, great day with 54,000 singing for Brian. When the show was over, Freddie didn't want to leave the stage and called on the other members of the band to play more songs. What a night!

I WAS THERE: TONY WALSH

I FIRST SAW Queen on *Top of the Pops* doing 'Seven Seas of Rhye' when I was 11 and heavily into The Sweet. I couldn't believe what I was seeing and hearing. Everybody was talking about it at school the next day. I was unable to secure tickets for Wembley so I got tickets to see them in Cologne on Brian May's 39th birthday and, yes, they did play ''39'! Brian also joined Marillion for 'Market Square Heroes'. They then announced they would play Knebworth and I got tickets for that as well. To this day, I still don't know why I didn't see them in the Seventies.

Tony Walsh saw Queen in Cologne

NEPSTADION
27 JULY 1986, BUDAPEST, HUNGARY

I WAS THERE: MERCÉDESZ WINDISCHMANN

THE TICKET WAS very expensive. By the time I'd saved up enough money to buy a ticket they'd sold out. Luckily, a friend of a friend who worked there as a security guard let me in when the doors opened. He made me stay in the same place in case someone asked me for the ticket I didn't have.

LES ARÈNES DE FRÉJUS
30 JULY 1986, FREJUS, FRANCE

I WAS THERE: ERIK LE BACCON, AGE 18

I WENT WITH two friends. The show should have taken place in Italy but something went wrong and they had to find another place and settled on Frejus, a little town on the French Riviera. It was such a small arena. There were perhaps only 2,000 people there. I was jumping with friends into the water close to the palace in Cannes when I saw a plane advert in the sky – 'Queen en concert a Frégus' – and I immediately went and bought my tickets!

Erik le Baccon saw Queen play in Frejus

I WAS THERE: CAMPBELL CUNNINGHAM

WE WERE CAMPING in the south of France. We had travelled down in the car with two kids in the back and Queen's *Greatest Hits* playing on the tape most of the way. We had heard on the news that the Queen concert in London had lost its inflatables and caused havoc in the air space but I hadn't got tickets as they were all sold very quickly. We arrived safely at our holiday destination after the 1,000 mile drive and set up camp in Frejus. One morning, I was out on my early morning jog down into Frejus town when I saw a poster advertising Queen at the Roman arena. Now this was news to me as I knew all the tickets for their concert in Nice or Cannes had sold out, so I stopped and read the advert. They were going to be on that week - the Nice concert had been cancelled – and tickets were going on sale the next day. I got there early, joined the queue and got four tickets for us all as a family.

The seats were quite far back, right at the top of the arena, but still we were

Campbell Cunningham saw Queen at the Amphitheatre in Frejus

in there for the magic – literally! Our kids were nine and seven years of age. They said it was the best day of their lives and now in their forties they still vividly remember it. We sat eating our snacks of sandwiches and digestive biscuits with a flask of tea before the start. Meanwhile the Dutch and German fans behind and around us were smoking weed. I smuggled a tape recorder in and recorded some of the concert and I've still got the tape somewhere - but most of the recording is of me singing!

RAYO VALLECANO STADIUM
3 AUGUST 1986, MADRID, SPAIN

I WAS THERE: MANUEL SANCHEZ, AGE 18

I WAS WORKING in an office, and had the money for the ticket to the concert but none of my friends had the money to go with me. It was a beautiful summer's day in Madrid, the Rayo Vallecano Stadium was full of people with smiles on their faces and most of them were foreigners on holiday. Queen started with 'One Vision' and what a song to start with.

Manuel Sanchez was 18 when Queen came to Madrid in 1986

ESTADIO MUNICIPAL
5 AUGUST 1986, MARBELLA, SPAIN

I WAS THERE: DAN MCEACHRAN, AGE 7
I WAS ON holiday with my parents in Spain. We did not intend to go to Spain to see Queen but the opportunity came to us as a result of the holiday rep selling tickets on the morning of the concert. I didn't have any knowledge of Queen the band. When I was told we would be seeing Queen that evening, I really did think I was going to meet Her Majesty Queen Elizabeth II. We got to Marbella Football Stadium quite a few hours before the gig started. As we were in the stadium early, we had a walk around to see

Dan McEachran was 7 when his dad took the family to see Queen

what seats to have. The front of stage was obviously busy, with standing room only, and as I was young my parents wanted us to have seats for the gig. We found front row seats on the left side section as you looked at the stage. We were quite far back and only just above ground level.

The warm up acts seemed to go on forever but when Queen fired up the whole place came alive. Having no idea about who Queen were or any of their songs, I was completely hooked on the energy coming from the stage and how everyone in the stadium was completely hooked on it as well. It has always stayed with me just how fantastic the atmosphere was.

As a 12-year-old boy in 1991, I remember I was sat having breakfast watching BBC television before school when I first heard the news of Freddie Mercury's death. I ran into the kitchen to tell my parents. As the years went on and I became an adult, I have seen various Queen tribute bands and I have seen Queen and Adam Lambert in Birmingham November 2017. I would absolutely sell my soul to the devil if I could go back in time as an adult to watch that concert again!

The world didn't know it but Queen's appearance at Knebworth Park in the summer of 1986 was to be their last live appearance with Freddie. Performing in front of over 150,000 fans in the grounds of Knebworth House in leafy Hertfordshire, Queen were treading in the footsteps of the Rolling Stones, Led Zeppelin and Pink Floyd. There could no longer be any doubt as to whether Queen were a serious rock band.

KNEBWORTH PARK
9 AUGUST 1986, STEVENAGE, UK

I WAS THERE: SAMMY SHACKLETON

I SET OUT very early to hitch hike alone from Liverpool to Knebworth, hoping to be there for around noon. That was optimistic. I arrived at the venue two songs from the end of Big Country's set after getting lost somewhere between Hitchin and Stevenage. I was eventually picked up at Stevenage by a guy who was working security at the event and I was exhausted when I arrived. I had no ticket for the concert and I was wandering around the grounds of Knebworth, figuring how to get into the concert. It was during these wanders that I saw the Queen helicopter landing by Knebworth House.

I paid £9 for a ticket from a tout who'd been asking for £15. When I entered the actual concert, the guy who'd given me the lift earlier was working on the entrance and he didn't even look at my ticket. I could have just walked in! I was struck by the size of the crowd. It was massive. Some were estimating it at 120,000, others were saying 150,000. I saw Michael Jackson on his *Big* world tour and Queen's crowd was much bigger. There was a definite excitement in the air in the run up to the start of the concert and when the concert began with 'One Vision' the crowd went wild.

Freddie was at home on stage. He owned the venue, he owned the crowd, he owned the world. I've never seen a front man and lead singer as captivating. He was always moving and the crowd moved with him. We fed him and he fed us. It wasn't an especially long concert, and of course none of us knew that we were witnesses to music history, as it was to be Freddie's last live performance, but it's one I'll always remember. The world was a poorer place after he died.

I WAS THERE: ALAN LEECE

I SAW AN ad for Knebworth in the paper so me and my housemate, Roland, decided to try to get tickets. We lived on the Wirral peninsula, just off the Old Chester Road, so public transport did not seem like an option. But I had a car, kindly given to me by my dad, and I was willing to share costs getting there. Roland could drive, but was not insured. I agreed to drive and Roland would navigate.

My dad's old Chevette (or the Shove-it, as it became known) was our chariot for the day. We hit a service station just before heading east off

Alan Leece was at Knebworth for the final show with Freddie

the motorway and had problems getting started again, so just in case I joined the AA. We drove for miles but at the next stop it wouldn't start without being pushing. Roland pushed, I let the clutch out....

We made it to Knebworth Park, although the engine died and a bunch of fans had to push us to our parking space. After a bit of a trek to the field, we picked out a spot close enough to the stage, on the rim of the bowl. We were about a third of the way back from the stage. But we could see the stage and the screens and weren't too hassled. The stage looked amazing in the daylight.

There was a fairly long wait for the main act. The anticipation was building; the crowd started to get restless. The wait was possibly a little too long, or very finely judged. A helicopter appeared overhead. We, or I, didn't know it but that was Queen's arrival vehicle. It was dusk; the lights were taking over. And finally, on came Queen, to huge roars and excitement. The helicopter did a circle or two of the field as they went into the first number.

I remember hoping 'Seven Seas of Rhye', my first Queen song memory from 15 years before, would be played and it was, albeit part of the medley along with 'Now I'm Here'. I wasn't expecting 'In the Lap of the Gods' from *Sheer Heart Attack* but there it was. I just went from song to song, enjoying what I didn't know and loving what I did. The band were professional as anything, but they also looked like they were enjoying themselves. Freddie got us all to follow his singing - he had an amazing voice! - and swore at us because we were so good and/or too cocky! One voice versus 120,000 plus. It should have been no contest, but he could belt out, note perfect. Every. Single. Time.

It was a long trek back to the car after the gig, with the songs still ringing in our ears. Some idiot had turned the lights out, so we were all following those in front. Roland and I got to the car and – miracle! - it started. We joined the queue to get out of the parking field. It was a long time before we had moved even 100 metres, so we decided to sleep until the gates cleared, which they did at about 2.30am. We got driving and made it to Welwyn Garden City where the car gave out again.

We went into the police station to borrow the phone to call AA and let them know I was stuck on a double yellow. 'No problem,' they said. The AA man arrived, charged the battery for us and off we went to Roland's place in Shropshire. We napped there, had a meal with his folks and then headed for home on the Wirral. A few more indications that the car was not good, I drove on low lights and even without lights for some time to eke out the battery amps a little more.

We got home about 11pm, around 24 hours after Queen had left the stage. I had to get the day off and have the car looked at by my brother-in-law. It turned out that the charging circuit was intermittently broken by a dodgy charge indicator lamp on the dashboard. Sometimes the battery charged, sometimes it didn't, and we got home on the last few amps in it. At least the mystery was gone – I hated not knowing!

I WAS THERE: MICHELE DUGGAN, AGE 20

MY SISTER WAS a fan and had all three of the first albums, and was playing them at home a lot. When 'Bo Rap' was released, it went to a whole other level and from there I was firmly a fan. By the time of Knebworth, I was in with a crowd who were regular festival and concert goers. Four of us went, three lads and me. It was the biggest concert I have ever

Michele Duggan remembers Knebworth for a lot of reasons

attended, and it remains the best ever live concert I have been to. The other two wanted to go down the front but Simon was a bootlegger and needed to be in area where it was good for capturing the sound. Having fainted in the crush at *Monsters of Rock* watching Van Halen, I decided to stick with Simon. At the end, having split off from our driver, we realised we had no idea where the car was so spent hours searching for it without success. We found a phone box and called my boyfriend but he was over the limit and couldn't drive. So Simon called his dad who drove two and a half hours from Boston in Lincolnshire to fetch us. I slept on the floor of the local police station reception, along with a number of other people, while we waited for him to arrive. 30 minutes from home, we met up with our other friends who had spent all night looking for us!

I WAS THERE: DEAN HAYCOCK, AGE 15

I WENT WITH my mom and auntie to Knebworth. When we got there, I said, 'I'm going down the front' and, having arranged where to meet afterwards, off I went. The sun was beating down and stewards kept throwing water cartons from the stage into the crowd. I didn't catch any of them. There was an enormous bottle fight, with thousands of plastic bottles being thrown across the crowd. Jerry Stickles, the concert promoter, came on and said the show would be cancelled if it carried on. Thankfully it stopped.

Dean Haycock asked Brian why there was no video of the last ever show with Freddie

A couple of groups came on - Belious Some and Big Country. Quo and Queen fans were throwing grass clumps at both groups and it was actually very funny. Quo came on and were very good. Then Queen came on and blew my mind - it was a massive dream come true for me. I was right at the front - I saw John Deacon throw his guitar for some reason. I remember the cameras being there and always wondered why Queen's last concert was never released for us to watch. I wrote to Brian May 20 years to the day of the concert, asking him why it had never been put on film and released. Amazingly, he replied:

"This is well-timed, Dean, and that's a very good question. The answer is very simple, and very embarrassing. It is one of the biggest blunders in our history. The cameras were rolling, and visuals of the entire concert were relayed to the Idaphore screens simultaneously with the show. All it needed was for someone in our team to put a tape machine on the end of either the screen mix or the cameras themselves. No one did. So it all went into the ether. It would have been a great DVD to have, wouldn't it… Queen's Last Concert. Well, sadly, it will never happen."

I WAS THERE: JASON MOORE, AGE 21

THE FIRST TIME I heard of Queen was in 1982 at Elland Road Stadium in Leeds. I wanted to go, but never got a ticket for the gig. But I went down there about an hour into the concert and sat outside listening, along with thousands of other people. And that's what really got me into Queen. I'd never really bothered with them before that. I tried to get tickets for *Live Aid* which never came off, and then I got a ticket for the '86 Knebworth gig.

Jason Moore (left) had an unforgettable day

I lived in Leeds. I went out clubbing on the Friday night and woke up in someone's house. My mate was knocking on the door of this house at five o'clock in the morning to wake me up and I'd only got in at three. We set off down to Stevenage and I slept most of the way. As the day started to happen, I just remember horrendous traffic heading into Stevenage, getting towards Knebworth Park. We queued for three hours to get into a farmer's field and get parked. The parking was unorganised and total bedlam. And then we started walking towards Knebworth, along with thousands of other people. It was absolutely boiling hot. We had no shirts on and were getting sunburnt. We got in there and tried to get as close to the front as we could. We managed to get to within about 100 feet from the stage, so we were in for the day then. The atmosphere was unbelievable.

The first act that came on was a dance act called Belouis Some and they didn't go down too well with Queen fans. People had been drinking outside the park so there was a lot of hostility towards the band and they were getting bottled. I felt sorry for them. Status Quo were on next. Everyone expected them to come on just before Queen but they came on earlier because they were doing another concert that day and requested an earlier spot. They didn't go down well with the Queen fans either. The promoter was Harvey Goldsmith. He came on asking for calm and the Queen fans were just throwing objects at him, bottles full of sand and everything. He got hit on the head by a bottle. And the drum kit went over, and Francis Rossi got bottled. All anyone wanted to see was Queen.

Unfortunately, a guy got stabbed at the concert and bled to death 50 feet from the stage. I can vaguely remember seeing a melee around that area and there being a bit of a fracas. But with 150,000 people in a venue, you don't know what's going on. We only found this out afterwards. He got taken away by paramedics and that was it. Everyone just thought he was injured and off they went. But the poor guy had died.

The last act to come on before Queen was Big Country, and they were very, very good and went down a lot better than Quo. It was getting into the evening by now. It was chock-a-block and I can remember looking around behind me and the furthest people from the stage were nearly a mile away.

All of a sudden, we heard the Queen helicopter coming in and they came straight over the top of the audience, just 50 metres above us. It just hovered above us, and everyone knew that Queen were on board. The Queen fans all went crazy, and then it shot off again and landed behind the stage. And an hour later Queen came out and the place went mad. It was just the best performance I've seen by a live band. Nothing ever beat that. Freddie Mercury was on top form. Queen played about two hours and they finished with the usual stuff – 'God Save the Queen' and 'We are the Champions'.

One thing that will always stick in my mind is trying to get out of the place, because if you can imagine 160,000 people all trying to get out of the place at the same time it was ridiculous. We ended up making our way back to the field where we'd parked and sleeping in the car. Well, we didn't sleep really. We didn't get out until nine o'clock the next morning, and so we started driving up the A1 from Stevenage to Leeds. My mate fell asleep at the wheel and we ended up in a field. The car was a bit worse for wear but we weren't badly injured, and we ended up getting back to Leeds and lived to tell the tale. I'll never forget that day. It was fantastic. But it just showed you how big Queen were. You didn't realise that until you saw the size of that audience.

I WAS THERE: ADRIAN SMITH

FOUR OF US went. I was a postman, Neil was a printer, the other Neil was a postman and Dave was a diesel fitter. We had a boot full of beer going up as it was a scorching hot day but swapped some for programmes outside of the concert. I was right in front of the stage. They were superb that night. They finished with 'We are the Champions', with Freddie dressed in a red robe and crown. Freddie also squashed any rumours of them breaking up which had apparently been circulating.

I WAS THERE: ALEX NEWTON, AGE 15

I WAS A massive Queen fan and it was my first ever gig. I remember that the day was one of the hottest of the summer and the atmosphere was absolutely buzzing. I was towards the back of the crowd but felt that added more to the experience, especially on tracks like 'Radio Ga Ga' and 'We Will Rock You' with the customary hand clapping. Knowing now that it was Freddie's last gig makes the experience even more special.

I WAS THERE: JACQUELINE HUBBARD

I GOT UP, feeling so excited. A group of friends were meeting up, one of whose dads was taking us up there in his brand new Range Rover. We arrived at Knebworth with all our drinks, only for them to be confiscated by staff at the entrances. The doors opened and we ran towards the front of the stage. We were about a quarter of the way back, and had a fantastic view. I remember thinking, 'I can't go to the loo because if I do, I will lose my place and never find my friends again.'

Jacqueline Hubbard was at Knebworth

All of a sudden the atmosphere of the crowd changed. We looked into the skies and there in front of us was Queen's helicopter, circling around us. The excitement was building even more now, and the audience was almost in a frenzy waiting for the off. Then – BAM! - the music, the mist and it was 'One Vision'. The crowd went wild. The feeling was incredible right from the off. I remember suddenly jumping up and down to the music, although there was no choice - the crowd took you with them, whether you wanted to jump or not. We were treated to hit after hit and it was electrifying. With 'Radio Ga Ga' everyone was clapping in unison. Freddie worked the crowd and drove us crazy, strutting across the stage. What a showman. And Brian May on the guitar – well, what can I say? Just 'wow! To be part of such an event was in my eyes an honour and a privilege. It is one concert I will never forget until the day I die.

I WAS THERE: MOYA MAHONEY

I WENT WITH my oldest friend, Anne, who was (and is) a massive fan. I always liked Queen from first hearing them around 1975 when I was at college. They were even better than expected live, a truly stand out experience.

Moya Mahoney (left) and friend Anne were at Knebworth

I WAS THERE: MARK WALLINGS

TWO MATES FROM work, Pete and Don, had a spare ticket and asked if I wanted to go. We left on Friday night, six of us in a Transit van, and started off on the A5. We stopped off at the Bull Inn pub in Atherstone and stayed there for a couple of hours before carrying on to Milton Keynes to stay overnight with one of the lads' brothers. Next day, we found a pub closer to Knebworth and played drinking games, although the driver didn't take part and I didn't drink too much, which was lucky as I'm not much of a drinker. The traffic at Knebworth

Mark Wallings got a spare ticket off mates from work

was bumper to bumper so we parked up on the verge on the main road and walked.

The traffic going to Knebworth was bumper to bumper

Me and the driver got to the gates and went in, leaving the rest of the lads to play rugby with another group of lads. We walked round the edge of the crowd and got along way down but found it hard to get through. Luckily for us, four girls from the Isle of Wight seemed to get through so we just followed them until we were five deep from the stage. It wasn't squashed and they had food and drink and shared it with us. It was dusk when Queen started and you could see the crowd were buzzing. It's still about the best concert I've been to. The music, the atmosphere, the crowd made it a fantastic experience.

I WAS THERE: NEVILLE JAMES

I WENT THROUGH love of, then hatred of, 'Bo Rap' as it was number 1 too long for me, but I loved 'We are the Champions' because it coincided with my favourite football team, Liverpool, winning the league and European Cup. When Queen's *Greatest Hits* came out and the football team I played for did the whole *Wayne's World* style 'Bo Rap' singalong, I went into the whole back catalogue. My experience of the day was just how vast the audience was and that my hearing might be permanently damaged by being too near the huge speakers. The live show was a greatest hits compilation of Fred's showmanship, but at the same time it felt professional and clinical rather than the personality he is famed for.

I was delighted to have seen the mighty Queen

But I was delighted to have seen the mighty Queen and looked forward to seeing them again to see if the next show would be different. Knowing since that I was blessed to see the last ever performance by the original line up, I felt ungrateful for the memory.

I WAS THERE: KEVIN PARKER

I LIVE ON the Knebworth estate and have seen every concert there and worked on most of the early ones. On one of the previous concerts, I was lucky enough to make friends with a guy named Wally Gore. Wal had worked for Queen from the very start and he was John Deacon's right hand man. He also, along with John 'Tunbridge' Wells, ran Queen's security. We sadly lost Wally in 2011. He used to have me in stitches with some of his stories. The Queen concert for me was a bit disjointed, as I was catching up with a few people, eg. Neville Keighley (known as Belouis Some) was a support act and I had supplied the trained hawk on the 'Imagination' video in London, which was I believe the first music video to contain full frontal nudity! Years before, when we first met and I was 15 years old, Wal had given me the nickname 'the Yoof'. Him being a cockney lad, it sounded right. I was told that when someone went to find Wal for me, Wal was with Freddie. When the guy said 'the Yoof is looking for you, Wal', Freddie was very amused by my nickname!

I WAS THERE: RITA DAVIS

AT THE END Freddie put his crown on and cloak on and did a couple more songs. Everybody held lighters up to salute him and stood swaying to his music. I was so sad when they announced he had died. He would still be making perfect records if he was still here. I'm so glad I got to see him.

I WAS THERE: MATTHEW THOMAS, AGE 16

I'D SEEN THEM before, in Birmingham when I was only just 14. At Knebworth me, my mate Martin and my older brother Richard all went to Leeds very early on the day of the show to get a bus. It seemed to take forever to get there but we got in the park around 4pm and, considering there was supposed to be anything between 100,000 and 250,000 there, we got a good spot. My brother went off on his own while Martin and I just stood around waiting for Queen. It was very warm and we only had a very small bottle of pop between us, so we had to ration it.

Matthew Thomas's Knebworth ticket

After watching the support acts there was a gap of what seemed hours but finally the lights dimmed and the place filled with smoke as Brian May ripped into 'One Vision'. For a couple of 16-year-olds, this was just beyond incredible. The band and Freddie were imperious that night, although his choice of language wasn't the best. Two and a half hours later the whole place was in darkness and it seemed to take forever to get out and find our bus as they all looked the same, but we managed it. As we got on the bus my brother also arrived, begging for someone to give him a drink. The bus set off but we didn't get out for about two hours. We finally got back to Leeds around 7am, extremely hungry and tired but very happy.

If everyone who said they were there that day actually was, there must have been about two million people there. Obviously, it was the last show they ever did which brings mixed memories. I'm happy that I was there but sad that it was the last show with Freddie.

I WAS THERE: LESLIE LANE

THIS WAS A show that I couldn't miss. I live in Stevenage and Knebworth Park is right next door. My mate Eric and his wife Karen joined me. The field was enormous and we placed ourselves around a hundred metres from the stage. We didn't want to be crushed down the front, and it was going to be a long day.

Status Quo had changed their slot so they could dash off to try and break a Guinness world record of playing three gigs in 24 hours in three different countries. One of their roadies had climbed onto the roof of the stage with a giant cardboard guitar and played to the crowd. The crowd responded to the roadie and rumour has it he was later sacked when Quo realised what he'd done and that he was getting a better reaction than them.

After Big Country, a few plastic bottles started to be thrown through the air, what started out as a little harmless fun but soon turned into a quite scary situation as more and more bottles started to be thrown, including ones still full of liquids. Thankfully, the bottle throwing died down when it was time for Queen.

As at Wembley, they bounded out to 'One Vision', 'Tie Your Mother Down' and 'In the Lap of the Gods', the 120,000 plus crowd going mad and loving it all. Freddie said, 'This is what you wanted, this is what you're gonna get,' before going into 'Seven Seas of Rhye'. A few songs in, Freddie stood on the edge of the stage and said, 'This is an enormous place. From up here it looks beautiful.' It was the same set as Wembley so we got 'Under Pressure', 'A Kind of Magic', 'I Want to Break Free', the rock 'n' roll medley and they finished with 'Bohemian Rhapsody', the crowd loving every moment. They returned to encore with 'Radio Ga Ga'. The stage lights lit up the whole Knebworth crowd for the chorus and I stood on tiptoes to see a sea of clapping hands all doing the hand claps perfectly in time.

'We Will Rock You' thundered out and the crowd were in great voice as they sang along. 'Friends will be Friends' followed, which I always felt spoilt the flow before 'We are the Champions.' 'Champions' brought one of my favourite parts of the show, when Freddie sang, 'You've brought me fame and fortune and everything that goes with it, I thank you all,' and raised his hand to the crowd as a show of thanks. This moment always brought a shiver to my spine in a good way, as if Freddie really did appreciate the fans. Then it was over. The band took their bows and Freddie said, 'Thank you beautiful people, see you around.'

Little did any of us then know that we would never see him around again, but what a concert to finish a career on. Queen went out at the top of their game.

I WAS THERE: WILLIAM MARTIN

WE HAD HOPED to get tickets for the two dates at Wembley Stadium in July but they had sold out. I will never forget this show. I was in front of the stage, in the centre and about halfway back. The whole concert was brilliant and perfect in every way. The only downside was it took about five hours to get out of the car park at the end after such a great concert. Little did we think this would be the last time they played in the UK. I was lucky to have seen them three times.

I WAS THERE: PETER SNEESBY

I SAW QUEEN on their '84 and '86 tours at Wembley and at Knebworth. It was truly amazing and, in my opinion, they are the best live band ever. Freddie was the real McCoy and the best ever, God bless him. I also went to see Queen in 2008 when Paul Rodgers fronting the band at the London O2 when they did the *Cosmic Rocks* tour, but I don't care much for Adam Lambert fronting the band. I

Peter Sneesby was at Knebworth

wish they would dig some more Queen live gigs out of the vaults and release them on CD or DVD, especially the 1979 show at Hammersmith Odeon. That was a great show, during the *Live Killers* era. There are so many good live shows still locked away in the vaults - Hyde Park (1976), Earls Court (1977) and Buenos Aires (1981) all deserve a proper release. They're on YouTube!

I WAS THERE: PAUL PHILLIPS

NO ONE KNEW this would be the last gig for the original Queen line up. The band arrived in a chopper carrying the *A Kind of Magic* logo. I was about a quarter of the way back in an audience of around 250,000 people. Freddie seemed to connect to all of us. It was an amazing way to end up saying goodbye to him.

I WAS THERE: RICHARD ROGERS

HAVING SEEN THEM at Wembley Arena and then *Live Aid*, I joined the fan club and went to the first fan convention in 1986 in Great Yarmouth. I went to Wembley Stadium and bought a ticket outside at face value. All the inflatables broke free from their moorings and escaped, and Freddie did 'Big Spender'. I went on a coach trip to Maine Road, Manchester just a few days afterwards. And then I saw them at Knebworth for the final time. They never actually announced that they had retired from live performance. Towards the end of the *Magic* tour, Freddie was struggling with things but it wasn't obvious to the public. I think it was the following year that he might have started to become ill. I remember seeing him appear at the Brit Awards and he looked extremely gaunt. But they carried on recording and still made some great records. In all I got to see Queen five times and they were all great concerts. They were the best ever live band I've seen.

I WAS THERE: TOMMY WEIR

I HAD SPENT years trying to convince my oldest and best friend, who took me to my first ever Queen concert, to come and see them again but he had always refused. This time, I was not taking no for an answer. Eight of us met up in Glasgow late on Friday evening to catch the organised overnight coaches down to Knebworth, meaning we would be amongst the first to arrive. We had the good old Glaswegian concert survival pack for our jaunt down south, a carry out comprising numerous cans of booze, a few bottles of spirits and of course a few rolls to soak up the said liquid. Like good old *American Express*, we never leave home without it!

Arriving in Knebworth, the coaches were all parked on a huge industrial estate and roads were closed to allow fans freedom of movement. I remember the walk to the park - there were numerous stalls selling their dubious wares, but I was only interested in the usual concert merchandise of programme, t-shirt or sweatshirt. Going through the gates into the grounds of the park, I thought Knebworth House looked quite regal. The weather was perfect. It was going to be an absolute scorcher. Having arrived very early, we made our way to the front and pitched our spot approximately 15 metres from the stage and just off centre.

As dusk began to come down, the dry ice started wafting from the stage area and the huge video screens flickered into life. The roar went up. This was it, the *Magic* tour was coming to an end and we were ready for a party. We'd already had a sneak preview of what was to come, as their Wembley gig had been broadcast on television in July, but this was the icing on the cake for me, the end of the tour and in the company of my oldest and best mate who'd introduced me to Queen all those years ago.

Similar to the *Works* tour, the lighting rig flickered into life and started to rise up from the stage, with all the lights flashing to the strains of the intro to 'One Vision'. The band ripped right into top gear with Freddie, resplendent in his white trousers, yellow jacket and yellow vest, sprinting from side to side, up and down the catwalks, cajoling the crowd into hysteria. He had us eating out the palm of his hand from the off.

'Tie Your Mother Down' blasted out and the crowd absolutely bounced in unison. This was brilliant to be part of and to see. A little snippet of 'Lap of the Gods' with a snippet of 'Liar' thrown in followed, before we moved on to 'Seven Seas of Rhye'. It was a stunning 100mph start to the show and there was no let up as they tore into 'Tear It Up', Freddie sounding as good as ever.

Things took a small drop in level as the intro to 'A Kind of Magic' played and four huge inflatable Queen members appeared like massive hot air balloons and soared up into the dusky Knebworth sky. Two of them managed to break free from their guy ropes so the air traffic controllers will have had their work cut out. Freddie then stripped off his jacket and indulged in the traditional crowd ritual of 'ay-ohs'. The crowd, three times bigger than the *Live Aid* audience, lapped it up and played along, only louder and bigger than anything the band had experienced in the UK before.

We got 'Under Pressure', which Freddie owned without Bowie, 'Another One Bites the Dust' and 'Who Wants to Live Forever?' Was Freddie giving us a message? Brian's guitar solo was set against billowing dry ice and an impressive back drop of blazing white lights. He went through his repertoire and into 'Now I'm Here' before the quieter part of the show and 'Love of my Life' and 'Is This the World we Created?'

Freddie then took us on a little rock 'n' roll journey back in time with 'You're So Square', 'Hello Mary Lou' and 'Tutti Frutti', dashing up and down his walkways, his enjoyment all over his face. Knebworth was his kingdom and he was the queen. They finished with 'Bohemian Rhapsody' and 'Hammer to Fall', the crowd off again in a bouncing and frenzied mass of air guitars, everyone thinking they were Brian May.

The band came back for 'Radio Ga Ga' and the huge sea of hands lit up by the stage lights for all to see was breathtaking. At the end, I vividly remember John Deacon smashing his bass guitar into his amps and thinking 'he must be angry at something or someone'. Perhaps Freddie had told them what was going on with him personally and John was letting his frustration out.

I WAS THERE: JULIAN WOLFENDALE

I WAS NINE years old and into Slade, Sweet and T. Rex. I was pop music mad and used to win all the pop quizzes at school. Then my older brother, whose Zeppelin, Who and other stuff I'd hear through the bedroom door, brought home *Sheer Heart Attack*. This was different. They already sounded like a mega rock band. They were outstanding at Knebworth. Queen came on when it was dark and suddenly there was Freddie, stood atop a giant staircase and wearing an ermine gown and a crown. What a star that man was. He was punching the air along with the thousands in the audience. He shouted something I couldn't hear and that was it – they

Julian Wolfenden first heard Queen through his brother's bedroom door

started. I stood spellbound for the entire set. Everyone seemed to know all the words. You were drawn in right from the start. It was like being in a shared dream. It was just absolutely amazing.

I WAS THERE: CARL TANNER

I HAVE A few wonderful memories of seeing Queen for the first time at Wembley in '86 and at Knebworth a month later. The first sight of the stage, the smiling crowds – and not a mobile phone in sight. The atmosphere at both were electric but the finality of it all was not present during those final bars of 'God Save the Queen' on that August evening. Officially 125,000 were at Knebworth but it was more like 250,000 plus. The coach we travelled up from Portsmouth on got stuck in traffic so we had to walk five miles to get in, missing the first act. It seems to be a great topic of conversation now when I say that I have actually seen Freddie Mercury live.

Carl Tanner saw the Knebworth show

One other story is regarding Spike. As a Portsmouth lad he was regularly spotted playing with local Portsmouth and Gosport bands one minute and then on stage with Queen the next. One band I roadied for in 1990 was The Rhino Men, who Spike occasionally played keyboards for and who is credited on their album 'Makin Tracks'. Suffice to say when I roadied for them, he was gigging elsewhere.

In my eyes Queen were and still are the most diverse and talented band on the planet, with all credit now to the songs and of course Brian and Roger for keeping it all alive. Not forgetting Spike, it goes without saying!

INNUENDO LAUNCH PARTY
QUEEN MARY
4 FEBRUARY 1991, LONG BEACH, CALIFORNIA

I WAS THERE: BRIAN LEE SOLAR

I HAVE SEEN Queen live a few times, but post Freddie and John. I became a hardcore Queen fan in the US in 1983, the year after they last toured America with Freddie and John. I put down a deposit at a local ticket agency to get good seats when the band came around on their next tour, but that tour never happened. I did sort of make up for that disappointment of not seeing the original band line up. With a friend who was also a Queen fan, we snuck into the *Innuendo* album release party aboard the Queen Mary ship docked in Long Beach, California. In the days before 9/11 security, all we had to do was look over the shoulder of the person with the guest list, tell him or her the names we picked off the

Brian Lee Solar gatecrashed the *Innuendo* launch party

list, and we were in - no ID shown. So, taking the identity of Bo Boyd, a now-deceased Disney executive, I was able to meet Brian and Roger at the party. (I'm sure Bo still got into the party). But no Freddie and John at the release party either.

FREDDIE'S DEATH
24 NOVEMBER 1991, LONDON, UK

RUMOURS ABOUT FREDDIE'S health began circulating in the British press in October 1986 and he was later reported to have received an AIDs diagnosis in April 1987. Queen ceased performing, but continued to make music, with an increasingly gaunt Freddie appearing in a number of the band's videos. Freddie's last public appearance was at the Brit Awards in London on 18 February 1990, when he and the rest of Queen collected the Brit Award for Outstanding Contribution to British Music. Freddie Mercury died on 24 November 1991 of bronchial pneumonia due to complications arising from AIDS.

I REMEMBER WHERE I WAS: MARK MAHAL
I HAD A soccer match with the team I was playing for. As I was parking my car, it came across the radio that Freddie Mercury had died. At that moment it was as if a part of my youth also died that day. But in reality Farrokh Bulsara and Freddie Mercury will live on forever in the hearts of those such as I. A long time, tried and true fan, I have since seen one show with Paul Rodgers and two with Adam Lambert. I applaud Brian and Roger for carrying on.

I REMEMBER WHERE I WAS: STEVE JAMES

IT WAS A Sunday night. I was out with a girlfriend in Ilford, Essex and we were driving out for something to eat when it came on the radio that Freddie Mercury had announced that he had AIDS and he wanted the fans to know. And I thought, 'Oh, there'll a cure for that and he'll probably be all right.' Next day I was driving to work at eight in the morning and they were playing Queen songs relentlessly and they just said he'd passed away. It was a bit of a shock. At work, I was saying he was a fantastic singer and a genius and some guys were ribbing me, saying he was gay and he deserved what he got and all that kind of thing. Not everyone was open minded in those days.

I REMEMBER WHERE I WAS: LISA VENTURA

I GREW UP with Queen from the moment I was born. I can honestly remember listening to the first few Queen albums when I was in my playpen in the old house I used to live in with my parents. My mum was a huge Queen fan and often played their albums when my dad was out at work in the day, before he went onto the nightshift with his job as a mechanical engineer. I can remember listening to the first five albums by the

Lisa Ventura grew up with Queen

time I was just two years old. But more than that, even at that young age, I was drawn to Freddie Mercury in a big way.

There was something very captivating about him, with his exotic looks and long black hair. I would stare at Queen's album covers, completely drawn to him. I didn't know what Freddie had, but whatever it was, he had it in spades. When I was three years old my mum took me to see *Bedknobs and Broomsticks* at the Odeon cinema in Foregate Street, Worcester. Just up the road from that used to be WH Smiths – today it is the Flames Grill and Restaurant. At the back of the store was the record department, and I remember going in there after the film because my Mum wanted to buy the new Queen album, *News of the World*, and when we got home she put it on the record deck. I can remember so vividly at three years old clapping along to 'We Will Rock You', a song that is entrenched firmly in my mind to this day along with 'We Are the Champions', which became my song and the anthem of my life.

I was looked after by my beloved Aunty Marie during the school holidays. We would sit in her upstairs sewing room listening to Queen, me writing stories and reading books and her sewing away on her machine. The walls were covered with Elvis posters, just as my bedroom had posters of Queen and Freddie Mercury on all the walls. Bless her, she let me play Queen to my heart's content, and I bet she got fed up of hearing 'The Prophets Song' and 'Bohemian Rhapsody'.

As each Queen album was released, I learnt the lyrics off by heart. Some were a bit questionable for someone of such a young age, especially songs like 'Get Down Make Love', but learn them I did. I knew everything there was to know about Queen and soaked up information and knowledge about every band member like a sponge, collecting and reading books and articles in the press.

Hearing Freddie's line in the film *Bohemian Rhapsody* where he tells Jim Reid at EMI records, 'We're four misfits who don't belong together, playing for other misfits. They're the outcasts right at the back of the room. We're pretty sure they feel that they don't belong either. But we belong to them' was like having a lightbulb go off in my head. I finally understood why Queen and Freddie Mercury had such an impact on me. Queen were indeed a band of misfits, for misfits. They aimed to appeal to those who didn't quite fit in, who felt that they didn't have a place in the world, and they did that incredibly well.

As someone who felt that I didn't fit in and didn't belong from as far back as I can remember, I could completely relate to this. When I was 44, I was diagnosed as being on the autistic spectrum, and so much made sense to me about why I was the way I was. As someone who is neurodiverse, I don't fit into the 'normal' conventions, but I do still contribute a lot to the world. With Queen I did belong, I did have a place in the world, and they belonged to me. They were my band, and they showed me the way.

The excitement I felt whenever Queen released a new album was palpable, and I couldn't wait for my mum to buy each one as it came out. From *Jazz* to the *Flash Gordon* soundtrack to *The Game*, *Hot Space* and *The Works*. I would be like a cat on hot bricks waiting for each album to be released. As each album represented a change of direction for Queen, Freddie Mercury also changed with the passing of time. He cut off his gorgeous long black hair, grew a moustache and lost his flamboyant Zandra Rhodes-designed stage costumes in favour of tight jeans and t-shirts. I didn't understand the significance of this change at such a young age, but eventually I did understand it and why Freddie did it.

In 1985 my cousin Maria, a singer and actress, landed a role as one of the three backing singers in the musical *Time* at the Dominion Theatre in London, written by Dave Clark and starring Cliff Richard. As a solo artist, Freddie Mercury recorded the title track to the musical, also called 'Time'. My parents and I went to see my cousin in the show when it first opened, and we got to go backstage to meet Cliff. Had we gone the day before, Freddie Mercury was there, and I would have met him. While it was exciting at the age of 11 to meet such a famous person as Cliff, he certainly wasn't Freddie Mercury! I was so upset. My cousin said that she once knocked on Cliff's dressing room door when Freddie was at the theatre recording the video for 'Time', and he was sprawled out on a sofa in there and said to her, 'Hello darling, come and join us!' My cousin got to meet him and I didn't. I was so jealous!

The day Freddie died, 24 November 1991, is a day I will never forget. I woke up to the news that he had passed away aged 45, and I was inconsolable for days. I was 17 years old and it honestly felt like a member of my family had died. No-one could replace Freddie Mercury in Queen for me, and I'm glad they didn't try. Freddie was unique, with a voice you could listen to for hours and a stage presence that no-one else before him or since him has possessed.

RIP Freddie… I still love you. xx

FREDDIE MERCURY TRIBUTE CONCERT WEMBLEY STADIUM
20 APRIL 1992, LONDON, UK

I WAS THERE: JOANNE SETTERS

I WAS AT the Freddie Mercury tribute concert and extremely honoured to have been there for such a legend. I was a huge fan, and still am. I went with my sister and our husbands. The music was great, the bands were awesome and the atmosphere was amazing. But Queen music is not quite the same without dear Freddie's voice.

I WAS THERE: STEVE JAMES

I USED TO read the *NME*. I remember the 'Is this man a prat?' headline. Freddie stopped doing interviews on the basis that they got you nowhere, so what was the point? He let his music do the talking. I was at the Freddie Mercury Tribute Concert. I went with my brother. It was pretty chocka. We were standing about halfway back. As they came on, the crowd started moving and we were trapped. You couldn't push forward or back. But it evened out a bit later on. It was a good concert. All the acts came on and did a tribute to him. But it wasn't the same without Freddie there! It was a bit karaoke, really, but still a good send off.

It's good with Adam. If they pack it in you've got nothing. You've just got the albums. Carrying on playing brings the younger generation into the game. I went to see the musical *We Will Rock You* and there's kids aged 10 years old, reading the programme and pointing out the members of the band. The new generation are getting into it. It's the music that stands out. Queen's music appeals to all ages.

It's like The Beatles.

Queen's music appeals to all ages. It's like The Beatles

ENCORES

MAPLE LEAF GARDENS

21 NOVEMBER 1977, TORONTO, CANADA

I WAS THERE: ANNE-MARIE KLEIN

A concert review:

QUEEN'S SHOW AT Maple Leaf Gardens last night was indeed a pleasure, mostly a visual one. Because the show was enjoyable, many flaws can be forgiven. It all began rather optimistically, despite a frisbee attack on a fan, with a spectacular and typical entrance by Freddie Mercury, who was dressed as a chessboard in his celebrated jumpsuit. Stylish attire, topped by a black leather jacket, promising that 'we will rock you'. After a quick disappearance to enable guitarist Brian May to conjure the song's guitar solo, Roger Taylor, the drummer, bashed out before the last member, bassist John Deacon, came into the picture to start us off.

Freddie led us into a medley of their hits, featuring mainly his compositions, with such favourites as 'Somebody to Love', 'Good Old-Fashioned Lover Boy' and 'The Millionaire Waltz', his contributions to their *Day at the Races* LP. He did include Deacon's AM ditty, 'You're My Best Friend'.

Freddie's 'Death on Two Legs' number brought excitement as he delivered the crucial line 'now you can kiss my ass goodbye!' and the crowd of 17 000 cheered its' approval. After a lovely rendition of 'Love of my Life' on acoustic guitar, a newer Mercury-May duet spot, Deacon and Taylor rejoined them for May's soft folk song "39'. The show went into a languid drop as they plunged into May's protest song, 'White Man'.

Compared to the first half of the show, where Queen had tried very hard to bring in their new material – successfully - the old hard number lacked feeling and interest. The band, led by Freddie who was doing his share (and more!) to keep the bored and boring crowd interested, tried to blend the lyrical harmonies of May's 'Prophet's Song' into the previous number, and 'listen to the wise man' echoed in the concert venue. After an unsuccessful attempt by Freddie to make this bit captivating, May came up with a 15-minute guitar solo he could and should have avoided. By then, the song's drive had been completely lost. It was all uphill again as the rest of the quartet returned in the spotlight with old goodies like 'Keep Yourself Alive' and 'Liar', both from their first record, and May's brilliant 'Brighton Rock'.

The reunited efforts of 'Stone Cold Crazy', a song the four wrote together, woke the crowd up. Taylor's hard rock number, 'I'm in Love with my Car' gave Queen enough energy and power to lead them to a victory. Mercury, who had already thrilled one fan by tossing his tambourine into the audience, came on with their mammoth hit and now classic, 'Bohemian Rhapsody'.

During the tape segment, the band disappeared to return promptly 45 seconds later, with Mercury dressed as an earring and Taylor's stage in full lighting. Smoke filled the stage as two smoke bombs blew them off to the hard rock part of the song. Mercury showered the fans with carnations and excitement was finally in the air, leading Queen to a much-deserved five minute standing ovation and three encores until they were much too tired to go on.

The flicking of the Bics brought them back on for three songs, notably 'Tie Your Mother Down' where, although Freddie's voice was drowned by screams and loud guitars, the fans were practically rushing the stage. It was followed by their current single, 'We are the Champions' and its B-side, 'We Will Rock You', their theme song. Indeed, they had kept their promise and survived through a few lows. They left with a queenly goodbye, to the sounds of their version of 'God Save the Queen', a song that should have been entitled 'Mercury Saves Queen'.

REGENT THEATRE
7 AUGUST 2003, 2003, MELBOURNE, AUSTRALIA

I WAS THERE: FIONNA SHEPHEARD
I MET BRIAN May and Roger Taylor at an after party for a *We Will Rock You* opening night meet and greet after party in Melbourne. We were lucky enough to see them play a couple of Queen songs and they did a Led Zeppelin song. I spoke to Brian for a bit about what he is up to these days, etc. and about his astro science (which went over my head!). He had such a presence, and was very charming. I told him I had just read a Queen biography, which he hadn't heard of.

QUEEN+PAUL RODGERS NEWCASTLE ARENA
3 MAY 2005, NEWCASTLE, UK

I WAS THERE: PETER SMITH

OF COURSE, IT was never going to be the same. When I heard that Queen were going out on tour again with Paul Rodgers as front man, I could hardly believe it. How was that going to work? What would it be like? However, as an old Queen, Free and Bad Company fan I felt I should go along and support them and see the new line-up for myself. My wife Marie, my son David and youngest daughter Laura all came along, and we were glad that we did. The way in which the show involved and showcased all of the band members was excellent. There were a few Free / Bad Company songs thrown in for good measure, which worked well. Indeed, the show didn't hide from the fact that this was a new, very different incarnation of Queen and celebrated all of what the band had to offer.

The show also didn't deny the band's history and legacy, with frequent videos of Freddie placing him at the forefront of everyone's minds and often at the front of the performance. You had to give it to them; they managed to pull off what many thought was the impossible, to go out with a new front man and make it work. All credit to Paul Rodgers for the way in which he approached this. The show was slick, still relevant and a great tribute to Freddie's legacy.

QUEEN+ADAM LAMBERT BARCLAYS CENTER
28 JULY 2017, BROOKLYN, NEW YORK

I WAS THERE: TERRY PARRETT, AGE 16

WHEN THEY STARTED again with Paul Rodgers, I watched the DVD they put out. I thought, 'Okay, it's not Freddie but it's still Brian and Roger so it's worth going to see.' I saw them at the MGM out in Vegas and it was just such a mismatch. Paul Rodgers is a great singer in his own right but he's not right for any of that music. He doesn't have the charisma and it wasn't really like seeing Queen at all. It wasn't even like seeing a tribute band. It was just very ill fitting. It wasn't a terrific experience and I figured that was the end of them.

And then when they started touring with Adam, in 2017 they did the Barclays Center in Brooklyn and it was incredible. Again, Adam's not Freddie but he sure does a heck of a job paying tribute to the music. It's respectful and it's very well done. His voice is great. He's not trying to imitate Freddie and it's a great thing to hear that music being done live by the band, no matter who's singing it if they're singing it well. And boy he sure does.

There's a chemistry with Adam that there wasn't with Paul Rodgers. Brian and Roger seem to really enjoy how outrageous he is. It's like Freddie, in that they're in the background letting him do his thing. I'd love to see them put out a studio album with Adam. I think it's something a lot of people would enjoy.

PPG PAINTS ARENA
31 JULY 2019, PITTSBURGH, PENNSYLVANIA

I WAS THERE: ANDREW DURANEY

I SAW THEM in 2019. Brian May was outstanding. In fact, the whole show was great. My daughter who is 15 became a big fan so I took her. She loved it. Adam Lambert did a great job. The sound was incredible and the tribute to Freddie was great.

CENTRAL LONDON
SEPTEMBER 2019, LONDON, UK

I WAS THERE: RICHARD LEWIS

I HAVE BEEN a Queen fan for 48 years since I was first introduced to their music at a concert in London in 1971. I had never been to a gig and seeing them live on stage totally blew me away – nothing I had seen on TV could have prepared me for them. I still remember locking myself in my bedroom and playing Queen on cassette over and over again, eventually wearing the tape so thin I had to do constant repairs to get it to play! I even managed to get into fights at school defending Queen against the then 'establishment bands' as other schoolboys didn't take kindly to the new kids on the block.

In September 2019 it was my 60th birthday and my partner, Suzanne, arranged numerous surprise treats for me which included going to the Hard Rock Café in London for their 'Freddie for a Day' tribute night where Monarchy put in a great shift on a very limited stage - and we sang our hearts out remembering Freddie.

Suzanne had also arranged for my best friend and fellow Queen fan Mick and his partner Margaret to join us in London for a few days. Had it not been for the Queen Fan Club Convention we would never have met them as they live in Leicester and we live in Kent and our paths would probably never have crossed, but we did meet in 1992 and hit it off straight away and have been the best of friends ever since.

We were staying in a central London hotel and Suzanne told us we had to all be in reception at 9am on the Saturday but gave no other clues, so we assembled ready with no idea of what lay ahead. She then introduced us to Lee who kept up the mystique for a while until they eventually told us we were doing a Queen tour of London, something I had never done despite growing up and working there. We loaded ourselves into the comfortable mini bus and set off in search of Queen!

We visited Imperial College, the venue of my very first Queen experience and also the scene of a fan club event many years later; it still sends shivers through my body. We stopped off at Garden Lodge too and paid our respects to Freddie before visiting a studio in Soho just round the corner from where I worked many years ago but I didn't even know it was there! One of our last stops was at the new Hard Rock Hotel to see Freddie's piano which was a treat in itself, but the overriding enjoyment was the dialogue we had with Lee. He was very knowledgeable and had even taken our very own Jim Jenkins on a tour with some Italian journalists. Even if you have visited some or all of the places that are part of Queen's London history, the conversation with Lee and his general knowledge of the whole music industry is well worth the trip.

I WAS THERE: KEITH RICHARD WILLIAMS

ALTOGETHER I THINK I saw Queen 13 times. I was 17 when I saw them at Hyde Park. I went down with my friend from school. His name was Vincent Delaney. It was my first time ever down in London. My mum told all the neighbours I was going down to see the Queen!

Freddie was just a fantastic performer. I was 60 in 2020 and I was given a life-sized Freddie Mercury cake for my birthday. We had 180 people in a hotel and the cake was behind a gold curtain. It was a surprise. I knew nothing about it.

I liked every single album they ever released. It was always something different. Who else but Queen could do something like 'Mustapha' and *Jazz* and then go on to something like 'Crazy Little Thing Called Love'? Queen have got to be the most diverse group ever musically. I just love their music. Unfortunately, my partner doesn't. But it was nice of him to get that cake for me.

Keith Richard Williams got a life-sized Freddie cake for his 60th birthday

Bill Harrison's ticket stubs

Craig Taylor saw Queen in 1985

Queen at CNE Stadium, 1980

Dianne Mack was at Manchester's
Free Trade Hall in 1975

Janet Kamal's tickets for
Newcastle City Hall.

Martin Docherty was at
Maple Leaf Gardens in 1978

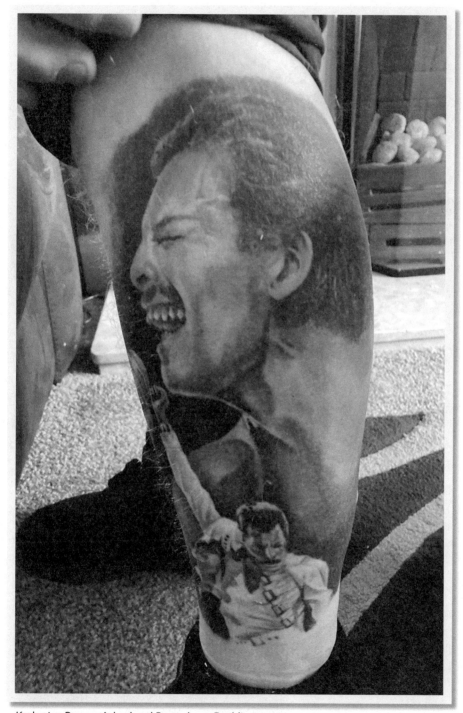

Katherine Bennett's husband Benny has a Freddie tattoo

Russell Wilson saw Queen with Adam in Tacoma

Martin Sladdin was at Manchester's Free Trade Hall in 1975

Nicolet de Ruiter is a big Queen fan

FORTHCOMING TITLES FROM SPENWOOD BOOKS

THIN LIZZY – A PEOPLE'S HISTORY

SLADE – A PEOPLE'S HISTORY

NEIL YOUNG – A PEOPLE'S HISTORY

Got a music memory you'd like to share?
Write to **iwasatthatgig@gmail.com**.